PATERNOSTER DIGITAL LIBRARY

The Fire that Consumes

*The Biblical Case for
Conditional Immortality*

A full listing of all titles in this series will be found at the close of this book.

PATERNOSTER DIGITAL LIBRARY

The resources of modern printing technology now enable us to respond to the on-going demand for classical biblical and theological studies which would otherwise have been too expensive to keep in stock. All titles in the series are important scholarly works in their own right and fresh titles will continue to be added at regular intervals. Readers who missed these books when they originally appeared now have the opportunity to enhance their collections, and new theological libraries in developing countries will welcome this opportunity to update their holdings with essential textbooks.

PATERNOSTER DIGITAL LIBRARY

The Fire that Consumes

*The Biblical Case for
Conditional Immortality*

Edward William Fudge

Revising Editor
Peter Cousins

Copyright © 1994 Edward William Fudge

First published 1994 by Paternoster

This Digital Edition 2005

Paternoster is an imprint of Authentic Media,
9 Holdom Avenue, Bletchley,
Milton Keynes, MK1 1QR, UK.
and
P.O. Box 1047, Waynesboro,
GA, 3080-2047, U.S.A.

11 10 09 08 07 06 05   7 6 5 4 3 2

The Right of Edward William Fudge to be identified
as the Author of this Work has been asserted in accordance
with Copyright, Designs and Patents Act 1988.

*All rights reserved. No part of this publication may be reproduced, stored in a retrieval system,
or transmitted in any form or by any means, electric, mechanical, photocopying, recording or
otherwise, without the prior permission of the publisher or a license permitting restricted
copying. In the U.K. such licenses are issued by the Copyright Licensing Agency,
90 Tottenham Court Road, London W1P 9HE.*

British Library Cataloguing in Publication Data
a Catalogue record for this book is
available from the British Library

ISBN 1-84227-304-3

Printed and bound in Great Britain
for Paternoster
by Nottingham AlphaGraphics

Contents

Foreword	ix
Foreword to the Original Edition	ix
Preface	xi
Abbreviations	xiv

1 Why Talk about Final Punishment?   1
Our point of view   2
'Orthodoxy' and the pains of hell   4
'Orthodoxy' and immortality   6
Modernism, fundamentalism and human destiny   7
Recent discussion   8

2 *Aiōnios* – How Long is 'For Ever'?   11
Derivation of *aiōnios*   12
'Everlasting' things that last for ever ... and some that don't   12
The quality of another aeon   13
'Eternal' with words of action   16
Summary concerning 'eternal'/*aiōnios*   19

3 'If a Man Lives Again, can he Die?' (The Question of Immortality)   21
Uneasiness within orthodox ranks   22
The biblical view   26

4 'The Soul is Immortal, But ...' (The Philosophers versus the Fathers)   32
Immortality and the Reformation: a (theological) tug of (sectarian) war   35
Summary and Conclusion   38

5 'Sheol': Do the Godly Go to 'Hell'?   41
Human existence in the Old Testament   41
Death apart from God   42
Sheol in the Old Testament   43
Etymology and translation   44
Sheol's inhabitants   45
Summary   46

6	**The End of the Wicked in the Old Testament**	47
	I. Passages containing moral principles of divine judgment	49
	II. Passages describing specific divine judgments in space-time history	53
	III. Passages concerning messianic or eschatological judgment	59
	Summary	66
7	**Between the Testaments**	68
8	**The End of the Wicked in the Apocrypha**	73
	Tobit	73
	Sirach	73
	Baruch	74
	Judith	75
	1 Maccabees	75
	2 Maccabees	75
	Wisdom of Solomon	76
	Other Apocryphal Works	77
	Summary	77
9	**The Pseudepigrapha and the Sinner's Doom**	78
	The Sibylline Oracles	79
	Fragments of a Zadokite Work	79
	Dead Sea Scrolls	80
	The Psalms of Solomon	82
	Fourth Ezra (Fourth Esdras)	83
	The Assumption of Moses	84
	Testaments of the Twelve Patriarchs	84
	The Life of Adam and Eve	85
	The Book of Jubilees	85
	First (Ethiopic) Enoch	88
	Second (Syriac) Baruch	90
	Second (Slavonic) Enoch	91
	Fourth Maccabees	91
	Summary	91
10	**Final Punishment in the Teaching of Jesus**	93
	Matthew 3:10, 12	94
	Matthew 5:20	95
	Matthew 5:22	95
	Matthew 5:25f.	99
	Matthew 5:29f.	100
	Matthew 7:13f	100
	Matthew 7:19	101
	Matthew 7:23	102
	Matthew 7:27	102

Matthew 8:11f.	103
Matthew 10:28	105
Matthew 10:39	109
Matthew 11:22ff.	110
Matthew 12:31f.	110
Matthew 13:30, 40–43	111
Matthew 13:48ff.	112
Matthew 18:8f.	112
Matthew 21:33–44	112
Matthew 22:13	116
Matthew 24:50f.	117
Matthew 25:30	118
Matthew 25:41, 46	119
Matthew 26:24	125
Luke 16:19–31	126
John 3:16	129
John 3:36	130
John 5:28f.	130
Summary and conclusion	130

11 Golgotha and Gehenna: Jesus' Death and the Punishment of the Lost — 135
Eschatology is an aspect of christology — 135
Calvary reveals God's final judgment — 137
Jesus' death was 'for sin' — 138
Jesus died the sinner's own death — 142
Jesus' death involved total destruction — 143

12 The Wages of Sin in the Writings of Paul — 146
The Thessalonian correspondence — 146
The Major Epistles — 156
Paul's language in its philosophical context — 166

13 Final Punishment in the Rest of the New Testament — 169
Hebrews — 169
James — 173
Acts of the Apostles — 174
1 Peter — 175
2 Peter — 177
Jude — 179
1 John — 181
Revelation — 182
The element of mystery — 196

14 Universalism's New Face — 199
Some 'Proof-Texts' of Universalism — 201
A Twofold Criticism — 203

15 Doubts: and how to resolve them	207
Bibliography	211
Index of Authors	220
General Index	222
Index of Foreign Words	224
Biblical and Extra-Canonical Literature	225

Foreword

For sixty years I have believed and taught what Edward Fudge so lucidly expounds in this book, but in all these sixty years it has been difficult in Britain to get hold of any publication which sets out the case for conditional immortality in a thorough and systematic way. Now this book, first published in the United States in 1982, has become available in a British edition, which has been skilfully revised and slightly abridged by Peter Cousins.

Christians in general and evangelicals in particular have in recent years become confused about the inspiration of the Bible and it has become all too easy to let the awful doctrine of hell disappear from sight in this general confusion. Fudge believes in the inspiration of the canonical scriptures of the Old and New Testaments without reserve and has researched the whole subject with painstaking care, trying to extricate the pure doctrine of the Bible from the accretions of later centuries. Fudge's clear-headedness and fair-mindedness are apparent throughout. He rejects the notion that humans have immortality without new birth, they *gain* immortality by becoming partakers of the nature of the God 'who alone has immortality'. The terror of the fires of hell is that they burn up all that is unfit for heaven. God's world in the end will have no place where sinners live on unreconciled to their maker; all will be light and glory.

I believe that this book will help many to worship God more wholeheartedly and to proclaim the gospel more confidently.

JOHN WENHAM
Oxford, 1994

Foreword to the Original Edition

While the subject of this study by Mr. Fudge is one on which there is no unanimity among evangelical Christians, it is at the same time one on which they have often engaged in fierce polemic with one another.

If there is no unanimity here among people who are agreed in accepting the Bible as their rule of faith, it may be inferred that the biblical evidence is not unambiguous. In such a situation polemic should have no place. What is called for, rather, is the fellowship of patient Bible study. It is the fruit of such study that Mr. Fudge presents here.

All immortality except God's is derived. The Father, who has life in Himself, has shared with the Son this privilege of having life in Himself. All others receive life in the Son. This is true in a measure even of natural life. 'In Him was life, and the life was the light of mankind.' But it is of spiritual and eternal life that we are now thinking.

Nor are biblical writers alone in insisting that God only has inherent immortality. Plato in the *Timaeus* points out that, if there is a morally good creator of the world, then all souls apart from himself exist by his will, even if his will decrees their immortality. It is a truism that Plato's teaching has profoundly influenced Christian anthropology. But the main difference between Plato's teaching and the biblical doctrine lies here: whereas Plato predicates immortality (albeit *derived* immortality) of the soul, when the New Testament writers speak of immortality in relation to human beings they predicate it of the *body* – of the body revived or transformed in the resurrection age.

Christian theologians chiefly disagree over the destiny in the Age to Come of those who live and die without God. The New Testament answer to this question is much less explicit than is frequently supposed. Paul is reported in Acts as declaring before Felix that he looked for 'a resurrection of both the just and the unjust.' But the only resurrection on which he enlarges in his letters is the resurrection of believers, viewed as their participation in the resurrection of Christ. 'If we believe that Jesus died and rose again' provides a far more secure basis for the Christian hope than any theory of the innate immortality of the soul, but it throws little light on the destiny of unbelievers.

It gives me pleasure to commend Mr. Fudge's exposition of this subject. All that he has to say is worthy of careful consideration, but there is special value in those chapters where he examines the testimony of successive sections of the Holy Scriptures.

I suppose that, as the terms are defined in this work, I would be regarded as neither a traditionalist nor a conditionalist. My own understanding of the issues under discussion would be very much in line with that of C. S. Lewis. Lewis did not systematize his thoughts on the subject (and I have not done so either); Mr. Fudge would no doubt ask (and rightly so) if our exegetical foundation is secure.

'It is a fearful thing,' we are assured by the writer to the Hebrews, 'to fall into the hands of the living God.' True – and yet into whose hands could anyone more confidently fall? King David knew how fearful a thing it was; but when it came to the crunch, he made the right choice: 'Let us fall into the hand of the Lord, for His mercy is great.' Christians have the assurance, both for themselves and for others, that the God and Father of our Lord Jesus Christ will never do anything unjust or unmerciful: He cannot deny Himself.

F. F. BRUCE

Preface

I did not set out to write this book. From childhood I had learned that those who go to hell will never die but will burn for ever. The prospect of someone suffering endless torment did not make me glad, but neither did it trouble me to a noticeable extent. Mostly I thought about something else. When an invitation came to research final punishment for a small theological publisher, I accepted more for the pleasure of study than for any dissatisfaction with my traditional understanding.

When my research began to uncover biblical and historical data challenging the traditional view, I was not eager to accept the conclusions to which that information seemed to lead. Yet the demands of Christian scholarship compelled me to share these findings with others and to invite critical dialogue. At the very least, I thought, proponents of the majority tradition will have to write a better book than ever before in defence of everlasting torment. So I wrote *The Fire that Consumes* with a desire to be biblical, reverent and fair, and to state objectively and comprehensively what my own research had found.

This book exemplifies God's sovereign use of the weak and poor to further his cause and bring him glory. Despite a teaching and writing ministry of over twenty years, I was largely unknown outside my own fellowship of Churches of Christ. This book went out on the strength of its merits, not on the reputation of its author. Yet God has seen fit to use it as a catalyst to call the evangelical church worldwide to rethink this biblical topic.

This book also exemplifies God's gracious providence. I had no idea, years earlier, that my master's studies in biblical languages at Abilene Christian University would some day be put to this use. Nor that my theological training at Covenant Theological Seminary and Eden Theological Seminary would eventually bear such fruit. Years of participation in the Evangelical Theological Society – as an active member, regional officer and contributor to its scholarly *Journal* – as well as publication by *Christianity Today*, *Moody Monthly* and other evangelical periodicals, all provided uncalculated credibility to this work when it called long-held beliefs into serious question. I see God's hand also in the invitation to research, the funding of four printings in the first edition, selection by Evangelical Book Club, and association with the present publishers in this new edition. To him be all the glory!

During the past twelve years there have been many responses to this book and its ideas, including dissertations, theses and at least six books in the UK and USA. I interact with most of those in footnotes throughout this new edition. Unfortunately these responses have not substantially advanced our exegetical understanding of relevant biblical texts. I am sorry to say it, but it is still true that the traditional view simply ignores much scriptural teaching on this subject. It is all the more apparent that its real foundations are ecclesiastical tradition and a vague notion (often overtly denied but constantly reappearing in print) that even the wicked have a soul (or some other aspect or substance) which will always exist, even cut off entirely from God and subjected to his consuming wrath. Yet not one passage of Scripture ever hints that it is the case.

This topic does not affect our salvation and it should not disrupt our fellowship. Equally capable and godly scholars affirm the reality of hell but disagree about its precise nature and result. Yet this subject is important, for it colours our view of God's character and human nature, and it shapes our attitude towards others and the way we share the good news of life in Christ.

Most of all, this subject may test the depth of the evangelical church's practical commitment to the authority of Scripture. It is very easy to *profess* that the Bible is our final standard and measure of doctrine. It is quite another matter to actually scrutinize a cherished doctrine, long held by a majority of Christians, in the bright pure light of God's Word. That is the challenge of this book. Indeed our evangelical *will* – not our orthodoxy – is now on the line. May God make us faithful in deed as in word.

Finally, I wish to think Peter Cousins for his valuable and substantial contribution in revising and condensing this new edition, a task which he performed with extraordinary enthusiasm and skill.

Chief Abbreviations

BZNW Beihefte zur Zeitschrifte fur die neutestamentliche Wissenschaft
CBQ   Catholic Biblical Quarterly
ChrT Christianity Today
ET   Expository Times
JBL   Journal of Biblical Literature
JBR   Journal of Bible and Religion
JETS Journal of the Evangelical Theological Society
JTS   Journal of Theological Studies
NTS   New Testament Studies
SJT   Scottish Journal of Theology

1

Why Talk about Final Punishment?

Hell is not a popular topic, even though one hears the word almost daily. Few people want to study the subject since 'liberals' do not believe in it and 'conservatives' are satisfied that they already have the answers. The number of people who are concerned to learn more is limited.

Hell is also a depressing subject. 'In over seventy years,' a recent writer began, 'I have met only two men that I can remember as having pleasure in talking about hell.'[1] Any who have a right to discuss the subject wish they did not have to. 'Today I must confess that there still lingers an aversion on my part to declare that there is no hope' for the unrepentant after death, says Lehman Strauss.[2] Hell is 'the ultimate horror of God's universe,'[3] the 'dark side of the far hereafter.'[4] But the Bible talks about an inescapable day of judgment for every human being (Acts 17:31; Heb. 9:27), followed by an irreversible and unending retribution for those who have finally rejected God's mercy (Matt. 25:46). So anybody who takes the Bible seriously must sooner or later face the issue.

As painful as it may be, there are good reasons for thinking about hell. It remains true that, as Isaac Watts argued, while such an exercise 'is not a direct ministration of grace', it can still be used of God to awaken sinners 'to a more piercing sight, and to a more keen sensation of their own guilt and danger . . . [leading people to] betake themselves to the grace of God revealed in the gospel'.[5] As Roger Nicole reminds us, this doctrine is 'an integral and vital element of our Christian faith'. It often provides the necessary background for an understanding of 'the true gravity of sin, of the magnitude of the human soul, of the depth of Christ's redeeming work, of the power of divine grace which plucks man out of the abyss like firebrands, of the urgency of the Gospel call, and of the supreme importance of the ministry of preaching and of missions.'[6]

Hell, along with death, the last judgment and heaven, make up the quartet of subjects traditionally treated under the heading of 'eschatology' or 'Last Things'. The doctrine of final punishment is not only important

1. L. A. King, 'Hell, the Painful Refuge', *Eternity* Jan. 1979, p. 28.
2. *Life after Death: What the Bible really teaches* p. 48.
3. John Wenham, *The Goodness of God* p. 27.
4. This is the title for the chapter on hell in Gerald C. Studer's *After Death, What?*
5. *The World to Come* p. 298. After he had written this book, which sets forth an 'eternal torment' view, Watts wrote another in which he suggested that the second death might mean the death of soul as well as body and that infants who died unbaptized might be annihilated in hell rather than suffer eternal torment.
6. 'The Punishment of the Wicked' *ChrT* (9 June 1958) p. 15.

within itself, but in the same way that eschatology is important in general. And eschatology 'is an indispensable dimension of Christian thought and action. Without it the church becomes static, ineffective, and usually heretical. For eschatology contributes a compelling dynamic to Christian action and obedience. It also sets boundaries and gives direction to Christian thinking about God, salvation, and obedient action in the world. When the basic eschatological perspective of Scripture is minimized or lost, Christian thought becomes heretical and Christian social action merely secular.'[7]

Perhaps the greatest reason for talking about hell is also the simplest and most obvious. Jesus spoke of it more than once and in the most serious tones. Whenever he speaks, we will do well to listen – and to do so with care. It is easy to hear Jesus against such background noise that we confuse what he is saying with sounds of our own surroundings. We must not only listen to Christ reverently – we must also listen carefully.

Our point of view

What one says about final punishment depends largely on where he stands in relation to other things. Is he a theist, an atheist or an agnostic? If a theist, is he a Christian? If he professes to be a Christian, is he liberal, evangelical or fundamentalist? Is he open to learn on this biblical subject, or does he suppose that the answers are already clear and settled? If he is open to study, what will be his determining authority? Is he committed most of all to a particular Confession, to what he thinks 'the church has always taught', to philosophy and reason, or to the words of the Bible itself? If he professes the last, does he reason from a specific truth such as God's love, wrath or justice or from an overall gathering and inductive weighing of passages on the subject from both the Old and New Testaments? What will be the final criteria if, as might at times happen, these various standards do not point in the same direction? Is he willing to confess an element of mystery where he cannot find full answers or does he then bend and stretch some scriptures to cover the gap left in others? The matter of authority is not a simple one, even to the reader with good intentions.

I am a theist, a Christian and an evangelical, persuaded that Scripture is the very Word of God written. For that reason I believe it is without error in anything it teaches and that it is the only unquestionable, binding source of doctrine on this or any subject. Negatively, this eliminates anything else as an unquestionable or binding source of doctrine. Positively, it requires that we actually use Scripture as a final authority, not being content to simply praise it as adequate for that purpose.

Such a high view of Scripture does not mean a lack of respect for the common opinion of the universal church through the centuries. If someone believes they alone have discovered a certain truth, they have good reason to doubt its validity. We can know nothing definitive about final punishment that has not come from the Word of God. At the same

---

7. David E. Holwerda, 'Eschatology and History: a look at Calvin's eschatological vision' in *Exploring the Heritage of John Calvin* p. 139.

time, the church's greatest theologians and most devout believers have always realized that God can continually cause new light to break forth from the Word that has been there all the time. One mark of a living church is that it is always reforming, with the guidance of the Holy Spirit and under the authority of the Word.

These are not mere words. They are the standards by which this book is to be critically measured. Not a day has passed during this research and writing without my earnest prayers for divine leading and wisdom. A number of special friends have also supported this work in regular prayer. After reading thousands of pages by uninspired and often conflicting authors, it is very comforting to remember that all they say has absolutely no bearing on what the truth finally is. The best any of them can do is repeat and explain what Scripture says. Any child of God can ask assistance in weighing the message of uninspired authors while beseeching a spirit of wisdom and revelation in the knowledge of the things God has said (Eph. 1:17f.; James 1:5–7). This not only comforts; it creates a sense of humility and of responsibility (James 3:1). We must open Scripture prayerfully and then handle it with care. We must then listen to it without objection or argument. It is the Word of the living God.

The doctrine of eternal torment is either true or it is not. Traditionalists says it is. Conditionalists say it is not. But only the Word of God can give an authoritative answer. The Christian's duty is to humbly receive whatever the Scripture says – on this or any subject – and then faithfully proclaim it as befits God's stewards. If we reject the traditionalist doctrine we must not do so on moral, philosophical, intuitive, judicial or emotional grounds, nor are we much concerned with the arguments of any who do. The only question that matters here is the teaching of Scripture.[8]

This book is not committed to a literalistic view of the fate of the wicked. The future age will be qualitatively different from the present

---

8. Morey, for example, characterizes conditionalists as people seeking to 'silence their conscience,' 'justify their wicked lives' and 'defend their evil ways' as they capitulate to 'liberalism' and a 'weak view of Scripture' (*Afterlife*, 157, 203). Television host John Ankerberg accuses conditionalists of teaching 'doctrines of demons' (*The Facts on Life After Death*, Harvest House, 1992, p.37). Dixon implies that those who reject the tradition of everlasting torment share 'modernism's mindset', form doctrinal positions based on 'tolerance of all viewpoints', or tailor their beliefs to achieve 'a 'kinder and gentler' evangelicalism' (*Other Side* pp. 182, 16, 9). In the first edition of *Whatever Happened to Hell?* Blanchard mistakenly calls me an Adventist, which for him means 'cultic' (pp. 166, 212, 219). I am actually an ordained elder and minister in the Churches of Christ, a past officer of the Evangelical Theological Society (USA) and a contributor to *Christianity Today* and other mainline evangelical publications. Morey falsely describes Verdict Publications (the sponsor of the original research project which ultimately resulted in this book) as a 'covert Adventist operation' which tried to hide its true identity by moving from Australia to America and then changing its publishing name (*Afterlife* pp. 202f.). In fact, *former* Seventh-day Adventist Robert Brinsmead founded Verdict Publications to propagate Reformation principles of justification by grace through faith within the SDA community. Brinsmead named his magazine 'Present Truth' after a pioneer SDA journal to emphasize that the 'present truth' for today is justification through trust in Christ's work alone and not reliance on Ellen G. White or novel interpretation of prophecy related to 1844, and later changed it to 'Verdict' to avoid confusion with Herbert W. Armstrong's periodical of a similar title.

world of space and time and we must allow for many surprises. Many previous conditionalists have been as literalistic as their traditionalist counterparts. What seems beyond question, however, is that the Old and New Testaments alike, in a multiplicity of ways, terms, figures, pictures, expressions and examples declare that the wicked will pass away and be no more, that righteousness will then fill the universe and that God will then for ever be all in all.

This is why the case presented here rests on a detailed examination of many biblical passages. They are considered in context, according to regular rules of hermeneutics. The tools used are, for the most part, either written or generally accepted by evangelical traditionalists. It follows that objections to the thesis ought not to be philosophical, dogmatic or pragmatic, but exegetical. Because many of the objections raised against the idea of everlasting extinction have started at the wrong end, they have frequently missed or avoided the basic exegetical issues.

I was reared on traditionalist teaching. I accepted it because it was said to rest on Scripture. Closer investigation has shown this claim to be mistaken. Careful study has shown that both Old and New Testaments teach instead a resurrection of the wicked for the purpose of divine judgment, the fearful anticipation of a 'consuming fire', irrevocable expulsion from God's presence into a place where there will be 'weeping and grinding of teeth', such conscious suffering as divine justice requires of each individual – and finally, the total and everlasting extinction of the wicked with no hope of resurrection, restoration or recovery.

So my beliefs have changed – as a result of careful study. Mere assertion and denunciation will not refute the evidence presented in this book, nor will a reaffirmation of ecclesiastical tradition. The case finally rests on Scripture. Only Scripture can disprove it.

'Orthodoxy' and the pains of hell

Anybody who queries traditionalist beliefs about hell is soon confronted with the barrier of 'orthodoxy'. Even today, many of us are understandably anxious not to cast 'orthodoxy' aside without good reason. But the fact is that when we begin to investigate the nature of 'orthodox' belief about hell, we find the situation a good deal more confused than many people imagine it to be. 'Orthodoxy' is a relative term, used in a historical sense, and the orthodoxy of traditionalism proves to cover a very large spectrum indeed.

At one end are High-Church ecclesiastics such as Pusey, who found strength beyond his years to hold up the orthodox standard as he understood it. Yet Pusey is widely quoted today by many who would be shocked out of their chairs if a contemporary preacher suggested some of the points he stated with great firmness. At the other end of the spectrum are conservative fundamentalists whose literalistic grasp of the traditional doctrine puts belief in 'real fire' on all but the same level of importance as the deity of Christ. Somewhere between the two lies a range of orthodox evangelicalism.

Contrary to what is often implied, there is no such thing as a uniform, standardized, detailed traditionalist orthodoxy. Traditionalist writers agree that the wicked will remain alive for ever, in sensible punishment of some description, so that neither they nor it will ever pass away. They disagree among themselves on how the wicked will be able to exist for ever when totally cut off from God, the extent of their number, the case of unevangelized pagans or deceased infants, the degree and nature of the punishment, and even the matter of possible salvation beyond the present life.

At the end of the nineteenth century, F. W. Farrar criticized 'the common opinions respecting Hell,' which he summarized in four parts: (1) 'The physical torments, the material agonies of eternal punishment'; (2) 'the supposition of its necessarily endless duration for all who incur it'; (3) 'the opinion that it is thus incurred by the vast mass of mankind'; and (4) 'that it is a doom passed irreversibly at the moment of death on all who die in a state of sin.'[9]

Pusey defended the 'orthodox' position. But he said that one need not think of hell in terms of physical pains or torment other than that which comes from being deprived of all good. Furthermore, the number of those lost will probably be relatively few.

> Belief to the contrary: . . . has no solid foundation whatever; it exists, probably, only in the rigid Calvinistic school, in which Dr. Farrar was educated, and from which his present opinions are a reaction. . . . The fourth is probably a misconception. . . The first is a point, not declared to be essential to the belief in Hell.[10]

Pusey therefore insisted only on Farrar's second point: 'the supposition of its necessarily endless duration for all who incur it.' Even that he later weakened considerably by allowing for a bare minimum of pain, caused perhaps only by the deprivation of all good rather than infliction by an external source. Pusey's 'orthodoxy' therefore reduces to this single point: endless conscious existence for a relatively small number of the damned, who will be cut off from all association with God and suffer to whatever extent that fact might require.

Although Pusey felt that 'perhaps millions have been scared back from sin' by the dread and fear of hell (conceding in another place that the poor in particular were susceptible to being motivated by such preaching), he finally stated regarding physical sufferings that 'it may suffice to say, that neither the Church nor any portion of it has so laid down any doctrine in regard to them, as to make the acceptance of them an integral part of the doctrine itself.'[11]

'As to "pains of sense," the Church has nowhere laid down as a matter of faith, the material character of the worm and the fire, or that they denote more than the gnawing of remorse. Although then it would be very rash to lay down dogmatically, that the "fire" is not to be understood literally, as it has been understood almost universally by Christians, yet no one has a right to urge those representations, from which the imagination

---

9. From Farrar's *Eternal Hope*, quoted by E. B. Pusey in his *What is of Faith as to Everlasting Punishment? In Reply to Dr Farrar's Challenge* . . . pp. 5f.
10. Pusey op. cit. pp. 6f.
11. Ibid. p. 18.

so shrinks, as a ground for refusing to believe in hell, since he is left free not to believe them.'[12]

Pusey seems to be content for preachers such as Spurgeon to scare the poor by preaching hellfire, but if a more intellectual person questions the Christian faith on such a basis, then it is 'not a matter of faith', even though such pain 'has been understood almost universally by Christians' as being physical! Is such reasoning fair? And what has become of the argument which rests so much on what has been 'universally' believed for so long?

Other traditionalists agree with Pusey that physical pain is not essential to the 'orthodox' view. Baptist theologian A. H. Strong concedes

> 1. that future punishment does not necessarily consist of physical torments, – it may be wholly internal and spiritual; 2. that the pain and suffering of the future are not necessarily due to positive inflictions of God, – they may result entirely from the soul's sense of loss, and from the accusations of conscience; and [even] 3. that eternal punishment does not necessarily involve endless successions of suffering, – as God's eternity is not mere endlessness so we may not be forever subject to the law of time.[13]

Across the Calvinistic fence, Louis Berkhof says it 'is impossible to determine precisely what will constitute the eternal punishment of the wicked, and it behooves us to speak very cautiously on the subject', though he goes on to say it will include both 'positive pains and sufferings in body and soul' as well as such 'subjective punishments as pangs of conscience, anguish, despair, weeping and gnashing of teeth.'[14]

In spite of the caution displayed by such thinkers, it is probably safe to say with another writer that, for much popular traditionalist preaching and writing, the fire of hell has been 'almost invariably understood as a real, material, inextinguishable fire, ceaselessly tormenting the damned.'[15] Advocates of 'orthodoxy' themselves have disagreed about the not unimportant topic of the nature of the punishment inflicted on the wicked.

The evangelist, Billy Graham, recently said:

> 'The only thing I could say for sure is that hell means separation from God .... When it comes to a literal fire, I don't preach it because I'm not sure about it.' Billy Graham, quoted in *Time* 74 (November 15th 1993).

'Orthodoxy' and immortality

Around the world in recent years, the conviction has been increasing that traditional orthodoxy needs to launch an 'anti-pollution' effort aimed at filtering out pagan ideas of Greek philosophy which early Christian apologists took for granted and which have passed largely unnoticed through the centuries.

Chief among these 'Grecian' remnants said to contradict biblical teaching is the idea that a person's 'soul' is an entity separable from the

---

12. Ibid. p. 23.
13. *Systematic Theology* 3:1035.
14. Louis Berkhof, *Reformed Dogmatics* 2.345.
15. D. W. Lotz, 'Heaven and Hell in the Christian Tradition', *Religion in Life* 48 (Spring 1979) 85.

body, which can remain conscious even when the body is dead, and which (unlike the body) possesses some quality which makes it indestructible. The traditional belief about the unending punishment of the wicked is based on this concept. In the words of a classic Reformed theologian: 'If the Bible says that the sufferings of the lost are to be everlasting, they are to endure for ever, *unless it can be shown either that the soul is not immortal or that the Scriptures elsewhere teach that those sufferings are to come to an end.*'[16]

Modernism, fundamentalism and human destiny

However, during the opening years of the twentieth century there were powerful forces discouraging evangelicals, especially in the North America, from addressing such issues. The fundamentalist-modernist controversy had an immense impact on religious life and thought.

'Liberal' Christianity, which was increasingly popular at the turn of the century, advocated a faith which is often summarized as 'the fatherhood of God and the brotherhood of man.' Since God is pure benevolence, it affirmed, he is certainly too good to consign anyone to the traditional hell. Every person has a divine spark; Jesus as the perfect teacher and example brings us to our full potential. And since all are God's children by nature, neither Jesus nor Christianity is uniquely supernatural.

Although it was originally a Catholic term for liberalism, the word 'modernism' soon passed into Protestant polemics as well, where it worked its way into the 'fundamentalist' thesaurus and still does active duty today, if not always with the same precision. In America, 'modernism' shared a bed with the 'social gospel'. During the early years of the early twentieth century the stage was set in the United States for a battle royal. The Baptists and Presbyterians were most affected by the controversy, followed closely by the Methodists and Disciples of Christ. Truly, the 'fundamentals' of Christianity were at stake; emotions rightfully ran high. Since 'modernists' denied that anyone would burn for ever in conscious torment it came to pass that anyone who even looked askance at the traditionalist hell came under immediate suspicion as a latent or closet 'modernist'.

'Fundamentalism' was born and christened in the year 1909, when it made a literary debut in the first of twelve volumes entitled *The Fundamentals: A Testimony to the Truth*. The books were sponsored by two wealthy California laymen who distributed them without cost to over three million church leaders and students around the world. Authors represented all major branches of historic Protestantism, including such men as James Orr, B. B. Warfield, Sir Robert Anderson, H. C. G. Moule, W. H. Griffith-Thomas, R. A. Torrey, Dyson Hague, A. T. Pierson and G. Campbell Morgan. The 'fundamentals' of faith they defended regarded the Bible (its inspiration and authority), Jesus Christ (his deity, virgin conception, miracles, substitutionary atoning death, bodily resurrection and personal return), and such topics as the reality of sin, the necessity for personal regeneration by the Holy Spirit, the power of prayer, and the obligation to evangelize.

---

16. Charles Hodge, *Systematic Theology* 3.876. Italics supplied.

These were the doctrines which elicited *The Fundamentals* and which bound their evangelical proponents into an amorphous group that became known as 'fundamentalists'. In 1910 the General Assembly of the Northern Presbyterian Church issued a list of five specific items which it termed the 'fundamentals of faith and of evangelical Christianity'. Again, these included the inspiration and infallibility of Scripture, the deity of Jesus Christ, his virgin birth and supernatural miracles, his substitutionary death for sins, and his physical resurrection and personal return. Later 'fundamentalist' organizations adopted the General Assembly's list, by and large, and today it serves a still broader range of evangelical institutions.

In May 1919 a conference convened in Philadelphia, resulting in a group called The World's Christian Fundamentals Association. This organization required members to affirm nine points of doctrine. The ninth point went slightly beyond some earlier lists, specifying the resurrection and final disposition of all men to either eternal blessedness or eternal woe. In fundamentalist circles today one finds popular, grass-roots lists of doctrines or questions intended for use in identifying persons suspected of 'modernism.' Such lists almost always include adherence to the doctrine of everlasting conscious torment, and often they specify literal fire. Ivory-tower evangelicals may scoff at the notion, but they need not drive far off the campuses to find this kind of 'orthodoxy' very much alive and well.

Such reactionary theology is easily understood, and we are wholly sympathetic with its intentions. At the same time, it has greatly hindered the exercise of the anti-tradition principle of Protestantism and (far more important) the biblical injunction to 'test all things' and 'hold fast what is good'. Because of this situation, most American evangelicals have shied away from the subject of final punishment, neither studying it themselves nor allowing others to do so. This is certainly not the only reason for lack of study, but it must be included if the whole picture is to be seen.

In Britain, by contrast, even non-evangelicals were never taken with the methods of German criticism or the dogmas of the older liberals in quite the same manner as their American cousins. Whether this was due to an inherent English conservatism, to American softness for anything novel, or to the 'defusing' effect of a British state church which itself found room to harbour all manner of theological creatures and birds, we cannot be sure.

Recent discussion

Whatever the cause, British evangelicals did not feel the same 'modernist' pressure that threatened American orthodoxy, and consequently 'fundamentalism' was never a British phenomenon either. American evangelicals sometimes find it difficult to remember this difference in backgrounds when British brethren approach questions with an obviously different perspective. British evangelicals, in turn, keep reminding Americans that it is indeed a fact. Partly for this reason, perhaps, and partly because of Anglicanism's official openness on the question, British evangelicals inside and outside the state church have been somewhat less hesitant than those in America to consider the case for final extinction of the wicked.

Writing in 1974, John W. Wenham described himself as 'encouraging the case for serious consideration of the case for conditional immortality' although he intended also to 'discourage those who hold traditional orthodoxy from surrendering it lightly'.[17] In other books Wenham argues powerfully for the historicity of Scripture and his cautious but positive reference to conditional immortality is highly significant. In a chapter contributed to *Universalism and the Doctrine of Hell*[18] he affirmed his belief in conditional immortality as the biblical doctrine.

Wenham refers also to two other twentieth century British authors, both firmly committed to the inspiration and final authority of Scripture, who were drawn to conditionalist conclusions. Harold Ernest Guillebaud was born in 1888 and went to Africa in 1925 as a missionary with the Church Missionary Society. He wrote several books, including a popular work on the atonement entitled *Why the Cross?* In it he took for granted the traditional view of hell. A few years later his publishers, the Inter Varsity Fellowship, asked him to write a book on *The Moral Difficulties of the Bible*, including a final chapter on the doctrine of everlasting punishment. When he came to write this, he found himself unable to answer the question to his own satisfaction, so the chapter was omitted from the book when it was published in 1941.

Guillebaud then began an intensive personal study of the subject, which resulted in another book, entitled *The Righteous Judge*, setting forth the conditionalist views to which his study had led. It was published privately in 1964 after the author's death.[19] Guillebaud believed that every soul survives bodily death but that the wicked will finally perish, both body and soul, in the second death.

Another significant evangelical figure in this connection was Basil F. C. Atkinson. Born in 1895, he served as Under-Librarian of Cambridge University from 1925–1960. He became renowned in evangelical circles and was a valued guide for many years to the Cambridge Inter-Collegiate Christian Union, members of which included future evangelical leaders such as John Stott, Robert Brow, David Watson and Derek Prince. He was a vigorous and outspoken supporter of traditional evangelicalism. Among his numerous books was one entitled *Life and Immortality*, subtitled *An Examination of the Nature and Meaning of Life and Death as they are Revealed in the Scriptures*. His appeal throughout is to the authority of Scripture and that alone. He holds a unitary view of man, seeing death as a period of unconsciousness, and believing in a universal resurrection and judgment, everlasting life for believers, and 'complete extinction and destruction out of the creation of God' for all 'unrepentant sinners, the devil, evil angels, sin and death and evil of all kinds'. Wenham describes this scholarly book as 'the fruit of a lifetime of study' and 'a remarkable piece of sustained argument'. Like Guillebaud's book, Atkinson's was published privately.

Atkinson and Guillebaud were little known outside the United

---

17. *The Goodness of God* (IVP 1974) p. 41.
18. *Universalism and the Doctrine of Hell* N. M. de S. Cameron (Ed.) (Baker/Paternoster 1993).
19. *The Righteous Judge: A Study of the Biblical Doctrine of Everlasting Punishment* (Phoenix Press nd).

Kingdom. But in 1988 John Stott, who is generally regarded as the dean of world-wide evangelicalism, wrote sympathetically of conditionalism, pleading that 'the ultimate annihilation of the wicked should at least be accepted as a legitimate, biblically founded alternative to their eternal conscious torment'.[20] Other well-known evangelical scholars have also recently expressed public support for a conditionalist stance.[21]

The question many evangelicals are currently facing is thus not whether human beings will exist for ever in their own right. Christian theologians have always denied that. Nor is it whether God, who created us, can also bring us to total extinction. That also is conceded by all. Neither is it whether God is able to make even the wicked immortal if he so chooses. No one denies this. The question being asked today by growing numbers of evangelicals is whether or not Scripture teaches that God will make the wicked immortal (along with the righteous) in the resurrection for everlasting life in pain rather than everlasting life in bliss, or whether, by contrast, immortality in the Age to Come is a boon promised only to the righteous on the basis of Christ's redemption and victory over sin and death.

There is only one satisfactory way to find the answer to that question. Wenham is surely correct when he says, 'For a Christian, one simple sentence of revelation must in the end outweigh the weightiest conclusions of man-made philosophy.'[22] Although almost half a century has passed since he wrote them Guillebaud's words will find a response among evangelicals today:

> Only God knows the facts, and if His revelation of them is rightly interpreted, no tradition (even an Evangelical tradition) has a good claim to be heard against it .... Evangelicals, who criticize the Roman Church for putting tradition on a level with the Bible, must be very careful that we ourselves do not unwittingly fall into the same snare ... The question is simply, *What do His words mean?* ... No Protestant should object to being asked to re-examine any traditional belief in the light of the Word of God, searching the Scriptures to see whether these things be so.[23]

---

20. D. Edwards and J. R. W. Stott, *Essentials* Hodder 1988 pp. 320–329.
21. P. E. Hughes, *The True Image* (Eerdmans/IVP 1989) ch. 37. Michael Green, *Evangelism in the Local Church* (Hodder 1990) pp. 69f.
22. *The Goodness of God* p. 29.
23. *Righteous Judge* pp. 46, 47, 49.

2

Aiōnios – How Long is 'For Ever'?

Discussion about final punishment has usually been accompanied by controversy concerning the Greek adjective *aiōnios*. Does this word describe time in unending duration ('everlasting'), some unknown quality of the Age to Come ('eternal'), both of these, or neither? Are these usual translations satisfactory or should we coin some new adjective such as 'aionic' or 'aionian'?

Jesus himself spoke in a single sentence of 'eternal' life and 'eternal' punishment (Matt. 25:46). Since Augustine, most theologians have insisted that the punishment must last as long as the life. But some have disagreed. This chapter will survey some of the approaches that have been made in trying to understand the New Testament meaning of *aiōnios* and its parent noun *aiōn*.

Some advocates of the traditional view of hell have insisted that these words signify only endless time. W. G. T. Shedd denies any sense of quality. 'The truth is', he flatly states, 'that *aiōn* is a term that denotes time only, and never denotes the nature and quality of an object.'[1] A recent popular writer calls the idea that *aiōnios* denotes a quality 'nonsense'; a 'Biblical word game' that 'denies the truth of God' and 'has no basis in fact.'[2] Some objectors to the traditional doctrine have been equally extreme in their response. F. D. Maurice said the word was purely qualitative, having nothing to do with time and speaking only of things that are spiritual, essential, beyond present categories of thoughts.[3] The article in *DCG* concludes that 'it is clear that "eternal" and "everlasting" are not

---

1. *Punishment* p. 87.
2. Braun, *Whatever Happened?* p. 162. Like many other traditionalist writers, Braun seems unaware of the conditionalist position. Although he makes a passing use of the term, he equates it with 'annihilationism' and mistakenly limits it to the belief that the dead will never be raised (p. 49). His charge that conditionalists 'wanted to be universalists but just couldn't bring themselves to justify it' (p. 49) is as uncharitable as it is inaccurate and is the kind of exaggeration that has brought needless opposition to the traditionalist position. His assumption that no one in 2,000 years has suggested the transliteration 'aiōnic' or 'aiōnian' instead of 'eternal' overlooks even Shedd's use of the terms. His statement that 'the Greek used in the NT does not have a single adverb with the meaning the same as the English "forever" ' (p. 159) ignores the Greek adverb *pantote*, which means 'always' and is indeed so cited by Baker (*Dispensational Theology* p. 651) in reaching the same view of hell as Braun advocates.
3. Don Cupitt, 'The Language of Eschatology: F. D. Maurice's Treatment of Heaven and Hell', *Anglican Theological Review* 54 no. 4 (Oct. 1972) pp. 305–317.

interchangeable'.[4] Farrar denied there is any authority whatever for rendering it 'everlasting'.[5] Clearly we shall not settle the matter by merely quoting claims.

Derivation of *aiōnios*

Even the derivation of *aiōnios* is disputed. One writer traces our English word 'eternal' through the Latin *aeternus* to *aeviternus* to *aevum*, which he says matches the Greek word *aei* that gives *aiōnios*. 'Thus the basic sense in both Greek and Latin is of everlasting existence', and the word clearly means 'always'.[6] Another insists that 'an appeal to the ancients, like that of Aristotle, can never sustain the assertion that eternity is the original sense of *aiōn*', that this sense was unknown to the Greeks for many centuries and came into use only in the later ages of the language.[7]

Non-biblical sources from early Christian times offer little help. Moulton and Milligan cite papyri from the first and second centuries A.D. There *aiōn* is used for the 'life' of a person as well as the life wished for a Caesar, or earlier for a Pharaoh. They give no evidence outside the New Testament for a qualitative meaning of *aiōnios*, saying that in their sources 'it never loses the [time] sense of *perpetuus*.' They conclude that the word's roots are too deep to dig for and that in general it 'depicts that of which the horizon is not in view, whether the horizon be at an infinite distance . . . or whether it lies no farther than the span of a Caesar's life'.[8]

We should probably conclude that both 'eternal' and *aiōn* have roots signifying time in both English and its Latin ancestor and in Greek. But in biblical interpretation, as elsewhere, usage matters at least as much as etymology. How does Scripture use *aiōn* and *aiōnios*?

'Everlasting' things that last for ever . . . and some that don't

Nicole observes that 51 times in the New Testament, *aiōnios* applies to the 'eternal felicity' of the redeemed, and there 'it is conceded by all that no limitation of time applies'.[9] On the other hand, Pétavel insists that at least 70 times in the Bible, this word qualifies 'objects of a temporary and limited nature', so that it signifies only 'an indeterminate duration of which the maximum is fixed by the intrinsic nature of the persons or things'.[10] The word means 'for ever', but within the limits of the possibility inherent in the person or thing itself. When God is said to be 'eternal', that is truly 'for ever'. But 'everlasting' mountains last only for a very long time – as long as they *can* last. Pétavel points out that Scripture frequently uses *aiōn*, *aiōnios* and their Hebrew counterparts (*olam* in

---

4. W. H. Dyson, 'Eternal Punishment', *DCG* 1:540.
5. *Eternal Hope* p. 197.
6. Cupitt, op. cit. p. 314.
7. Beecher, *History of Opinions on the Scriptural Doctrine of Retribution* p. 140.
8. *Vocabulary* p. 16.
9. Roger Nicole, 'The Punishment of the Wicked' *CT* 9.6.58 p. 14.
10. *Problem* p. 574.

various forms) of things which have come to an end. The sprinkling of blood at the Passover was an 'everlasting' ordinance (Ex. 12:24). So were the Aaronic priesthood (Ex. 29:9; 40:15; Lev. 3:17), Caleb's inheritance Josh. 14:9), Solomon's temple (1 Ki. 3:12f), the period of a slave's life (Deut. 15:17), Gehazi's leprosy (2 Ki. 5:27) and practically every other ordinance, rite or institution of the Old Testament system. These things did not last 'for ever' as we think of time extended without limitation. They did last beyond the vision of those who first heard them called 'everlasting', and no time limit was then set at all. According to this view, held by Pétavel, Froom and others, this is the meaning of *aiōnios* in the Bible. It speaks of unlimited time within the limits determined by the thing it modifies. Yet Beecher, a critic of the traditional doctrine of hell, dissents, arguing that the Mosaic ordinances and the possession of Palestine 'might have lasted to the end of the world, but did not'.[11]

The quality of another aeon

While it is unquestionably true that the Bible uses *aiōnios* to describe the Trinity, as also the redemption, salvation and final bliss of the redeemed, it is clear that the New Testament sometimes uses the word in a qualitative sense. This seems to reflect the common Jewish view that time is divided into two ages, the Present Age and the Age to Come (Matt. 12:32: Luke 20:34f). Jesus speaks of the cares (Matt. 13:22: Mark 4:19), the sons (Luke 16:8) and the end of this age (Matt. 13:39f; 24:3; 28:20). Paul also speaks of this age with its debaters (1 Cor. 1:20), wisdom and rulers (1 Cor. 2:6, 8; 3:18), course of life (Eph. 2:2), world rulers (Eph. 6:12, Received Text) and the rich (1 Tim. 6:17). Over against this age he also contrasts the Age to Come (Eph. 1:21).

The Present Age is under Satan's dominion (2 Cor. 4:4), and Christ gave himself for our sins to rescue us from it (Gal. 1:4). The Age to Come is of another order which may be called 'eternal' (*aiōnios*). To be guilty of an 'eternal' sin (Mark 3:29) is to be guilty of one which will not be forgiven even in the Age to Come (Matt. 12:32). That the Age to Come is eternal in quality is seen in the fact that the life of the Age to Come

11. *Opinions* p. 149. Beecher argues for the meaning 'age long' or 'dispensation'. He insists that the NT meaning of *aiōnios* is formed off this root by the translators of the LXX and so passes into NT use (pp. 140–147). To the extent that this is correct – and there is no question that the NT vocabulary contains much fruit born from the union of the Hebrew OT with the Greek language in the LXX – *aiōnios* in the NT is loosed from classical meanings discovered through strict etymology.

Harry A. Wolfson ('Immortality and Resurrection in the Philosophy of the Church Fathers', *Immortality and Resurrection* p. 65) says Origen used the Hebrew *olam* to argue that *aiōnios* means not everlasting but a very long time. Geerhardus Vos, on the other hand, argues from the same Hebrew word for the sense of perpetuity and unendingness (*The Pauline Eschatology* pp. 288f).

'Everlasting' equals ten generations in Deut. 23:3, 6. Salmond (*Immortality* p. 654) discounts all references to temporary things which are called 'everlasting' in the OT by saying that 'for the moment the imagination of the speaker or writer gives to the things the quality of the eternal'.

(eternal life) is possible even in the Present Age through faith in Jesus.[12] Where John talks of 'eternal life', the other Gospels generally speak of the 'kingdom', though these expressions are used interchangeably in the Synoptics (Matt. 19:16f, 23; Mark 9:45, 47) and in John (John 3:3, 5, 15f). To inherit the kingdom is to enter into eternal life (Matt. 25:34, 46).

Based on this Jewish eschatological usage, *aiōnios* sometimes suggests 'quality of being, almost meaning "divine" rather than enduring'.[13] It describes things which are bound to the kingdom of God, so that it is 'almost the equivalent of Messianic'.[14] The adjective 'eternal' is applied to things 'resulting from the final intervention of God, when he will establish the new world'.[15] It 'takes us into a sphere of being' where we view things 'in their relation to some eternal aspect of the Divine nature'.[16] The word speaks of 'being of which time is not a measure'.[17]

Given this definition, 'eternal' punishment or 'eternal' fire are those which 'partake of the nature of the *aiōn*', which are 'peculiar to the realm and the nature of God'.[18] The real point is the 'character of the punishment . . . .that of the order of the Age to Come as contrasted with any earthly penalties'.[19] When the New Testament speaks of 'eternal' life, in this view, the adjective *aiōnios* refers to 'the quality more than to the length of life'.[20]

This does not detract from the endlessness of the bliss, for Scripture explicitly states that nothing can ever separate God's people from his love, even things to come (Rom. 8:38f). They will 'always' be with the Lord (*pantote*, literally 'every then', 1 Thess. 4:17). God will glorify them and

---

12. This is true especially in the writings of John. The adjective *aiōnios* occurs 17 times in the fourth Gospel and six times in 1 John, always with the noun 'life'. It indicates 'a life that is different in quality from the life which characterizes the present age' (W. Hendriksen, *John* p. 141), although it carries a quantitative connotation. For more bibliography see J. W. Roberts, 'Some Observations on the Meaning of "eternal life" in the Gospel of John', *Restoration Quarterly* 7, no.4 (Fourth Quarter, 1963) pp. 186–193.

13. David Hill, *Greek Words and Hebrew Meanings: Studies in the Semantics of Soteriological Terms* (Cambridge: SNTS Monograph Series, no. 5 1967) pp. 163–201, summarized by D. E. H. Whiteley, 'Liberal Christianity in the New Testament', *Modern Churchman* 13, no.1 (Oct. 1969) p. 25.

14. Dyson, *DCG* p. 540.

15. J. Burnier, 'Judgment in the New Testament', *A Companion to the Bible*, ed. J. J. von Allmen p. 213. While both Gerald C. Studer (*After Death, What?* p. 127) and Froom (*Conditionalist Faith* 2:949) quote Burnier on this point, it is interesting that Froom stops shorter than Studer, who continues the quotation as follows: 'Moreover, every attempt to determine exactly what awaits men beyond judgment comes up against the undefined nature of a concept which was elaborated not to satisfy our curiosity, but to cause us to fear the God who offers us His pardon and eternal life in the fellowship of His Son.' Froom would profit from this warning against oversimplification of eternal matters since his SDA position leaves very little to the imagination. In Froom's defence, however, he quotes Burnier only to show broad support for what is sometimes thought to be a peculiar sectarian view.

16. Archibald Bisset, 'Eternal Fire', *DCG* 1:537.

17. B. F. Westcott, quoted by Dyson, *DCG* 1.540.

18. Baird, *Justice* p. 233.

19. Alan Richardson, *Introduction* p. 74.

20. Donald G. Bloesch, *Essentials* 2:229.

give them a body that cannot die (1 Cor. 13:33f). The endless joy of the saved does not finally depend on the meaning of *aiōnios*, for even if that word spoke only of a quality, Scripture sufficiently assures believers of everlasting happiness. To say that *aiōnios* has a qualitative meaning is not a 'linguistic smokescreen'[21] but represents the sober thinking of a cross-section of scholars, including several who hold the traditional view of hell.[22] Nor does it satisfy everyone!

Shedd concedes that Scripture speaks of two ages or *aiōns* and that the adjective *aiōnios* is related to this concept. But he points out that while the Present Age will end, the Age to Come will never end. Both ages are described by the Greek *aiōn* and the Hebrew *olam*. Things in both ages are described as *aiōnios*. The crucial question, according to Shedd, is '*in which of the two aeons*, the limited or the endless, the thing exists to which the epithet is applied . . . . If anything belongs solely to the present age, or aeon, it is aeonian in the limited signification: if it belongs to the future age, or aeon, it is aeonian in the unlimited signification.'[23]

H. A. A. Kennedy agrees with Shedd. Although in many passages *aiōnios* loses its time quality to become 'virtually equivalent to "transcendent, perfect"', Kennedy argues that 'the age of God's dominion is necessarily final. If St. Paul does not describe it as "eternal," in so many words, it is because the conception is self-evident to his readers.'[24]

Just as traditionalist Buis concedes a qualitative sense for *aiōnios*, but insists that it retains a quantitative meaning as well, so conditionalist Guillebaud says that 'though "eternal" is more than endless, the idea of permanence is an essential part of it'.[25] He cites several passages which contrast the temporary with the permanent (Luke 16:9; 2 Co. 4:17; 5:4) to support this conclusion. The evidence urges us to stand on this solid ground. Shedd and Braun are wrong to deny any qualitative sense. Maurice and Farrar are wrong to say there is no other sense. Buis and Guillebaud differ on the nature of final punishment, but both men rightly concede here and meet in the middle.

But if 'eternal' describes both quality and quantity, character and duration, what precisely does it signify about final punishment? Traditionalists and conditionalists may agree concerning the word, but they immediately draw swords when they begin to apply it to hell. The wicked go into *eternal punishment*. Does that refer to the act of retribution or to its

---

21. As charged by Jon Zens, 'Do the Flames Ever Stop in Hell?' *Free Grace Broadcaster*, (Mar.–Apr. 1987) p. 2.
22. In addition to Westcott and Bloesch, cited above, see Buis, *Eternal Punishment* pp. 49f.
23. Shedd, *Punishment* pp. 84f. Vos, on the other hand, sees no relation between the adjective *aiōnios* and 'the formal eschatological distinction' between the two ages (*Pauline Eschatology* p. 289).
24. H. A. A. Kennedy, *St Paul's Conceptions of the Last Things* p. 318.
25. Guillebaud, *Righteous Judge* p. 7. Another approach to the qualitative sense of *aiōnios* which I have not seen suggested elsewhere concerns the qualitative nature of *all* adjectives, formed as they are on nouns. This is particularly relevant in the present case, where the Hebrew construct state often serves in the absence of adjectives and, in the Septuagint and NT, sometimes becomes attributive genitives and sometimes Greek adjectives. On the phenomenon see M. Zerwick, *Biblical Greek* p. 14, 40.

effect? Which is 'eternal', the punishing or the punishment? As so often happens in exploring this cavernous topic, we finally kindle a light in one dark room, only to discover that it leads into a still deeper cave. We now move into that one.

'Eternal' with words of action

Of the 70 usages of *aiōnios* in the New Testament, six qualify nouns signifying acts or processes, as distinct from persons or things. These cases call for special consideration. They are 'eternal salvation' (Heb. 5:9), 'eternal redemption' (Heb. 9:12), 'eternal judgment' (Heb. 6:2), 'eternal sin' (Mark 3:29), 'eternal punishment' (Matt. 25:46) and 'eternal destruction' (2 Thess. 1:9). Three occur in Hebrews: all six have to do with final judgment and its outcome.

Here we see again the *other-age* quality of the 'eternal'. There is something transcendent, eschatological, divine about this judgment, this sin, this punishment and destruction, this redemption and salvation. They are of an entirely different nature from merely human, *this-age* matters. Yet something about this judgment, sin, punishment, destruction, redemption and salvation will have no *end*. Although in one sense timeless, they are in another sense without temporal limits. They belong to that Age to Come which is not bound by time and which will never end.[26]

Eternal judgment (Heb. 6:2)

Among the 'elementary teachings' which make up the 'foundation' of Christian teaching are 'the resurrection of the dead and *eternal judgment*'. This is literally the resurrection 'of the dead ones' (pl. *nekrōn*) seemingly both good and bad,[27] and it is linked to that judgment which is of the Age to Come, not merely a judgment made by man or God in the here and now. That is its *quality*, but what of its *duration*? How is the last judgment 'eternal' in the sense of *everlasting*? The act of judging will certainly not last for ever. But we notice that the text speaks of judg*ment* (*krimatos*), not of judg*ing*. There will be an act or process of judging, and then it will be over. But the judging results in a judgment and that will never end. The action itself is one thing: its outcome, its issue, its result, is something else. 'Eternal' here speaks of the result of the action, not the action itself. Once the judging is over, the judgment will remain – the eternal, everlasting issue of the once-for-all process of judgment.

---

26. We here bypass a larger issue concerning the philosophical and theological nature of 'time' and 'eternity.' On this see O. Cullman, *Christ and Time* pp. 37–68 and James Barr, *Biblical Words for Time* pp. 135–158.

27. It has frequently been stated that, as a general rule, when the NT speaks of the resurrection *of* the dead (*tōn nekrōn*), it has in view a general resurrection comprising both good and evil. When it speaks of a resurrection *from* the dead (*ek nekrōn*), it usually has in view a resurrection of the righteous unto life. Joachim Jeremias makes a contrary distinction in one important passage, however. See ' "Flesh and Blood Cannot Inherit the Kingdom of God" (1 Cor. xv.50)' *NTS* 2 (Feb. 1956) p. 155.

Eternal redemption (Heb. 9:12)

Christ has entered upon his high priestly service through the greater heavenly tabernacle 'not ... by means of the blood of goats and calves: but by his own blood, having obtained *eternal redemption*'. It is clear that 'eternal' here also has a qualitative aspect. These matters are of that order which is not a part of this creation (v.11). They pertain to the 'eternal Spirit' (v. 14), not the flesh. They belong to the new covenant and the 'eternal inheritance' (v.13). By faith these 'eternal' things are already operative and even visible (Heb.11), though they are of an order different from space–time creation.

This redemption is also 'eternal' in the sense of *everlasting*. Not that the act or process of redeeming continues without end: Christ has accomplished that *once for all.* Our author emphasizes that Christ did not have to suffer 'many times since the creation'. Rather, 'He has appeared once for all at the end of the ages to do away with sin by the sacrifice of himself' (Heb. 9:25f). But this once-for-all act of redeeming, now finished, which can never be repeated or duplicated, issues in an 'eternal redemption' which will never pass away.[28] 'Eternal' speaks here again of the result of the action, not the act itself. The 'eternal' result of the once-for-all redeeming action will never pass away.

Eternal salvation (Heb. 5:9)

By his obedience, Jesus became 'the source of *eternal salvation* for all who obey him'. This salvation partakes of the eternal *quality* of the new order – that order in which Jesus may be a priest like Melchizedek (v. 10). It is already a reality (Heb. 4:15f), for it partially intersects the present order even while it transcends it. But this salvation is also 'eternal' in the sense that it will never end. Jesus is not for ever saving his people: he did that once for all, as we have already seen. As with 'eternal redemption', this salvation is eternal because it is the everlasting result which issues from the once-for-all process or act of saving. The expression 'eternal salvation' here may come from Isa. 45:17. There God promised that 'Israel will be saved by the Lord with an everlasting salvation.' The following words show that the focus is on the result God will accomplish rather than the act he will perform. 'You will never be put to shame or disgraced, to ages everlasting.' Once the saving has taken place, the salvation remains. The 'eternal' outcome of God's finished action will never pass away.

Eternal sin (Mark 3:29)

In a controversy with some teachers of the law, Jesus said that whoever blasphemes against the Holy Spirit 'will never be forgiven: he is guilty of an *eternal sin*.' Verse 30 explains the nature of this 'eternal sin'. This sin of attributing to the demonic the Holy Spirit's power manifested in Jesus had a unique quality. It was 'eternal' because it resisted and contradicted the

---

28. This is all the more striking here since 'redemption' is in a form (*lutrōsis*) which, if anything, points to the process involved.

power of the Age to Come. It stood in opposition to the inbreaking kingdom of God, as Luke points out in the parallel passage (Luke 11:20). Matthew says it will not be forgiven, even in the Age to Come, which for Matthew is equivalent to saying it is an 'eternal sin' (Matt.12:32). Here too the act (of sinning) does not continue for ever. It was committed on that occasion in Jesus' ministry and may possibly never be repeated in exactly the same way. Punishment in hell is due for sins committed during this *Present Age*, not for evil done following the last day (Rom. 2:6–16). This 'eternal' sin was committed once. But its result remains for eternity.

Eternal destruction (2 Thess. 1:9)

When Jesus comes, he will punish those who have rejected the gospel. They will be punished with everlasting destruction and shut out from the presence of the Lord and from the majesty of his power.'[29]

This destruction clearly partakes of the Age to Come. It belongs to those eschatological realities which are now unseen and mysterious to our Present Age. In that sense it is 'eternal' in quality. It is also everlasting and unending. The NIV uses two verbs to describe the fate of the wicked. They will be 'punished' (with everlasting destruction), and they will be 'shut out' from the Lord's presence and power. The second verb, however, is not in the Greek but is supplied by the NIV translators. There is more to say about this, but for now we note that whatever happens will happen 'on the day he comes' (v. 10). It will not be happening for ever, but when he has brought about their destruction, its results will never end.

In keeping with the rest of the teaching of both Old and New Testaments, we suggest that this 'eternal destruction' will be the extinction of those so sentenced. This retribution will be preceded by penal suffering exactly suited to each degree of guilt by a holy and just God, but that penal suffering is not *itself* the ultimate retribution or punishment. There will be an act of destroying, resulting in a destruction that will never end or be reversed. The act of destroying includes penal pains, but they will end. The result of destruction will never be reversed and will never have an end.

Eternal punishment (Matt. 25:46)

The Parable of the Sheep and Goats ends with the statement that the wicked 'will go away to *eternal punishment*, but the righteous to eternal life.' Both the life and the punishment partake of the quality of the Age to Come. We have some experience here and now of *life* and of *punishment*. But we cannot know now what the *eternal* life will be in its fullness nor can we know now what the *eternal* punishment will be in its actual horror. There is more to either than a timeless extension of what we can now experience. We are acquainted to some extent with the nouns: the

---

29. There is no valid reason why the NIV should here follow the KJV in translating *aiōnios* as 'everlasting' instead of 'eternal' (as in the RSV, NEB, NASV and others). It is particularly strange since the NIV has 'eternal' punishment in Matt. 25:46.

adjective tells us they will then be of a quality we do not yet comprehend. There is clearly a qualitative aspect to 'eternal' punishment.

At the same time, the life and the punishment of this passage are never to end. They are 'eternal' in the sense of everlasting. But we need to note, as in the five cases above, that 'punishment' is an act or process. In each case so far, and indisputably in the first four, the act or process happens in a fixed period of time but is followed by a result that lasts for ever. In keeping with that scriptural usage, we suggest that the 'punishment' here includes whatever penal suffering God justly awards to each person but consists primarily of the total abolition and extinction of the person for ever. The punishing continues until the process is completed, and then it stops. But the punishment which results will remain for ever.[30]

Conclusion

This is a powerful argument which conditionalists have pressed with vigour.[31] In all the literature covered by this study, no traditionalist writer has dealt with it at all except perhaps to assert that it is false without giving any reasoning or evidence – and that but rarely. Like most of the conditionalist arguments, this one has simply been ignored. If the traditional understanding of hell is to stand, a cogent and persuasive answer must be forthcoming. Since all we want to know is God's truth as revealed in Scripture, no one need be threatened on either side of the discussion. This is a challenge which calls for careful exegesis and prayerful study within a commitment to the final authority of the Word of God.

Summary concerning 'eternal'/*aiōnios*

We have seen that the adjective *aiōnios* distinctly carries a qualitative sense. It suggests something that partakes of the transcendent realm of divine activity. It indicates a relationship to the kingdom of God, to the Age to Come, to the eschatological realities which in Jesus have begun already to manifest themselves in the Present Age.[32] It reminds us that while the nouns it modifies may be familiar, they are somehow set apart from our present experiences. There is more than meets the eye, a depth

---

30. Some have objected that such absolute destruction by extinction would not be sufficient 'punishment' or that it would not suit the description 'eternal'. We will consider both objections later, noting here only that these points are conceded by Augustine and by Jonathan Edwards.

31. Pétavel, *Problem* pp. 194f ; Froom, *Conditionalist Faith* 1:288–291. Guillebaud says: 'We do not claim to have proved that this interpretation is certainly right, but to have shown that it is legitimate and possible, and cannot (so far as the texts containing the word "eternal" are concerned) be called a forcing of Scripture to suit a theory' (*Righteous Judge* p. 11).

32. The Holy Spirit's descent upon the Christian church at Pentecost is also related to this. The Spirit not only guarantees to believers fulness of life in the age to come (Rom. 8:16–23; 2 Cor. 5:4; Eph. 1:13f, 2:7); He is also even now the mediating source by which God demonstrates the power of that age among his people (1 Cor. 14:24; Eph. 3:16, 20; Heb. 6:5). There is an *already* to this *not yet*, though there is so much more to come!

we do not fathom. Those traditionalist writers who deny any qualitative sense in *aiōnios* have overreacted. Their zeal for one truth has blinded them unnecessarily to another. Unless we coin a more appropriate word such as 'aionion' or 'aionic', this aspect of *aiōnios* is best represented by the word 'eternal'. We have also seen that the adjective *aiōnios* has a temporal aspect, indicating something that will never end. God himself has no limitation, including the limits of time. The Age to Come partakes of that limitlessness. So do the works of God which Scripture calls 'eternal'.

Those non-traditionalist writers who deny any temporal sense in *aiōnios* have also overreacted. They have not needed to deny the unendingness of the 'eternal' in order to hold to its otherness. Both are true. Many writers holding both positions have happily admitted as much. This unending aspect of *aiōnios* is best represented by the word 'everlasting' until someone finds a word more appropriate. Finally, we have seen that when the word *aiōnios* modifies words which name acts or processes as distinct from persons or things, the adjective usually describes the issue or result of the action rather than the action itself. This is indisputably true in four of the six New Testament occurrences. There is eternal salvation but not an eternal act of saving. There is eternal redemption but not an eternal process of redeeming. The eternal sin was committed at a point in history, but its results continue into the coming age which lasts for ever. Scripture pictures eternal judgment as taking place 'on a day', but its outcome will have no end. We suggest therefore that Scripture expects the same understanding when it speaks of 'eternal destruction' and 'eternal punishment.' Both are acts. There will be an actual destroying, an actual punishing. Both will issue in a result which will never end.

Yet a question remains and it has to do with human personality. Regardless of what one may think about the word 'eternal', can human beings ever be completely destroyed? Does not the immortality of the soul require that they continue to exist for ever? And does that not require the doctrine of conscious torment that will never end? Let us move on.

3

'If a Man Lives Again, Can He Die?' (The Question of Immortality)

While scholars define 'eternity', popular preachers and ordinary Christians are often talking about a different subject: human nature itself, and particularly that unseen 'part' commonly called the 'soul.' Physical death cannot, allegedly, touch this because it possesses immortality, and so at the last judgment God will sentence the wicked, then banish their never-dying-souls to conscious torment throughout the never-ending age. 'You have an immortal soul,' urges the revivalist, 'and it will spend eternity in either heaven or hell.' Theologians also fall back at times on the doctrine of man's immortality in this context. 'If man is admitted to be immortal,' writes Pusey, 'and punishment is not to be endless, there is no other conclusion but that he should be restored.'[1] Shedd notes that Scripture speaks of but two aeons, which cover and include all human existence, and concludes, 'If, therefore, he is an immortal being one of these must be endless.'[2] Hodge links the two and completes the traditional argument as it is often made. 'If the Bible says that the sufferings of the lost are to be everlasting, they are to endure for ever, unless it can be shown either that the soul is not immortal or that the Scriptures elsewhere teach that those sufferings are to come to an end.'[3] Shedd is bolder than most in his expression, but he clearly presents this common understanding of innate immortality. He even awes himself as he states what he believes.

> But irrepressible and universal as it is, the doctrine of man's immortality is an astonishing one, and difficult to entertain. For it means that every frail finite man is to be as long enduring as the infinite and eternal God: that there will no more be an end to the existence of the man who died today than there will be of the Deity who made him. God is denominated 'The Ancient of Days'. But every immortal spirit that ever dwelt in a human body will also be an 'ancient of days' . . . Yes, man *must* exist. He has no option. Necessity is laid upon him. He cannot extinguish himself. He cannot cease to be.[4]

If someone inquires why this does not fly into the face of Scripture's statement that God alone possesses immortality (1 Tim. 6:16), proponents answer that human immortality concerns only the soul, which survives bodily death.

---

1. *What is of Faith?* p. 27.
2. *Punishment* p. 86.
3. Hodge, *Systematic* 3:876.
4. *Punishment* p. 490.

God is immortal in the sense that he cannot die ... God 'only hath immortality' such as this. Man is immortal in the sense that there is in him that which does not die. His body dies, but his soul survives. It lives on after it has left the body. His identity is not lost when he dies: his true self, the ultimate being and personality of the man, remains as it was before death .... Not all of him dies: there is a part of him, and by far the more essential ....[5]

These theologians frankly admit that the expression 'immortal soul' is not in the Bible but confidently state that Scripture assumes the immortality of every soul. A popular writer says, for example: 'The Word of God assumes the eternal existence of every soul regardless of its destiny. Every man's soul is immortal and can never be annihilated.'[6] He later notes, 'They that are Christ's' tells us who shall become immortal, and "at his coming" ... tells us when we shall become immortal',[7] but still says, 'As a matter of fact the soul never lost its immortality.'[8] Since Calvin, whom we shall consider later, Reformed writers in particular have viewed human immortality as resulting from being formed in God's image and quickened by God's breath of life.[9] Buis is careful not to claim too much but says that while 'this cannot be considered absolute proof of the natural immortality of man, it certainly points in that direction.'[10] Although advocates sometimes present this view in a slightly tentative manner, they seem constrained to insist because here they perceive the supernaturalist view withstanding the anti-supernaturalist. The anti-supernaturalist says that for humankind death is the end. These orthodox thinkers know this is not so, and try to distinguish themselves from their unbelieving opponents by insisting there is a part which does not die. This 'immortal soul' escapes the death to which the body succumbs.

Uneasiness within orthodox ranks

The feeling has persisted, however, that something here does not fit.[11] While some orthodox writers have continued to affirm the immortality of

---

5. H. B. Swete, *Life of the World to Come* p. 3.
6. Lehmann Strauss, *Life After Death: What the Bible Really Teaches* p. 14. Blanchard (*Hell* 68f.) denies that the body can be destroyed either: 'The human body is a part of the material universe, and it has long been established that no material object in the universe can be destroyed in the sense of being wiped out of existence. Even if it disappears it is immediately reconstituted either as matter or energy. As this is a law which operates everywhere in nature, the human body is literally indestructible, and that being the case the extinction of the soul would be out of character with everything else that God has created.'
7. Ibid. p. 17.
8. Ibid. p. 16.
9. Calvin's corner of the Reformation has carried the heaviest end of the immortality log the past 400 years. The mortalist position has been widely held among Lutherans, Baptists and particularly Anglicans throughout Protestant history. Fundamentalism seems to have acquired the immortalist position through its 'Old Princeton' Calvinist ancestry, and the doctrine has since settled in with the unquestioned authority of a venerated relative.
10. Buis, *Eternal Punishment* p. 8.
11. Hodge (*Outlines* pp. 549-552), Shedd (*Dogmatic Theology* 2:612) and Berkhof (*Systematic* p. 672) all defend immortality as a biblical doctrine. Hermann Bavinck calls it a

the soul, though often with a look over the shoulder, many others have charged that the doctrine has serious deficiencies. The doctrine of inherent immortality is pagan in origin, they say, and crept into Christian thinking through Platonic philosophy. The Bible places hope for life after death in a bodily resurrection, not in an 'immortal soul'. They point out that the passages which speak of immortality attribute it to a future glorified body, not to the present soul; immortality is God's gift for the saved, not the inherent birthright of every person born into the world.

'The dream that death is an emancipation of the spiritual essence from a body that imprisons and clogs it, and is in itself the entrance on a freer, larger life, belongs to the schools, not to Christianity', writes James Orr.[12] Salmond points out that Paul, who gives more 'of a seeming psychology' than any other New Testament writer, 'never contemplates a simple immortality of soul: he never argues for man's survival merely on the ground that there is a mind or spirit in him. He proceeds upon the Old Testament view of man.' That view, Salmond continues, 'is essentially different from the Hellenic idea which ruled the scholastic theory, and has exercised a deep and unfortunate influence on modern systems of doctrine.'[13] Westcott notes that 'on principles of reason there seems to be no ground whatever for supposing that the soul as separate from the body is personal'. Such a statement, he admits, goes against popular language and belief, which 'are so strong in the assertion of the personal immortality of the soul . . . that it is very difficult for us to realise the true state of the problem'.[14] Writing in 1918 (*This Life and the Next*, p. 68), P. T. Forsyth expressed similar doubts. 'We can be more sure about the new creation than about the natural immortality of the soul. I do not wish to prejudge the question about conditional immortality. But I venture to suggest that it is better to approach the matter theologically than philosophically, in terms of the first creation and the second, of nature and of grace . . . Immortality is a gift, a creation.'

Dispensationalist J. N. Darby expressed his conviction that the idea of the immortality of the soul 'is not in general a gospel topic: that it comes, on the contrary, from the Platonists: and that it was just when the coming of Christ was denied in the Church, or at least began to be lost sight of,

---

'mixed article' demonstrated better by reason than by revelation. (Bavinck, *Gereformeerde Dogmatik*, 4th edition., 4:567; 3rd ed., 4:648). G. C. Berkouwer comments that 'Scripture is never concerned with an independent interest in immortality as such, let alone with the immortality of a part of a man which defies and survives death under all the circumstances, and on which we can reflect quite apart from man's relation to the living God' (Berkouwer, *Man: The Image of God* [Eerdmans 1962] p. 276). For these and other references see Hoekema, *The Bible and the Future* p. 89.

12. James Orr, *The Resurrection of Jesus* p. 282.

13. *Immortality* p. 573. Salmond was ahead of his time in noting the tension between the biblical and philosophical attitudes regarding man. Although he comes out in the end against the annhilation of the wicked, he considers the possibility and makes some objections.

14. *The Gospel of the Resurrection*: pp. 146f. In a footnote Westcott exempts from his comments here quoted the intermediate state of the soul between death and resurrection.

that the doctrine of the immortality of the soul came in to replace that of the resurrection.'[15]

George Beasley-Murray agrees. Philosophical arguments for surviving death 'usually proceed without reference' to Jesus' resurrection, he observes, and therefore 'cannot strictly be termed Christian'. In the end they are therefore 'irrelevant, for the Resurrection is itself a sufficient revelation both of the fact and the nature of immortality'. The kind of liberal preaching which dissolves Jesus' resurrection into an example of human immortality in general is unworthy of the gospel; it 'bears little relation to the New Testament'.[16]

Such statements could be mutiplied.[17] Traditionalists may no longer claim that the Bible assumes the immortality of the soul even though it does not teach it. Wenham throws down the gauntlet. That 'so important a truth should not be explicitly taught is strange. The onus of proof is on those who say it is assumed.'[18]

It has generally been thought that the immortality of the soul was a necessary tool for Christian theology. Today, however, the doctrine is increasingly regarded as a post-apostolic innovation, not only unnecessary but positively harmful to proper biblical interpretation and understanding.[19]

---

15. J. N. Darby, 'Hopes of the Church', *Works, Prophetic* (London Geo. Morrish, 1866) 1:463, quoted by Pétavel, *Problem* p. 111. The statement was weakened in a later edition of Darby's book, though the gist remained.

16. G. R. Beasley-Murray, *Christ is Alive!* p. 153.

17. They are – by Froom, *Conditionalist Faith* 2:247–1048. These pages trace the conditionalist witness from 1800. Froom's massive work was published after most of the traditionalist books on final punishment so far and has not received critical attention by such writers. In spite of an obviously polemical tone and a tendency to over-generalize at the expense of disagreeable evidence, Froom's encyclopaedic presentation must be considered in any thorough discussion of this subject in the future.

Froom cites many sources which carry little weight among evangelicals, and he tends at least to give the impression of extravagance in evaluating material. In spite of these weaknesses (in which he is certainly not alone, perhaps including this writer!), Froom convincingly establishes his claim of legitimacy for the minority conditionalist position in Christian understanding through the centuries. By constantly ascribing Platonism to immortalists (overlooking important distinctions), he detracts somewhat from the primary thesis, which he firmly establishes. It would be unfair of critics to simply note these subsidiary errors and offhandedly pass by the great mass of Froom's material.

18. Wenham, *Goodness* p. 35, note 4.

19. D. W. Gundry writes that 'although St Paul mentions Judaism in *Galatians* as a schoolmaster to bring us to Christ, within the apostolic period itself Hellenistic philosophy soon appears as another schoolmaster. Nor, indeed, did it prove any exception to the failing of schoolmasters at large – that of becoming an intellectual tyrant whose domination of the pupil lingers long after the pupil has left school' (Gundry, 'The Ghost in the Machine and the Body of the Resurrection', *SJT* 18, no. 2 [June 1965]:164).

The popular view of man's immortal soul has replaced the resurrection as ground of comfort in actual practice, according to several writers. See James J. Heller, 'The Resurrection of Man' *TT* 15, no. 2 (July 1958) p. 217f.; Hans Hofmann, 'Immortality or Life' (op. cit. 231); Gundry, op cit. p. 169; Joseph Blenkinsopp, 'Theological Synthesis and Hermeneutical Conclusions', *Immortality and Resurrection* p. 119; Helmut Thielicke, *Death and Life* pp. 197ff. Herhold looks at the modern rash of testimonies about 'after-death experiences' and comments, 'One does not need Easter if the spirit or soul is immortal. But it is precisely because "when you're dead, you're dead" that the resurrection

Critics further charge that the traditional view of immortal souls is without support either from Scripture[20] or from human wisdom.[21]

The relation between the doctrine of the soul's immortality and the doctrine of final punishment is real, though its clarity is deceptive. If every soul lives for ever, the traditional view of hell as unending conscious torment seems to follow. This presupposition has wielded tremendous influence on biblical interpretation in intertestamental Judaism and through most of the Christian centuries. One of Froom's main theses is that 'innate Immortal-Soulism' is the villain behind the traditionalist view of hell. Like the persistent officer of *Les Misérables*, he ferrets out the offender, then dogs his heels through nearly 2500 years and practically as many pages.[22]

Yet further reading suggests that much of Froom's energy might be misspent. For orthodox writers through the centuries from the apologists of the second and third centuries after Christ, to Augustine, to Calvin, to Reformed theologians today have usually been careful to qualify their claim for human immortality.[23] This means, they say, that something about human beings survives physical death and ensures a life beyond the grave. They emphasize that we are not immortal in the same way God is. Human immortality was a gift from the Creator and that same Creator is at perfect liberty to recall it. We are immortal or 'deathless', they say, in the sense that physical death will not be our final end. But that does not mean human beings are inherently indestructible. Just as Christian advocates of general immortality have qualified their view by saying that God can annihilate the soul, so Christian 'mortalists' have recognized that God can grant deathlessness and incorruptibility to any person he wishes. In the view of the first, the final annihilation of the wicked is possible – if God so wills. In the view of the second, the eternal preservation of the wicked is possible – if God so wishes. The crucial question is not really

---

is such incredibly good news' (R. M. Herhold, 'Kubler-Ross and Life after Death', *Christian Century*, 14 April 1976 p. 364).

20. Cullmann, *Immortality or Resurrection?* pp. 19–39; Murray Harris, 'Resurrection and Immortality: Eight Theses' *Themelios* 1 no. 2 (Spring 1976) pp. 50–55.

21. A Lutheran philosopher critiques the arguments of Plato (pp. 113–118), Aquinas (pp. 19–126) and Kant (pp. 126–132) for immortality and finds them all wanting (Reichenbach, *Phoenix*).

22. If Froom attributes Augustine's dualistic view of man to Plato, so his critics might trace Aquinas' monistic view to Aristotle. Both Greek philosophy and medieval scholasticism encompassed much. It is a form of 'grandstanding' to ignore the philosophical precedents of one's own position while charging one's opponent with philosophical presuppositions. For a critique of the monistic view of man from a philosophical standpoint, see Reichenbach, *Phoenix*.

23. A theologian describing himself as a 'convinced evolutionist' has argued that human immortality is not 'borrowed' but 'bestowed', affirming that 'something bestowed is bestowed for ever' (S. Dockx, 'Man's Eschatological Condition', *SJT* 27, no. 1 [Feb. 1974] p. 26). Origen is also an exception to this general rule. He proposed the eternality of souls, including their pre-existence, and reasoned to the ultimate restoration of all men. This view was condemned under Pope Vigilius in 543 according to M. E. Williams, 'Immortality of Human Soul', *NCE* 12:468f.

about natural mortality or immortality, therefore, for both sides concede the ultimate point to the greater sovereignty of God. The issue really becomes a matter of exegesis. Since God is able to preserve or to destroy his human creature, what does Scripture indicate that he will do to those finally expelled to hell?

Misunderstanding and overstatement have also frequently clouded the historical picture. As a matter of fact, the immortality of the soul has not been the universal faith of the church. It has always been questioned by some of her faithful children, as Froom clearly documents and other conditionalists have shown. It was championed, however, by the Roman Catholic tradition and, later, by the Calvinist. Today the doctrine is under attack in both those houses as well[24] – not in the name of science or philosophy but, as the direct result of work in biblical theology, attempting to purify the stream of tradition from pollutants produced by the philosophical factories which for nearly two millennia have contaminated its waters. Furthermore, a great portion of the Protestant world has roots in another view of human nature which does not insist on innate immortality. These include the Lutheran, Anglican and Anabaptist traditions, which all either sprang from or have from earliest times included the outlook known as 'Christian mortalism.'[25]

The biblical view

The Western church, along with the larger culture, bears the unmistakable stamp of the philosophies of ancient Greece and Rome. Biblical scholars continue to identify these alien traces in theological thought and attempt to distinguish them from what is authentic. Human nature has become a kind of focal point in this enterprise. Measured by the systematic and analytical standards of Greek philosophy, the Bible meets us here with what one writer has called a 'resounding silence'.[26] What it does say is often presented as the exact antithesis to 'the Greek view', and writers regularly talk of 'the Hebrew view' as if the term had a clear

---

24. See Calvinist sources in note 11, 32, 43–44 among others. Roman Catholic critics of natural immortality include: Andre-Marie Dubarle, 'Belief in immortality in the Old Testament and Judaism', *Immortality and Resurrection* pp. 37f.; S. B. Marrow and M. E. Williams, in articles under 'Soul' and 'Immortality', *NCE*.

25. The term belongs to Norman T. Burns and refers to 'the belief that according to divine revelation the soul does not exist as an independent conscious substance after the death of the body' (*Christian Mortalism* p. 13). Burns says many authors confuse two incompatible types of immortalism. He distinguishes between them. 'Annihilationists' deny a resurrection of the body, while 'soul sleepers' believe in a resurrection which will include the personal soul as well as body (p. 13). The latter ground is further divided between those who believe that the entire person dies together and those who believe in a personal soul which does not die but sleeps until resurrection (pp. 13f).

This same confusion is evident in much traditionalist literature concerning final punishment when 'Jehovah's Witnesses' (who deny that the wicked will be raised) are put in the same basket with Seventh-day Adventists (and others who affirm a resurrection of just and unjust with the ultimate annhilation of the wicked).

26. Gatch, *Death* p. 35.

and single meaning.[27] Careful scholars have criticized such oversimplifications.[28] They remind us of the rich diversity of thought found among 'Greeks' as well as 'Hebrews', particularly at the beginning of the Christian era.[29]

Many evangelical scholars are among those suggesting that traditional orthodoxy has passed lightly over the biblical material relating to human personality. The church, they say, has often drawn hasty conclusions and has frequently over-generalized in stating them. They point out that while humankind is made in God's image (Gen. 1:27), immortality is no more an essential quality of God than omnipotence or omniscience, yet no one has considered these to be inherent in the human creature. Even if the image of God included immortality, that might have been lost with the fall, for Adam 'begat a son in *his own* likeness, after *his* image' (Gen. 5:3).

The tree of life represented immortality in fellowship with God; but sin brought death and exile from the garden. As for Adam becoming a 'living soul', the identical Hebrew words are translated 'living creature' in the same context (Gen. 2:19; 9:12) and are applied to brute animals. Furthermore, the 'living souls' were told that if they disobeyed God, they would 'surely die'.

Jesus' quotation of the declaration, 'I am the God of Abraham, the God of Isaac, and the God of Jacob' (Matt. 22:32), has often been used to support belief in human immortality. But Jesus uses the quotation to

---

27. H. Wheeler Robinson, for example, commenting on the view of certain church fathers: 'This doctrine of resurrection, a common article of the Church's faith, shows the Hebrew parentage of the anthropology of the Church, just as the conception of immortality is largely due to Greek influences' (Christian Doctrine of Man p. 170).

28. Notably James Barr, (*Old and New in Interpretation* p. 39). Acknowledging this criticism, G. E. Ladd 'deliberately' speaks of 'the Greek view' in spite of Barr's objections. He justifies this designation for Platonic dualism in terms of its later influence on Christian theology. For an excellent discussion of the Platonic attitude over against the biblical (if not always 'Hebrew' or 'Jewish') outlook, see George Eldon Ladd, *The Pattern of New Testament Truth*, especially the chapter entitled 'The Background of the Pattern'.

29. 'It is indefensible to assert that Christianity owes its doctrine of resurrection to Jewish thought but its concept of immortality to Greek philosophy,' says Murray Harris. He cites the variety of thought found in Jewish literature between the Testaments, some of which we will consider later in detail (Harris, 'Resurrection and Immortality' p. 52). We recognize the diversity of Jewish thought concerning man and his destiny, and acknowledge the validity of the objection that 'the Hebrew view' is often grossly oversimplified and unfairly singularized. At the same time, one *might* speak of 'the Hebrew view' as here defined. Judaic literature of the intertestamental period and thereafter often reflects 'the Greek view' even if the authors were Jewish.

Nevertheless, it is easy to overstate conclusions and oversimplify material. Thus traditionalist writers have frequently assumed that by his relative silence Jesus endorsed the Pharisees' belief in the immortality of the soul. Jewish thought of Jesus' time is then represented as having only two strains – outright Platonic dualism (held by the Pharisees) and utter materialism (held by the Sadducees). Since the Gospels record Jesus' rejection of the Sadducees' doctrine, it is assumed that he agreed with the Pharisees. Such reasoning overlooks the diversity of Jewish thought illustrated in the sources. It also proves more than orthodox theologians would wish to affirm since Josephus may indicate a Pharisaic belief in transmigration of souls.

prove, not immortality, but the resurrection![30] The Lukan parallel (20:37f.) says that 'to him all are alive', but both the context and the argument point to the resurrection of those who belong to God, not the immortality of every person.[31] When the Bible uses expressions such as 'salvation of the soul' (cf e.g., Mark 8:35ff; Heb.10:39 KJV; 1 Pet. 1:9), it is utilizing such passages as Psalms 16:9ff, 49:15 and 73:24, in which the psalmist expresses his hope for abiding fellowship with God, who will not let his own perish. 'The "soul" . . . does not stand in dualistic contrast to the body, but signifies man himself whom God seeks and saves for life eternal.'[32] The soul, for New Testament writers as well as Old, generally stands for 'the natural life of man . . . in his limitedness and humanity over against the divine possibilities and realities'.[33]

Man in the Old Testament

Man is described as a 'soul' (Hebrew: *nephesh*, Gr. *psychē*) over 130 times in the Old Testament and about 16 times in the New. The Old Testament displays *nephesh* in such a rainbow of shades that English translators have rendered it 45 different ways![34] God forms Adam of dust, breathes into him 'breath of life', and he becomes a 'living soul'. This resembles our saying that a man or animal *is* a conscious being and also *has* conscious being.[35] The Old Testament applies the same terms to both man and the animals.

This is true of *nephesh*/soul-life (Gen. 9:5), *ruach*/spirit-breath (Gen. 6:17) and *neshamah*/spirit (Gen. 7:22). 'Soul' is the most comprehensive term for man in his wholeness, and its meanings range from 'neck', 'life', 'self' and 'person' to what seems the opposite of life – 'corpse' (Num. 19:31).[36]

'The soul is not only the upholder of certain states: it is the full soul

---

30. Orr, *The Resurrection of Jesus* p. 283.
31. Guillebaud, *Righteous Judge* p. 3.
32. Karel Hanhart, *The Intermediate State in the New Testament* pp. 238f.
33. Ridderbos, *Paul* p. 120. See also pp. 54 9f.
34. Atkinson, *Life and Immortality* p. 3. This book, though small, makes an exhaustive study of the biblical usages of words involved in the four topics which are the heads of Atkinson's chapters: 'The Nature of Man,' 'Rest and Darkness,' 'Resurrection and Glory,' and 'The Doom of the Lost.' Morey argues that the Septuagint used *psychē* for *nephesh* because its translators believed in the immortality of the soul and this Greek word everywhere had that meaning. (*Death and the Afterlife*, Bethany House, 1984 p. 50.) In fact, *psychē* was used by Greeks who believed the soul died with the body and also by those who believed it lived forever and always had.
35. Ibid. p. 2.
36. Heller, pp. 220f. The KJV has 'living soul' in Gen. 2:7 but translates the same Hebrew phrase 'living creature' in verse 14, where it is applied to the animals. Norman Snaith calls this 'most reprehensible . . . . It is a grave reflection on the Revisers that they retained this misleading difference in translation . . . . The Hebrew phrase should be translated exactly the same way in both cases. To do otherwise is to mislead all those who do not read Hebrew . . . . The tendency to read 'immortal soul' into the Hebrew *nephesh* and translate accordingly is very ancient, and can be seen in the Septuagint rendering of Lev. 24:18, where the Greek translators omitted the word' (Norman Snaith, 'Justice and Immortality,' *SJT* 17, no. 3 [Sep. 1964] pp. 312f).

substance with special qualities and powers.'[37] It 'is man himself viewed as a living creature'.[38] Wolff breaks down according to its primary terms the Old Testament view of human nature in its wholeness. *Soul* speaks of 'needy man', *flesh* is 'man in his infinity', *spirit* points to 'man as he is empowered', and *heart* signifies 'reasonable man.'[39] Nikolainen summarizes the Old Testament's wholistic anthropology thus:

> Man is an indivisible whole. Seen from different points of view, he is by turns body, flesh and blood, soul, spirit, and heart. Each of these portrays a specific human characteristic, but they are not parts into which man may be divided. Body is man as a concrete being; 'flesh and blood' is man as a creature distinguished from the Creator; soul is the living human individual; spirit is man as having his source in God; heart is man as a whole in action. What is distinctively human is in every respect derived from God. Man is in every cell the work of God (body), he is in all circumstances the property of God (soul), he is absolutely dependent on God (spirit), and in all his activity he is either obedient to God or disobedient (heart). The God relationship is not merely the life of the 'highest part' of man. The whole man 'from top to bottom' exists only by relation to God.[40]

All these details lead to a single conclusion.

> When *death* occurs, then it is the soul that is deprived of life. Death cannot strike the body or any other part of the soul without striking the entirety of the soul . . . . It is deliberately said both that the soul dies (Judg. 16, 30; Num. 23, 10 et al.), that it is destroyed or consumed (Ez. 22, 23, 27), and that it is extinguished (Job 11, 20).[41]

This is the consistent witness of the Old Testament.

Man in the New Testament

The New Testament does not take a different view of the matter. Paul uses 'soul' (*psychē*) only 13 times, usually with reference to the natural life of humankind. The adjectival form of this word designates the unspiritual or carnal person as opposed to the spiritual one (1 Cor. 2:14ff), or the

37. Johannes Pedersen, *Israel: Its Life and Culture* 1–2:152.
38. Ladd, *New Testament Truth* p. 37.
39. Hans Walter Wolff, *Anthropology of Old Testament*, Contents.
40. T. A. Kantonen (*The Christian Hope* [1954] pp. 30ff) so summarizes Aimo Nikolainen's 1941 Finnish-language study, *Man in the Light of the Gospel*. Quoted here from Heller, *The Resurrection of Man*.
41. Pedersen, *Israel* p. 179. Froom quotes part of Pedersen's statement here as evidence that in the OT view 'the soul dies'. Yet one wonders if Froom is reading Pedersen with Greek eyes himself. Pedersen says earlier: 'This does not mean that *nephesh* means life or soul interchangeably; still less does it mean, as has been maintained, that *nephesh* does not mean soul at all, but only life . . . . But the fact is that soul as well as life with the Israelites means something else than it usually does with us' (p. 152). Pedersen seems to say that, given the Hebrews' wholistic view of man, it was natural that they should speak of 'the soul' dying; he is not taking sides on whether or not 'the soul' (in a dualistic or Platonic sense) either can or does 'die'.

natural body of the present life in contrast to the spiritual body of the life to come (1 Cor.15:44).

For the biblical writers, every expression of hope after death, of vindication beyond the present life, or of communion with God beyond the grave, is grounded on the faithfulness of the living God, who has shown himself so true in life and will not forsake his own people in death. David expects to 'dwell in the house of the Lord for ever' for the very same reason he anticipates 'goodness and love all the days' of his earthly life (Ps. 23:6). That reason is the fidelity he has always seen in God, who keeps covenant, not any death proof substance he discovers in his own self. Like Jesus (Luke 23:46), Stephen (Acts 7:59) and Paul (2 Tim. 1:12), the Christian believer's hope is in the faithfulness of the Creator (1 Pet. 4:19), who is able to raise the dead (Rom. 4:17; 1 Pet. 1:21).

Reichenbach's study leads him to conclude that 'the doctrine that man as a person does not die . . . is apparently contrary to the teachings of Scripture . . . . There is no hint that the only thing spoken about is the destruction of the physical organism, and that the real person, the soul, does not die but lives on.'[42] Donald Bloesch underscores this conclusion. 'There is no inherent immortality of the soul. The person who dies, even the one who dies in Christ, undergoes the death of both body and soul.'[43]

Hoekema concludes that 'we cannot point to any inherent quality in man or in any aspect of man which makes him indestructible.'[44] F. F. Bruce warns that 'our traditional thinking about the "never-dying soul," which owes so much to our Graeco-Roman heritage, makes it difficult for us to appreciate Paul's point of view.'[45] Helmut Thielicke denies that Paul speaks of some 'immortal substance which would victoriously break through our mortal fate'. Our hope is altogether in God, who 'has given us the hope that on the other side of the great fissure he continues to be Lord and does not allow his history to be ruptured, that he is for us a God of life and resurrection, that he remains the Creator *ex nihilo* and his initial instalment of this hope is the Spirit (2 Cor. 5:5).'[46]

---

42. *Phoenix* p. 54. Contrast Morey, who exclaims that 'once man dies, he . . . becomes a disembodied supradimensional energy being and is capable of thought and speech without the need of a body' (*Afterlife* p. 79). Such a notion not only lacks any scriptural basis but also eliminates the need for a bodily resurrection since this 'disembodied supra-dimensional energy being' gets along so well without a body and might even travel faster unencumbered by one! To his credit, Morey elsewhere (p. 44) explains that 'soul' and 'spirit' do not refer to 'separate entities' in man but rather describe the human being's 'multi-dimensional functions and relationships'.

43. Bloesch, *Essentials* 2:188.

44. Hoekema, *The Bible and the Future* p. 90.

45. F. F. Bruce. 'Paul on Immortality,' *SJT* 24, no. 4 (Nov. 1971) p. 469. The quotation apears also in *Paul* p. 311.

46. Thielicke, *Death and Life* p. 133. Thielicke scrutinizes anthropology and soteriology side by side, then contrasts Luther's view with Roman Catholic teaching. Luther saw man in need of God's constant creative gift of life – and of imputed righteousness by grace through faith. Rome pictured man as having immortality in his own soul – and receiving an infused righteousness and grace in himself. Thielicke comments: 'Just as no creature on the level of death and life has any inherent qualitative immortality, so also on the level of sin and justification no man has inherent qualitative righteousness' (p. 107). Later he writes that 'both righteousness and *zōē* [life] remain exclusively at God's disposal' and that

Murray Harris offers eight theses concerning resurrection and immortality, concluding: 'Man is not immortal because he possesses or is a soul. He becomes immortal because God transforms him by raising him from the dead.' Platonic thought made immortality 'an inalienable attribute of the soul,' he continues, 'but the Bible contains no definition of the soul's constitution that implies its indestructibility'.[47]

That gifted apologist and theologian, Edward John Carnell, cut through the humanist's optimism, the scholastic's tradition and the philosopher's wisdom to focus on man before God, man as *creature*, man as *sinner*. He stood on the solid rock of biblical faith, surrounded by the best of orthodoxy's heritage, when he concluded:

> Instead of teaching that man is of such infinitely incontestable value, that God, to be worthy of his name, must preserve him immortally, the Christian follows Paul's judgment that there is none righteous, no not one (Romans 3:10). Man, then, deserves death, not life. The Christian cannot appeal to the rationality of the universe, for all rationality is from God. He cannot claim an independent rule of goodness and justice to assure him of life, for all goodness and justice flow from God. In short, the Christian knows that man, a vile, wretched, filthy sinner, will receive immortal life solely and only by God's grace: man neither deserves immortality nor is worthy of it. Unless he that made man sovereignly elects to give him salvation and life, by grace and not by works, man is absolutely without hope. Man came into this world naked and it is certain that he will depart in exactly the same manner: and he Who gave life in the first place can also recall it either to damnation, blessedness, or annihilation.[48]

'I participate in them only to the degree that fellowship with God in Christ vouchsafed to me ... for no intrinsic reason at all' (p. 197).

Here, he says, 'the reformers' biblical understanding of justification reaches, as it were, its high point. Just as I stand with empty hands before God and remain standing, just as I can only beseech God nevertheless to accept me, in just this fashion do I move into my death with empty hands and without any death-proof substance in my soul, but only with my gaze focused on God's hand and with the petition on my lips, "Hand that will last, hold me fast!" ... I remain in fellowship with him who is Alpha and Omega and with this knowledge I walk into the night of death, truly the darkest night; yet I know who awaits me in the morning' (pp. 198f). Calvin's predisposition toward the immortality of the soul prevented him from grasping this connection between man's nature and his salvation.

47. 'Resurrection and Immortality,' p. 53. Morey speaks for traditionalists in general in affirming that 'man is always and absolutely dependent upon the Creator for this life as well as for the next life,' and that 'life in this world and in the next must always be viewed as a gift from God' (*Afterlife* p. 94). Like some modern defenders of unending conscious torment, he also acknowledges (but seemingly does not factor into his reasoning) that whenever Scripture uses the terms 'immortal' or 'incorruptible' of human beings, it always describes the *resurrection body* of the *saved* (p. 95).

48. *An Introduction to Christian Apologetics* pp. 344f.

4

'The Soul is Immortal, But...'
(The Philosophers versus the Fathers)

Many Christian writers through the centuries have spoken of the 'immortal soul'. In the last chapter we remarked in passing that such theologians generally have not meant that the soul is immortal in an absolute sense. There was a time, they say, when it did not exist. They further acknowledge that a time could come when it will cease to exist unless God sustains it of his own will. This chapter will take a closer look at that distinction and its implications regarding eternal punishment.

The immortality of the soul was a principal doctrine of the Greek philosopher, Plato, who was born about the time the last Old Testament book was being written.[1] In Plato's thinking, the soul (*psychē*) was self-moving and indivisible or 'simple'. Degenerated and eternal, it existed before the body which it inhabited, and which it would survive. To be apart from the body was the soul's natural and proper state: to be imprisoned in a body was its punishment for faults committed during a previous incarnation.[2]

Plato came to these conclusions by several roads. One was his theory of knowledge. All education, he said, is actually reminiscence. When we think we are learning, the soul is really recalling something from a previous existence. If this is true, the soul must have its own life independent of its successive bodies. Plato gave this as a 'likely account', while acknowledging that 'the greatness of the subject and the weakness of man' prohibited certainty.[3] His teaching about the soul was given to illustrate his other principles. He did not intend his words to be taken literally, since 'about the other world or worlds we can speak for the most

---

1. See any standard source book of philosophy. A. A. Hoekema, pointing out that the idea of the immortality of the soul is not a concept peculiar to Christianity, says it 'was developed in the mystery religions of ancient Greece, and was given philosophical expression in the writings of Plato' (Hoekema, *The Bible and the Future* p. 86).

2. I. C. Brady, 'Soul, Human, Immortality of,' *NCE* 13:464. According to Leonard Hodgson the argument that the soul is immortal because it is a simple and not composite substance and therefore cannot suffer disintegration comes from later Platonists, not Plato. Hodgson also says that Plato did not originate the later idea that the body was evil or the source of evil (L. Hodgson, 'Life after Death: The Philosophers Plato and Kant' *ET* Jan 1965, p. 108).

3. Quoted by Brady (op. cit.) from the *Phaedo* (107A).

part only in figure or allegory'.[4] But Plato's successors, like those of many another great thinker, literalized and systematized what he had said. In doing so they lost all the 'disarming tentativeness'[5] of Plato's original dialogues.

Many Christian writers of the second and third centuries wanted to show their pagan neighbours the reasonableness of the biblical faith. They did it the same way the Jewish apologist, Philo of Alexandria,[6] had done long before. They wrapped their understanding of Scripture in the robes of philosophy and worldly wisdom, choosing whatever might adorn it best. Paul had often warned against contemporary philosophy (1 Cor. 1:19–2:5; Col. 2:1–10) but these apologists, zealous for their new-found faith, set out to battle the pagan thinkers on their own turf. They freely borrowed the Platonic conception of the soul, the chief characteristic being its separability from the body.[7] When arguing for the resurrection and last judgment, they often used the pagan doctrine of immortality to show that these concepts were not 'logically absurd'.[8]

Yet the Christian writers persistently distinguished their concept of the soul's 'immortality' from that held by contemporary Platonists. The soul is not *inherently* immortal, insisted the fathers. It had a *beginning* – from God. And though it survives the death of the body, its *future* existence also depends entirely on God's will.[9] Even Origen[10] and Augustine,[11] who did sometimes speak of the soul's *natural* immortality, made this distinction

---

4. E. G. Selwyn, 'Image, Fact and Faith,' *NTS* 1, no. 4 (May 1955) p. 238; Gatch, *Death* p. 32.

5. Gatch, *Death*.

6. Responding to objections from some who minimized Philo's influence on the church fathers, H. A. Wolfson cites his book, *The Philosophy of the Church Fathers*. He then adds: 'Whether even without Philo the Fathers of the Church would have attempted to harmonize Scripture and philosophy is a plausible assumption. Whether the result of their harmonization would have been the same as it is now is a matter of conjecture. But it happens that Philo came before them and it also happens that all kinds of evidence show the influence of Philo upon them' (H. A. Wolfson, 'Notes on Patristic Philosophy,' *Harvard Theological Review* 57, no. 2 [April 1964] p. 124.

7. Harry A. Wolfson, 'Immortality and Resurrection in the Philosophy of the Church Fathers.' *Immortality and Resurrection* p. 79.

8. Ibid., pp. 90f; Brady, *NEC* p. 464.

9. See Wolfson op. cit. p. 57 for detailed quotations and references in support of this thesis. Included are Justin Martyr (*Dialogue with Trypho* 5), Irenaeus (*Against Heresies* 2. 34.4), Tatian (*Oration to the Greeks* 13), Theophilus (*Ad Autol.* 2.27; 2.24) as well as the undisputed conditionalists, Arnobius and Lactantius.

10. Robert L. Wilken, 'The Immortality of the Soul and Christian Hope,' *Dialog* 15, no. 2 (Spring 1976) p. 114. A debate continues whether or not Origen was consistent in this position. Wolfson says he was ('Notes on Patristic Philosophy,' pp. 125ff). Consistent or not, both sides agree that Origen conceded God's the right to destroy the soul. His remark that the soul cannot have 'essential' (*substantialis*) corruption means, according to Wolfson, 'that the soul, having been created by God as partaking of his own nature, will not be destroyed by God; it does not mean that God could not destroy it, if he so willed' (Wolfson, op. cit. pp. 59f).

11. Wolfson, op. cit. p. 60. Froom makes Augustine a thorough-going Platonist: in Augustine 'Immortal-Soulism' reached the high-water mark of post-Nicene times' (*Conditionalist Faith* 1:1073).

clear. Others, like Justin Martyr and his pupil Tatian,[12] viewed the pagan doctrine of immortality as a challenge to the resurrection and fought against it openly.[13]

Sometimes these writers gave theological reasons for human immortality. Ignatius saw it as the abolition of the punishment of sin, Irenaeus as the restoration of human destiny, Tertullian as the vindication of God's justice.[14]

Participants in the discussion about final punishment have fiercely debated the precise sense the fathers attached to the immortality of the soul. Froom and other conditionalists insist that the earliest fathers all rejected innate immortality. Pusey argues just as passionately that they espoused it.[15] Robert L. Wilken, a Lutheran professor at the University of Notre Dame and an outsider to this discussion, probably sizes up the situation correctly. 'The fathers', he says, 'modified the notion of the immortality of the soul as it was understood within the Greek philosophical tradition. Yet, in its main lines, they adopted the idea, adapting it where necessary to the requirements of Christian faith and they gave it a prominent place in Christian piety.'[16]

---

12. J. Pelikan, *The Shape of Death: Life, Death and Immortality in the Early Fathers* pp. 14, 21f.

13. Although popular books often cite Arnobius as a father of the conditionalist position on hell, he actually said very little on final punishment. His primary thrust was directed against the Platonic world-view as such, especially its anthropology. The Neo-Platonism which formed the backdrop for the fathers of the fourth and fifth centuries was itself in a state of flux. Its fundamental problem was to 'locate the soul metaphysically by defining its relation on the one hand to the visible world which it inhabits, and, on the other hand, to the intelligible world, the intellectual substance, with which it is naturally affiliated'. (R. A. Norris, *Manhood and Christ: A Study in the Christology of Theodore of Mopsuestia*, p. 13). Norris warns against the tendency to equate every dualistic statement of the fathers with 'Platonism,' showing that Platonism of the period included both dualistic and monistic elements which were never fully reconciled (pp. 14ff). At the same time, he stresses that 'Christian theology of the fourth and fifth centuries owed to middle Platonic and Neo-Platonic thought much of the conceptual structure in terms of which it interpreted the Church's gospel.' He also notes that 'the presuppositions of this philosophical outlook' became, 'whether in a disguised or an explicit fashion, part of the framework of Christian theological discussion' (p. 18).

Gatch observes that a contemporary issue within Platonism of the time was the question whether or not the soul was created (Gatch, *Death* p. 165). The inconsistency which even a created 'immortal soul' posed for the biblical view of man was felt by the fathers, says Norris, who adds that 'no patristic thinker of this period is willing to pursue the logic of the philosophical tradition which he had inherited to its normal conclusion' (op. cit. pp. 18f).

14. This summary comes from Marjorie Suchocki, 'The Question of Immortality,' *Journal of Religion* 57, no. 3 (July 1977) p. 294, who offers process theology as a fitting modernization of the biblical and patristic hope. We appreciate her insight into these three writers but disagree completely with her primary point. The statements above from Norris, Wolfson and Gatch represent a refinement in patristic studies, since even H. Wheeler Robinson overlooks the distinction they make between the fathers and the philosophers (H. Wheeler Robinson, *The Christian Doctrine of Man* pp. 169f.). Froom would likewise have profited from these works.

15. Froom, *Conditionalist Faith*, 1:757-927; E. B. Pusey, *What Is of Faith?* pp. 172–177.

16. Wilken, 'Immortality of the Soul' p. 114.

Immortality and the Reformation: a (theological) tug of (sectarian) war

Any attempt to describe the thinking of people who lived in a distant time faces a special danger. Unless one exercises great care, one easily yields to the temptation to smooth over the rough spots of diversity in the data, painting a more uniform – and probably partisan – picture. The literature concerning final punishment contains many such 'polished' accounts of thought in various periods, from Old Testament teaching through the fathers to the Reformers. At the same time, if one can keep his head and dodge the whizzing bullets while walking through these embattled fields, he will also hear some harmonious notes.

The immortality of the soul was a matter of great interest during the sixteenth and seventeenth centuries. The fortunes of this doctrine among the reforming churches make a fascinating tale. We will be aware of the danger of oversimplifying the material as we relate the high points of that story.

Luther

Luther said little about man's supposed natural immortality or about the 'soul' as a separable part. He often wrote of death as a 'sleep.' Between death and resurrection, Luther pictured the deceased as having no consciousness of anything – although this sleep was sweet and peaceful for the righteous. In the resurrection, believers would hear Christ's gentle voice calling them and arise. Their period of death would then seem only a moment, as when one falls asleep at night and 'instantly' wakes to find the morning.[17] In keeping with this view of man – totally dependent on God for his existence day by day – Luther rejected the philosophical doctrine of innate immortality. In one vehement outburst against Roman traditions he classes the immortality of the soul among the 'monstrous fables that form part of the Roman dunghill of decretals'.[18]

17. 'We should learn to view our death [as] . . . a fine, sweet and brief sleep, which brings us release from . . . all misfortunes of this life, and we shall be secure and without care, rest sweetly and gently for a brief moment, as on a sofa, until the time when he shall call and awaken us together with all his dear children to his eternal glory and joy' (*A Compend of Luther's Theology* p. 242). 'We Christians . . . should train and accustom ourselves in faith to despise death and regard it as a deep, strong, sweet, sleep; to consider the coffin as nothing other than a soft couch of ease or rest' (*Works* 6:287f). These quotations are documented by Froom, *Conditionalist Faith* 2:74–77; similar ones are given in *Christian Mortalism* pp. 28–32.

Without noting any of these statements, Donald G. Bloesch quotes Luther's commentary on Genesis that 'the soul does *not* sleep but is awake and enjoys the vision of angels and of God, and has converse with them' (*Essentials 2:205*, note 32).

18. On June 15, 1520, Leo X issued the bull *Exsurge Domine*, condemning 41 theses from Luther's writing. It was published in Germany that September, and Luther was given 60 days to recant under threat of excommunication. When Alexander and Eck, prominent Catholic adversaries, ceremonially burned the offending works, Luther replied in kind. He burned the papal bull outside the gates of Wittenberg on Dec. 10, 1520 and issued four works, (two in Latin, two in German) defending his condemned propositions. The quotation comes from his reply of Nov. 29, 1520. The Latin reads: '. . . *omnia illa infinita portenta in romano stequinilio Decretorum*,' (quoted in Pétavel, *Immortality* p. 255. For a historical account and a translation of one of the German responses, see Luther's *Works* vol.32, *Career of a Reformer, II*.

Tyndale

When Sir Thomas More attacked Luther's teaching of 'soul-sleeping', William Tyndale came to the Reformer's defence in England. 'The true faith', Tyndale wrote, 'putteth the resurrection, which we be warned to look for every hour. The heathen philosophers, denying that, did put that the souls did ever live. And the pope joineth the spiritual doctrine of Christ and the fleshly doctrine of philosophers together; things so contrary that they cannot agree, no more than the Spirit and the flesh do in a Christian man. And because the fleshly-minded pope consenteth unto heathen doctrine, therefore he corrupteth the scripture to establish it.'[19]

Although the moderate reforms of the English church left much of the Roman doctrine untouched, including the immortality of the soul, Christian mortalism was preached to the people of Protestant England from the earliest times. Although established churchmen denounced this teaching, they 'rarely examined the concept on its theological merits and only occasionally and superficially considered the scriptural arguments on which it was based.'[20]

Anabaptists

The term 'Anabaptist' is a very general description which is applied to a wide diversity of Reformation Christians who rejected the state churches of Luther and Calvin. The designation 'Anabaptists', meaning 're-baptizers', was given by their opponents and based on the practice of establishing churches of believers who were baptized upon a profession of faith. Anabaptists differed from the Lutherans and Calvinists also in their attitude toward the state (taxes and war) and the relationship the church should have to government and society in general. They stressed the authority of the Word of God apart from creeds and confessions of faith. They also championed the right of the individual to study the Scriptures, relying on the Holy Spirit alone for guidance.

Whatever benefits or abuses attached to such views, they encouraged willingness to question established ideas. One such was the immortality of the soul. Along with this, many Anabaptists held conditionalist views about final punishment. These minority ideas were perpetuated in England in the seventeenth century by many of the General (Arminian) Baptists. Yet while 'the soul-sleeping view was reasonably commmon in sectarian circles during the first century of the English Reformation, it remained a decidedly minority view which most churchmen ... did not examine on its own merits'.[21]

Calvin

The Anabaptists met perhaps their most furious opponent in John Calvin, who was especially vehement in his denunciation of the 'Anabaptist' doctrine of 'soul-sleeping'. Calvin felt this called the hope of eternal life into question, and he attacked soul-sleeping with special passion in his

---

19. Quoted by Burns, *Christian Mortalism* p.101; Froom, *Conditionalist Faith* 2:94.
20. Burns, *Christian Mortalism* p.99.
21. Ibid. p.192.

first theological book, *Psychopannychia*.[22] Quistorp almost understates the case in saying that this essay 'is distinguished by the special acrimony of his polemic against Anabaptists'.[23] Calvin outlined this work in 1534 and published it in 1542.

Although Calvin and Luther differed on the soul's state after death, Calvin's intense zeal outweighed Luther's depth of commitment. It is the distinct contribution of Burns that he has detailed the way in which Luther's opinion was conceded in the interests of Reformed unity, its defence passing to the hated Anabaptists. As a result, Calvin's view became first the dominant and finally the orthodox doctrine of most established Protestant churches.[24] Burns writes:

> When the Lutheran reformers failed to give vigorous support to psychopannychism, soul sleeping lost what small chance it might have had to be considered a debatable doctrine, a thing indifferent. Once it was identified solely with the Anabaptists, there was no hope for a hearing before respectable Protestants . . . . Unchallenged by the doctrine of a Reformation church of comparable stature, the view of the churches of Geneva and Zurich (and of Rome) on the nature of the soul had to prevail in England.[25]

Heinrich Bullinger, the gifted pastor of Zurich and a man of enormous influence, linked Calvin's view with the later orthodoxy. Because of his friendship with the British exiles during Mary's Catholic reign, his translated works carried much weight in England. Through the enormous influence of the Second Helvetic Confession of 1566 (which Schaff says Bullinger wrote almost single-handedly), Calvin's view was widely adopted as the authoritative standard for Reformed churches throughout the world.[26]

Calvin's 'conditional' immortality

Calvin held that the soul received immortality from the stamp of God's image, although he agreed with the earlier apologists that the soul had a beginning. He often denigrated the body, calling it a 'prison',[27] a 'rotting carcase' and even 'wretched dung'. Quistorp sharply criticizes Calvin's dualistic view of man as philosophical and unbiblical,[28] and Gatch says Calvin 'betrays a greater concern with immortality than with the resurrection'.[29] James P. Martin shares Gatch's opinion.[30] But Holwerda defends Calvin against the charge that his view of immortality overshadowed or negated the biblical hope. Holwerda does not deny that

---

22. The title comes from a Greek word meaning 'to be awake [or watchful] the whole night through,' which represented Calvin's position against those who taught soul-sleeping.
23. Quistorp, *Last Things* p.55.
24. *Christian Mortalism* pp. 31ff.
25. Ibid. pp.32f.
26. Ibid. p.25.
27. *Institutes* 3.9.4.
28. *Last Things* pp. 60,73. He cites many such statements from Calvin.
29. Gatch, *Death* p.120.
30. *The Last Judgment in Protestant Theology from Orthodoxy to Ritschl* pp.16f.

Calvin was powerfully influenced by the philosophical doctrine of the immortality of the soul. Rather, he cites passages in which Calvin rests *ultimate* hope for life and blessedness on Christ, the second advent and the resurrection to come. Whatever Calvin's roots, Holwerda insists that the fruit of his hope carried the aroma of Christ and the flavour of eschatology.[31]

For all his influence on popular piety and religious expression, however, another aspect of Calvin's doctrine of immortality matters more to our study. That is the fact that Calvin, like the fathers of the earlier centuries, expressly and repeatedly stated that the soul depends on God for its existence and that God can put it out of existence if he so desires.

Commenting on Psalm 103:15ff, Calvin said: 'Although the soul after it has departed from the prison of the body remains alive, yet its so doing does not arise from any inherent power of its own. Were God to withdraw his grace, the soul would be nothing more than a puff or a blast, even as the body is dust; and thus there would doubtless be found in the whole man nothing but mere vanity.'[32] And in a sermon on 1 Tim.1:17ff: ' . . . our souls are not immortal of their power, nor is the life in them enclosed in themselves, as though it had roots there. Where is there life then? In God.'[33] The soul's immortality, he said in another sermon, is '*not natural*. For whatsoever had a beginning may have an end, and may come to decay, and even perish utterly.'[34]

Calvin scholars call attention to this point. T. F. Torrance notes that Calvin taught that the 'soul survives the death of the body only at the mercy of God, and has no durability in itself'.[35] He cites commentaries, sermons and other works in which Calvin stresses that the soul is as much a *creature* as the body and that both depend for their being 'entirely on the grace of God'.[36] According to Torrance, Calvin's view means that if God were to withdraw for even an instant the presence of his Spirit, 'we would drop into the nothingness from which we are called into being'. So far as Calvin is concerned, Torrance says that is 'just as true of the soul of man as of his body'.[37] Quistorp quotes a sermon in which Calvin, referring to man's immortal soul, says that 'everything which has a beginning can also have an end, can perish'.[38] Even Holwerda, who defends Calvin against some of Quistorp's charges, agrees fully on this point.[39]

Summary and conclusion

In the matter of the soul's immortality, advocates of the traditional orthodoxy have had to deflect attacks from both right and left. Church

---

31. 'Eschatology and History: A Look at Calvin's Eschatological Vision,' *Exploring the Heritage of John Calvin* pp.116, 120f, 134.
32. Quoted in T.F. Torrance, *Calvin's Doctrine of Man* p.27.
33. Ibid.
34. Ibid., note 5. From a sermon on 1 Tim. 6:15f.
35. Ibid.. pp.26f.
36. Ibid.. p.26.
37. Ibid.. p.29.
38. Quistorp, *Last Things* p.70.
39. Holwerda, 'Eschatology and History' p.114.

fathers of the first five centuries faced Platonic and Neo-Platonic adversaries who denied the Christian resurrection but affirmed the inalienable immortality of the soul. The philosophers themselves disagreed on some of the fine points. In this setting the apologists reasoned for bodily resurrection of all, both good and evil. The common doctrine of the soul's immortality was a convenient tool.

Being men of their age, these Christian writers accepted (with exceptions) the common Platonic view of the soul as a component separable from the body and unhurt by physical death. In this they agreed with their opponents, but on the eternity of the soul fathers and philosophers parted company. To the soul's *immortality* (survival of the death of the body) the Platonists generally added *eternality*. There the fathers stood firm, insisting that although the soul enters and leaves the body, and even survives its death, it is not eternal. It had its beginning by the creation of God, and God – if he pleases – can also make it extinct. Only God possesses *that* kind of 'immortality'.

With rare and disputed exceptions, this is the common witness of theologians who affirmed the soul's immortality – from the days of the earliest Greek apologists until and including John Calvin and his descendants today. 'Immortality' has not meant 'eternality.' Christian writers have used the concept as an illustration for their apologetics and as a weapon against anti-supernaturalists who denied the resurrection. Only by a kind of reflex action have they used it as the basis for argument concerning final punishment. Then, like some hidden footlight, the doctrine has tinted exegesis, its own scriptural legitimacy frequently a matter of doubt. Ironically, the writer with the most *biblical* defence of the soul's immortality was probably Origen, who likely bought into the *Platonic* system further than any Christian theologian before him or since.

On the other side, traditional advocates of the immortal soul have faced biblical theologians who charged them with denying God's unique immortality. The apologists of the fourth and fifth centuries felt this inconsistency, and later theologians have not resolved it either. Whenever this objection is raised, Christian advocates of the immortal soul paint the doctrine in faint pastels. Although it is part of their baggage – stamped with the initials of the church – it keeps getting in the way, and no one quite remembers what it really contains.

Faced with this two-pronged attack, reinforced by a secondary doctrine that only gradually joined the troops, traditional orthodoxy has resorted to a holding action. It has rushed first to one front and then to the other, attempting to keep its own forces intact while repelling the particular adversary of the moment. Today the traditional dualistic dogma of soul-immortality is under increasing suspicion as an interloper. Orthodox writers are concluding that the church will not suffer by its expulsion but, rather, that this would eliminate an unnecessary inconsistency from the rationale of orthodoxy.

Crisscrossing all of this flows the stream of Christian mortalism. Freshly issuing from springs opened by Luther and Tyndale, and fed by tributaries of recent biblical theology, this understanding appears as the sparkling water of pristine Christianity. Today, more than ever, orthodox evangelical scholars are taking its claims seriously.

In *neither* case – among mortalists or immortalists – is there any reason why anthropology should govern eschatology. For the Christian, the truth about final punishment must finally stand only on a thorough exegesis of the Word of God. Into this sanctuary pagan philosophical presuppositions may not intrude. That the history of Christian doctrine permits their dismissal we have seen in this chapter and the last. For, while orthodox theologians have often spoken with the accent of Plato's philosophy, they finally have rested all hope on God alone. The immortal soul survives physical death, they say, but it cannot resist the power of God. If God wishes, he can reduce even the immortal soul to nothing.[40]

---

40. Vincent Taylor laments the modern turn from the traditional doctrine of the soul's immortality, calling it 'a dark night through which the world is passing' and 'a valley of humiliation through which we have to travel with a quagmire on the one side and hobgoblins of the pit on the other'. He speaks not so much of the claim to a biblical monism, however, as a secular rejection of hope for life after death (Vincent Taylor, 'Life after Death: The Modern Situation,' *ET* 76 no. 3 [Dec.1964] p. 77).

Modern philosophical alternatives to the traditional view of immortality of the soul are discussed in John Hick, *Death and Eternal Life*, and Paul Badham, *Christian Beliefs about Life after Death*. On the claim of process theologians to combine the biblical view with modern philosophy, see Tyron Inbody, 'Process Theology and Personal Survival,' *Iliff Review*. 31, no. 2 (Spring 1974) p. 31–42: Suchocki, 'The Question of Immortality' pp.288–306. This view might satisfy the demands of modern philosophy, but it falls far short of the personal and corporate hope which NT writers expect to be actualized in the new cosmos at the return of Jesus Christ.

5

'Sheol': Do the Godly Go to 'Hell'?

What does the Old Testament teach about life after death? Not much, according to many writers. Harry Buis, a responsible and respected advocate of the traditionalist view, warns that the Old Testament 'contains little information about the eschatological future of the individual, and almost all of this is concerned with the future of the godly rather than that of the ungodly.'[1] He also cautions against the common tendency to read 'back into the Old Testament concepts which were not held until much later in the history of doctrine.' But, he notes, a high view of inspiration does call for us to read the Old Testament in the brighter light of the New.[2]

Other authors of various viewpoints agree. An article in *ET* concludes that 'even in the few Old Testament apocalyptic writings ... the future state of righteous and wicked ... is described only in the most general terms'. [3]

Conditionalists have discovered more fertile fields in the Old Testament. Like the spies returning from the valley of Eshcol, these writers sometimes returned enthusiastically with a cluster of texts greater than one person can carry.[4] Perhaps traditionalist authors have gone in search of a particular fruit and, returning empty-handed, have reported that the land was barren.

Human existence in the Old Testament

The Old Testament view of human nature begins with Genesis 1–2. God, who said, 'Let the land produce living creatures' also 'formed the man from the dust of the ground'. Once man did not exist. The living creatures are described as 'having the breath of life' in them. So too with the man: God 'breathed into his nostrils the breath of life and he became a living soul'.[5] It is impossible to view Old Testament man correctly apart from

---

1. Buis, *Eternal Punishment* pp. 1f.
2. Ibid. p. 2.
3. S. H. Hooke, 'Life after Death: The Extra-Canonical Literature,' *ET* 1965 p. 273. See also Gerald C. Studer, *After Death, What?* p. 19; *New Catholic Encyclopedia* 13:467; *NIDNTT* 2:206f.
4. Pétavel, *Problem* pp. 88ff; White, *Life in Christ* pp. 387–390; Atkinson, *Life and Immortality (passim)*; Froom, *Conditionalist Faith* 1:29–180.
5. The NIV recognizes this and correctly translates *nephesh* in Genesis 2:7 as 'living being'. See also H. W. Wolff, *Anthropology of the Old Testament*; G. E. Ladd, *Pattern of New Testament Truth*, especially the chapter entitled 'The Background of the Pattern'. See also special issues of *Verdict* on 'Man,' parts 1–3 (Aug., Sep., Dec. 1978).

this placing within God's creation.[6] Because of our origin, we exist in a double relationship – vertically with God and horizontally with the rest of creation. Because humankind had no existence until God formed them and gave them life, they should view life each moment as God's immediate gift of grace. Without God's constant provision of life, we have no claim on our own existence. Because human beings bear God's image they can know God in a personal way, but they are still God's creatures. Mankind does not live or exist independent of God, although capable of lusting after that position. Every attempt to be its own god is doomed to failure because of what man is – dust, scooped from the earth. When God takes back the breath of life, 'they die and return to the dust' from which they were taken. Men and women can rejoice in a hope beyond death – but only in God. The very name 'Adam' also means 'dust'. Thus we should not despise our 'physicalness,' or disregard the rest of creation. We are not constitutionally superior to these things so may not look on them with disdain.[7] The Old Testament invites human beings, as a part of God's good creation, to enjoy 'a healthy materialism, a reverence for the dignity of the body which is human life in the concrete'.[8] But all this enjoyment is 'under God.' God is the giver and sustainer of life. The Old Testament shows us that 'life is manifested in God's entering into covenant with his people .... The righteous can have life only by holding onto the God of salvation who is the God of life. Life is understood as a gift.'[9] Traditionalists are right to point out that 'life' means far more than bare 'existence'. Thielicke describes the God-related quality of true life in the Old Testament:

> Wherever God is, there is life. Where God is not, there is death (Ps. 104:29–30; Job 34:15) .... Whoever does not have this contact with the breath of God, whoever lives in protest against him or in internal detachment from him, is already dead regardless of how much vitality he might have externally (Eph. 2:5; Rom. 5:21; 7:10; 1 John 3:14–15). His life is disconnected from its actual source of power, though still rolling along 'in neutral' according to the law of inertia.[10]

Death apart from God

The opposite is also true. The most notable characteristic of the dead in the Old Testament is that they are cut off from God. Death means lack of relationship with God.[11] Here human beings differ from the animals, who

---

6. Thomas E. Ridenhour ('Immortality and Resurrection in the OT,' *Dialog* 15 [Spring 1976]: 104–109) surveys Old Testament scholars, H. H. Rowley, H. W. Wolff, Gerhard von Rad, R. Martin-Achard and O. A. Piper, and finds agreement that the OT views human life relationally in respect to God and to his covenant people.
7. An excellent popular treatment of man's place in creation is Francis A. Schaeffer, *He Is There and He Is Not Silent* (Tyndale House, 1972), pp. 1–88.
8. Bruce Vawter, 'Intimations of Immortality and the Old Testament,' *JBL* 91, no. 2 (June 1972) p. 170f.
9. Ridenhour, 'Immortality ' p. 104.
10. Thielicke, *Death and Life* pp. 106f.
11. Wolff, *Anthropology of the Old Testament* p. 107.

share their earthly origin and gift of life. Thielicke paints a vivid picture of human uniqueness among God's creatures – aware of being related to God, of sinfulness, and of mortality.

> The flowers and the grass, the whales and the mountains know nothing of being thus related to God. Only man knows this. Only he with his solitary awareness of death protrudes above the creaturely realm and thus has a different form of perishability, as though his were raised to a higher power. He alone must pose the question of the meaning of God's action that comes to expression in his death . . . . Because he is compelled to pose the question, it becomes evident that man's returning to dust is qualitatively different from the simple physical returning to dust of a simply physical being . . . . He sees clearly a decision being made against him here with which he must come to terms.[12]

The first man and woman tasted this death-fear when they ate the forbidden fruit, then heard God approaching in the Garden. They must have supposed that God was coming even then to inflict the promised penalty of death. But an eternal purpose had outweighed the historical action. Already grace was abounding more than sin. The right to exist had indeed been forfeited, but God willed to 'bring many children to glory!' 'The existence of our race then is a boon beyond the limits of law.'[13] But Cain soon murdered his brother, and before long the entire first family is dead. What becomes of the human race then? The Old Testament does not share the optimism expressed by Socrates as he awaited death with his disciples.[14] Man is not an eternal soul trapped in a crude body: we came from the earth, and to it we return. The Old Testament speaks of the state after death under the picture of Sheol.

Sheol in the Old Testament

A few traditionalist writers have argued that Israel perceived Sheol as the place of unending future retribution. Shedd calls it 'a fearful punitive evil, mentioned by the sacred writers to deter men from sin',[15] threatened 'as the penalty of sin, to the wicked, but never to the righteous';[16] it has 'the same meaning as the modern Hell'.[17] Braun repeats Shedd's views, equating Sheol with the modern conception of hell – the extent of his findings concerning future punishment in the Old Testament.[18] These

12. Thielicke, op. cit. p. 138.
13. White, *Life in Christ* pp. 116, 119.
14. See Cullmann, *Immortality or Resurrection?* pp. 19–27.
15. Shedd, *Endless Punishment* p. 21.
16. Ibid p. 24.
17. Ibid p. 23.
18. Braun, *Whatever?* pp. 130–142. Braun concedes that *sheol* sometimes means the physical grave, but insists it refers also to a place of punishment for the wicked. Buis strengthens his argument by some honest concessions (see notes 1, 24–25); Braun hurts his argument by a bombastic tone in the absence of evidence: thus, 'I have seen pompous claims by some that . . . Sheol is the expectation of the wicked and the righteous alike' (p. 133). Specific data supporting his view would carry more conviction.

claims simply do not stand up under the light of biblical usage. The 'liberal' *IDB* flatly states: 'Nowhere in the OT is the abode of the dead regarded as a place of punishment or torment.'[19] The 'conservative' *Baker's Dictionary of Theology* says Sheol is 'uniformly depicted in the OT as the eternal, amoral abode of both righteous and unrighteous alike'.[20] Buis corrects Shedd, describing Sheol as the 'place of shadowy existence where the good and the evil continued to exist together after death'[21] and 'where good and evil alike share a similar dreary fate'.[22] He quotes 'the fine conservative scholar,' Oehler, that 'in no part of the Old Testament is *a difference in the lot* of those in the realm of death distinctly spoken of'.[23] Anyone with a concordance can verify these statements. Faithful Jacob expected to go 'down to Sheol' when he died (Gen. 37:35; 42:38; 44:29, 31). Righteous Job longed to hide in Sheol until God's anger passed him by (Job 14:13). David, the man after God's heart, viewed Sheol as his resting place, though he trusted God to redeem him from its grasp (Ps. 49:15). Even Jesus Christ, the Holy One of God, went to Sheol (Gk. *hadēs*) upon his death (Ps. 16:10; Acts 2:24–31). There is simply no basis for making Sheol exclusively a place of punishment for the wicked.[24]

Etymology and translation

According to D. K. Stuart, the word 'Sheol' appears only once outside the Old Testament – in a fifth century B.C. Aramaic papyrus from the Jewish settlement at Elephantine.[25] The etymology is uncertain. Most modern scholar tend to think it comes from a root meaning 'ask' or 'inquire'. Older writers sometimes suggested a root meaning 'to bury oneself'. The idea of something hidden appears in synonyms of several languages. The German *Holle* comes from *Höhle*, a cavern. The Greek *adēs* literally means the 'unseen' realm. The English word 'hell' comes from the Anglo-Saxon *helan*, meaning 'to cover' or 'to hide.'[26] The Old Testament uses the word *sheol* 65 or 66 times. The KJV translators followed their own conception of things and made it either 'hell' (31 times), 'the grave' (31 times) or 'the pit' (3 times). The ASV did not try to translate but left 'Sheol'. The NIV usually translates 'grave,' though at least once 'the realm of death' (Deut. 32:22). This aligns with Froom, who distinguishes sheol from the material grave but suggests 'gravedom' as a suitable translation.[27]

19. T. H. Gaster, 'Dead, Abode of the *IDB* 1:788.
20. Robert B. Laurin, 'Sheol,' op. cit. p. 484.
21. Buis, *Eternal Punishment* p. 3.
22. Ibid p. 12.
23. Ibid p. 5.
24. Shedd argues (and Braun repeats) that Sheol equals modern 'hell' because it is never threatened to the righteous. But God threatens not the righteous but the wicked! Scripture shows the righteous going down into Sheol, however, as well as the wicked. For a thorough study of the term see Atkinson, *Life and Immortality* pp. 42–53.
25. *ISBE* vol 4 p. 472. (Published 1988, since when other instances may have been found.)
26. Pétavel, *Problem* p. 91, note 1.
27. Froom, *Conditionalist Faith* 1:160–165.

Sheol's inhabitants

Even if the noun is limited to the Hebrew language, the picture conveyed is not. The common understanding of at least a particular region is seen in the Gilgamesh Epic. The dead hero, Enkidu, returns to tell his friend of the wretched state of those in Erkallu, the Land of No Return.

> Looking at me, he leads me to the House of Darkness,
> ... To the house which none leave who have entered it,
> On the road from which there is no way back,
> To the house wherein the dwellers are bereft of light,
> Where dust is their fare and clay their food.
> They are clothed like birds, with wings for garments,
> And see no light, residing in darkness.[28]

Job also describes 'gravedom' as 'the place of no return ... the land of gloom and deep shadow, ... the land of deepest night, of deep shadow and disorder, where even the light is like darkness' (Job 10:21f.). In Psalm 88:12 it is 'the place of darkness' and 'the land of oblivion'. It is 'the land of dust, forgetfulness and forgottenness, silence, monotony, loneliness, and sleep'.[29] Although individuals are sometimes pictured as conversing in Sheol or engaging in similar lifelike pursuits (Isa. 14:9–18), they are not whole persons but mere shades, personified for dramatic purposes.[30] Their state cannot be called 'life' in any meaningful sense. It is 'such a pale and pitiful reflexion of human existence that it has no longer any reality, and is only a metaphorical expression of non-being'.[31] This is mythological language for the most part, no doubt owing something to pagan roots, but not so different from the way we speak of the sun 'rising' and 'setting' or use the names January or Saturday (originally honouring Roman gods), or refer to other days of the week by names relating to other pagan gods. We should not suppose, however, that Israel took the language literally or used it with its original pagan meaning. John B. Burns has shown how the Old Testament 'demythologized' such language, using it only for effect, contrast or literary purposes.[32] Because the Old Testament defines human life in terms of its relationship to God, Sheol is evil. It removes people from their place on earth, where they rejoiced in God's fellowship and praised him for his goodness (Isa. 38:11, 18f.). Yet Sheol is not beyond God's reach (Job 26:6; Amos 9:2). Righteous men

---

28. Pritchard, *ANET* p. 87. S. H. Hooke gives a slightly different translation in 'Life after Death: Israel and the After-Life,' *ET* May 1965 p. 236. On Egyptian ideas of the afterlife see S. G. F. Brandon, 'Life after Death: The After-Life in Ancient Egyptian Faith and Practice,' *ET* April 1965 pp. 217–220. On the relation between Israelite and pagan attitudes regarding this subject and their different use of some common language, see John Barclay Burns, 'The Mythology of Death in the Old Testament,' *SJT* no. 3 (Aug. 1973) p. 327–340.
29. Burns, op. cit. p. 332. *Jewish Encyclopedia* (vol. 11, col. 283) says: 'Sheol is a horrible, dreary, dark, disorderly land.'
30. They are the *rephaim* (Job 26:5; Ps. 88:10; Prov. 2:18; 9:18; 21:16; Isa. 14:9; 26:19). 'For the member of the community of Israel, the dead were beyond his interest for they had ceased to live and praise Yahweh' (Burns, 'Mythology of Death,' p. 339).
31. R. Martin-Achard, *From Death* p. 17.
32. Burns, 'Mythology of Death.' pp. 327–340. esp. p. 339.

and women repeatedly express confidence that God will restore them from Sheol to enjoy life once more in fellowship with him (1 Sam. 2:6; Ps. 16:9–11; 68:20). Having experienced the joy of God's presence and faithfulness on earth they want to live with him for ever; his past faithfulness gives them confidence that they will.[33] The patriarchs died in hope, according to Hebrews 11, but their hope was in the power and love of God, not in a philosophical dogma or any immortal part of man.

As Old Testament believers faced death, they were confident in their knowledge alike of God's ultimate purpose, and of his grace and power (Gen. 26:3; 49:29; 50:25; Exod. 13:19; Joshua 24:32). Nothing less will explain the intensity of the Old Testament hope and expectation (John 8:56).[34] Job's poignant expression of hope is deeply touching: 'If a man dies, will he live again? All the days of my hard service I will wait for my renewal to come. You will call and I will answer you; you will long for the creature your hands have made' (Job 14:14f.).

Summary

The Old Testament's concept of Sheol belongs to its larger view of humankind before God. This perspective, framed in light of the creation, determines the Hebrews' attitude toward both life and death – and hope beyond that. Sheol is the common fate of all mortals. It is not a place of punishment. In most of the Old Testament the wicked have no reason to expect to leave Sheol. The righteous do, however, for they know and trust the living God! Nothing is hid from his eyes, and no power can withstand his deliverance. His people lie down in peace, fully expecting to live again. In a few places this hope is stated explicitly but it pervades the entire Old Testament. So far as the destiny of the wicked is concerned, Sheol is not a final word. The Old Testament does say much about the end of the wicked, however. We will consider that positive teaching now.

---

33. Throughout both Testaments God's faithfulness is the ground of his people's hope. Since the resurrection and ascension of Jesus Christ, believers have had historical verification that God is faithful and that he will not forsake them even in death.

34. Norman A. Logan, 'The Old Testament and a Future Life,' *SJT* 6, no. 2 (June 1953) p. 170.

6

The End of the Wicked in the Old Testament

The Bible is not a work of philosophy or mysticism, but of history. It shows God at work in history within his world and with his people, enacting the saving plan, which he purposed even before creation. But the Old Testament ends on an unresolved chord: Jesus Christ must come to resolve it. It is not surprising that Old Testament teaching often leaves us in suspense, awaiting God's revelation in Jesus Christ.

These earlier Scriptures foreshadow, hint, suggest, outline, prefigure, illustrate and promise. The New Testament Scriptures fill in the details, flesh out the bones, tint the colouring, fine tune the picture and complete the canonical revelation. Concerning life and immortality we are in the dark until Jesus brings them to light in the gospel (2 Tim. 1:10). God's wrath also is hidden until it is revealed in the gospel (Rom. 1:15–18). The old saying:

'The New is in the Old concealed/The Old is in the New revealed'

is still valid.

The New Testament tells us that the Old Testament is preserved for our instruction and example (Rom. 15:4; 1 Cor. 10:11ff). Alongside the New, it is profitable for every teaching situation (2 Tim. 3:15ff). Yet Christians have in general neglected the Old Testament Scriptures when thinking about the final punishment of the wicked. Traditionalist writers appear to have thought they offered at best vague hints contained in two or three passages. Conditionalist writers have made more use of Old Testament material but have presented their arguments largely in summary form.

A modern example of the conditionalist approach is Froom. He says the Old Testament uses 50 different Hebrew verbs to describe the final fate of the wicked and notes that they all signify different aspects of *destruction*.[1] Such verbs are buttressed, he says, by figurative or proverbial expressions which also speak 'everywhere and always' of 'the *decomposition, of the breaking up of the organism* and *final cessation of the existence of being* – never that of immortal life in endless suffering'.[2] By combining both lists

---

1. *Conditionalist Faith* 1:106.
2. Ibid. p. 107. For example, the wicked will be as: a vessel broken to pieces, ashes trodden underfoot, smoke that vanishes, chaff carried away by the wind, tow that is burned, thorns and stubble in fire, vine branches pruned off, wax that melts, fat of sacrifices, a dream that vanishes, etc.

Pétavel speaks of the 'multitude of proverbial expressions, a long succession of images which sometimes seem to exclude each other, but which always, by association of ideas, and like fractions reduced to a common denominator, are found to be in accord when used

into one, Froom produces an alphabetical list of some 70 English expressions which the Old Testament uses to describe the wicked's end. The list is cumulatively most impressive, particularly in view of the resounding silence which meets it in traditionalist works.[3] Yet one could wish for more.

Several of Froom's 70 examples seem not altogether applicable, and a few appear to be completely out of place. Some simply call on God to judge the wicked or give the righteous victory over their enemies, with no apparent reference to Last Things (Ps. 55:23; 60:12; 94:23; 104:35; 139:19). Others praise God for deliverance over the wicked (Ps. 118:12; 119:119; Isa. 43:17). One simply states temporal blessings given or withheld by God (Prov. 13:9). Another prescribes the ultimate penalty of excision under the Law of Moses[4] (Exod. 22:20). Closely akin are three passages which speak of sin's original death penalty, itself the subject of much debate (Gen. 3:19; Ezek. 18:4,20). Two others seem to refer only to God's power to sustain life – a relevant point but needing more explanation than here given (Ps. 75:3; Isa. 40:24). Read in context, many of Froom's passages do seem relevant to final punishment; it is no reflection on his contribution and that of others cited in the following pages for us to inquire further.

For the present study we will examine a number of relevant Old Testament passages under three headings. First are texts which state moral principles of the divine government. From these we may learn general truths which shed light on the end of the wicked, at least by implication. We do not want to make too much of such statements, but neither do we wish to make too little. Second are a selection of texts concerning specific divine judgments within history. Some involve Israel; some involve pagan nations or cities. They add further light on God's punishment of sin. Perhaps most important, they exemplify much of the symbolism the Bible uses to describe divine judgment against sin. Finally we look at a number of Old Testament statements concerning the wicked's end which appear in contexts that are clearly either messianic or eschatological.[5] These have special value since they look beyond

---

to describe the end of the existence of evil and of obstinate evildoers. Everywhere we find the notion of a final cessation of being, of a return to a state of unconsciousness, never that of a perpetual life in suffering' (*Problem* pp. 88f.).

3. *Conditionalist Faith* 1:108ff. Dixon does not mention the dozens of verbs or scores of metaphors and similes which OT writers employ to foretell the end of sinners – all of which sound like total extinction. Blanchard briefly considers five Hebrew verbs for destruction, but concludes that the wicked will not really be destroyed in hell because (1) the words may have metaphorical meanings and (2) Old Testament victims of human or divine extermination were not technically annihilated since there remained either smoke or ashes or dust (*Hell* pp.234ff.). Froom's list is quite impressive and has sent the present writer to the text in search of more information.

4. This is not irrelevant to the subject but needs to be viewed in theological perspective. That perspective comes at Calvary, where God's wrath as well as his justice (righteousness) is revealed. We consider this in a separate chapter.

5. I. Howard Marshall calls 'eschatology' a 'slippery word' because of its frequent careless use in at least nine different senses. ('Slippery Words: Eschatology,' ET, June 1978 pp. 264–269).

circumstances of ancient history to the grand revelation of God's salvation and the final manifestation of his wrath – the two aspects commonly involved in divine judgment.

I. Passages containing moral principles of divine judgment

General references in the poetic books

Job's 'comforters' are sure they know how God acts in the world. As they accuse their friend on the basis of the popular orthodoxy they describe how the wicked are punished and the righteous flourish. Bildad (Job 18:5–21), Zophar (Job 20:4–29), Eliphaz (Job 22:15–20) and Elihu (Job 34:10–28) all describe the fate they expect will overtake the wicked. We cannot derive a doctrine of final punishment from the statements of Job's miserable comforters. They reflect an uninspired orthodoxy, to whatever extent it should prove correct; and the hero, Job, objects throughout to their arguments. However, Job raises a point we do well to consider. Given the moral government of God over humankind, why can the wicked die rich and the righteous languish in misery? Even Job's own final restoration does not erase this troubling issue.

In the Psalms and Proverbs we find language similar to that of Job's companions – but with apparent divine sanction. According to numerous psalms, the wicked will go down to death and Sheol, their memory will perish, and they will be as if they had never existed. On the other hand, God will rescue the righteous from death and they will enjoy him for ever (Ps. 9; 21:4–10; 36:9ff; 49:8–20; 52:5–9; 59; 73; 92). Proverbs offers the same hope. The wicked will pass away, be overthrown, be cut off from the land, be no more, their lamp put out. The godly will endure and their house will stand, for they have an everlasting foundation (Prov. 2:21f; 10:25; 12:7; 24:15–20).[6]

The reader might argue that these texts refer only to the present life. Nothing in the contexts or in the explicit language demands otherwise. If we had only these passages in Job, Psalms and Proverbs, we might well suppose that the wicked will all perish in death, from which they will have no redeemer, but that God will redeem the righteous from death and they will inherit the earth for ever. These poetic books do not specifically threaten a resurrection of the wicked, a final judgment after death, or any ultimate punishment beyond temporal death itself.

Yet there is more to be said. For Job's problem also surfaces in Psalms and Proverbs. Where do we see all this happening to the wicked? They often prosper – and the righteous die. Is this the last word about God's justice? Because of this apparent injustice, such passages may fairly be said to suggest a final reckoning and judgment of the wicked beyond temporal death. But they give no information concerning such events, nor

---

6. Blanchard admits that if the biblical writers intended to say that the wicked will become extinct, they could have expressed that in the very words they used (p. 234). However, he denies that is what they meant because the words are used elsewhere in a figurative or secondary sense (*Hell* pp. 234ff).

do they even explicitly require it. It is an implication drawn from the divinely revealed principles of divine government. Six psalms in particular strongly point in this direction.

Psalm 11:1-7 Even now God rules from his heavenly throne, observing both righteous and wicked (vv. 4, 5). Evildoers sometimes destroy the very foundation of moral society, and the godly feel powerless (v. 3). Yet they may know that God is on the throne; a day of reckoning is coming when God will reverse the roles and even the score. 'On the wicked he will rain fiery coals and burning sulphur (brimstone, KJV); a scorching wind will be their lot' (v. 6). Then 'upright men will see his face' (v. 7).

This world does not reward virtue or punish evil, but a day of divine reckoning will surely come. This psalm pictures the wicked's fate in terms taken from the punishment of Sodom, when 'the Lord rained down burning sulphur' (Gen. 19:24) and 'overthrew' city, people and vegetation (Gen. 19:25). He 'destroyed' the wicked in a 'catastrophe' so thorough that the next day Abraham could see only 'dense smoke rising from the land, like smoke from a furnace' (Gen. 19:28f).

Psalm 34:8-22 This psalm praises God, who delivers his people from their troubles. Peter uses it to encourage suffering Christians, quoting from verses 8 (1 Pet. 2:3) and 12-16a (1 Pet. 3:10ff).

The psalm contrasts the fates of those who trust God and those who do not. Those who fear God and take refuge in him will find him good (v. 8). They will lack for nothing good (vv. 9f).

God will be close to them in need (v. 18), see their plight, hear their cries (vv. 15, 17), and deliver them from trouble (vv. 17,19). They may enjoy a long and good life (vv. 12f); in the end God will redeem his servants so that none of them will be condemned (v. 22).

By contrast, God turns his face against the evil (v. 16), who finally are slain by their own wickedness (v. 21). At the last, God will condemn them (v. 21) and cut off their memory from the earth (v. 16).

The contrasts are striking. Whether we are good or evil, God is the One we must finally face. The righteous may expect to be delivered and vindicated because God is their mighty saviour. The wicked must know that their adversary and judge will be God, not man.

But as often as not, these destinies are not reached in earthly life. The righteous sometimes die in unjust suffering and shame; the wicked sometimes die in prosperity and peace. So the psalm looks beyond the present life for its infallible fulfilment, seeking, in that sense at least, for blessing and punishment in the world to come. Whatever we see now, the psalm promises a day when the righteous will shine (v. 5) but the wicked will be no more (v. 16). This is God's word on the matter, and he will bring it to pass.

Psalm 37:1-40 The psalmist describes the security of those who trust in God and the insecurity of the wicked. He has seen the wicked flourish: '... but he soon passed away and was no more; though I looked for him, he could not be found' (vv. 35f). This is the way, he boldly says, with the wicked in general.

Job's objection returns: where do we see this happening to the wicked? The answer must be that we do not yet see their end. This is made more certain by Jesus' use of the promise from verse 11 that 'the meek will inherit the earth' (Matt. 5:5), a reward which is there synonymous with the kingdom of God. The meek do not inherit the land – now. But like the writer of Hebrews, Jesus and David speak of the pilgrim's future homeland (Heb. 11:8–16) in the world to come (Heb. 2:5). They look, with Peter, for the new heaven and earth, the home of righteousness (2 Pet. 3:13).

In this light the couplet in v. 10 to the expression Jesus quotes becomes more significant. 'A little while, and the wicked will be no more; though you look for them, they will not be found.' This is said not once but repeatedly throughout the psalm. The wicked

> will soon wither like the grass and die away like green plants (v. 2);
> will be no more so they cannot be found (v. 10);
> will be laughed at by the Lord, for their day is coming (v. 13);
> will be pierced by their own swords, and their bows broken (v.15);
> will be broken in power (v. 17);
> will perish like the beauty of the fields and vanish like smoke (v.20);
> will be cut off (vv. 22, 28, 34, 38);
> will be destroyed (v. 38).

Here 'die' and 'destroy' are defined by a variety of figures from nature. These are not the mere hollow hopes of Job's shallow and uninspired friends. They are the solemn promises of David as he speaks by the Holy Spirit (Matt. 22:43; Acts 2:30). Those who trust in God might not see it happen now. But they are to wait patiently for the Lord's time, confident that he will bring his word to pass (vv. 7, 34). This psalm is surely instructive concerning the final fate of those who mock at God.

Psalm 50 God judges both the righteous and the wicked. He comes in fire and tempest to judge his people (vv. 3–6). 'Call upon me in the day of trouble,' he invites the godly; 'I will deliver you, and you will honour me' (v. 15). But to the wicked: 'What right have you to recite my laws or take my covenant on your lips?' (v. 16). 'Consider this,' he says to those who forget God, 'or I will tear you to pieces, with none to rescue' (v.22).

The symbolism is familiar: God comes in a fire storm for judgment. The words are chosen for impact rather than literal description. But they teach something, and what they teach is conveyed to the emotions by the threat, 'I will tear you to pieces, with none to rescue.'

Psalm 58 Imprecatory psalms have long disturbed Christian readers. How can godly people call for vengeance on their enemies? Should they not, rather, ask God to forgive them? It is important for us to understand that David's enemies are also God's enemies (which is ultimately why they are David's) and that David is turning all vengeance over to God. In this context we observe what David expected to happen when God took vengeance.

We must not read back into the Old Testament what is not there. Rather, we must listen to each passage for its own message, however shadowy or vague that message might be. Here is how the psalmist describes God's just punishment:

> their teeth will be broken in their mouths (v. 6);
> they will vanish like water that flows away (v. 7);
> they will melt like a slug as it moves along (v. 8);
> they will not see the sun, like a stillborn child (v. 8);
> their blood will bathe the feet of the righteous (v. 10).

The ultimate result will be God's honour. People will exclaim: 'Surely the righteous still are rewarded; surely there is a God who judges the earth' (v. 11).

Psalm 69:22–28 New Testament writers frequently quote this imprecatory psalm. They apply its words to Jesus (v.9/John 2:17 and Rom.15:3; v.21/John 19:28f) on the one hand, and to Judas (v.25/Acts 1:20) and unbelieving Israel (vv. 22f/Rom.11:9f) on the other. Here is the desperate cry of a righteous man, outnumbered and overpowered by wicked enemies, calling on God for vindication (justification) and deliverance (salvation).

He longs to see God's wrath poured out on the wicked (v. 24), their place deserted and their tents empty (v. 25). He is sure they will have no part in God's salvation (v. 27) but will be blotted out of the book of life (v. 28). God will finally hear the righteous (vv. 32f); they and their children will inherit Zion (vv 34ff).

In this psalm the end of the wicked is that they cannot be found! Their place is empty; they are not listed among the living. They are victims of the righteous wrath of God. The righteous, meanwhile, enjoy God's salvation. The language is figurative, the style is poetic, but the meaning is clear and the message is true.

Summary

Throughout the Old Testament, God teaches us about the end of the wicked in various ways. The books of poetry – Job, Psalms and Proverbs – reflect on the meaning and value of life 'under the sun'. What will be the difference between godly and ungodly in the end? How does it 'pay' to serve God? Why do the righteous sometimes die in poverty while the wicked lie down in fame and prosperity?

To answer these questions, the poetic books take us behind the scenes. There they point to the sovereign God on his throne, telling us that this God who already rules will also one day judge. They reassure us again and again that he will vindicate all who trust in him. In various ways they tell us how the godless will come to nothing. They will perish, will disappear, will not be found. Their place will be empty and they will be no more. Their bows will be broken, their own spears will slay them. The godly will wipe their feet in the wicked man's blood. The wicked man's name will not be found in the register of the living. Those who trusted in God will rejoice in his salvation. They will endure for ever. They and their children will inhabit Zion. They will be vindicated when they see God and dwell with him. They will inherit the earth.

These things do not happen now, so we look for their fulfilment in the world to come. Jesus and the New Testament writers do in fact quote from these psalms and apply their words to the coming age. They tell men and women of faith today that the same moral principles of divine government rule behind the scenes. They give us also the hope expressed by Job and David and Solomon.

Figurative language is not to be taken literally. (God's people will not literally paddle in the blood of wicked men.) But, as we shall point out again and again, a poetic figure must correspond to what it illustrates. Without some genuine correspondence, such symbolism misleads. Without being literal, therefore, we may learn from these passages of Scripture. Is it significant that they say nothing of conscious unending torment? That none of them hints at a fire which tortures but does not kill? That they do not envision the presence of the wicked for ever – even in a distant place? What they do portray, by contrast, is a time and a world where the wicked will not be; where the meek will rejoice in God's presence for ever. Every living creature will praise God, who has shown himself to be a righteous judge.

Some readers may wish to find the traditionalist picture elsewhere. That is a permissible pursuit. But as we leave these passages of Scripture, we must remember two things: (1) They do tell us something, and we must include them as we form a total biblical picture. (2) The picture they describe is the one we have just stated.

II. Passages describing specific divine judgments in space-time history

The laws given by God to Israel appear in two forms. There are specific commandments ('do not murder,' 'honour father and mother'), and case laws ('If a bull gores a man or woman, it shall be put to death'). One might think of theory and practice. God stated the absolute principles, but also illustrated their application in specific, concrete situations. The Old Testament teaches similarly in the matter of the end of the wicked.

We have considered passages from the poetic books which state moral principles of divine judgment. Such statements are scattered through the other books as well. But besides stating these principles God has also illustrated how they operate in specific situations. We can learn not only from the principles and promises of the Psalms but also by observing God's acts of judgment. In this section we examine some examples of the severity of God.

Genesis 6–9 In one sense, the story of the Flood closes the story which begins with creation.[7] This cataclysmic[8] judgment brought an end to one world and ushered in a new (Gen. 6–9; 2 Pet. 2:5; 3:4ff). It becomes a

---

7. Gary V. Smith applies structural analysis to Gen. 1–11 and finds the Flood story occupying a prominent theological position. See 'Structure and Purpose in Genesis 1–11,' *JETS* 20, no. 4 (Dec. 1977) p. 307–320.

8. The Greek translation of the Old Testament (the Septuagint, abbreviated LXX) and the Greek N.T. both use the word *kataklysmos* for the 'Flood'. The verb form *kataklyzō* ('to overwhelm with water') appears in 2 Peter 3:6.

standard biblical model for later crises and judgments. Later writers point to its unexpectedness (Matt. 24:38, 39; Luke 17:26f), its victims (2 Pet. 2:5,9), those it saved from the world's wickedness (1 Pet. 3:20ff; 2 Pet. 2:5, 9), Noah's faith (Ezek. 14:14, 20; Heb. 11:7), as well as God's patience preceding the judgment (1 Pet. 3:20; 2 Pet. 3:4ff) and the certainty of his covenant which followed it (Isa. 54:9). Jesus (Matt. 24:38f; Luke 17:26f.) and Peter (2 Pet. 2:5,9; 3:3–7) both use it to illustrate elements of their teaching about Last Things.

Because of their total depravity ('every inclination of the thoughts of his heart was only evil all the time,' Gen. 6:5), God decided to 'wipe mankind ... from the face of the earth' (Gen. 6:7). God tells Noah his plan 'to put an end to all people' (v. 13), 'to destroy both them and the earth' (v. 13), 'to destroy all life under the heavens, every creature that has the breath of life in it. Everything on earth will perish' (v. 17). Seven days before the Flood, God again tells Noah, 'I will wipe from the face of the earth every living creature I have made' (Gen. 7:4). Only life in the ark would survive.

The event itself is as severe as the threats. The Flood brings universal death: to 'every living thing that moved on the earth', to 'everything on dry land that had the breath of life in its nostrils', to 'every living thing on the face of the earth ' – 'men and animals and the creatures that move along the ground and the birds'. They 'perished', 'died', were 'wiped out' and 'wiped from the earth'. Only Noah was left, and those with him in the ark (Gen. 7:21ff.).

After Noah and his family leave the ark, God promises that he will never again 'destroy all living creatures' (Gen. 8:21); never again will there be a flood 'to destroy the earth' (Gen. 9:ff.). He formalizes his promise in a covenant with Noah and his sons, and seals the covenant with the sign of the rainbow. Whenever people see the rainbow, they can remember God's promise and realise that he will be faithful to the covenant (Gen. 9:8–17).

Sometimes words such as 'perish,' 'destroy' or 'die' may be metaphorical or figurative. Here there is no doubt about their meaning. In this actual example of the end of the world, these terms clearly mean literal death. Here evildoers meet the precise end described so often throughout Psalms and Proverbs.[9]

Since Jesus and Peter use this event to describe the earth's final destruction by fire, we need to consider its significance carefully. The Holy Spirit might have inspired many pages of philosophical discussion about the exact meaning of 'destroy' and 'perish' and whether they signified 'annihilation' or merely 'making inactive.' Instead, God points back to what he has already done once, warning that it is an example of what the wicked may expect again.

Genesis 19:24–29 The destruction of Sodom and Gomorrah ranks alongside the Flood as a historical demonstration of divine judgment. The

---

9. Not their final end, in view of the resurrection and judgment to come, but one typical of it according to NT writers. Dixon ignores the Flood as a biblical paradigm of final destruction, while Blanchard sets aside its clear meaning because the Flood did not physically annihilate the planet (*Hell* p.238).

name becomes a synonym for wickedness,[10] its chief survivor a model of one receiving God's mercy (2 Pet. 2:7ff).

Following Abraham's unsuccessful attempt to save the city through intercession (Gen. 18:16–33) and the inhabitants' shameful attack on their two angelic visitors (Gen. 19:1–11), Lot escapes with his family (Gen. 19:12–23).

> Then the Lord rained down burning sulphur on Sodom and Gomorrah – from the Lord out of the heavens. Thus he overthrew those cities and the entire plain, including all those living in the cities – and also the vegetation in the land. But Lot's wife looked back and she became a pillar of salt. Early the next morning Abraham got up ... He looked down toward Sodom and Gomorrah ... and he saw dense smoke rising from the land, like smoke from a furnace. (Gen. 19:24–29).

Biblical writers find this story instructive in many details. Isaiah is impressed by the total destruction of the entire wicked population – not one escaped! (Isa. 1:9). Paul quotes Isaiah's words with the same purpose (Rom. 9:29).

Jesus emphasizes the suddenness of the judgment. When God acts against the wicked, the righteous had better drop everything and run! (Luke 17:26–33.) The godly survivors are themselves like sticks snatched from the fire (Amos 4:11; Jude 23). Even the agent of destruction becomes a biblical symbol for divine punishment. This is the origin of 'fire and brimstone' in the Bible, with brimstone (sulphur) suffocating by its fumes, and fire consuming completely.[11]

In keeping with other passages on the fate of the wicked, Sodom's destruction also resulted in a barren and empty land void of human inhabitant. Moses later stresses this (Deut. 29:23), as do Jeremiah (49:18) and Zephaniah (2:9).

Even more significant, this desolation is to be perpetual. Centuries later, when God foretells Babylon's punishment of everlasting ruin, Sodom is the chosen example (Isa. 13:19–22; Jer. 50:40). The same thought appears in what Jude says about Sodom being 'an example of those who suffer the punishment of eternal fire' (Jude 7). The actual burning of Sodom was notably quick – in that regard even merciful (Lam. 4:6). God's wrath struck, 'burning them to ashes,' and made them 'an example of what is going to happen to the ungodly' (2 Pet. 2:6). But we have already seen how the New Testament applies the adjective 'eternal' to the results of a process, and that fits all the evidence here as well.[12]

---

10. Deut. 32:32; Isa. 1:10; 3:9; Jer. 23:14; Ezek. 16:46–56; Rev. 11:8. Yet Jesus says judgment will be more tolerable for Sodom and Gomorrah than for the cities which rejected his personal ministry and miracles (Matt. 10:15; 11:23f.; Luke 10:12).

11. Brimstone ('sulphur' in the NIV) forms part of the divine retribution against apostates in Israel (Deut. 29:23; Job 18:15; Ps. 11:6), against Assyria (Isa. 30:33), Edom (Isa. 34:9), Gog (Ezek. 38:22), idolaters (Rev. 14:10), the beast and false prophet (Rev. 19:20), Satan (Rev. 20:10) and sinners in general (Rev. 21:8). Pétavel speaks of its suffocating vapour as an agent of destruction (*Problem* p.193). The final outcome of 'fire and brimstone' in the prototypal historical judgment of Sodom was the complete extermination of every sinner and the desolation of their land. When the 'fire and brimstone' had passed, nothing but smoke was left.

12. See chapter 3, under ' "Eternal" with Words of Action'.

The fire fell from heaven and burned the wicked to ashes, resulting in a total desolation that would never be reversed![13]

Following Sodom's destruction, Abraham saw dense smoke rising from what had been a prosperous city – a grim reminder of the severity of divine justice. This picture, too, becomes part of the prophetic vocabulary of God's judgment and the fate awaiting the wicked (Isa. 34:10; Rev. 14:11; 19:3).

The biblical writers repeatedly point to Sodom as an example of God's impending judgment. We must not ignore this host of witnesses; biblical examples may sometimes illustrate more than other writers of Scripture explicitly state, but they certainly teach no less. All we ask here is that Sodom's destruction be given the same place and significance in our own thinking that it receives from Moses, Isaiah, Jeremiah and Zephaniah, Peter, John and Jesus.[14]

Deuteronomy 29:18–29 Near the end of his life Moses leads Israel in a renewal of the Sinai covenant. In solemn assembly before the Lord (vv. 10–15) he warns them to avoid idols and keep their hearts for Jehovah (vv. 16ff). Anyone who enters the covenant hypocritically, thinking he can avoid God's punishment, will bring disaster on himself and the people.

> The Lord will never be willing to forgive him; his wrath and zeal will burn against that man. All the curses written in this book will fall upon him, and the Lord will blot out his name from under heaven. The Lord will single him out from all the tribes of Israel for disaster, according to all the curses of the covenant written in this Book of the Law (29:20f).

Here is the Old Testament counterpart to the unforgivable sin of Matt.12:31f. 'The Lord will never be willing to forgive him.' We recall the unbeliever on whom Jesus says God's wrath abides (John 3:36). The situation also closely parallels the crisis described in Heb.12:15, with its warning about the 'bitter root' that may grow up to their great harm (v. 18).

Moses pictures the outcome of God's continuing wrath against the land, comparing it to a previous divine judgment.

> The whole land will be a burning waste of salt and sulphur – nothing planted, nothing sprouting, no vegetation growing on it. It will be like the destruction of

---

13. Constable drives home the conditionalist argument. 'In the days of Abraham, four rich and populous cities flourished in the plain of Jordan. On a sudden, fire descended from heaven, and, after a period of terror, regrets, and pain, the inhabitants were deprived of life.

'They and their works were burnt up; and this ruined, lifeless, hopeless, condition has remained to the present time ... The whole transaction conveys the idea of conscious pain for a time, followed by ruin and death for ever. This is, according to Scripture, to "suffer the vengeance of eternal fire"' (*Punishment* p. 141).

14. Blanchard correctly cites Sodom's destruction as an example of what awaits the ungodly (*Hell* pp.99, 139, 196), but misses the whole point by insisting that 'perish' requires technical annihilation (p. 239). Is it not sufficient that Scripture writers say that God destroyed the Sodomites? Because smoke and ashes remained when the people were gone, are we required to conclude that 'perish' and 'destroy' really mean living forever in torment?

Sodom and Gomorrah . . . , which the Lord overthrew in fierce anger. All the nations will ask: 'Why has the Lord done this to this land? Why this fierce, burning anger?' And the answer will be: 'It is because this people abandoned the covenant of the Lord, the God of their fathers' (Deut 29:23ff.).

The terrible effects of God's covenant wrath are portrayed very specifically. We might relate this passage to the judgment which fell on Jesus at Calvary. There he, who was always faithful to God's covenant, became this man under the covenant's curse.[15] In both Testaments God's salvation springs totally from sovereign mercy. In both cases he establishes it in a covenant with his people. This covenant contains stipulations and blessings, but it also threatens despisers with the direst of curses.

In this Old Testament paradigm the curse of the broken covenant is unmitigated disaster, destruction from off the land, leaving only the grim reminder of a desolate and fruitless earth (cf. Heb. 6:4–8). The execution of this penalty surely includes great terror, anguish and pain. But when the divine wrath has swept past, no sound is heard. The silence following the judgment is unbroken.

Isaiah 1:27–31 The book begins with an oracle against rebellious Judah and Jerusalem. God has already chastened his people through the Assyrians (Isa. 1:7ff), but they have not repented (vv. 4ff). The punishment will continue but it will be cleansing, leaving a purified remnant faithful to God. 'I will turn my hand against you; I will thoroughly purge away your dross and remove your impurities . . . Afterward you will be called The City of Righteousness, The Faithful City' (vv. 25f). Those who accept correction will be blessed; those who resist God will face a punishment even more severe.

Isaiah uses vivid symbolism to contrast these two fates:

> Zion will be redeemed with justice, her penitent ones with righteousness. But rebels and sinners will both be broken together, and those who forsake the Lord will perish. . . . You will be like an oak with fading leaves, like a garden without water. The mighty man will become tinder and his work a spark; both will burn together, with no one to quench the fire (1:27–31).

The picture is one of total desolation. Like Sodom and Gomorrah, Judah will be left without survivor or remnant (Isa. 1:9). Metaphors emphasize this: the people will burn like tinder; because the fire will not be quenched, it will destroy completely. Only destruction, emptiness, and ruin will remain. The wicked will be no more.

This passage threatens a specific historical judgment but it confirms what we know of the prophetic symbolism, the divine vocabulary of judgment. Again we note the outcome – total desolation with no survivors, described in terms of a burning fire which is not quenched and which therefore destroys completely.

---

15. Heb. 3:2,6. The expression 'the faith of Christ' (Gal. 2:16, 20 et al.) may well refer to Christ's own faith(fulness) to God as a man under the covenant. Although Jesus kept faith with God by perfect obedience to the covenant stipulations and thereby earned the covenant blessings, he willingly 'became a curse for us' (Gal. 3:13).

Isaiah 5:24f. God's woes and judgment-warnings to Jerusalem continue. The land will be emptied, and its inhabitants will go into captivity (vv. 9, 13). Mockers may rise and tempt God now, but their day will come (vv. 19ff). The prophet pictures their fate:

> Therefore, as tongues of fire lick up straw and as dry grass sinks down in the flames, so their roots will decay and their flowers blow away like dust . . . . Therefore the Lord's anger burns against his people; his hand is raised and he strikes them down. The mountains shake, and the dead bodies are like refuse in the streets. Yet for all this, his anger is not turned away, his hand is still upraised.

Again God shows us an empty land. Only corpses line the streets. The wicked are as helpless against God's judgment as straw and dry grass are against fire. Nothing of them is left – 'their roots decay and their flowers blow away like dust.'

Here again a prophecy relating to a specific historical event employs symbolic language. Again, fire is part of the vocabulary used. We should not interpret this language literally. Isaiah's hearers did not puzzle over the inconsistency of corpses in the streets on the one hand and destruction by fire on the other. Such prophetic language is intended to strike hard. God is not purveying information or satisfying curiosity; he is arresting the hearers' attention and enlivening their conscience. One writer compares such prophetic language to Picasso's abstract painting, 'Guernica'. This portrays the terrible tragedy that befell a particular Basque town on April 28, 1937. It is not a photograph but an expressionist painting. By 'de-calendarizing' the scene, Picasso universalizes it. It is still specific, but it has become far more. Now it symbolizes the ravages and trauma of war throughout history.[16]

Nahum 1:2–15 Nahum's prophecy targets a specific pagan people – Nineveh (Nah. 1:1). God comes in stormy fire for judgment (vv. 3–6; cf Ps. 50). His wrath is like fire which no one can endure (v. 6). He pursues his enemies into darkness (v. 8). He brings their plots to an end, never to reappear (v. 9). They are consumed like dry stubble (v. 10). God cuts them down and they pass away, completely destroyed and left without descendant (vv. 12, 14f).

Again we get the 'feel' of the prophetic judgments. The metaphors are mixed: thus God comes in fire and pursues into darkness. No one should stop and ask how fire and darkness can coexist. The mention of 'fire' calls for one emotional response; 'darkness' elicits another. Both are true. Later in the prophecy the plundering of Nineveh is graphically described in literal terms (Nah. 2:3–10; 3:1–3), but that language is no more fearful than this.

We note that Nineveh's judgment is pictured in terms of fire and darkness and that it consumes the people so entirely that they pass away without descendant or any hope of return.

---

16. The illustration is Vernard Eller's (*Most Revealing* pp. 87ff). The book is an excellent introduction (and more) to reading biblical prophecy, particularly the opening chapter.

Zephaniah 1:14-18 The 'day of the Lord' is the usual prophetic expression for a time of divine judgment against a city, nation or the whole world. Then God is clearly in charge. This day stands in sharp contrast to 'man's day' (the literal expression in 1 Cor. 4:3), when the wicked may occupy the throne and the righteous suffer.

Zephaniah paints an ominous picture of the 'day of the Lord' soon to come on Jerusalem by the agency of the Babylonian armies.

> The great day of the Lord is near – near and coming quickly. Listen! The cry on the day of the Lord will be bitter, the shouting of the warrior there. That day will be a day of wrath, a day of distress and anguish, a day of trouble and ruin, a day of darkness and gloom, a day of clouds and blackness, a day of trumpet and battle cry . . . . Their blood will be poured out like dust and their entrails like filth. Neither their silver nor their gold will be able to save them on the day of the Lord's wrath. In the fire of his jealousy the whole world will be consumed, for he will make a sudden end of all who live in the earth.

The prophet describes God's 'day of judgment' (here a specific historical judgment against Jerusalem) from its victims' point of view. It is a day of wrath, distress and trouble – words Paul also uses of the final day of judgment (Rom. 2:5-9). It is a day of anguish – the best one-word description of the New Testament's 'weeping and grinding of teeth.' It is a day of darkness but also of consuming fire – expressions also repeated in the New Testament warnings of the End.

Zephaniah helps us see again how the Old Testament prophets, by the Spirit of God, pictured God's approaching punishment. We should not always assume that 'the day of the Lord' refers to the eschatological end of the world. But we may be sure that it describes a visitation of divine wrath on the wicked (usually accompanied by divine mercy for true believers).

As we become familiar with the symbolism used by Old Testament prophets, we learn to grasp the meaning of the same language when it is used in the New Testament, by Jesus and the men he chose, to warn us of the great 'day of the Lord'. To that same extent we will be freed from the temptation to attach to biblical expressions other meanings of modern derivation, meanings which have no basis in Scripture and which sometimes contradict its consistent normal usage.

III. Passages concerning messianic or eschatological judgment

In addition to texts which state moral principles and those illustrating temporal judgments, a number of Old Testament passages clearly speak of a messianic or eschatological judgment. Because these texts or their contexts are so applied in the New Testament, we too may read them in that light. We will consider nine such passages here. Others probably could be found. But these are representative and consistent with the other texts which we might have adduced.

Psalm 1:3-6 The psalm contrasts the life and end of the wicked and the righteous. The godly man is like a well-watered tree. Its leaves never wither, and it is fruitful all the year around (v. 3). The picture reminds us of the Garden of Eden in Genesis or of the Eternal City in Revelation.

The wicked, by contrast, are 'like chaff that the wind blows away'. They will not be able to stand in judgment, and their path will finally perish (vv. 4ff). The picture is one of exclusion, expulsion, disintegration and desolation. At that the psalm stops. Other passages say more of the fate of the wicked but none contradicts what is said here.

Psalm 2:9–12 This 'royal' psalm is clearly messianic and is quoted frequently in the New Testament.[17] Verses 9 and 12 describe the Son's wrath against his enemies.

> You will rule them [or break them] with an iron sceptre; You will dash them to pieces like pottery. . . . Kiss the Son, lest he be angry, and you be destroyed in your way, for his wrath can flare up in a moment.

The rather colourless word 'perish' is further described as the result of the Christ's kindled wrath, his breaking with an iron sceptre. In this psalm it is compared to being shattered like earthenware. The picture – one of destruction in the ordinary sense of the word – teaches us about Christ's coming judgment.

Psalm 69:22–28 The New Testament use of this psalm suggests it could also be treated as in some sense messianic. It also fits the category of passages which deal with moral principles of divine government, and we have already discussed it there.

Isaiah 11:4 The chapter is clearly messianic. Paul applies the words of v.10 to his gospel ministry among the Gentiles (Rom. 15:12). Each of the first five verses is paraphrased or echoed by New Testament writers. Verses 6–9 have been variously interpreted as describing the gospel age, the millennium, or the new heavens and earth – in each case the fruit of Jesus' work of redemption.

The Messiah judges justly, vindicating the poor. The wicked also feel his judgment, for 'he will strike the earth with the rod of his mouth; with the breath of his lips he will slay the wicked' (v. 4). The language recalls Psalm 2. They may scoff at God's King now, but one day he will be their judge. From his lips now flow life and peace; by them the wicked will then be slain. The picture is symbolic, but its import is clear. The passage fits the larger pattern, and it is part of the whole biblical picture.

Isaiah 33:10–24 Oppressors afflict Israel now, but a brighter future is in store. When God 'arises', the scene will change (v. 10). The attempts of the wicked to protect themselves will be as futile as conceiving chaff or giving birth to straw. The wicked will ignite themselves by their own sins (v. 11), which will then 'consume' them (v. 11). They will burn 'as if to lime', blazing like 'cut thornbushes' (v. 12). The picture of total destruction could scarcely be more graphic.

---

17. Matt. 3:17; 15:5; Acts 4:26; 13:33; Heb. 1:5; 5:5; 1:2; Rev. 2:26f.; 12:5; 19:15.

All the same, some traditionalists have found everlasting conscious torment prefigured in verse 14.

There are three objections against this interpretation.

1. The context of verses 11ff speaks against it, picturing instead a total destruction by fire that could not possibly be more complete. The 'fire' of this passage does not preserve – it consumes! This explains why no wicked person can 'dwell' with it.

2. The language of v.14 is most naturally interpreted as referring to the eternal holiness of God himself, not the fire of hell. God is a 'consuming fire' (Deut. 4:24; Heb. 12:29). Isaiah had already used this figure (Isa. 5:24f.; 10:16ff), and he will use it again (Isa. 47:14). The fire of God's holiness always destroys whatever is not pure. As with Nadab and Abihu, the same fire which sanctifies the altar destroys the irreverent (Lev. 9:23–10:3). The 'everlasting burning' of Isaiah 33:14 parallels the 'consuming fire' of verse 11, and both refer best to God in his holiness.

3. Verse 14 asks a question which may be answered by the verses that follow. Just as Ps. 15 inquires who can dwell with God, then gives the answer, so in this passage. The answer of verses 15ff is strikingly similar to that of Ps. 15. Only one who 'walks righteously and speaks what is right,' who rejects extortion and bribes, who avoids evil in every form, can 'dwell' on the heights. Only this one can dwell with the God who is a consuming fire, whose holy glory is an everlasting burning against all sin.

That the passage is eschatological is indicated by verses 17–24. Redeemed Zion will 'see the King in his beauty and view a land that stretches afar' (v. 17). They will look on the eternal Jerusalem (v. 20), where none will be ill and all sins will have been forgiven (v. 24).

The 'everlasting burning' of this passage does not torment perpetually. Like a blaze devouring dry thorns, it consumes the wicked. Only those walking uprightly, their sins forgiven, can dwell with such a God.

Isaiah 51:3–11 Israel may suffer in exile, but present distress only foreshadows a glorious restoration. Those who trust in God will rejoice in his salvation. Those who mock his law and reproach his people will feel his wrath.

This passage is in a messianic context. It is preceded by one of the 'Servant Songs' (Isa. 50:4–10) and followed by another (Isa. 52:13–53:12). It looks forward to God's righteousness and salvation. Jesus has already procured these blessings, and the Holy Spirit now administers them. Their consummation will come at the End. The contrasting picture of righteous and wicked also may have some fulfilment now, but it waits till the second advent for complete actualization. Thus we may add such a passage to the Old Testament witness concerning the destiny of the wicked.

God will restore his people to a new Eden ringing with glad thanksgiving and songs of joy (v. 3). Even the Gentiles will share in God's righteousness and salvation (vv. 4,5), which will last for ever (vv. 6b, 8b). The wicked will have no part in this paradise. Earth's inhabitants will 'die like flies' when the heavens 'vanish like smoke' and the earth wears out 'like a garment' (v. 6). When the righteous thrive, the wicked will perish.

'For the moth will eat them up like a garment; the worm will devour them like wool' (v. 8).

This language is symbolic but true. We therefore take it seriously but not literally. God does not intend us to picture the damned as being consumed by insects and their larvae. The figure is just that — a figure. But it stands for something. It truly describes the reality for which it stands. What is the significance of the heavens and earth vanishing like smoke or wearing out like a garment, if not a complete passing away so that no trace is left? What does it mean that the wicked will be eaten up by moths and worms like wool and other garments? Is it not total destruction, again without a trace? While it is important that we recognize the symbolic nature of such passages, it is equally vital to allow the pictures to speak for themselves. They must describe a reality which truly corresponds to the significance of the symbol. This passage also can teach us something about the end of the wicked if we let it speak in its own terms.

Isaiah 66:24 This is arguably the most ignored biblical passage concerning final punishment, although it contains the scriptural phrase which is probably quoted most often. Earlier in the chapter, God contrasts the peace and comfort promised the humble (Isa. 66:2,12ff.) with the 'fury' he will show his foes (v. 14). The language is typically symbolic. God executes judgment 'with fire and with his sword' (v. 16). When the visitation has ended, 'many will be those slain by the Lord' (v. 16b). The wicked 'meet their end together' (v. 17) but the righteous and their descendants endure for ever (v. 22). 'All mankind' comes to worship God (v. 23) — the wicked are no more. This is the setting of the crucial verse 24.

> And they will go out and look upon the dead bodies of those who rebelled against me; their worm will not die, nor will their fire be quenched, and they will be loathsome to all mankind.

Jesus quotes these words (Mark 9:48), and they have formed the basis for much subsequent Christian teaching on hell, so we shall examine each phrase.

The righteous 'go out and look' on their enemies' corpses. Although clearly a symbolic picture of the future, this may well be based on an actual incident which Isaiah witnessed. In one of the greatest acts of divine deliverance since the Exodus and the Red Sea, God had answered Hezekiah's prayer and saved Jerusalem overnight from certain defeat by the Assyrians (2 Kings 18:17–19:36; Isa. 36, 37). Isaiah had strengthened Hezekiah with the Lord's encouraging message (Isa. 37:21–35). That night

> the angel of the Lord went out and put to death a hundred and eighty-five thousand men in the Assyrian camp. When the people got up the next morning — there were all the dead bodies! (Isa. 37:36)

Now Isaiah declares that a similar scene will be reproduced on a vaster scale at the end of time. In the historical event of Isaiah's day (Isa. 37:36) and in his prophetic picture of the future (Isa. 66:24), the righteous contemplate with satisfaction 'the dead bodies' of the wicked. They look at corpses (Heb. *pegerim*), not living people. They view their destruction, not their misery.[18]

Other Bible verses mention 'worms' in connection with dead bodies.[19] Several kinds of flies lay eggs in the flesh of carcasses.

The maggots hatched from them serve a beneficial purpose in hastening decomposition. But they are also a symbol of ignominy 'precisely because they attack only bodies deprived of burial'.[20] To the Hebrew mind, even if a man could live to be 2,000 years old and have 100 children, without a proper burial he would better have been stillborn (Eccles. 6:3–6). Like Jezebel, these corpses are left unburied; they are 'loathsome' to all who see them (2 Kings 9:10). Jeremiah also predicts this ultimate disgrace for God's enemies:

> At that time those slain by the Lord will be everywhere – from one end of the earth to the other. They will not be mourned or gathered up or buried, but will be like refuse lying on the ground (Jer. 25:33).

Such discarded corpses are fit only for the worms and fire. Although death by burning was not unknown to the Old Testament,[21] that is not the picture here. To burn a corpse might identify it as utterly accursed or devoted to God for destruction (Josh. 7:25). It also was an act of inhuman contempt (Amos 2:1).[22]

Because this fire is 'not quenched' or extinguished, it completely consumes what is put in it. The figure of unquenchable fire is frequent in Scripture and signifies a fire that consumes (Ezek. 20:47f), reduces to nothing (Amos 5:5f) or burns up something (Matt. 3:12).[23] Both worms and fire speak of a total and final destruction. Both terms also make this a 'loathsome' scene. The righteous view it with disgust but not pity. The final picture is one of shame, not pain.

Traditionalist writers interpret this passage in the light of their conception of final punishment rather than forming an understanding on the basis of the passage. Jesus' use of the language is generally handled the same way. Rather than studying this passage, determining the sense of its figures and interpreting the New Testament references on that foundation, traditionalists persistently begin with the New Testament references, interpret them in the light of church positions, and ignore the Isaiah text altogether.

Buis does quote the verse as one of those 'which hint at future retribution' but does not attempt to explain its figures. Instead, he cites Delitzsch as saying that it speaks of 'the eternal torment of the damned'.[24]

---

18. On God's people viewing the carcasses of their enemies with satisfaction, see also Exod. 14:30 (the prototypal event); Ps. 58:10; 91:8; Ezek. 39:9–22; Mal. 4:1ff.
19. Isa. 14:11. Job speaks thus of himself as one already dead in Job 7:5; 17:14; 21:16.
20. Pétavel, *Problem* p. 323.
21. 'Death by burning is prescribed for two sexual offences (Lev. 20:14; 21:9); in the story of Gen. 38:24 it is for harlotry' (M. Greenberg, 'Crimes and Punishment,' *IDB* 1:741).
22. Pedersen reads later ideas into the text in his comment: 'When the worms gnaw the dead body, the soul feels it' (J. Pedersen, *Israel: Its Life and Culture* 1–2:180).
23. See also 1 Kings 22:17; Isa. 1:31; Jer. 4:4; 21:12; Mark 9:43, 48.
24. Buis, *Eternal Punishment* p. 13.

Braun ignores the passage entirely and Dixon barely mentions it. Blanchard quotes or cites it several times, but without regard to its context, historical background or transformation by apocryphal Judith from a disgusting scene of dead corpses to a sadistic one of conscious sinners in unending pain.[25] Isaac Watts concludes that there would be 'no punishment at all' if the text meant what it pictures, and therefore allegorizes the gnawing worm into 'the remorse and terrible anguish of conscience which shall never be relieved'. He then interprets the unquenchable fire as 'the pains and anguish which come from without'.[26] Calvin judges it a mistake to say these things 'related absolutely to the last judgment', although he does 'not deny that they extend as far as to that judgment'.[27] He supplies no exegesis but asserts that 'the plain meaning' is

> that the wicked shall have a bad conscience as an executioner, to torment them without end ... and finally, that they shall tremble and be agitated in a dreadful and shocking manner, as if a worm were gnawing the heart of a man, or a fire were consuming it, and yet thus consumed, he did not die.[28]

Luther also makes the worm 'the bite of the conscience', an interpretation suggested also by Augustine.[29] This allegorical interpretation, based on reading into the text something not there while passing over all that is, is thus very ancient, dating at least to the intertestamental apocryphal book of Judith.[30] But search as we may, one simply cannot find anything in Isaiah 66:24 about conscious suffering, much less for ever. One might wish to argue the point from some other passage. But any fair use of the phrases originating here must at least take account of the sense of this passage without reading into its picture extraneous ideas from a later time and place. Careful exegesis demands as much, but that is what traditionalist writers have consistently failed to supply. Conditionalist authors have repeatedly pointed out this deficiency, but they have customarily been ignored.

Salmond, who defended the traditionalist view of hell, is a notable exception. He wrote, 'This is the picture at least of an absolute overthrow, an irreversible punishment overtaking the rebellious. At a later period the word [hell] was used to designate the place of future retribution.'[31] Later he notes that, while the terms of Jesus' teaching are based on this passage, 'it does not follow that they are limited to the use which is made of them

---

25. *Hell* pp. 130–143.
26. *The World to Come* . . . , pp. 300f. Since Tertullian, many traditionalist authors have been concerned that the wicked not be punished too 'lightly' even if achieving this meant strengthening the plain teaching of Scripture to something more harsh.
27. *Commentary on Isaiah* 4:438.
28. Ibid. p. 439.
29. *Works* vol. 17, 'Lectures on Isaiah' p. 416.
30. In the last chapter of Judith the heroine, following a great deliverance from the Assyrians, leads the people in a song of victory. Clearly alluding to Isaiah 66:24, she says: 'Woe to the nations that rise up against my race: / The Lord Almighty will take vengeance of them in the day of judgment, / To put fire and worms in their flesh; / And they shall weep and feel their pain for ever' (Jth. 16:17).
31. Salmond, *Immortality* p. 354.

there' and that they become 'figures of a retribution of another order than any that takes effect on earth'.[32]

We agree with that statement most heartily. The adjective 'eternal' includes a qualitative aspect, as we have already seen, and it suggests something belonging to the Age to Come. The final punishment of the wicked will indeed be 'of another order' than that of any temporal judgment. But Scripture describes what it will be in terms taken from specific occasions of divine judgment within history. We ask only that any explanation of those terms at least begin with the scenes they first described, and then that any extension of their meaning be grounded on biblical exegesis and not traditional or dogmatic fancy.

Daniel 12:2f. Even scholars who tend to discount Old Testament references to the final resurrection acknowledge it in this verse.[33] The passage looks forward to a resurrection of both good and evil,[34] but it is not clear whether it reveals it as universal in scope. One author discusses the text in the light of its larger whole (Dan.11:2–12:3), 'whose theme is judgment,' and sees the resurrection here as 'a solution to the problem of the defense of the righteous in persecution'.[35] Another argues that the resurrection is of members of the chosen people alone.[36] We do not have to pack all God's word into any one verse; further revelation makes clear what may here be obscure.

Among traditionalist writers, Buis calls Daniel 12:2 'one very clear reference to future punishment,' but he makes no further comment on the passage.[37] Braun does not even mention the verse in his chapter on the Old Testament.[38] Concerning the wicked, the text says only that of the 'multitudes' who awake from the dust of the earth, with 'some to everlasting life,' there will be 'others' who awake 'to shame and everlasting contempt'. The Hebrew word translated 'contempt' also appears in Isaiah 66:24, where it is translated 'loathsome' and describes unburied corpses. Conditionalist writer, Pétavel, notes that 'the sentiment of the survivors is disgust, not pity.'[39] Nothing will change this sentiment; there is 'everlasting contempt'.

Malachi 4:1–6 These verses stand on one side of the great period of divine silence, reaching out expectantly to the story resumed in the

---

32. Ibid. p. 376.
33. H. H. Rowley calls Daniel 12:2 'the only clear and universally recognized reference to resurrection in the Old Testament,' according to Thomas E. Ridenhour, 'Immortality and Resurrection in the Old Testament,' *Dialog* 15 (Spring 1976) p. 107.
34. Dubarle disputes this. 'It is not until the New Testament (John 5:38) that resurrection for punishment is foreseen.' He suggests an alternative explanation: that the wicked here are 'condemned to rot away for ever in the earth, arousing the abhorrence of all flesh' ('Belief in Immortality in the Old Testament and Judaism,' *Immortality and Resurrection* p.41).
35. Ridenhour, 'Immortality and Resurrection,' p. 107.
36. Dubarle, 'Belief in Immortality,' p. 41.
37. *Eternal Punishment*, p. 12.
38. *Whatever?* pp. 130–142.
39. Pétavel, *Problem* p. 323.

Gospels 400 years after. Jesus himself says John is this passage's 'Elijah' (Matt. 11:14; Mark 9:11ff; Luke 1:17). Like the book of Revelation in the New, this last book of the Old Testament Scriptures (in time, not Hebrew or Greek order) contrasts the final destinies of good and evil.

The 'day' of God is coming (v. 1), the 'great and dreadful day of the Lord' (v. 5). For those who revere God it will bring joy. They will leap like frolicking calves as they rejoice in the healing rays of the Sun of righteousness (v. 2). This day will also bring their vindication, for they will trample down the wicked, who will be 'ashes under the soles' of their feet (v. 3).

Arrogant evildoers will become like 'stubble,' and the coming day will 'set them on fire' with an all-consuming fire which will leave 'not a root or a branch' (v. 1). The expression eliminates every possibility of remnant or survivor. When God promised Judah a surviving remnant on another occasion, he used language just opposite (2 Kings 19:30; see the same figure applied to Jesus in Isa. 11:1; 53:2). It will be too late then for remedy; there is no hope of restoration or chance to escape. The godless will be 'ashes under the soles' of the feet of the righteous (v. 3).[40]

We need not literalize this prophecy or try to schedule it. But the reality these symbols convey must be in keeping with the sense of the pictures, which correspond to the fulfilment, not contradict it. The picture portrays the righteous rejoicing in God's salvation and the wicked gone for ever. The picture does not include perpetual torment, though it does include a total consumption by destroying fire. With these sobering verses Old Testament revelation ceased. God's next prophet would cry in the desert, demanding repentance in view of the approaching fire of God (Matt. 3:7–12).

Summary

The Old Testament has much to say about the end of the wicked. Job, Psalms and Proverbs repeatedly affirm the moral principles of divine government. The wicked may thrive now and the righteous suffer but that will not be the final picture. Repeatedly these books reassure the godly that those who trust will be vindicated, they will endure for ever, they will inherit the earth.

The wicked, however proud their boasts today, will one day not be found. Their place will be empty. They will vanish like a slug as it moves along. They will disappear like smoke. Those who search for them will not find them. Even their memory will perish. On these pillars of divine justice the world stands, and by these principles the Lord God governs his eternal kingdom.

The historical books of the Old Testament offer another insight. Not only does God declare what he will do to the wicked; he has shown his justice in action. When the first world became too wicked to exist, God destroyed it completely, wiping every living creature outside the ark from the face of the earth. That, says the New Testament, is a model of the

---

40. Blanchard quotes Malachi 4:1 but reasons as if verse 3 did not exist (*Hell* p. 137). Dixon also cites 4:3 but dismisses its figure without exegesis (*Other Side* p.79).

fiery judgment awaiting the present heavens and earth. When Sodom became too sinful to continue, God rained fire and brimstone from heaven, obliterating the wicked inhabitants in a moment so terrible it is memorialized throughout Scripture as an example of divine judgment. From this terrible conflagration no survivor emerged – even the ground was left scorched and barren. Only the lingering smoke remained, a grim reminder of the fate awaiting those who attempt to quarrel with their Maker.

Cities and nations also tasted God's wrath. Edom and Judah, Babylon and Nineveh in turn experienced temporal judgments. Some were spared a remnant. Others were not. The Spirit of God describes these divine visitations in terms of fire and darkness, anguish and trouble. Unquenchable fire consumed entirely until nothing was left. Again smoke ascended, the prophetic cipher for a ruin accomplished.

The inspired declarations of the prophets combine moral principle with historical fate. The details of actual destructions wrought on earth become symbols for another divine visitation. While they speak to their own times, the prophets also view the distant future. A day is coming when God will bring an end to all he has begun. That judgment will be the last.[41] Righteous and wicked will be gathered alike to see the justice of the Lord they have served or spurned. Again there will be fire and storm, tempest and darkness. The slain of God will be many – corpses will lie in the street. Amidst this scene of utter contempt worms and fire will take their final toll. Nothing will remain of the wicked but ashes – the righteous will walk over them. God's kingdom will endure for ever. The righteous and their children will inherit Mount Zion. Joy and singing will fill the air. All the earth will praise the Lord.

Such is the Old Testament picture of the end of the wicked.

---

41. P. T. Forsyth wrote: 'For the Bible as a whole ... history is viewed under the category of judgment (though saving judgment) and not under that of progress. ... The course of historic events is that of a series of judgments ... a long crescendo of judgment, ending in a crisis of all the crises, a harvest of all the harvests which had closed one age and begun a new, a grand climacteric of judgment, a last judgment, which dissipates for ever in a storm the silting up of all previous judgments, because ending a temporal world and opening an eternal' (*The Justification of God* p. 185, quoted by Morris, *Judgment* p. 60).

7

Between the Testaments

The period from Malachi to Matthew has been described as 'the 400 silent years,' but in terms of literature it was anything but quiet. Within a century after Malachi, Alexander the Great had conquered his world. He took tribute of one kind but left another of his own. The Greek language became the common tongue of the civilized world, linking peoples scattered since Babel.

The Jews were widely dispersed. Large populations had settled in Egypt; others remained in Babylon and Persia; exiles spread in all directions. Those who returned to Palestine were soon under foreign occupation once more. The Seleucids of Syria and the Ptolemies of Egypt competed for the mastery of this land-strip between them, finally relinquishing it to the Romans, who in 40 B.C. installed the half-breed family of Edomite Herods.

During the last two centuries B.C. Israel's faith was tried in the fire. The Syrian tyrant, Antiochus IV (175-164 B.C.),[1] one of the cruellest men in history, determined to unify his territory by enforcing Greek religion, custom and law. To this end he outlawed on pain of death every important practice of Jewish faith, including Sabbath observance, circumcision and the laws concerning food. He committed the ultimate blasphemy when he caused an altar of Zeus to be erected in the temple at Jerusalem, compelling the Jews to participate in his heathen worship. This 'abomination that makes desolate' (probably described in Daniel 11:31) had its impact but also its repercussions.

Open rebellion finally came in 167 B.C. at the little village of Modin. A faithful priest named Mattathias, resisting an act of sacrilege, killed the king's representative, then fled to the countryside with his family and an ever-enlarging band of volunteers. Mattathias died the next year, but the guerrilla movement continued under his son Judas, who became known as 'The Hammer' (Maccabeus). Antiochus would have exterminated the Palestinian Jews entirely, but eastern revolts forced him to respond there instead. Judas' courage rose with his faith (probably celebrated in Hebrews 11:34); he defeated the king's army at Emmaus and then at Beth-zur. On the 25th of Chislev, 165 B.C., Judas rededicated the temple and restored the daily sacrifices, an event still celebrated in the Feast of Hanukkah.

---

1. Antiochus took the surname 'Epiphanes' ('The Manifest [God]'), prompting some of his enemies to call him 'Epimanes' ('The Madman'). This brief history of the period reflects N. Turner's article, 'Antiochus,' *IDB* 1:150f.

Such times reveal apostates and make martyrs. They also generated a special type of literature known today as 'apocalyptic'. Parts of Daniel in the Old Testament fit this pattern, as does Revelation in the New. This literature mirrored the minds of the steadfast struggling souls. Among its common traits were: (1) a strong sense of the otherness of God, (2) the conviction that the end of the world is at hand, (3) a sense of man's existence in historical time, and (4) the use of mysterious and secret revelations.[2] This apocalyptic literature 'located the believer in a minority community and gave his life meaning by relating it to the end, soon to come, which would reverse his present status.'[3] Both Jews and Christians produced such material until about A.D. 100.

Some of these books were included in the Septuagint (though not in the final Hebrew canon) and are regarded as biblical by the Roman Catholic Church but not by most Protestants. Generally called the 'Apocrypha,' these 14 or 15 books (depending on their division) are the best known of the 'outside' books, but they are by no means the most important.

Of far greater interest for the present purpose are the writings often called the 'Pseudepigrapha.'[4] James H. Charlesworth, a specialist in the area, lists 77 known works under this category and leaves the list open for further additions.[5] The fascination these writings hold for scholars today is seen in Charlesworth's bibliography of 1,494 articles or books on the subject, all published between 1960 and 1975!

Generalizations abound concerning this intertestamental literature as a whole and regarding its teaching on final punishment. Opinions reputable scholars held as late as the 1950s have had to be modified or abandoned in the light of new discoveries, among them the Dead Sea Scrolls, a vast collection first found in the late 1940s and still being translated and analyzed.

2. William E. Beardslee, 'New Testament Apocalyptic in Recent Interpretation,' *Interpretation* 25, no. 4 (Oct. 1971) p. 424f.
3. Ibid. p. 424. Another scholar reminds us that 'theological conceptions and the literature that contains them do not evolve in a vacuum. They are the products of real people, living in concrete historical situations' (Nickelsburg, *Intertestamental* p. 10).
4. Literally 'false writings,' so called because authorship is attributed to OT figures such as Moses, Baruch, Solomon, Enoch, the twelve patriarchs and others. Scholars who specialize in this genre urge against any modern connotation of fraud or deceit. 'Rather than being spurious,' says Charlesworth, 'the documents . . . are works written in honor of and inspired by Old Testament heroes. It is anachronistic and misrepresentative to suggest that there is anything innately fraudulent about the Pseudepigrapha' (Charlesworth, *Pseudepigrapha* p. 25).
R. H. Charles suggests a practical reason for this practice of attaching ancient names as authors of more recent works. By the third century B.C. the Law had come to be regarded as God's supreme and final revelation; it not only took the place of the pre-exilic prophets – the possibility of any new word from God was now unthinkable. If anyone would gain a hearing for a new work, it must be in the name of an ancient worthy, when prophecy was still allowed to have taken place. Charles concludes: 'All Jewish apocalypses, therefore, from 200 B.C. onwards were of necessity pseudonymous if they sought to exercise any real influence on the nation; for the Law was everything, belief in inspiration was dead amongst them, and their Canon was closed' (*APOT* 2:viii–ix). While this was probably one factor, other scholars caution that it was not the only one.
5. *Pseudepigrapha and Modern Research* pp. xi–xiv.

It is tempting to try to neatly box intertestamental thought, to clearly distinguish between ideas, and to label views precisely. It is also impossible. The literature cannot be easily categorized – whether by place of origin (Palestine or Diaspora), authorship (Hellenistic Jews or those loyal to Law and tradition), or even by its precise time.[6] Some books show clear signs of later Christian 'editing' and additions. The Judaism which produced this literature also includes great diversity of thought. One who searches here for doctrinal patterns finds that the 'picture is far from clear or coherent.'[7] Expectations of the End were 'varied and unsystematized'.[8] These books present 'a heterogeneous mass of ideas in constant flux'.[9]

Yet it is possible to overstate the influence of the pseudepigrapha on the New Testament. Charlesworth is undoubtedly correct in saying that the 'often bizarre, usually rich apocalyptic traditions upon which the Pseudepigrapha almost has a monopoly were determinative for the thoughts of Dante, Bunyan, and Milton'.[10] It is another matter entirely to say that 'most of the ideas regarding the future life which are found in the New Testament writings had their origin in the apocalyptic writings'.[11] Although the New Testament repeats some concepts and language found in the intertestamental material about final punishment – including the place-name 'Gehenna' itself – its *teaching* clearly originates in the Old Testament.[12]

---

6. 'Not only was Palestine deeply hellenized, at least in scattered sections, but the diaspora itself contained islands of Jews loyal to Torah and traditions.' Furthermore, 'the geographical origin of a composition is usually the most difficult issue to resolve' (ibid. p. 24). Nickelsburg says there was 'no single Jewish orthodoxy' in intertestamental eschatology, the very idea of 'a unitary Jewish view' being 'a pure fiction' (*Intertestamental* p. 180).

On diversity regarding eschatological anthropology in Palestinian Judaism, see Gunter Stemberger, *Der Leib der Auferstehung: Studien zur Anthropologie und Eschatologie des palastinischen Judentums im neutestamentlichen Zietalter (ca. 170 v. Chr.–100 n. Chr.)*, AnBib 56 (Rome: Biblical Institute, 1972). On the great diversity found in the eschatological expectations of western Diaspora Judaism, see Ulrich Fischer, *Eschatologie und Jenseitserwartung im hellenistischen Diasporajudentum*, BZNW 44 (Berlin/New York: de Gruyter, 1978). Fischer identifies both wholistic and tripartite anthropologies, individualistic and cosmic hopes, and (confirming our present findings) various 'final punishments' of the wicked, including total annihilation.

7. S. H. Hooke, 'Life after Death: The Extra-Canonical Literature,' *ET*, June 1965, p. 276.

8. 'Eschatology,' *HDB* p. 266.

9. R. H. Charles, *A Critical History of the Doctrine of a Future Life* p. 362. F. F. Bruce uses the intertestamental literature to illustrate the 'varieties of expectation among religious Jews in the last two centuries B.C.' in 'Paul on Immortality,' *SJT* 24, no. 4 (Nov. 1971) p. 459. The same material appears in his *Paul* p. 302.

10. *Pseudepigrapha* p. 25.

11. C. T. Fritsch, 'Apocrypha,' *IDB* 1:164.

12. Writers advocating any position only confuse matters when they hastily equate similarity of language with agreement – or even worse, origin – of thought. An orthodox view of Scripture would seem to require that we give the Old Testament precedence over any extrabiblical materials as the proper background for viewing and understanding the NT. In expressing this conviction, I acknowledge but would slightly modify the growing

Traditionalist writers also have made too much of the intertestamental literature. They have found certain texts describing unending conscious torment (an idea not contained in the Old Testament, as we have already seen) and have simplistically assimiliated these ideas to the language of Jesus. Shedd quotes Edersheim (1883) as saying that the first-century Jews taught eternal punishment, and leaves it at that.[13] Pusey also argues from this single point of view, though in fairness we should note that he was responding to Farrar's similar overstatement in the opposite direction.[14] Buis cites the Pharisees' belief in this kind of eternal punishment, then argues from Jesus' silence that he approved of their doctrine.[15] One modern writer even quotes Philo of Alexandria as giving

---

idea 'that the proper approach to the historical Jesus is via documents and traditions contemporaneous with him' (Charlesworth, *Pseudepigrapha* p. 26).

Harmon has charged that this book 'overemphasizes the Old Testament background at the expense of the intertestamental literature' when interpreting NT passages ('Case' p. 206). I simply urge that when we set out to define biblical words, we begin with the earlier biblical material and that we enlarge or modify definitions based on early revelation only with the warrant of revelation given later. Harmon correctly notes that, by NT times, a tradition existed for interpreting intertestamental language. In view of the diversity of that tradition regarding disputed points, I see no reason to change the common OT meaning of the language of final judgment – all of which suggests total, irreversible extinction in hell. That understanding is further corroborated by the testimony of the Apocrypha (with the single exception of one text in Judith), most of the Pseudepigrapha, and all of the Dead Sea Scrolls translated thus far. Harmon says I 'admit' that the intertestamental evidence on this topic is quite diverse. 'Emphasize' would be a better word. Advocates of the traditional view are the ones who must 'admit' the diversity, since their position has often depended in part on assuming that intertestamental and first century Jews were all of one mind on this subject in favour of eternal conscious torment. I therefore laboured to show the intertestamental diversity of opinion, and concluded that we must come to grips with NT language on final punishment without relying on such shortcuts as assuming some 'uniform Jewish view,' as many traditionalists have done.

13. Shedd, *Punishment* p. 14, note 1. Shedd could plead ignorance of 20th century discoveries to the contrary, but Morey's 1982 book falls headlong into the same error of relying on Edersheim to prove that eternal torment was 'the' Jewish view at the time of Christ (*Afterlife* pp. 89, 119, 126f.). Interestingly, Morey later (pp. 268f) quotes Edersheim to the contrary, noting that both Shammai and Hillel taught that some would stay in Gehenna while others would return from it, and Jochanan ben Zakkai was so uncertain about the wicked's final fate in hell that he didn't know whether God would bind them with eternal fetters, be angry with an eternal wrath, or kill with an eternal death.

14. 'The Jews believed in eternal punishment before or at the time of the Coming of our Lord, and called the place of that punishment Gehenna' (*What Is of Faith?* p. 49). Pusey was responding to F. W. Farrar, who had said that 'the Jews ... never did ... normally attach to the word Gehenna that meaning of endless torment which we attach to "Hell" ' (*Eternal Hope* p. 80). Farrar erred in citing rabbinic sources too late for the view of Christ's day; Pusey erred in noticing too little of the evidence, singling out one view to the neglect of another equally well documented.

15. Buis, *Eternal Punishment* p. 24. As noted earlier, the Pharisees probably believed also in the preexistence of souls (Josephus, *Wars* 2. 8. 14; *Antiquities* 18. 1. 3); perhaps reflected in John 9:2. F. F. Bruce cautions concerning Josephus' 'eagerness to assimilate' his account of the Pharisees' teaching 'to the Greek outlook' (*Paul* p. 301). Conditionalist Edward White notes: 'The points in which alone the doctrine of the Pharisees was defended both by Christ and Paul against the Sadducees, were those of the existence of

'the generally-held view of both the orthodox Jews and the Judeo-Christian community of that period.'[16] This is roughly comparable to the situation of an archaeologist in the year A.D. 4,000 uncovering a twentieth-century Christian Science reading room and proclaiming it the key to understanding Protestant beliefs of the period.

There is no question that the traditionalist understanding of hell is very ancient, nor that it finds expression in the intertestamental literature of the Jews. But that literature also contains the view we have seen in the Old Testament that the day will come when the wicked will cease to be. Salmond, who defended the traditional doctrine, recognized this alternative of annihilation in the intertestamental writings and called attention to it.[17] Strack and Billerbeck, acknowledged authorities in the field of later rabbinical literature, go even further. They suggest the possibility that the term 'eternal punishment' in the Pseudepigrapha was itself synonymous with everlasting annihilation.[18] The implications of this statement, if it is correct, are staggering, turning upside-down a major traditionalist presupposition.

We make no claims here of being either exhaustive or final. This apocalyptic field covers a vast territory, and its literature is most complex. We will simply ask two questions, then seek to answer them. First, what views did the Jews hold concerning final punishment at the beginning of the Christian era as discerned in this apocryphal literature 'outside' the canon? Second, to what extent did such views coincide with the divine revelation contained in the Old Testament?

---

spirits, and the "resurrection of the just and unjust." ' He warns against the danger of assuming 'that whatever ... Christ did not explicitly condemn He sanctioned by His silence' and correctly observes that Jesus 'taught by affirmation rather than denial' (*Life in Christ* pp. 220f).

16. Leslie H. Woodson, *Hell and Salvation* p. 43.

17. S. D. F. Salmond concludes that 'the class of literature which is the most relevant witness to the state of Jewish belief in Christ's time, shuts us up to a choice between annihilation and a penal immortality as the prevalent conception of the future of the impenitent but they have no place for the idea of a universal restoration of the perverse' (*Immortality* p. 359). We will note a view that the wicked will all be converted before the end. This is different from saying they will go to 'hell' and later be restored – a view later expounded by Origen and others.

18. 'The punishment of the godless, regardless if they were judged in the catastrophic judgment or the regular judgment, lasts forever. But the Pseudepigrapha also speak about the destruction or the annihilation of the godless, so that one may be in doubt if to them the everlasting condemnation of the (judged) guilty simply had become synonymous with everlasting annihilation' (Hermann L. Strack and Paul Billerbeck, *Kommentar zum Neuen Testament aus Talmud und Midrasch* 2:1096).

The German text states: 'Die Bestrarung der Gottlosen, gleichviel ob sie im Katastrophengericht oder um ordentlichen Gerichtsverfahren gerichtet sind, wahrt ewig. Daneben reden die Pseudepigraphen aber auch vom Untergang oder von der Vernichtung der Gottlosen, so das man im Zweifel sein kann, ob innen die ewige Verdamnis der Gerichteten nicht vielfach gleichbedeuten gewesen ist mit deren ewiger Vernichtung.'

8

The End of the Wicked in the Apocrypha

Christian attitudes to the books of the Apocrypha vary widely. Some regard them as fully canonical; others as valuable but not authoritative in the same sense as the books of the Old and New Testaments; others again as having very little spiritual significance.

But for our present purpose these books are important since they reflect at least some views current among Jews during the inter-testamental period and may help us in understanding the significance and context of the teaching of Jesus. Introductory material in this chapter regarding the authors and the times and places of origin of the apocryphal books comes from appropriate articles in *IDB*.[1] Some of the underlying issues are debatable but certainty about authorship and date are not of great significance in this context.

Tobit

This didactic romance may date from about 200 B.C., though some Roman Catholic scholars argue for a seventh-century origin. The hero's dying words to his son Tobias describe the end time, concluding with:

> they that love God in truth shall rejoice, and they that do sin and unrighteousness shall cease from all the earth (4:6ff.).

There is no mention here of a resurrection. Righteous Israelites who are alive will inherit the promised land and rejoice for ever. Sinners simply 'shall cease from all the earth.' Whether they are executed and consumed, as in the Old Testament, or are converted *en masse* is an open question, though the text suggests the latter. Conscious unending torment is nowhere in the picture.

Sirach (or Ben Sira)

Also called Ecclesiasticus, this book of wisdom purports to be the Greek version of a Hebrew work written by the translator's Palestinian grandfather. The Greek version probably comes from Egypt somewhere between 195–171 B.C. The author is acquainted with and hostile to Hellenism.

His view is that of the Old Testament. Those led astray by wine and women 'will perish.' 'Mould and worms will take possession' of them

---

1. Quotations in this chapter are from R. H. Charles, *APOT* vol. 1.

(19:2f.). The sinner's end will be as with fire. 'Like tow wrapped together is the assembly of the ungodly, and their end is the flame of fire' (21:9). Isaiah also compared the wicked's end to tow or tinder, no sooner ignited than consumed (Isa. 1:31; see also Judg. 16:9).

Sirach says the wicked will so perish when their slick path slides them into 'the pit of Hades' (21:10).

Sirach also speaks of 'the glowing fire' in which the wicked will 'be devoured' and 'find destruction' (36:7-10). The Greek text has a 'fire of wrath', and the Syriac text says 'in anger and in fire'. Another passage warns: 'In the assembly of the wicked a fire is kindled, and in an apostate nation doth wrath burn' (16:6). The following verses compare this fate to the destruction of Sodom, the extermination of the Canaanites, and an unidentified occasion on which 600,000 enemy footmen were destroyed.

The imagery of fire begins to change significance during this period. Instead of the Old Testament fire which cannot be quenched until it totally consumes, the literature begins to speak of a fire which torments its victims but does not destroy them. R. H. Charles notes signs of this transition in 7:17. Here the Hebrew text says 'the expectation of man is decay,' and a later rabbinic quotation repeated it as 'the hope of man is the worm' (Pirqe Aboth 4.7). But when Ben Sira translated his grandfather's words into Greek, he included an additional thought. Instead of 'decay' or 'the worm,' he put 'fire and the worm.' Although the shift is discernable, the statement concerns not the wicked as such but humankind in general. And even 'fire and the worm' could totally consume (as in Isa. 66:24) rather than torment for ever. Still, the change seems to reflect a current opinion.

Baruch

This work, attributed to the secretary of the prophet Jeremiah, addresses the Jews in Babylon. It may date from about 150 B.C. The author urges the righteous to suffer patiently, using a figure familiar to the Old Testament. 'My children, suffer patiently the wrath that is come upon you from God: for thine enemy hath persecuted thee; but shortly thou shalt see his destruction, and shall tread upon their necks' (4:25).

Later Baruch describes the coming end of Israel's enemies in terms used by Isaiah and Jeremiah and later by John in Revelation.

> Miserable are the cities which thy children served:
> Miserable is she that received thy sons.
> For as she rejoiced at thy fall,
> And was glad of thy ruin:
> So shall she be grieved for her own desolation. . . .
> . . . For fire shall come upon her from the everlasting, long to endure;
> And she shall be inhabited of devils for a great time' (4:32-35).

The words about the destruction and burning of Babylon recall Jeremiah 51:58, 62f. The statement that the city would 'be inhabited of devils for a great time' may reflect Isaiah 13:19-22. Baruch uses the established language of the Old Testament prophets, referring probably to temporal rather than eschatological judgment.

Judith

This tale of a heroic Jewish maiden who saves her people may come from 150–125 B.C., though the date is disputed. At the end of the story the heroine, Judith, leads Israel in a song of victory over their former oppressor:

> 'Woe to the nations that rise up against my race;
> The Lord Almighty will take vengeance of them in the day of judgment,
> To put fire and worms in their flesh;
> And they shall weep and feel their pain for ever (16:17).

The fire and worms probably come from Isaiah 66:24, but now the transition hinted at in Sirach 7:17 is completed. Where Isaiah saw the unburied corpses of God's enemies exposed to the abhorrent destruction of fire and worms, Judith introduces a completely different idea of everlasting conscious pain. Her 'fire and worms' do not destroy; they sensibly torment. They are not outside agents which consume their victim; they are internal agonies inside his flesh. The victims are not destroyed but 'feel their pain for ever'.

Umistakably, these words describe the traditionalist hell. Equally unmistakably they are a new departure. In all the Old Testament's inspired pictures of the wicked – in the historical, poetic or prophetical books – we have nowhere found such a picture of unending conscious torment. But here it is, in the apocryphal Book of Judith.

1 Maccabees

This historical narrative of the Maccabean liberators and their valiant deeds was probably written about 110 B.C. by an author sympathetic to the Hasidic element in Judaism, which produced the Essenes and the Pharisees. In sectarian terms the book is nonpartisan, espousing the distinctive views of neither the Pharisees nor the Sadducees.

1 Maccabees does not speak clearly about the eschatological end of the wicked. One passage reflects the same Old Testament outlook we have already seen, that the sinful man will meet his end in the earth. The author exhorts:

> And be not afraid of the words of a sinful man, for his glory shall be dung and worms. Today he shall be lifted up, and tomorrow he shall in no wise be found, because he is returned unto his dust, and his thought is perished' (2:62ff.).

2 Maccabees

Judas Maccabeus is the hero of this book, which may have been written slightly before 1 Maccabees, whose saga it continues. This author goes beyond any apocryphal literature we have seen yet in clearly affirming a bodily resurrection, though it seems to be limited to the righteous. So far as the wicked are concerned, the martyr heroes here stand fast on the sovereignty and justice of God. They are sure he will punish their tormentors but they say comparatively little about the details.

90-year-old Eleazar disdains to escape martyrdom by renouncing his God: 'Even were I for the moment to evade the punishment of men, I should not escape the hands of the Almighty in life or in death' (6:26). As his wife and their seven sons face death they encourage each other in hope of a bodily resurrection, in which they warn their adversary he will have no part. God will be his judge, they say again and again, without being more specific.

Thus the second brother challenges the king: 'Thou dost dispatch us from this life, but the King of the world shall raise us up . . . and revive us to life everlasting' (7:9). The fourth brother similarly faces his executioner. 'Tis meet for those who perish at men's hands to cherish hope divine that they shall be raised up by God again; but thou – thou shalt have no resurrection to life' (7:14). The fifth brother warns that God's 'sovereign power will torture thee and thy seed!' (7:17); the sixth brother says, 'Think not thou shalt go unpunished for daring to fight against God!' (7:19); the seventh: 'But thou, who hast devised all manner of evil against the Hebrews, thou shalt not escape the hands of God' (7:31). Later he adds, 'Thou shalt receive by God's judgment the just penalty of thine arrogance' (7:36). His prayer is that God will make the persecutor acknowledge 'in torment and plagues, that he alone is God' (7:37).

This punishment may well be expected in the present life and culminate in a death from which the brothers anticipate there will be no return. Their tormentor will have no part in the resurrection to life, and they do not seem to expect a resurrection of any other kind. If they held any views of conscious unending torment for the wicked, this would be an ideal occasion to express it. But they do not, although they do warn him of God's certain vengeance.

Wisdom of Solomon

Probably written during the first century B.C., this is an outstanding example of Hellenistic Jewish writing. Some have detected in 2:21–39 the unbiblical concept of a bodiless reward for immortal souls but the language used about the wicked could come from Psalms or Proverbs. Two passages illustrate this agreement.

> But them the Lord shall laugh to scorn.
> And after this they shall become a dishonoured carcass,
> And a reproach among the dead for ever:
> Because he shall dash them speechless to the ground,
> And shall shake them from the foundations,
> And they shall lie utterly waste, and be in anguish,
> And their memory shall perish   (4:18f.).

> The hope of the ungodly is like chaff carried off by the wind,
> And like a thin spider's web driven away by a tempest;
> And like smoke which is scattered by the wind,
> And passeth away as the remembrance of a guest that tarrieth but a day.
> But the righteous live for ever,
> And the Lord is their reward,
> And the care for them with the Most High   (5:14f.).

Nickelsburg notes that while the Wisdom of Solomon attributes immortality to the soul of the righteous man already, neither life nor immortality are inherent to the soul but are the result of the godly man's actions in this life. For this reason, he says, even in the Wisdom of Solomon immortality is ascribed only to the righteous, while the 'wicked bring death upon themselves, death in an ultimate sense'.[2]

Other Apocryphal Works

The Apocrypha also includes 1 Esdras (a historical work which closely parallels Ezra-Nehemiah), 3 Maccabees (an alleged historical work of the period before 2 Maccabees but generally regarded as less reliable), and several smaller additions to canonical books (1 Baruch, Epistle of Jeremy, Prayer of Manasses, and additions to Daniel and to Esther). None of them adds anything to what we have so far discovered.

Summary

The Apocrypha stands between the divine revelation of the Old Testament and the fanciful imagination of some of the Pseudepigrapha. On the fate of the wicked this literature overwhelmingly reflects the teaching of the Old Testament. The wicked will not escape God's judgment. They will surely die. Worms will be their end. They will pass away like smoke or chaff, or burn up like tow. The righteous may hope for a resurrection and blessed life with God, but the wicked will have no part in it.

Judith contains the single explicit reference to conscious everlasting pain. The Greek version of Sirach changes the Hebrew in one passage to what might reflect the same view. This expectation is clearly present, but it is not the general one. On the other hand, the total, irreversible destruction of the godless was clearly anticipated by some Jews by the first century.

---

2. *Intertestamental* pp. 88, 179.

9

The Pseudepigrapha and the Sinner's Doom

Although the books described as 'pseudepigrapha' stand well outside the canon of Scripture, biblical scholars today are keenly interested in them. Some writers have exaggerated their worth, as if they were the true source of New Testament teaching about the last things and judgment. Yet even a modest estimation of these assorted writings, dated from approximately 200 B.C.–A.D. 100, acknowledges their importance in providing historical perspective for New Testament studies.

Judaism of the intertestamental period comprised living, thinking folk who sometimes differed vigorously from each other on theological matters. This unsurprising fact has not always come across in popular writings about the period, not least in respect of beliefs about final punishment.[1] Traditionalist authors have tended to imply that this literature is filled with references to everlasting conscious torment,[2] that this doctrine simply carried the Old Testament teaching a proper and natural step further, and that New Testament teaching should be interpreted accordingly.

Recent scholarship acknowledges this diversity and this chapter will therefore avoid bold claims and sweeping generalizations. A simple survey of a representative sample of pseudepigraphical literature from the period 200 B.C.–A.D. 100 will suffice to illustrate the variety.[3]

We will pass over detailed questions of authorship, place and date of origin, or schools of thought represented.[4] We begin with books which teach the final extinction of the wicked and move across the spectrum to those teaching everlasting conscious torment. In each case we begin with the books generally thought to be the oldest and work forward to the early

---

1. An excellent summary of intertestamental literature on this subject is Terence Forestell: 'Christian Revelation and the Resurrection of the Wicked,' *CBQ* 19, no. 2 (April 1957) 165–189. Yet a thorough reading of the sources suggests several oversimplifications even here. Only one who has tried to analyze and categorize pseudepigraphal thought can properly sympathize (and tremble a little) in making such a criticism. Also very helpful is George W. E. Nickelsburg Jr., *Resurrection, Immortality, and Eternal Life in Intertestamental Judaism.*

2. The cautious and conservative Reformed author, Harry Buis, is a good modern example. In *Eternal Punishment* Buis notes the extravagance of certain intertestamental material but implies that eternal torment was the common Jewish view of final punishment at the time of Jesus (pp. 16–22).

3. The field of Pseudepigrapha is vast and still increasing. Here we survey those works included in R. H. Charles, *APOT* vol. 2, from which all quotations are also taken.

4. For introductory material we have relied on Charlesworth, *Pseudepigrapha*, along with specific articles in *IDB*.

Christian decades which also saw the writing of the New Testament. The question to be answered will be whether these writings imply there was some standard 'Jewish view' on the subject, or whether we ought to examine the New Testament on its own terms and understand it on the basis of ordinary biblical exegesis.

The Wicked will Totally Pass Away

The Sibylline Oracles

This is a composite work of uncertain date. Books 3–5 are generally thought to come from a Jewish author of perhaps the second century B.C. Some other parts seem much later in origin and are salted with Christian interpolations.

The Jewish core says the wicked will be totally destroyed. The author warns 'Babylon' that 'from the air above there shall come to thee . . . eternal perdition. And then thou shalt be as thou wast before as though thou hadst not been born' (l. 307–310). Crete, too, faces 'a scourge and a dread eternal destruction,' when it will be 'wreathed in smoke and fire shall never leave thee but thou shalt burn' (ll. 504–507). God 'shall burn with fire the race of stubborn men' (l. 761).

This seems to take place in a mighty conflagration which will destroy the whole earth along with all its sinners. Book 4 tells how God will carry this out.

> And he shall burn the whole earth, and consume the whole race of men, and . . . there shall be sooty dust. But when at last everything shall have been reduced to dust and ashes and God shall quench the giant fire, even as he kindled it, then God himself shall fashion again the bones and ashes of men, and shall raise up mortals once more as they were before. And then the judgment shall come wherein God himself shall give sentence, judging the world once again. And to all who have sinned with deeds of impiety a heap of earth shall cover again, and murky Tartarus and the black recesses of hell. But all who are godly shall live again on earth when God gives breath and life and grace to them, the godly (4:76–90).

This conflagration reappears in book 5, where it involves a 'battle of the stars' and results in 'a new creation' (5:207–213). God will 'utterly destroy' his enemies 'so that dead bodies shall remain on the earth more numerous than the sand' (5:298–305).

Fragments of a Zadokite Work

Otto Betz dates this around 68–63 B.C., noting its kinship to certain Dead Sea Scrolls.[5] Here the wicked face God's 'power and might and great fury with flames of fire . . . so that there should be no remnant, nor

---

5. Charles includes this among the Pseudepigrapha, but Charlesworth does not. Betz wrote the article on this book in *IDB*.

any to escape of them' (2:4, 5). They await 'destruction' (9:12, 13), when they will be 'cut off from the midst of the camp' (9:49).

Dead Sea Scrolls

The discovery in 1947 of the library and headquarters of an ancient ascetic Jewish commune near Qumran, northwest of the Dead Sea, was of immense importance to our understanding of the development of Judaism.[6]

The Qumran sect was evidently organized by a 'Teacher of Righteousness' and functioned for about two centuries before the Roman invasion of Palestine in A.D. 66–73. These pious Jews repudiated the Hasmonean high priesthood in Jerusalem and denounced its liturgical calendar. They saw themselves as the righteous remnant, whom God would use to execute judgment at the rapidly-approaching End. Meanwhile, they would quietly perfect their own holiness and offer pure worship, meekly enduring whatever suffering the wicked establishment might cast their way.

These 'covenanters' read their Old Testament in the light of their own movement. Isaiah's 'Assyrian,' Habakkuk's 'Chaldean' and Daniel's 'king of the North' all referred to the Romans ('Kittim') according to the Teacher of Righteousness. God had used these pagans to punish Israel's wicked priests, but God would soon punish them as well. The Qumran community would become God's guerrillas in a final war against the 'sons of darkness'. The last battle would be won by the direct intervention of Michael, the archangel, ushering in the kingdom of God's saints and the end of the old world. The new covenant and the new age would be a reality.

Josephus' Testimony

Writers on final punishment have often cited Josephus' description of Essene belief concerning souls. In *Wars of the Jews* (2.8.11), Josephus claims that the Essenes held the common Platonic view of immortal souls trapped during life in mortal bodies but freed at death to their natural sphere. Souls of wicked men would finally be judged and enter everlasting torment, according to Josephus' account of Essene belief. He identified this doctrine with Greek philosophy, calling it a 'lure' not easily resisted by those who 'once tasted their wisdom'.

This evaluation must now be seriously questioned if the Qumran sectarians were indeed Essenes, as is commonly thought. The Dead Sea Scrolls 'speak plainly' of 'annihilation for the wicked'[7] (see below).

---

6. The Dead Sea Scrolls do not properly fit under the category Pseudepigrapha; we include them because of their obvious overlapping with the other literature and their conspicuous bearing on the subject at hand. This historical summary is paraphrased from F. F. Bruce, 'A Reappraisal of Jewish Apocalyptic Literature,' *Review and Expositor* 72, no. 3 (Summer 1975) pp. 307–310.

7. F. F. Bruce, 'Paul on Immortality,' *SJT* 24, no. 4 (Nov. 1971) pp. 459f. The quotation also appears in Bruce, *Paul* p. 303.

G. W. E. Nickelsburg (*Intertestamental* p. 169) concludes that the Essenes had 'a belief in, or akin to, immortality of the soul, but not resurrection'.

W. S. LaSor summarizes, 'There would be suffering and distress for Israel but destruction for the wicked.'[8]

Testimony of the Scrolls

God had sent the Teacher of Righteousness 'to make known to the last generations what He would do to the last generation, the congregation of traitors,' according to the Damascus Document (CD 1.11, 12). The document continues with a lengthy description of the end of sinners, comparing it to the fate of the antediluvians who perished in the Flood and of the unfaithful Israelites who fell in the wilderness. God's judgment of sinners will leave 'no remnant remaining of them nor survivor' (CD 2.6, 7). They would be 'as though they had not been' (CD 2.20).

The wicked will end in the terrible Pit of fire and darkness. The Scroll of the Rule (Manual of Discipline) describes its horror in a formal curse against the 'men of the lot of Belial'.

> Be thou cursed in all the works of thy guilty ungodliness!
> May God make of thee an object of dread by the hand of the Avengers of vengeance!
> May He hurl extermination after thee by the hand of all the Executioners of punishment!
> Cursed be thou, without mercy, according to the darkness of thy deeds!
> Be thou damned in the night of eternal fire! (1QS 2.4–8.)

Such will be the fate of all who follow the Spirit of Perversity instead of the Spirit of Truth.

> And as for the Visitation of all who walk in this (Spirit), it consists of an abundance of blows administered by all the Angels of destruction in the everlasting Pit by the furious wrath of the God of vengeance, of unending dread and shame without end, and of the disgrace of destruction by the fire of the regions of darkness. And all their time from age to age are in most sorrowful chagrin and bitterest misfortune, in calamities of darkness till they are destroyed with none of them surviving or escaping (1QS 4.11–14).

Some evildoers will be destroyed in the eschatological War between the Sons of Light and the Sons of Darkness. They are given no hope of resurrection but will experience 'final destruction for all the lot of Belial'. Wickedness will 'be crushed without a remnant and without any survivor for [all the son]s of darkness' (1QM 1.5–7). The soldiers of Qumran are to inscribe certain war trumpets with the legend: 'God overflows all the sons of darkness: He will not withdraw His Anger till He has destroyed them' (1QM 3.9). The victors will 'pass like a flaming torch in the straw, devouring the wicked and returning not until the destruction of the guilty' (1QM 11.9–11).

Qumran commentaries on biblical books make the same point. The explanation (*pesher*) of Psalm 37 promises that 'all who rebel against being

---

8. Art. 'Dead Sea Scrolls' in *ISBE* vol 1 p. 892. See also Andre Dupont–Sommer, ed., *The Essene Writings from Qumran*, from which all quotations here are taken.

converted from their iniquity will be cut off' (4Qp Ps 37.1.3, 4). 'They will be wiped out and on the earth not a [wi]cked man will be found' (4Qp Ps 1.6–8). The wicked princes who oppressed God's people 'will perish like smoke which van[ishes before the wi]nd' (4Qp Ps 2.8). The commentary on Habakkuk tells how God will destroy the Wicked Priest. 'He will declare him guilty and will judge him with fire of sulphur' (1Qp Hab 10.3–5).

Like the Psalter of the Old Testament, the Hymn Scroll of the Qumran Community celebrates the terrors which await all the sinful enemies. Judgment comes for some at the hands of the Sons of Light (the warriors of Qumran). Then

> The Sword of God shall hasten and all his sons of tr[ut]h shall rouse themselves to [destroy] ungodliness and all the sons of transgression shall be no more. . . .
> They shall trample (them) underfoot unto destruction leaving no remn[ant]. (1QH 6.29, 30, 32.)

The rest will taste God's special terrors at the end of the world, a time when the earth will rumble, the mountains will crumble and dissolve, and the heat of God's wrath will turn earth's very foundations into a hellish river of molten ruin.

> And the bonds of Death tightened leaving no escape,
> and the torrents of Belial overflowed all the high banks
> Like a fire consuming all their shores,
> destroying from their channels every tree green and dry
> and whipping with whirlwinds of flame
> until the vanishing of all that drinks there.
> It devours all the foundations of pitch
> and the bases of the continent;
> the foundations of the mountain are prey to fire
> and the roots of flint become torrents of tar . . .
> And the eternal foundations stagger and shake
> and the host of the Valiant of heaven
> brandishes its whip in the world;
> and it shall not end until utter destruction.
> which shall be final, without anything like it (1QH 3.28–31, 35, 36).

The Psalms of Solomon

According to the common but not unanimous opinion, the Psalms of Solomon come from pre-Christian Hasidic Jews, those pious 'covenanters' whose spiritual offspring include both the Pharisees and the ascetic Essenes of Qumran. Their date is probably the middle of the first century B.C.

Like the Old Testament book their name suggests, these psalms anticipate a time when the wicked will vanish from the earth and never again be found. God 'bringeth down the proud to eternal destruction in dishonour' (2:35). He will 'recompense the sinners for ever according to their deeds' (2:38), which later is explained to mean their extinction. The sinner

> falleth and riseth no more. The destruction of the sinner is for ever, and he shall not be remembered, when the righteous is visited. This is the portion of sinners for ever. But they that fear the Lord shall rise to life eternal, and their life shall be in the light of the Lord, and shall come to an end no more (3:11–16).

Another passage says the slanderous tongue will perish in flaming fire (12:5). Israel may hope for God's salvation for ever, but sinners will 'perish together at the presence of the Lord' (12:7). When 'the life of the righteous shall be for ever', sinners 'shall be taken away into destruction, and their memorial shall be found no more' (13:9, 10). Their 'inheritance ... is destruction and darkness, and their iniquities shall pursue them unto Sheol beneath' (15:11). They will 'perish for ever in the day of the Lord's judgment, when God visiteth the earth with his judgment' (15:12). A few lines later the author repeats: 'sinners shall perish for ever' (15:15).

Fourth Ezra (Fourth Esdras)

Numerous writings circulated under Ezra's name during the early Christian centuries. Charlesworth calls this one 'one of the most brilliant and original of all apocryphal compositions'. Scholars generally recognize an authentically Jewish core in chapters 3–14, which they believe were composed in either Hebrew or Aramaic during the final decades of the first century after Christ, probably in Palestine. Two Christian compositions written in Greek, sometimes called 5 Ezra (chs. 1, 2) and 6 Ezra (chs. 15, 16), are thought to have been added later.

Like many other works of the period, 4 Ezra has the wicked suffering immediately after their death and before the final judgment. Here that suffering consists primarily of remorse for the past and dread of the future, which are described under seven headings (7:78–87). Before the end of the world there will come a series of messianic woes. Sinners who survive these will be converted, and all living people will hold to the truth (6:25–28).

The Messiah will reign in joy over his people 400 years on the earth, then he and all his subjects will die. Primeval silence will shroud the earth for seven days. Then the new age will begin, and the old order will be gone for ever (7:26–31). The earth will give up all its dead, and the Most High will set up his throne of judgment.

> Then shall the pit of torment appear, and over against it the place of refreshment; the furnace of Gehenna shall be manifest, and over against it the Paradise of delight (7:32, 33, 36).

When Ezra expresses sorrow that so few are finally saved, God compares them to his jewels. He rejoices over the few, he says, and continues:

> 'I will not grieve over the multitude of them that perish: for they it is who now are made like vapour, counted as smoke, are comparable unto the flame: They are fired, burn hotly, are extinguished!' (7:61.)

The Fate of the Wicked is Stated Ambiguously

The Assumption of Moses

The date of this work is uncertain. Guesses range from the second century B.C. to the first century A.D. One passage in particular speaks of the fate of the wicked, and it is ambiguous.

> For the Most High will arise, the Eternal God alone,
> And he will appear to punish the Gentiles . . .
> And thou shalt look from on high and shalt see thy enemies in Ge(henna)
> And thou shalt recognize them and rejoice,
> And thou shalt give thanks and confess thy Creator (10:7, 10).

In a footnote to the phrase 'in Ge(henna),' Charles acknowledges that his text actually has *terram* for the Greek *gē* ('earth'). Rather than having the saved see their enemies 'on earth,' Charles makes *gē* an abbreviation for ge(henna), thus amending the text to fit a view with better documentary support elsewhere in the literature. But 'Gehenna' is still ambiguous since it may either consume the sinner entirely or keep him alive in torment.

Testaments of the Twelve Patriarchs

Fragments of the Testaments have been discovered among the Dead Sea Scrolls and in the synagogue geniza (storeroom for discarded scrolls) at Cairo, Egypt. Charlesworth says the material existed in recognizable form about 100 B.C. and was based on more ancient works. The present manuscripts probably include several later Christian additions and changes.

The language of the Testaments is also capable of more than one interpretation. Reuben warns women who use facial adornment that 'every woman who useth these wiles hath been reserved for eternal punishment' (Test. Reuben 5:5). Levi sees 'fire, snow and ice made ready for the day of judgment' (Test. Levi 3:2). Those who bless God will be blessed, but everyone who curses him 'shall perish' (Test. Levi 5:6).

Unless men avoid lying and anger, they will 'perish' (Test. Dan 2:1) when Messiah comes to 'execute an everlasting vengeance' on Israel's enemies (Test. Dan 5:10). Besides an intermediate state of suffering after death (Test. Asher 6:5), readers are warned to avoid a punishment such as fell on 'Sodom, which sinned . . . and perished for ever' (Test. Asher 7:1). The context applies this statement to the Dispersion – the people are nowhere to be found in their homeland, but they are still alive and suffering somewhere else!

Benjamin closes the book with language borrowed from Daniel. 'Then shall we also rise,' he says, 'each one over our tribe, worshipping the King of heaven . . . . Then also all men shall rise, some unto glory and some unto shame' (Test. Benjamin 10:7, 8).

'Everlasting punishment and vengeance' might imply that the wicked perish for ever. It could also describe eternal conscious torment. The shame to which some will rise could possibly mean everlasting pain, although neither Daniel (12:2) nor Isaiah (66:24) pictures that in the canonical precedents to this language. This book will probably continue to be a bone of contention, and both sides in the debate will likely claim it for support.

The Life of Adam and Eve

This expanded version of Genesis 1–4 probably came in a Semitic tongue from a Jewish writer of the first century B.C. Its reference to the final doom of the wicked is also unclear.

> God will stir up for himself a faithful people, whom he shall save for eternity, and the impious shall be punished by God their king, the men who refused to love his law .... Therefore the Lord shall repel from himself the wicked, and the just shall shine like the sun, in the sight of God (29:7ff.).

Inconsistent Teaching about the Wicked's End

The Book of Jubilees

This important book from the second century B.C. retells the Bible story from creation through the Exodus in the Jewish commentary form known as midrash. It claims to be a history given by God to Moses on Mount Sinai. Portions of it appear among the Dead Sea Scrolls; it probably represents the same stream of Judaism which produced Essenism. The original language was likely Hebrew, although it is extant in full only in Ethiopic manuscripts.

Jubilees repeatedly stresses that the wicked will be utterly destroyed. One single passage apart, this is its exclusive word concerning the ungodly, and even the possible exception is capable of that interpretation. Abraham warns Isaac against following the way of sinners lest he 'sin a sin unto death before the Most High God.' God would then 'hide his face from thee,' Isaac is told, 'and give thee back into the hands of the transgression, and root thee out of the land, and thy seed likewise from under heaven, and thy name and thy seed shall perish from the whole earth' (21:22).

Later Abraham describes the idolaters' end.

> There shall be no hope for them in the land of the living;
> And there shall be no remembrance of them on the earth;
> For they shall descend into Sheol,
> And into the place of condemnation shall they go,
> As the children of Sodom were taken away from the earth
> So will all those who worship idols be taken away (22:22).

When Esau wants a fatherly blessing, Isaac tells him instead that he will 'sin a complete sin unto death, and thy seed shall be rooted out from under heaven' (26:34). Isaac's blessing of Levi includes the promise that those who hate him will 'be rooted out and perish' (31:16f.). Anyone who afflicts and curses Judah 'shall be rooted out and destroyed from the earth and be accursed' (31:20).

For the abominable sin of incest 'there is no atonement for ever to atone for the man.' He must be 'put to death and slain, and stoned with stones, and rooted out from the midst of the people of our God. For to no man who does so in Israel is it permitted to remain alive a single day on the earth, for he is abominable and unclean' (33:13f.). This unforgivable sin never has atonement precisely because the man is speedily executed before the sun goes down!

While these passages all speak of total destruction, it is not clear if the penalty follows a final judgment or is to be carried out wholly in time and history. A few other texts seem to refer clearly to an eschatological judgment.

God blesses Jacob with the words: 'I will give to thy seed all the earth which is under heaven, and they shall judge all the nations according to their desires, and after that they shall get possession of the whole earth and inherit it for ever' (32:19). This picture could be borrowed from numerous Old Testament passages which portray a similar scene. The wicked will be 'judged' (here at the hand of Israel) – never to be mentioned again – and the righteous inherit the earth.

One passage specifically describes an earthly Messianic kingdom, after which comes judgment. The spirits of the righteous rise in everlasting joy, but their bodies rest in the earth. This text says the wicked are judged, but their final fate is not specified.

> And all their days [the righteous] shall complete and live in peace and in joy, and there shall be no Satan [or 'satan' – accuser] nor any evil destroyer; for all their days shall be days of blessing and healing . . . . And the righteous shall see and be thankful, and rejoice with joy for ever and ever, and shall see all their judgments and all their curses on their enemies (23:29f.)

Because the Philistines mistreated Isaac, another passage curses them in view of a final day of judgment.

> And no remnant shall be left to them, nor one that shall be saved on the day of the wrath of judgment; for destruction and rooting out and expulsion from the earth is the whole seed of the Philistines (reserved), and there shall no longer be left for these Caphthorim a name or a seed on the earth . . . . And neither name nor seed shall be left to him on all the earth; for into eternal malediction shall he depart. And thus it is written and engraven concerning him on the heavenly tablets, to do unto him on the day of judgment, so that he may be rooted out of the earth (24:30, 32, 33).

'Eternal malediction' is their fate on 'the day of the wrath of judgment'. The passage specifically describes that destiny as expulsion and being rooted out of the earth, a destruction which leaves 'neither name nor seed' for ever.

One passage in Jubilees might be thought to imply conscious everlasting torment, although its context does not seem to require that meaning. Isaac warns Jacob and Esau of the punishment that will befall either of them who attacks his brother after Isaac dies. The penalty will begin in the present life. 'Everyone that devises evil against his brother shall fall into his hand, and shall be rooted out of the land of the living, and his seed shall be destroyed from under the heaven.' But that is not all, as the warning continues:

> But on the day of turbulence and execration and indignation and anger, with flaming devouring fire as he burnt Sodom, so likewise will he burn his land and his city and all that is his, and he shall be blotted out of the book of the discipline of the children of men, and not be recorded in the book of life, but in that which is appointed to destruction, and he shall depart into eternal execration: so that their condemnation may be always renewed in hate and in execration and in wrath and in torment and in indignation and in plagues and in disease for ever (36:9ff.).

These last words sound much like the unending conscious torment of the traditional hell, clearly seen already in Judith. But two considerations weigh against that interpretation here. First, if this is the author's meaning, it is the only place he reveals it in the entire book. Furthermore, it would seem to contradict what he consistently affirms whenever he otherwise mentions the subject. Second, the context itself suggests his more usual view of the wicked's destruction. The day of 'turbulence and indignation and anger' is also the 'day of execration'. He recalls the destruction of Sodom: 'with flaming fire as he burnt Sodom, so likewise will he burn his land'. The sinner is not found in 'the book of life' (i.e. listed among the living) but is 'appointed to destruction'. He departs into 'eternal execration' (i.e. he is cut off for ever). His condemnation is 'always renewed'; not being exhausted in this life, it extends into the Age to Come.

But does not the word 'torment' here necessarily imply everlasting conscious pain? The author of Jubilees sheds light on that question in describing how Simeon and Levi avenged the rape of their sister Dinah by the Shechemites.

> And Simeon and Levi came unexpectedly to Shechem and executed judgment on all the men of Shechem, and slew all the men . . . and left not a single one remaining in it: they slew all in torments because they had dishonored their sister Dinah . . . . And the Lord delivered them into the hands of the sons of Jacob that they might exterminate them with the sword and execute judgment upon them . . . . See how the Shechemites fared and their sons: how they were delivered into the hands of two sons of Jacob, and they slew them under tortures (30:4ff., 17).

The fate of the men of Shechem is clear. Simeon and Levi 'slew' them, 'executed judgment' on them, 'exterminated them with the sword'. What is interesting is that the author of Jubilees describes this by saying 'they slew all in torments' and later that 'they slew them under tortures'. The punishment involved torments and tortures, but its end was extermination. Might not the same scene be in view in the ambiguous passage we have just seen? If so, Jubilees gives a single, consistent view of the end of the wicked – final extermination. If this interpretation is not permissible, Jubilees offers an inconsistent picture. Several times it expects sinners finally to be exterminated, though one passage threatens everlasting conscious torment.

First (Ethiopic) Enoch

Often called Ethiopic Enoch to distinguish it from 2 (Slavonic) Enoch and 3 (Hebrew) Enoch, this book is extant in its entirety only in Ethiopic, preserved because of its canonical status in the Ethiopic Church. That text is based on a Greek version; the bulk of the work probably comes from the second century B.C.[9]

Enoch is divided into five major parts, four of which are quoted among the Dead Sea Scrolls. This book was widely read: it appears in allusion or quotation in the Book of Jubilees, the Testaments of the Twelve Patriarchs, the Assumption of Moses, 2 Baruch and 4 Ezra among the Pseudepigrapha. It contains the words which Jude attributes to 'Enoch,' as well as many phrases scattered throughout the rest of the New Testament.

Of its five sections, the one most relevant to New Testament doctrine is the 'Similitudes,' which speak of 'the [rather than 'a'] Son of Man'. Interestingly, this is the only section not yet found among the scrolls at Qumran, which might indicate a later date. According to Charles, the doctrine of a resurrection 'was made a commonplace of Jewish theology' by this book.[10]

Although it does not strictly concern our study of final punishment, we note in passing Enoch's detailed concern with detention and torment, even before the great judgment, for both wicked angels (19:1f.; 21:1–10) and certain sinful men (22:11ff.; 103:5–8). At times 1 Enoch has sinners finally exterminated; elsewhere they endure conscious pain for ever.

Sinners exterminated

In some passages sinners are 'driven from the face of the earth' (38:1) and 'perish' (38:5), their life 'at an end' (38:6). It had been better for such people never to have been born (38:2). Apostates will not be found in heaven or on earth after 'the day of suffering and tribulation' (45:1f.). Here Enoch seems to teach annihilation:

> I will transform the heaven and make it an eternal blessing and light:
> And I will cause mine elect ones to dwell upon it:
> But the sinners and evil-doers shall not set foot thereon. . . .
> But for the sinners there is judgment impending with me,
> So that I shall destroy them from the face of the earth (45:4ff.).

Enoch warns sinners in the next chapter that 'darkness shall be their dwelling, and worms shall be their bed, and they shall have no hope for rising from their beds' (46:4). When God judges, 'the unrepentant shall perish before him' (50:4). Sinners 'shall be destroyed before the face of

---

9. Bruce, 'Jewish Apocalyptic Literature' pp. 310ff.
10. Charles, *APOT* 2:185.

the Lord of Spirits, and they shall be banished from off the face of his earth, and they shall perish for ever and ever' (53:2).

Enoch saw 'the angels of punishment' preparing 'instruments of Satan' by which God's enemies would 'be destroyed' (53:3ff.). Elsewhere the angels 'execute vengeance' on the oppressors. The enemies 'shall be a spectacle for the righteous and for his elect' when God's 'sword is drunk with their blood'. The righteous 'shall never thenceforward see the face of the sinners and unrighteous' (62:11ff.). Sinners 'shall die with the sinners, and the apostate go down with the apostate' (81:7f.). (Charles surmises in a footnote that they 'go down' to Gehenna.)

Enoch sees a parable about wicked rulers and apostate Israelites. In it 70 shepherds and their blind sheep are

> judged and found guilty and cast into this fiery abyss, and they burned . . . .
> And I saw those sheep burning and their bones burning (90:25ff.).

Charles has rearranged the text which says that 'sin shall perish in darkness for ever, and shall no more be seen from that day for evermore' (92:5), which he thinks speaks of the flood in the days of Noah.

A clearer passage warns:

> Know ye that ye are prepared for the day of destruction: wherefore do not hope to live, ye sinners, but ye shall depart and die; for ye know of no ransom; for ye are prepared for the day of the great judgment, for the day of tribulation and great shame for your spirits (98:10).

A few verses later we read that sinners 'shall have no peace but die a sudden death' (98:16).

God uses fire to destroy the wicked. The heathen are 'cast into the judgment of fire, and shall perish in wrath and in grievous judgment for ever' (92:9). Sinners 'perish in the day of unrighteousness' (97:1), 'in shame and in slaughter and in great destitution' when their spirits are 'cast into the furnace of fire' (98:3).

'Ye shall perish, and no happy life shall be yours,' Enoch warns (99:1). This will come to pass when the wicked are 'trodden under foot upon the earth' (99:2) or are 'slain in Sheol' (99:11). They will burn in 'blazing flames burning worse than fire' (100:9) and will 'be utterly consumed' (99:12). One passage describes this fiery destruction in graphic and explicit terms.

> 'I will give them over into the hands of Mine elect:
> As straw in the fire so shall they burn before the face of the holy:
> As lead in the water shall they sink before the face of the righteous,
> And no trace of them shall any more be found.
> And on the day of their affliction there shall be rest on the earth,
> And before them they shall fall and not rise again' (48:8f.).

Sinners suffer conscious pain for ever

At other times 1 Enoch seems to expect the wicked to suffer for ever in conscious pain. Enoch sees an 'accursed valley' (Gehenna) outside Jerusalem which is described as the place of judgment for sinners. 'In the last days there shall be upon them the spectacle of righteous judgment in the presence of the righteous for ever' (27:1ff.). This might mean conscious pain that lasts for ever, though it could also describe a judgment of everlasting destruction in the sense of irreversible extinction.

In another place Noah sees a river of fiery molten metal with the smell of sulphur, flowing together with a valley of streams of fire. There fallen angels await judgment. There also wicked kings are punished after death as 'a testimony,' because 'those waters will change and become a fire which burns for ever' (67:4–13). Whether this fire will then consume sinners or only torment them we are not here told.

Finally, in what Charles calls an 'independent addition' to the book, it is said that sinners 'shall cry and make lamentation in a place that is a chaotic wilderness, and in the fire shall they burn; for there is no earth there.' An angel describes the scene as the place where 'are cast the spirits of sinners and blasphemers, and of those who work wickedness' (108:3–6). The passage also has 'their names . . . blotted out of the book of life,' 'their seed destroyed for ever,' and 'their spirits . . . slain,' so its meaning is not totally clear.

Second (Syriac) Baruch

Except for a Greek fragment, this whole book is extant only in one Syriac manuscript. By general consent it is said to have been composed during the final decades of the first century after Christ, but its original language is still debated. Some argue that this work teaches conscious eternal torment. There will be a judgment according to sins and righteous deeds (24:1–4) after the Messiah has an advent (back to heaven, Charles thinks) in glory (30:1).

> Then all who have fallen asleep in hope of him shall rise again . . . But the souls of the wicked, when they behold all these things, shall then waste away the more. For they shall know that their torment has come and their perdition has arrived. (30:2–5).

There is no doubt in 2 Baruch that the wicked will 'depart to torment' (44:12; 59:2; 64:7–10; 83:8) or that 'the dwelling of . . . many shall be in the fire' (44:15). The earth will give up the sinners just as it received them, that they might 'suffer torment.' They will see the righteous transformed into the splendour of angels; then they will 'depart to be tormented' (51:5f.). Whether the torment ends in extinction or continues in conscious pain the author does not here say.

Elsewhere, however, Baruch says clearly that 'a fire shall consume their thoughts' (48:39). Sinners go 'to corruption,' and there is no numbering of 'those whom the fire devours' (48:43). There will be no turning back then, no change of ways or place for prayer when the wicked come to judgment (85:12). All that remains is 'the sentence of corruption, the way of fire, and the path which bringeth to Gehenna' (85:13). God will then 'destroy those who are polluted with sins' (85:15).

In one passage Baruch multiplies similes like those found in the Old Testament psalms. God's enemies will 'be like a vapour' (82:3), 'be made like unto a drop' (v.4), 'be accounted as spittle' (v.5). 'As smoke shall they pass away' (v.6), 'as grass that withers shall they fade away' (v.7), 'as a wave that passes shall they be broken' (v.8). They 'shall pass away as a passing cloud' (v.9).

The Wicked will Suffer Eternal Conscious Pain

Second (Slavonic) Enoch

Most scholars think this 'Book of the Secrets of Enoch' was written in Greek, shortly before the destruction of the temple in A.D. 70, in either Palestine or Egypt. Like 1 (Ethiopic) Enoch, this Enoch sees angels (7:1f.) and men (41:1) waiting in torment before the judgment. The wicked will 'perish,' and they must anticipate 'the limitless judgment' (40:12).

Enoch sees a place where

> murky fire constantly flameth aloft, and a fiery river (comes) forth, and that whole place is everywhere fire, and everywhere frost and ice, thirst and shivering, while the bonds are very cruel, and the angels fearful and merciless, bearing angry weapons, merciless torture.

This, he is told, is prepared for sinners 'for eternal inheritance' (10:1–6). Every false speech (speaker?) 'will be cut with the blade of the sword of death, and thrown into the fire, and shall burn for all time' (63:4). One wonders even here if 'for all time' might describe the irremediable effect of the burning rather than conscious pain, especially since those thrown into the fire have already been 'cut with the blade of the sword of death.' This example illustrates the difficulty modern interpreters face when grappling with particular terms used by pseudepigraphical advocates of both eternal extinction and everlasting torment. The same problem arises in later literature on the subject from the New Testament onward. Unless an author is explicit in his view, his language will likely be disputed, and readers of opposing convictions will jointly claim him for support.

Fourth Maccabees

Eusebius and Jerome attributed this book to Josephus, but modern scholars regard it as the work of a Jew of Stoic leanings who had mastered both Greek thought and language. The hub of the book tells the story of martyrdom of the faithful mother and her seven sons (see 2 Macc. 7:1–42). Our author uses their case to illustrate victory through 'the supreme power of reason'.

The seven sons warn their wicked torturer of 'torment by fire for ever' (9:9), 'torments without end' (10:12), and an 'eternal doom' (10:15). This will be 'a more rapid and an eternal fire and torments which shall not leave hold on thee to all eternity' (12:12). Whoever transgresses God's ordinances must also know that 'a great struggle and peril of the soul awaits in eternal torment' (13:15).

Summary

The Pseudepigrapha offer a variety of expectations regarding the final end of sinners. It is clear that there is no such thing as 'the Jewish view' on the matter. Neither is it proper to say that everlasting conscious torment is the primary or predominant view. This expectation appears quite clearly in a handful of passages. It is a possible interpretation in several other cases. For present purposes we may allow them all.

It is also clear that this literature thoroughly documents the older view of the sinner's total extinction as one Jewish opinion current during the period 200 B.C.–A.D. 100. This doom is frequently accomplished by fire and is usually preceded by a period of conscious anguish and suffering. In expecting a time when sinners will perish from the face of the earth and never again be found these writers repeat the frequent testimony of the Old Testament. With the exception of one clear passage in Judith and one ambiguous text in Sirach, this is also the view in the Apocrypha.

Because of this unquestionable range of opinion, which can be so thoroughly documented, we cannot presume a single attitude among Jews of the time of Christ. We may not read Jesus' words or those of the New Testament writers with any presuppositions based on a supposed uniform intertestamental opinion. We must deny categorically the common assumption that Jesus' hearers all held to everlasting torment. We must not assume that Jesus endorsed such a view simply because he nowhere explicitly denied it. We are free to examine the teaching of the New Testament at face value and to determine the meaning of its terms according to the ordinary methods of proper biblical exegesis. The literary and linguistic background for this exegesis includes the Apocrypha and Pseudepigrapha, but towering above these we see the inspired revelation contained in the Scriptures of the Old Testament.

10

Final Punishment in the Teaching of Jesus

The ultimate support for the doctrine of the final punishment of unrepentant sinners is the teaching of Jesus Christ.[1] Yet Jesus' teaching has been received in various ways: 'It has been taken with absolute literalness; it has been spiritualized; it has been regarded as subject to interpolation, greater or less; or its originality is admitted, but its expected fulfilment is regarded as a mistake and an illusion.'[2] Some deny that Jesus ever taught what Matthew reports, dismissing these statements as 'bitter anti-Jewish sentiments' rising out of 'a mutual escalation of hatred caused by a poaching of converts'.[3]

Yet even the most radical of critics can scarcely avoid the conclusion that Jesus said a great deal about the terrible fate awaiting those who reject God's mercy. He spoke of exclusion from the kingdom, the severity of wrongdoing, the destruction of unrepentant sinners – and he taught that opportunity to repent was cut off at death. 'It is impossible to eliminate sayings of Jesus which give terrible warning as to the possibility of loss and exclusion.'[4]

Wenham points out the implications:

> We cannot escape, for we know who said these things, we know his tenderness, we know the authority of his words and we know that this is the language (be it more or less symbolic) which he regarded as best fitted to describe the price of impenitence. It is Love who speaks like this, it is God himself.[5]

One might approach Jesus' teaching from several directions. In this study we will page through the Gospels simply discussing and summarizing the data. We begin with Matthew, not so much because it is first in canonical order, but because it records more that Jesus said on this subject than the other evangelists. This should not surprise us when we remember that Matthew is writing particularly for a Jewish audience who

---

1. It is seemly, therefore, that the present chapter should be our most lengthy one.
2. J. A. MacCulloch, 'Eschatology,' *ERE* 5:381–382. On modern approaches to Jesus' eschatological message in general, see Howard C. Kee, 'The Development of Eschatology in the New Testament,' *JBR* 20, no. 3 (July 1952) pp. 187–193.
3. D. E. H. Whiteley, 'Liberal Christianity in the New Testament,' *Modern Churchman* 13, no. 1 (Oct. 1969) p. 26.
4. A. M. Ramsey, quoted by Alan M. Fairhurst, 'The Problem Posed by the Severe Sayings Attributed to Jesus in the Synoptic Gospels,' *SJT* 23 (1970) p. 79.
5. Wenham, *Goodness* pp. 20f.

would be especially interested in this theme of divine judgment.[6] Where Mark, Luke or John supply additional detail, we will include this. Finally, we will examine the few relevant gospel passages not found in Matthew, ending our inquiry with a summary and some conclusions.

Matthew 3:10, 12

The last verses of the Old Testament promise that Elijah will come to prepare Israel for the day of the Lord. At the outset of the gospel story we meet John the Baptizer, who is Malachi's 'Elijah,' and also Isaiah's 'voice in the wilderness'. Nazirite by commission and priest's son by birth, he is also a prophet – and much more! This prophet is Messiah's harbinger, a *martys* in the sense of 'witness,' but authenticating his message by a martyr death. His diet and dress evoke the ancient past, underscoring the impression that after four centuries of silence Israel's sovereign God was speaking once again.

Like Habakkuk before him, John calls on men to flee. He warns of imminent fiery judgment. When the Pharisees come to check him out, John compares them to desert reptiles, escaping a wilderness fire. He speaks of coming wrath (Matt. 3:7; Luke 3:7), a theme which continues through the New Testament.[7] This judgment can be avoided only by repentance followed by faith in the Lamb of God.

'The axe is already at the root of the trees,' he announces, 'and every tree that does not produce good fruit will be cut down and thrown into the fire' (Matt. 3:10). The figure would be instantly recognized; Jesus himself would choose it for his Parable of the Fig Tree (Luke 13:6–9). Trees with bad fruit are burned (Matt. 7:19), as are unfruitful vines (John 15:6) and useless weeds (Matt. 13:40). In Jesus' teaching, as in John's, these figures from the land represent sinners in the end-time. They stand for false prophets, hypocritical hearers, sunshine soldiers or fruitless disciples. In each case they are burned up.

The Coming One will 'baptize you with the Holy Spirit and with fire,' John says (Matt. 3:11). Luke records the same words, but Mark promises the Holy Spirit and stops, perhaps because his Christian readers in Rome would know well already a 'fire' of persecution; they needed encouragement now, not warning (Mark 1:7f.). This future baptism of fire is almost certainly to be understood alongside John's other references to fire; it is the fire of judgment, the judgment that would break first over the head of Jesus himself, qualifying him to administer it in turn to his enemies. Daniel had spoken of a river of fire flowing from the flaming throne of the Ancient of Days (Dan. 7:9f.). As the end-time Son of Man, Jesus would be immersed in that river even as John baptized him in the waters of Jordan. These two baptisms – in water and in fire – would form a great

---

6. Matthew's Jewish audience expected a final day of reckoning at the end of history. In the Old Testament, life on the earth has purpose and destiny in fellowship with God; contrary to the cyclical view of history held by many Greeks, for instance, although it becomes that if God is removed from the picture, as Ecclesiastes makes clear. (See Chapter 6 above.)

7. Rom. 2:5,8; 5:9; Eph. 5:6; Col. 3:6; 1 Thess. 1:10; 5:9; Rev. 6:16f.; 11:18; 19:15. On John the Baptist and his warnings see C. Scobie, *John the Baptist* p. 68.

parenthesis around the Saviour's earthly ministry; both must be accomplished before Jesus could baptize in the Holy Spirit.[8]

The Son of Man would suffer, the Lamb would die in silence, but John predicts that this same one would come again as Judge. 'His winnowing fork is in his hand, and he will clear his threshing floor, gathering the wheat into his barn and burning up the chaff with unquenchable fire' (Matt. 3:12). As in the Old Testament, 'unquenchable fire' represents a fire of judgment which cannot be stopped. On and on it comes, driven by the wind of God's righteous fury – burning irresistibly, until nothing is left but silence and smoke.[9] The Old Testament Scriptures give ample background for understanding this judgment-fire; like them, John sees it as 'burning up' the chaff.

Matthew 5:20

> 'I tell you that unless your righteousness surpasses that of the Pharisees and the teachers of the law, you will certainly not enter the kingdom of heaven.'

This verse may well be the key that unlocks the Sermon on the Mount. The Pharisees and scribes were concerned to achieve right standing before God's court (Rom. 9:31–10:5). Jesus refutes their rationalizing on six counts in chapter 5 (vv. 21,27,31,33,38,43).

In chapter 6 Jesus deflates all pseudo-piety toward men (v. 3), God (v. 5) or even self (v. 16). Only with the righteousness God provides can anyone enter his kingdom (Matt. 6:33). Jesus offers this righteousness freely to those who come confessing need and making no claims of their own (Matt. 5:3–12; Isa. 64:6/61:10). Exclusion from the kingdom will be the fate of those who lack true righteousness. We will meet this description again.

Matthew 5:22

One point at which Jesus countered the scribes' rationalizing was God's prohibition of murder. Jesus did not follow the traditional formula of scribal teaching – 'Rabbi X said that Rabbi Y said that Rabbi Z said thus' – but taught with divine authority (Matt. 7:29). In God's eyes, he said, anger in any degree is dangerous and culpable.

> Anyone who is angry with his brother will be subject to judgment ... Anyone who says to his brother, 'Raca,' is answerable to the Sanhedrin. But anyone who says, 'You fool!' will be in danger of the fire of hell.

These three figures of punishment – judgment, Sanhedrin and fire of hell

---

8. On the relation of Jesus' baptism to his larger ministry in the light of the entire Bible, see E.F. Harrison, *Short Life of Christ* pp. 66–78.

9. See Isa. 1:31; 34:10f.; Jer. 4:4; 7:20; 17:27; 21:12; Ezek. 20:47f.; Amos 5:6; contrast Ps. 118:12; Heb. 11:34. Dixon defines 'unquenchable' fire according to Webster (*Other Side* pp. 80, 146). Blanchard (*Hell* pp. 219f.) seems unaware of its common biblical usage to denote the irresistibility of God's judgment that consumes (Ezek. 20:47f.), reduces to nothing (Amos 5:5f.), burns up what is put into it (Matt. 3:12) and destroys both body and soul (Matt. 10:28).

– are not ascending but rather parallel phrases, seen in the similarity of the cause of the judgment. There is little difference between being angry with one's brother, insulting him, and calling him a fool.[10] There is apparently no basis for the common explanation that Jesus here describes a succession of greater Jewish crimes with penalties correspondingly severe.[11]

This is the Saviour's first specific reference to Gehenna, by now a technical term in Jewish sources for the fiery pit where the godless will meet their final doom. 'Entrance into hell indicates spiritual ruin in the starkest terms,' writes William L. Lane.[12] The word would mean nothing to Gentiles – it appears only once in the New Testament outside the Gospels, and that is in the very 'Jewish' epistle of James. It is not found in pagan Greek literature or even the Septuagint[13] or Josephus.[14] But to Jesus' hearers Gehenna had a long and sombre history.

The Greek word *gehenna* is a transliteration of the Hebrew 'Valley of (the sons of) Hinnom'. Several sites have been identified, but most authorities now locate it on the west and south of Jerusalem. A 'deep and yawning gorge' that never contains water, the valley descends over 600 feet from its original source. At the lower end are numerous rock tombs, indicating its possible use as a potter's field.[15]

The valley bore this name at least as early as the writing of Joshua (Josh. 15:8; 18:16), though nothing is known of its origin. It was the site of child sacrifices to Moloch in the days of Ahaz and Manasseh (apparently in 2 Kings 16:3; 21:6). This earned it the name 'Topheth,' a place to be spat on or abhorred.[16] This 'Topheth' may have become a gigantic pyre for burning Assyrian corpses in the days of Hezekiah (Isa. 30:31ff.; 37:36). Jeremiah predicted that it would be filled to overflowing with Israelite corpses when God judged the nation for its sins (Jer. 7:31ff.; 19:2–13). Josephus indicates that the same valley was heaped with dead bodies of the Jews following the Roman siege of Jerusalem about A.D. 69–70.[17] In what is probably the classic Old Testament passage behind New Testament teaching on hell, Isaiah pictures a similar scene following the Lord's slaughter of sinners at the end of the world (Isa. 66:15f., 24). Josiah desecrated the repugnant valley as part of his godly reform (2 Kings 23:10). Long before the time of Jesus, the Valley of Hinnom had connotations of whatever is 'condemned, useless, corrupt and forever discarded'.[18]

---

10. Baird, *Justice* p. 226.
11. W. D. Davies, *The Setting of the Sermon on the Mount* pp. 235–239.
12. *Mark* NICNT p. 349.
13. H. Bietenhard, 'Gehenna' *NIDNTT* 2:208.
14. Joachim Jeremias, 'Gehenna' *TDNT* 1:658.
15. George L. Robinson, 'Gehenna' *DCG* 1:635f. According to *JE* ('Gehinnom,', vol. 5, col. 583) the valley's modern name is Wadi al-Rababah.
16. 'Hell,' *The Protestant Dictionary* p. 287. See also Berkhof 2:344. Moloch may be Melech, the 'King-god,' vocalized with the vowels of *bosheth* ('shame'), perhaps the Baal (a Semitic word for 'Lord') of Tyre. So says Pilcher, *Hereafter* p. 83.
17. According to Pétavel, *Problem* p. 193. He refers to Josephus *Wars*, vi. 8, #5; v. 12, #7.
18. Calvin D. Linton, 'The Sorrows of Hell,' *CT* 16 (19 Nov. 1971) p. 12.

Between the Testaments a tendency arose in Jewish literature to relate visions of last things to names and persons from the Old Testament. Thus Armageddon, Jerusalem and the Garden of Eden all became stylized figures of things to come. The Valley of Hinnom became *gehenna*.[19] The thought of Gehenna as a place of eschatological punishment appears in intertestamental literature shortly before 100 B.C., though the actual place is unnamed.[20] It is 'this accursed valley' (1 En. 27:2f.), the 'station of vengeance' and 'future torment' (2 Bar. 59:10f.), the 'pit of destruction' (Pirke Aboth 5:19), the 'furnace of Gehenna' and 'pit of torment' (4 Esd. 7:36).

The imagery becomes almost commonplace in Jewish literature of this period, but there is contradictory testimony as to exactly what happens in Gehenna. We have already mentioned a few passages in the Pseudepigrapha which seemingly anticipate everlasting torment, as well as one such verse in the Apocrypha. Many other passages within the intertestamental literature also picture the wicked being punished by fire, but this is the consuming, unquenchable fire of the Old Testament which utterly destroys, leaving only smoke as its witness. Certainly to those who first heard the Lord, Gehenna would convey a sense of horror and disgust. Beyond that, however, one must speak with extreme caution.

It is commonly said that Gehenna served as Jerusalem's garbage dump, 'a necessary hygienic incinerator outside the walls,'[21] though some have asked for more evidence.[22] Here is one attempt to describe the scene:

> Here the fires burned day and night, destroying the garbage and purifying the atmosphere from the smell of rotten fish or decaying vegetation. In time of war the carcasses of vanquished enemies might mingle with the refuse, thus furnishing patriotic writers with a clue as to the destiny of their own persecutors. They were destined to be destroyed in the fires that were never quenched.[23]

If this was the case, Gehenna once more was a place of undying worm and irresistible fire, an abhorrent place of crawling maggots and smouldering heat.

In the rabbinic lore of later Judaism, Gehenna was greatly embellished. Originally a place of punishment for Israel only, its scope broadened to include all sinners. From about the days of the apostle Paul, Gehenna became the rabbis' general term for the intermediate state. Still later it became a purgatory.[24]

Some of these developments show traces of foreign influence, perhaps from the Zoroastrian eschatology of Iran. There, fire is the means of

---

19. T. H. Gaster, 'Gehenna' *IDB* 2:362.
20. Strack & Billerbeck, 2:1029.
21. T. G. Dunning, 'Heaven and Hell' p. 353.
22. A. Bisset says the statement from Kimchi comes too late (A.D. 1200) to be accepted without further evidence (A. Bisset, 'Eternal Fire', *DCG* 1:536). Shedd quotes Robinson that there is no evidence for a Gehenna garbage dump in Christ's day (*Punishment* 43).
23. J. Arthur Hoyles, 'The Punishment of the Wicked after Death,' *London Quarterly and Holborn Review*, April 1957, p. 118.
24. Strack & Billerbeck, 2:1032–1033; F. F. Bruce, 'Paul on Immortality,' *SJT* 24, no. 4 (Nov. 1971) p. 459. See also Bruce, *Paul* p. 302.

testing at the last judgment. The mountains, which are made of metal, melt and flow over the earth like a river. As people pass into this molten metal, they are either purified or destroyed. In the end, everything, including hell itself, will be purified by fire.[25]

The Greek philosopher, Heraclitus of Ephesus, also taught that each world era ends with a great conflagration, returning everything to the primal fire, from it producing a new world. The Stoics later included some of these ideas in their concept of the end of the world by fire (*ekpyrōsis*).[26]

Later rabbinic tradition placed Gehenna in an enormous underground cavern beneath the earth with the solid ground resting over it like the lid of a kettle over boiling water. Its entrance was narrow, somewhere in the neighbourhood of Jerusalem. There Abraham sat at its gate to see that no circumcized man entered. Some rabbis said the setting sun reflected the glare from the fires of Gehenna or that Gehenna's heat warmed the waters of the Sea of Tiberias.[27]

The Babylonian Talmud had the worst Jewish sinners sentenced to Gehenna for 12 months. Then 'their bodies are destroyed, their souls are burned, and the wind strews the ashes under the feet of the pious.' All who enter Gehenna come out, with three exceptions: those who have committed adultery or shamed their neighbours or vilified them. In the end, God would take the sun from its case, and it would heal the pious and punish the sinners. There would be no Gehenna in the future world.[28]

Some rabbis were sympathetic; others were harsh. Some described torment by snow, smoke, thirst and rebellious animals. Others spoke of the righteous observing the torments of the damned, 'tossing in their pain like the pieces of boiling meat in a cauldron'. Others, more benevolent, said light flooded even Gehenna each Sabbath, and the wicked, too, had a day of rest.[29]

There was disagreement about the duration of the punishment. Some believed that the pain would continue for ever with or without Gehenna, while others believed punishment would end with the last judgment. Whether this last view allowed a future life for the wicked or looked for their total annihilation cannot be determined conclusively.[30]

However interesting such rabbinic lore may be, it is largely irrelevant for biblical studies because it comes so late.[31] We are thrown back instead to the intertestamental literature to determine the popular concepts of

---

25. Scobie, *John the Baptist*, p. 68; H. Bietenhard, 'Fire' 1:653f. Concerning the probable influence of Persian concepts on Pharisaic doctrine, see Bruce, *Paul*, p. 47.
26. Bietenhard, 'Fire' pp. 653f.
27. Pilcher, *Hereafter* p. 89.
28. 'Ge-hinnom,' *JE* vol. 5, cols. 581–583.
29. Strack and Billerbeck, 2:1076; Pilcher, *Hereafter* pp. 85f., 91.
30. Forestell, 'Christian Revelation' *CB*19, no. 2 (April 1957) p. 176f.; Hedwig Wahle, 'Die Lehren des rabbinischen Judentums uber das Leben nach dem Tod,' Kairos: *ZWT* 14, no. 4 (1972) p. 302ff., 308f.
31. F. W. Farrar devotes 60 pages to Jewish eschatology in his *Eternal Hope*, concluding that 'rabbinic opinion was generally' that souls are punished according to faults, with annihilation the worst punishment possible (Excursus v). Salmond correctly notes that

Jesus' day, and there, as we have seen, we find contradictory opinions. At the end of our search we must come again to the fulness of Jesus' teaching – his warnings, his parables, his similes – as seen against the background of the Old Testament Scriptures and as illuminated by the post-Pentecost writings of the Spirit-filled men who later 'remembered' and 'understood' Jesus' teaching.[32]

Matthew 5:25f.

Regardless of the precise nature of final punishment, Jesus stressed the importance of using the present opportunity in order to avoid it:

> Settle matters quickly with your adversary who is taking you to court. Do it while you are still with him on the way, or he may hand you over to the judge, and the judge may hand you over to the officer, and you may be thrown into prison. I tell you the truth, you will not get out until you have paid the last penny.

This passage has often been used as a proof-text. Roman Catholic theologians use it in the interest of purgatory. Others think it favours the restoration position. Others claim it for eternal torment. Luke's parallel is no clearer (Luke 12:58f.), nor is the Parable of the Unmerciful Servant, which includes the same principle (Matt. 18:34f.).

We commend the following conclusions of Salmond, an advocate of eternal torment. He pointed to 'the helplessness of the man when once in the prison, the finality of his condition there, the hopelessness of discharging his debt'. Our Lord speaks here, he goes on, 'of a justice which is inexorable, a law of retribution which [the victim] cannot avert, a peril which cannot be stayed.'[33]

Traditionalists sometimes point to the 'tormentors' in the latter passage as proof of everlasting conscious pain. The verb form of the same word appears in Revelation 9:5, however, where the 'torment' specifically lasts for five months. The New Testament uses the word metaphorically and literally, physically and spiritually, in time and in eternity.[34] In the Septuagint, *basanos* usually translates *asham*, 'which regularly refers to God's destruction because of guilt'.[35] The word itself does not determine the duration of the torment it describes. H. E. Guillebaud, a conditionalist, argues that

---

Farrar's use of the rabbinic literature missed the mark because it failed to take into account the late date from which much of it came (*Immortality* pp. 364, 371).

32. John 14:16ff, 25f; 16:8–14. 'The doctrine delivered in the Gospels appears to need, and to promise, further explanations, combinations, and developments, The character of that ministry on the whole is introductory' (T. D. Bernard, *Progress of Doctrine in the New Testament* p. 74). Later Bernard writes: 'Though in the teaching of Jesus all the truth might be implied, it was not all opened; therefore the Holy Ghost was to add that which had not been delivered, as well as to recall that which had been already spoken' (p. 89).
33. *Immortality* p. 379.
34. Johannes Schneider, '*Basanos*' *TDNT* 1:561–563.
35. Baird, *Justice* p. 232.

> . . . a prisoner who never comes out of prison does not live there eternally. The slave who was delivered to the tormentors till he should pay two million pounds would not escape from them by payment, but he would assuredly die in the end: why should not the same result be at least a possibility in the application?[36]

Matthew 5:29f.

The end of sin is so terrible that one gains even if one has to discard a cherished member of the body in order to avoid it. Loss of one limb now is far better than total loss hereafter.

> If your right eye causes you to sin, gouge it out and throw it away. It is better for you to lose one part of your body than for your whole body to be thrown into hell. And if your right hand causes you to sin, cut it off and throw it away. It is better for you to lose one part of your body than for your whole body to go into hell.

Jesus uses verbs which emphasize the sense of being rejected, banished, expelled. 'Throw' (*ballō*) away eye or hand, he says – as men discard worthless salt (Matt. 5:13), dead grass (Matt. 6:30) or inedible fish (Matt. 13:48). That is better far than having your whole body 'thrown' away on the day of judgment! This word has many other uses, of course, and we do not suggest that it has any inherent eschatological significance. At the same time, it is interesting to note how frequently Matthew uses *ballō* when speaking of the doom of the lost (Matt. 3:10; 5:25; 7:19; 13:42, 50; 18:8, 9, 30). The second comparison in the passage also stresses the idea of banishment: better to lose one part of the body than for the whole body to 'go off away' (*apelthē*) into hell.

Again Jesus makes Gehenna the place of final punishment. Here he gives no graphic description of its destructive power or even its duration, saying only that those who enter it go from another place, having been discarded and expelled by God. The picture is one of total loss, and it is entirely in keeping with the Old Testament to see that loss as ultimately consummated in destruction by fire.

Matthew 7:13f.

The gate giving upon the way to life is narrow and small, Jesus warns. There is another gate – a wide one through which many now press – but it leads to destruction. Jesus admonishes the disciples:

> Enter through the narrow gate. For wide is the gate and broad is the road that leads to destruction, and many enter through it. But small is the gate and narrow the road that leads to life, and only a few find it.

Our Lord shows us the kingdom of God in the shape of a city. It is surrounded by a wall with gates which are opened each day but closed at night and in times of danger. Whenever the gates are closed, one can enter only by the narrow gate – a small gate built into the main gate – so

---

36. *Righteous Judge* p. 21.

small it can admit but one person at a time. Through this narrow gate only those can enter whose names are properly recorded on the city's roll of inhabitants (its 'book of life'). This is the picture A. J. Mattill draws in a careful study of the passage. He argues convincingly that 'life' here is the life of the kingdom of heaven; that the word translated 'narrow' (formed from *thlibō*) refers to end-time tribulations that come on God's people, and that Jesus' primary tone is one of urgency.[37]

The emphasis here is not on the doom of 'destruction' awaiting the many but on the need for haste to avoid this imminent doom. Mattill paraphrases Jesus' warning:

> Hurry, before the eschatological storm breaks loose, to enter into the city of God through the narrow gate, which is wide enough to admit only one registered citizen at a time. For wide is the gate and broad is the road which is free of persecution, the comfortable way which leads to destruction in hell, and there are many who enter through this gate. Because narrow is the gate and great are the end-time tribulations and persecutions on the narrow way which leads to eternal life in the kingdom of heaven, and only a few people find it.[38]

Here once more Jesus offers a choice: persecution now or destruction hereafter. To experience the 'destruction' of 7:13 means being thrown into Gehenna (Matt. 5:29f.). Putting it the other way, those thrown into hell will be destroyed.

Matthew 7:19

If Jesus warns of impending destruction, so did the prophets before him. Like them, he confronted false prophets, ready to usher the gullible through the broad gate onto the wide road. 'Watch out for false prophets,' Jesus continues in Matt. 7:15. You recognize them by their fruits. Then he speaks of their end:

> Every tree that does not bear good fruit is cut down and thrown into the fire.

We have met this figure already, and we shall see it again. Baird examines this saying in the light of the larger context. Jesus is giving a series of 'crisis contacts' comparing the condition and destiny of the children of the kingdom with that of the wicked (Matt. 7:13–27). He contrasts the few/life with the many/destruction (vv. 13f) and doer/kingdom with evildoer/depart (vv. 21ff.). In vv 24–27 we find wise/not-fall and foolish/destined-to-fall. This verse is part of a similar contrast. The good tree not cut down is compared with the bad tree destined to be cut down and thrown into the fire. Casting into the fire parallels destruction (v. 13), rejection (v. 23) and the ruin of a house (v. 27). Baird concludes: 'If one carries out the logical imagery here, the fire would seem to refer to the destruction of a tree already dead,' a saying similar to Luke 12:5, which we will note later.[39]

---

37. A. J. Mattill, Jr., 'The Way of Tribulation,' *JBL* 98, no. 4 (Dec. 1979) pp. 531–546.
38. Ibid. p. 546.
39. *Justice* p. 225.

Matthew 7:23

Alongside the threatening false prophets, Jesus now mentions hypocrites who at the judgment claim they have prophesied, exorcized demons and performed miracles in Jesus' name, and therefore should be admitted to the kingdom. Jesus does not question their accomplishments but disowns them nonetheless, saying they did not do the will of the Father (Matt. 7:21f). 'Then I will tell them plainly,' Jesus continues, 'I never knew you. Away from me, you evildoers!'

The last sentence is from Psalm 6:8 where the psalmist rebukes hypocrites who profess God's name but deny his power to save. The claim of those in Jesus' story to have prophesied in the name of the Lord also reminds us of similar words in Jer.14:14; 27:15. There God condemns certain false prophets who promised peace and an easy way, 'I did not send them, though they *prophesied in the name of the Lord.*'

Regardless of their sins, the point is clear: those who do not truly know Jesus on earth will be turned away by him at the judgment.

Matthew 7:27

In Matthew Jesus concludes the 'Sermon on the Mount' with this Parable of the Wise and Foolish Builders. The foolish man builds with no foundation, and his house crumbles before the storm. 'The rain came down, the streams rose, and the winds blew and beat against that house, and it fell with a great crash.'

Ben Sira also contrasted the heart of the fool with a solidly-constructed house.

'As timber girt and fixed into the wall is not loosened by an earthquake, so a heart established on well-advised counsel will not be afraid in time of danger' (Sir. 22:16). More pertinent is Ezekiel's portrayal of God's judgment-storm which will test all men and make false prophets evident by their destruction (Ezek. 13:1–16).

> Therefore this is what the Sovereign Lord says: In my wrath I will unleash a violent wind, and in my anger hailstones and torrents of rain will fall with destructive fury. I will tear down the wall you have covered with whitewash and will level it to the ground so that its foundation will be laid bare. When it falls, you will be destroyed in it, and you will know that I am the Lord (Ezek. 13:13f).

The house lacking foundation (cf. Matt. 16:18; Heb.11:10) has a 'great fall', if we read Matthew's Greek literally. Luke says it had a great 'ruin' (Luke 6:49).[40] The related verb is used of wine bottles bursting (Luke 5:37), nets ripping apart with fish (Luke 5:6), or maddened swine tearing someone to pieces with their teeth (Matt. 7:6). He also says the destruction came 'immediately' ('the moment the torrent struck,' NIV) and that it was great. One who has seen a house demolished by hurricane, tornado or flood can appreciate both the suddenness and the severity of

---

40. In the LXX this word stands for the Hebrew *negeph* used most often for a divine judgment of destruction. See Ex. 12:13; 30:12; Num. 8:19; 16:46f.; Josh. 22:17; Isa. 8:14.

such a destruction. Jesus' figure is forceful and almost universally understood.

Matthew 8:11f.

Again Jesus stresses the exclusion of the unrepentant. It will surprise them and will occasion great anguish and remorse. The saying is Jesus' response to the outstanding faith of a Roman centurion.

> Many will come from the east and the west, and will take their places at the feast with Abraham, Isaac and Jacob in the kingdom of heaven. But the subjects of the kingdom will be thrown outside, into the darkness, where there will be weeping and gnashing of teeth.

Those who come 'from the east and the west' are certainly Gentiles. Both the hope and the language are straight from the Old Testament (Ps. 107:3; Isa. 49:12; 59:19; Mal. 1:11). Instead of 'the subjects of the kingdom' (a Jewish concept characteristic of Matthew's Gospel), Luke has 'you yourselves,' which corresponds to Jesus' meaning (Luke 13:28). In his larger context Luke has combined Matt 8:12 with Matt 7:21ff. (Luke 13:27ff). Where Matthew has the false disciples report their miracles, Luke has them remind Jesus that they once ate with him in the streets of their city. Table fellowship is important throughout Luke-Acts. But all reminders and claims come to nothing. The Messianic banquet is reserved for those who come when God invites – regardless of their other interests and occupations – even if they are blind and halt and lame (as in the Parable of the Wedding Feast). Luke ends the episode with Jesus' statement that 'there are those who are last who will be first, and first who will be last' (Luke 13:30).

Here, too, those rejected are 'thrown outside' (from *ballō*, already noted, strengthened by *ek*, 'out') into the darkness. The 'outer darkness' of the older version conveys better the extent of this 'bouncing' beyond the area illuminated by the lights inside the house.

In the Old Testament, darkness was a characteristic of Sheol, but that is probably not in Jesus' mind here. More appropriate is the darkness associated with the judgment of the 'day of the Lord' in the prophets. Both Matthew and Luke have the adverb of place, 'there' (*ekei*), a point the NIV makes clearer in Matthew 8:12 with its 'where'. It is there, says Jesus, in that outer darkness, that there will be weeping and grinding of teeth. This expression 'recurs in verbatim fashion seven times in an eschatological framework, and each time as an elaboration on the nature of final punishment'.[41] (See below, p 104).

The Old Testament 'day of the Lord' was also a day of darkness. Then, too, 'the cry' is bitter (Zeph. 1:14). Zephaniah's picture ends with 'the fire of his jealousy,' by which 'the whole world will be consumed' (Zeph. 1:18).

Throughout our literature weeping is associated with fear, misery or extreme grief, often because of God's judgment on sinners. People weep, for example, when Jerusalem is destroyed (Isa. 22:12) or when far from

---

41. Baird, *Justice* p. 225

their homeland (Bar. 4:11). James warns the rich to weep for fear of God's coming judgment (James 5:1). The prophets picture people weeping over the death or destruction of others (Isa. 16:9; Jer. 9:1; 48:32; Rev. 18:9); one entire Old Testament book – Lamentations – is devoted to this.

In 4 Ezra 7:80–87 the damned weep seven ways during their intermediate detention before the judgment: in shame and remorse for the past, and in fear and dread of the future, but most of all as they glimpse the glory of God, before whom they will soon be judged. This portrayal is in keeping with the biblical references already cited. Together they appear to warrant Baird's statement that 'there is little precedent for interpreting Jesus' use of "weeping" as a symbol for the torment accompanying the actual punishment of the *eschaton*'.[42]

In these passages weeping speaks more of terror and extreme loss, not so much of actual pain. It is part of the 'fearful expectation of judgment,' and a powerful reminder that 'it is a dreadful thing to fall into the hands of the living God' (Heb. 10:27, 31).

Most often in the Bible, the grinding of teeth describes the wrath of an adversary about to kill his victim – the teeth belong to the tormentor, not the tormented (Job 16:9; Ps. 35:16; 37:12; Lam. 2:16; Acts 7:54). Psalm 112 may be the single exception. The psalm begins, 'Blessed is the man who fears the Lord' (v. 1), whom it describes in verses 2–9. The final verse points a contrast: 'The wicked man will see and be vexed, he will gnash his teeth and waste away; the longings of the wicked will come to nothing' (v. 10). As before, the wicked man's gnashing of teeth seems to express his rage against the righteous. But even while he grinds his teeth in impotent fury, he wastes away and comes to nothing.[43]

When we examine the seven Gospel occurrences of 'weeping and grinding of teeth', we find that the expression

- modifies 'throw into darkness outside' (Matt. 8:12; 22:13; 25:30);
- accompanies 'you yourself thrown out' (Luke 13:28);
- follows 'assign him a place with the hypocrites' (Matt. 24:51);
- modifies 'weed out of his kingdom' and 'throw away' (Matt. 13:41f);
- accompanies 'separate the wicked from the righteous' (Matt. 13:49f).

In each instance those consigned to 'weeping and grinding of teeth' are separated from others who are approved. Each time the expression accompanies a specific act of banishment, expulsion or rejection. The last two passages add that those excluded and banished are thrown into 'the fiery furnace,' something that is not necessarily associated with 'weeping and grinding of teeth,' as shown by all the other cases. There is no indication that God will miraculously intervene for these, as he did for Daniel's three friends, whose lives were thus prolonged. May we not suppose, then, that this 'fiery furnace' does to its victims precisely what

---

42. Ibid. p. 229.

43. Both Blanchard and Dixon surpass their traditionalist ancestors by pointing out that 'gnashing of teeth' denotes anger and not anguish. Dixon understands that the expression has that meaning in the rabbinic literature (*Other Side* p. 163). Blanchard knows that it signifies anger in the Bible as well (*Hell* p. 156). Neither author mentions Psalm 112:10.

the enemies of Shadrach, Meshach and Abednego hoped theirs would do to them? (Dan. 3:15-27). Unless God intervenes, where is any hope? Certainly no other god can save from such a fate! (Dan. 3:15, 28).

In scriptural usage the expression 'weeping and grinding of teeth' seems to indicate two separate activities. The 'weeping' reflects the terror of the doomed as they begin to realize that God has rejected them and as they anticipate the execution of his sentence. 'Grinding of teeth' seems to express their bitter rage and enmity toward God, who has sentenced them, and toward the redeemed, who will for ever be blessed. The common assumption that 'weeping and grinding of teeth' describes the everlasting agony of souls in conscious torment is the interpretation of a later age and lacks any clear biblical support.

In closing, we echo Paul's admonition to 'consider . . . the kindness and sternness of God' (Rom. 11:22). On the first point, we observe that every warning of weeping and grinding of teeth is addressed to someone who has rejected God's offered grace. Not one is directed to people such as the citizens of Nineveh or even Sodom and Gomorrah. Whatever awaits those who die without knowing the gospel, it certainly will not include the remorse of remembering such rejected opportunities or the terror of facing a God whose Son they have knowingly despised.[44] On the second point, these words remind us that 'the terrors and despair of the lost at the throne of judgment, as we find them portrayed in the Bible, cannot be exaggerated'.[45]

Matthew 10:28

Little wonder that Jesus warned:

> Do not be afraid of those who kill the body but cannot kill the soul. Rather, be afraid of the one who can destroy both soul and body in hell.

This context, too, includes divine rejection and expulsion, for Jesus says he will personally disown traitorous disciples in the presence of the Father (Matt. 10:33). Only God should be ultimately feared, Jesus says, and James echoes this, speaking of God as 'able to save and destroy' (James 4:12).

Lest one read into Matthew's account any Platonic dualism regarding man's being, we have Luke's record of the same words: 'Do not be afraid of those who kill the body and after that can do no more. But . . . fear him who, after the killing of the body, has power to throw you into hell. Yes, I tell you, fear him' (Luke 12:4f). This passage does not teach the immortality of every human soul but rather that God can kill the soul as well as the body. Unless Jesus is making idle threats, the very warning implies that God will execute such a sentence on those who persistently rebel against his authority and resist every overture of mercy.[46]

---

44. A survey of evangelical reflection on the fate of the unevangelized is *No Other Name: An Investigation into the Destiny of the Unevangelized*, by John Sanders (Grand Rapids: Eerdmans, 1992).

45. Atkinson, *Life and Immortality* p. 102.

46. Cullmann writes: 'We hear in Jesus' saying in Matthew 10:28 that the soul can be killed. The soul is not immortal. There must be resurrection for both [body and soul]; for

Human nature as a psychosomatic unity, created from nothing by the God who alone gives life, corresponds precisely to the words of the Lord. Baird elaborates:

> This is the dimension of death, which only becomes alive when that higher potential of the soul takes on the dimension of the Kingdom. If the individual rejects this Spirit, new life does not come and he remains in the physical realm of death ... When the body is killed, its psychosomatic counterpart, tied to the body and possessing nothing beyond itself, must suffer the same fate. As Matthew says, *both* soul and body are destroyed in *gehenna*.'[47]

This raises a most interesting point. For if human beings depend wholly on God for their existence day by day, and if the wicked are banished absolutely from God's presence and are deprived of any divine blessing, the question must arise how they can continue to exist for any period of time. But there is more. Not only does Scripture say throughout that life in any dimension is a gift of God; it is also a matter of record that 'immortality' and 'incorruption' are promised as exclusively to the righteous as are 'glory' and 'honour' (Rom. 2:7, 10; 1 Cor. 15:42ff, 50, 54). All will be raised, but some will 'rise to live' while others will 'rise to be condemned' (John 5:28f; Dan. 12:1f.).

On this matter traditionalist writers have for the most part been strangely silent. When they have spoken, they have often applied to the wicked descriptions of the resurrected body which Paul reserves for the righteous alone. Such an indiscriminate use of terms characterizes the writings of Athenagoras, Augustine and Chrysostom,[48] as of later traditionalist advocates. Calvin was aware of this problem, though he never seems to have met it head-on.[49] Luther posed the difficult question but declined to give it much thought.[50] It has often been observed that his chief concern was justification, not eschatology. Many modern authors, both Catholic and Protestant, seeing no biblical ladder down from this tightrope, simply leap into the philosophical net of the immortality of the soul.[51]

The conditionalist Henry Constable challenged the common notion that the wicked, too, will be raised incorruptible, arguing that resurrec-

---

since the Fall the whole man is 'sown corruptible" (*Immortality or Resurrection?* pp. 36f.). For similar statements see earlier chapters here on immortality of the soul.

Blanchard's traditionalism cannot allow the plain meaning of 'destroy' here, but only that 'there are those whose eternal fate will be to have God toss them aside, body and soul.' (*Hell* p. 131). Similarly, Dixon has to explain that God will not 'put the wicked out of existence,' lest someone take Jesus' words at face value (*Other Side* p. 125).

47. *Justice* pp. 222f. On the relations between body, Holy Spirit, resurrection, cosmos and the new age, see Joseph Blenkinsopp, 'Theological Synthesis and Hermeneutical Conclusions,' *Immortality and Resurrection* pp. 122–125.

48. See quotations and references in Constable, *Punishment* p. 81; Shedd, *Dogmatic Theology* 3:491f.; J. N. D. Kelly, *Early Christian Doctrines*, p. 483.

49. *Institutes* 3. 25. 9.

50. Ewald M. Plass, comp., *What Luther Says: An Anthology*, 2:628, #1922.

51. M. E. Williams, 'Soul, Human, Immortality of,' *New Catholic Encyclopedia* 12:469; Charles F. Baker, *A Dispensational Theology*, quotes Shedd with approval from his *Dogmatic Theology* 2:652. See further examples in chapter on immortality.

tion, as such, requires no essential change from a former state. Speaking of his traditionalist opponents, he wrote:

> They all tell us that a change will pass upon the wicked at their resurrection! We ask for proof. They cannot say that there cannot be a resurrection without a change; for, unfortunately for them, there have been resurrections where no change has taken place. All the resurrections before that of Christ were such. He was the 'first fruits from the dead,' because in the case of others raised before Him no change from mortality took place. They cannot say that there cannot be a resurrection followed by death; for, again, the cases of Jairus' daughter, and the widow's son, and Lazarus, would confront and confound them; for all these, after they were raised, died again. We ask them for proof that the bodies of the wicked will undergo any change at their resurrection.[52]

Had Constable lived a hundred years later, he would have found some scholarly support. F. F. Bruce, dean of evangelical commentators, says that it is curious though perhaps accidental 'that in Paul's letters there is no clear reference to the resurrection of the wicked'.[53] Murray Harris, a professor at Trinity Evangelical Divinity School, calls it a 'distinctive feature of the Christian view of resurrection' that the righteous dead are transformed as well as revived. He uses the same illustration as Constable. 'To be revived is not to be resurrected: the raising of Lazarus (Jn. 11:1–44) or of the widow of Nain's son (Lk. 7:11–17) was a restoration to temporary physical life (they came to life only ultimately to die once more), not a resurrection to permanent spiritual life.'[54] Harris observes that according to the New Testament there is a reanimation that leads to judgment, not to life but to the 'second death' (Dan. 12:2; John 5:29; Rev. 20:4ff, 11–15). He notes that

> in the Pauline Epistles resurrection seems to be depicted as a privilege reserved for the new humanity in Christ. In any event, whatever the anthropological state of the wicked dead after they have regained 'life', they are certainly not possessors of 'spiritual bodies', since the *sōma pneumatikon* [spiritual body] is imperishable and therefore not subject to 'the second death'.[55]

W. G. T. Shedd, a powerful advocate of everlasting conscious torment, recognized the problem, which he never entirely reconciled with his overall conclusion:

> The bodies of the wicked, on the contrary, are not delivered from the power of Sheol, or the grave, by a blessed and glorious resurrection, but are still kept

---

52. *Future Punishment* p. 83.
53. Bruce, 'Paul on Immortality,' p. 458; also *Paul*, p. 301.
54. Murray Harris, 'Resurrection and Immortality: Eight Theses,' *Themelios* 1, no. 2 (Spring 1976) p. 51f.
55. Ibid. p. 52. Paul Tillich has some good words on this, when taken at face value and apart from his special meanings: 'Condemnation can only mean that the creature is left to the nonbeing it has chosen. The symbol "eternal death" is even more expressive' (Paul Tillich, *Systematic Theology* [Chicago: University of Chicago Press, 1951, 1957] 2:78, quoted by C. C. Goen [with reservations, as here!], 'The Modern Discussion of Eschatology,' *Review and Expositor* 57, no. 2 [April 1960]: 124).

under its dominion by a 'resurrection to shame and everlasting contempt' (Dan. 12:2). Though the wicked are raised from the dead, yet this is no triumph for them over death and the grave. Their resurrection bodies are not 'celestial' and 'glorified,' like those of the redeemed, but are suited to the nature of their evil and malignant souls.[56]

This being the case, does it not follow that the wicked, deprived of any life from God and subjected to the destructive force of Gehenna besides, will eventually lose all vitality and truly die? May we not think of a glowing ember which, removed from the fireplace, finally loses all its fire? Or of an electric heater, now unplugged from its source of power, which glows for a short period but finally and inevitably goes out? This is how a contemporary conservative commentator describes the lake of fire:

> It is the second death, that is, the destiny of those whose temporary resurrection results only in a return to death and its punishment. Alford writes, 'As there is a second and higher life, so there is also a second and deeper death. And as after that life there is no more death ([Rev.] ch. xxi. 4), so after that death there is no more life' (pp. 735f.).[57]

Our Lord's warning is plain. The human power to kill stops with the body and is limited by the horizons of the Present Age. The death thus inflicted is not final, for God will call forth the dead from the earth and give the righteous immortality. God's ability to kill and destroy is without limit. It reaches deeper than the physical and further than the present. God can kill both body and soul, both now and hereafter.

In Matthew's account Jesus uses 'kill' and 'destroy' in parallel fashion, apparently making them interchangeable. Luke quotes Jesus as saying, 'Fear him who, after the killing of the body, has power to throw you into hell.' This is the identical sequence described in Isaiah 66. There, too, God first slays his enemies, then throws their dead bodies into the consuming fire (v. 24). Throughout Luke–Acts Luke shows a thorough acquaintance with Isaiah and a special affinity for the book's language and concepts. It is not surprising that Luke rather than Matthew repeats Jesus' words in a form which closely resembles Isaiah's picture of the eschatological punishment.

Far from lessening the anxiety of sinners, this understanding of Jesus' words intensifies their dread. 'Yes, I tell you,' Jesus says, 'fear him!' Here is an urgency our careless generation badly needs to learn. When morality is determined on the basis of human polls rather than divine precepts, we need to hear the thunder and see the lightning and feel the force of the voice of Almighty God.

Guillebaud drives the point home:

> But let none imagine that because eternal punishment does not mean everlasting torment, therefore it is a mild penalty which need not be dreaded .... No more dreadful mistake could be made than so to consider the matter

---

56. *Punishment* pp. 39ff.
57. *Revelation* NICNT p. 367. Henry Constable wrote: 'The unjust are not raised in incorruption; they are not raised in immortality .... For the bodies of the unjust are raised only in their old mortality. They are thus raised for punishment. Raised in their old mortality, the pains of hell will again, must again reduce them to a second death, from which there is no promise of a resurrection' (*Future Punishment* p. 94).

.... Having faced death once in this world, the lost soul must face it again, under circumstances of unutterable shame and horror. God will not then be One who can be ignored or patronized, He will be known for what He is, the One who fills heaven and earth. Then the Almighty King, who had offered him salvation and would so gladly have saved him, will reject him and pronounce him only fit for destruction.

The instinct, which so often makes even the suicide struggle desperately for life at the last, will surely be far more powerful as the soul faces the final disintegration of personality, the utter end, and what an awful end! How terrible the process of destruction will be will depend on the degree of each soul's guilt before God, ... how much light has been disobeyed. But in any case what an awful thing it must be to be rejected by God as worthless, and cast upon the bonfire as rubbish to be destroyed, realizing as never before what might have been if God's salvation had been accepted. Remember those words of the Lord Jesus Christ ... 'There shall be the weeping and gnashing of teeth.'[58]

Matthew 10:39

If nobody can ultimately destroy another's life, and if God can so kill men and women in their totality that nothing survives, life and death alike take on new meaning in the Present Age. Jesus points to this when he says:

> Whoever finds his life will lose it, and whoever loses his life for my sake will find it.

The same saying, set here in a context of the disciples' suffering, appears again in all the Synoptics in a discussion regarding Jesus' own death (Matt. 16:21–28; Mark 8:31–9:1; Luke 9:22–27). Jesus tells the disciples that he must be killed and rise again (Matt. 16:21). They must also deny their own selves and take up the cross daily (Matt. 16:24). His followers must not seek to save their own lives – although they will truly find them if lost for Jesus (Matt. 16:25). What is a man's advantage, Jesus asks, if he gains the whole world but loses his own life? (Matt. 16:26).

The NIV sentimentally keeps the KJV 'soul' in Matthew 16:26, though it inconsistently translates the identical word (*psychē*) as 'life' in v. 25. Instead of 'soul,' Luke simply says 'himself' (*heauton*, 'very self,' NIV), making it absolutely clear that Jesus used *psychē* in the wholistic Hebraic sense, not in the dualistic sense of Greek philosophy.

The context suggests that 'finding one's life' and 'losing one's life' should be taken at face value with the normal meanings. Jesus explains his own approaching death and resurrection to life (v. 21). He warns against attempting to save one's own life and promises that whoever loses their *life* for the Lord will find it in the end (v. 25). No one willingly exchanges their *psychē* (their very self) for any amount of riches (v. 26), a principle extended in Jesus' questions to the Age to Come. Some standing in sight of Jesus would see an advent of the Son of Man before they tasted *death* (v. 28). When Jesus comes in glory with the angels to reward each person, some will lose their *life;* others will find *life*.

58. *Righteous Judge* p. 45.

We do not question that 'life' includes more than mere existence – a point made as often by conditionalist writers as by traditionalists. Nor do we deny that 'life' and 'death' sometimes have figurative meanings in the Scriptures. The entire flow of thought in this context, however, as well as the general use here of these words, prompts two questions. First, since 'life' may mean more than mere existence but never (to our knowledge) means less, on what basis can 'loss of life' mean less than the loss of existence, even though here it obviously implies the loss of far more? Eternal 'death' involves more than temporal 'death,' but surely it involves no less. Second, what warrant does this context provide for making 'lose one's life' and 'find one's life' figurative in verses 25f when the same thoughts are so obviously literal in all the verses both before these and after?

Matthew 11:22ff.

Woe to you Korazin! Woe to you, Bethsaida!

It will be 'more bearable' for Tyre and Sidon on the day of judgment than for Korazin and Bethsaida, Jesus says. It will be 'more bearable' for Sodom then than for Capernaum.

Luke records essentially the same words (Luke 10:13ff). Jesus here indicates that there will be degrees of punishment at the end, based on degrees of culpability (see also Matt. 12:41f. / Luke 11:29–32). What will be Capernaum's fate? Will she be 'lifted up'? No! She will 'go down to Hades'. This language comes from the Old Testament prophets as they threatened Babylon (Isa. 14:13, 15) and Tyre (Ezek. 26:19ff). For them the temporal execution of the threat meant their disappearance, never to be found again, though others around them continued. Jesus here personifies cities, however, and we do not wish to make too much of these words in our study of the final punishment of individual sinners.

Matthew 12:31f.

Once, when Jesus healed a demon-possessed man who was both blind and mute, some Pharisees attributed his power to Beelzebub, the prince of demons. Jesus warned them sternly:

> The blasphemy against the Spirit will not be forgiven. Anyone who speaks . . . against the Holy Spirit will not be forgiven, either in this age or in the age to come.

Where Matthew uses the apocalyptic language of the two ages, Mark compresses the same idea into an eschatological adjective. The person 'will never be forgiven; he is guilty of an *eternal* sin' (Mark 3:29). Luke eliminates the language of eschatology altogether, stating simply that 'he will not be forgiven' (Luke 12:10). These parallels explain each other. The 'eternal sin' is not a sin committed without end, as if sinners in hell for ever continue to sin and therefore for ever feel the penal blows.[59] It

---

[59] A. A. Hodge says, for example: 'The instant a soul sins it is cut off from the communion and life of God. As long as it continues in that state it will continue to sin. As long as it continues to sin, it will deserve his wrath and curse. It is obvious that the sinful

was the specific sin of blasphemy against the Holy Spirit, the agent of divine power in the new age, by whom Jesus performed his miracles of the kingdom of heaven. This specific sin was committed at a particular point of time well within the bounds of earthly history. The 'eternal' sin denies and repels the only one who can forgive, and so can never be forgiven – even in the coming age of eternity.

To say the sin is never forgiven is not the same as saying its perpetrators will always endure conscious torment for committing it.[60] It is possible in our society for a convicted murderer to be pardoned. But if he is not forgiven, the form of his punishment is beside the point. He is no more pardoned if he is executed for his crime than if he spends a hundred years in prison. Salmond expressed the meaning well:

> The phrase in question is an absolutely exclusive phrase. It means that neither in the present nor in the future, neither in this dispensation nor in what follows it, neither before nor after Christ's Coming, is there forgiveness for this sin. It is difficult to see how the irremediableness of the condition could be more distinctly expressed.[61]

Matthew 13:30, 40–43

In this Parable of the Weeds the farmer tells his servants to let wheat and weeds grow together until the harvest. 'At that time,' the owner says, 'I

---

tempers and conduct indulged in hell will deserve and receive punishment as strictly as those previously indulged in this life' (*Outlines* pp. 584f.). Strong argues that eternal sin demands eternal punishment and that the depraved will continue to sin even in hell (*Theology* 3:1048f.). He creates a moral dilemma without seeming to realize it. On the one hand, he says that 'habit begets fixity of character, and in the spiritual world sinful acts ... produce a permanent state of sin, which the soul, unaided, cannot change' (p. 1049). On the other hand, he argues that benevolence in God may to the end permit the existence of sin and may continue to punish the sinner ... because [God] ... provides for the highest possible freedom and holiness in the creature through eternity' (p. 1053).

Constable responded to this type of argument by pointing out that (1) Scripture never suggests any such idea as sin in hell but (2) specifically states over and over that future punishment is for deeds 'done in the body' during present life in this age. 'Just fancy an earthly judge sentencing a criminal to a punishment too severe for the offence committed, and then gravely justifying his sentence by the observation that the criminal would be sure to deserve it all by his conduct in gaol [jail]!' (*Future Punishment* pp. 107ff.; quotation on p. 109).

60. A. A. Hodge is an example of one who presents the 'unpardonable sin' as evidence for everlasting conscious torment (Hodge, *Outlines of Theology* p. 582).

61. *Immortality* p. 381. In 1877 Frederick W. Farrar, archdeacon and canon of Westminster, stirred a British tempest when he preached a series of sermons in Westminster Abbey on final punishment. These were published (in self-defence according to his preface) as *Eternal Hope* in 1879. When (1880) Edward Bouverie Pusey replied with *What is of Faith?* Farrar responded (1881) with *Mercy and Judgment*. Farrar disagreed with both traditionalists and conditionalists, arguing most of all for a 'larger hope' beyond the bounds of the present life. Pusey had a kind of 'larger hope' of his own, insisting that Ahab, Absalom, Herod and even Antiochus Epiphanes may have experienced death-bed repentance and be saved (Pusey, *What Is of Faith?* pp. 12ff.). A modern conservative writer who argues for the possibility of conversion in the Age to Come is Brethren scholar, Vernard Eller, *Most Revealing* pp. 199ff. See also Sanders, *No Other Name*.

will tell the harvesters: First collect the weeds and tie them in bundles to be burned, then gather the wheat and bring it into my barn' (v. 30). We have already seen figures from agriculture which involve burning what is rejected. Jesus supplied his own interpretation:

> As the weeds are pulled up and burned in the fire, so it will be at the end of the age. The Son of Man will send out his angels, and they will weed out of his kingdom everything that causes sin and all who do evil. They will throw them into the fiery furnace, where there will be weeping and gnashing of teeth. Then the righteous will shine like the sun in the kingdom of their Father.

Two witnesses tell us this picture is eschatological. Not only does Jesus specifically apply the parable to 'the end of the age'; his language has that background in the Old Testament. Both Nestle's Greek text and the NASB cross-reference the expression, 'everything that causes sin and all who do evil,' to Zeph. 1:3. Although the words are not found in the standard English translations, the RSV and NASB give them in a marginal note and the NIV note says, 'Hebrew uncertain.' Some manuscripts of the Septuagint do have these very words in this prophetic passage which goes on to describe the terrible 'day of the Lord'.

Jesus' promise that 'the righteous will shine like the sun' seems to come from Dan. 12:3, which directly follows a major Old Testament passage regarding final punishment (see above p. 65). In Mal. 4:1–3 also the 'sun of righteousness arises' for the righteous while the wicked become ashes under the soles of their feet. In the present parable the workers pull the weeds up and burn them in the fire, a figure, says Jesus ('*as* . . . *so*') of what the angels will do to sinners at the end.

Matthew 13:48ff.

This Parable of the Net closely resembles the Parable of the Weeds in its word about final punishment. The net in the story drew 'all kinds of fish,' and the fishermen 'collected the good fish in baskets, but threw the bad away' (v. 48). Jesus explained the figure (vv. 49ff).

> This is how it will be at the end of the age. The angels will come and separate the wicked from the righteous and throw them into the fiery furnace, where there will be weeping and gnashing of teeth.

The Lord's emphasis here is clearly on exclusion. Many who profess to follow him do not really know him at all. Today they merge with the true disciples, but God's own time of separation is coming. Jesus makes this point in many of his sayings; it is an essential element in both the Greek (*krisis*) and English words for judgment. In the first century or the twentieth, people who profess to believe in hell tend almost always to think of it as for other people. Jesus checks us in that presumption: God's great separation will hold many surprises!

Matthew 18:8f.

The greatest in the kingdom of heaven is the person most like a little child, Jesus tells his competitive and ambitious disciples. And woe to whoever turns one of God's little ones out of the road or causes such a one to sin! Jesus repeats in essence what he had said earlier about forfeiting a member of the body in order to escape Gehenna (Matt. 5:29f.).

> If your hand or your foot causes you to sin, cut it off and throw it away. It is better for you to enter life maimed or crippled than to have two hands or two feet and be thrown into eternal fire [*to pyr to aiōnion*]. And if your eye causes you to sin, gouge it out and throw it away. It is better for you to enter life with one eye than to have two eyes and be thrown into the fire of hell [*tēn geennan tou pyros*].'

Gehenna here is called the 'eternal fire'. In another place Jesus says the 'eternal fire' was prepared for the devil and his angels (Matt. 25:41). This is paralleled by reference to the kingdom, which was 'prepared since the creation of the world' (v. 34). By implication the 'fire' seems to be at least as old as creation; it is clear that it will extend beyond the Present Age. It is therefore said to be 'eternal,' since it neither begins nor ends with the Present Age. The phrase does not convey what 'eternal fire' will do to those thrown into it. Whereas God designed the kingdom especially for the redeemed, the fire was made for the fallen angels (2 Pet. 2:4-9; Jude 6). God formed the human creatures for glory with himself, a destiny wholly of grace. Those who align themselves instead with the rebel creatures of a higher and previous order must finally share their fate.

Where Matthew has 'eternal fire,' Mark speaks simply of being 'thrown/going into hell' (Mark 9:43,45,47). As in the matter of 'eternal sin,' Mark uses the straightforward language of prose rather than the terminology of apocalyptic. It is generally agreed that both evangelists record words spoken originally in Aramaic. Matthew's language may add flavour and force, but it should not be naively interpreted in a way that contradicts Mark's. Luke's account of the incident stops short of this conversation (Luke 17:1f).

Jesus' chief thrust concerns care for the 'little ones'. Calvin captures this in his commentary, not elaborating on final punishment but simply urging 'whoever . . . desires to escape that fearful punishment' to 'stretch out his hand to the little ones who are despised by the world, and let him kindly assist them in keeping the path of duty.'[62] That Jesus should talk of self-mutilation in this pastoral context is interesting in the light of Zech. 11:17. There, too, the subject is God's concern for his helpless people, and the curse on a worthless shepherd is the loss of his right arm and right eye. Earlier the flock pay off their worthy shepherd with 30 pieces of silver, the Mosaic price of a wounded slave (Exod. 21:32). The shepherd throws the paltry sum to the potter in the house of the Lord (Zech. 11:12f).

Mark also adds to Matthew's record a phrase taken from Isa. 66:24. There hell is a place 'where their worm does not die, and the fire is not quenched' (Mark 9:48; some mss add the same words at vv. 44f). Instead of Isaiah's 'their fire,' Jesus says simply 'the fire,' showing there is no special significance to the pronoun, although 'their' agrees with Matthew's

---

62. *Harmony of the Evangelists* 2:336.

statement that while the fire was 'prepared' for others it will also be the fate of these.

The 'worm' here (*skōlēx*) is the kind that feeds on dead bodies; we have already examined this figure. Scripture supplies no basis for making the worm a metaphor for remorse, an interpretation now almost universal and documented as early as Origen. This is a devouring worm, and what it eats – in Isaiah's picture here quoted without amendment – is already dead.

The devouring worm is aided by a consuming fire. This understanding is supported, not only by the biblical references already noted to 'unquenchable fire', but by Homer's reference to 'unquenchable fire' used by the Trojans against the Grecian ships (*Iliad* 16. 123, 194; 1.599) and the church historian Eusebius' 'unquenchable fire' which burns a martyr to ashes (Eccl. *Hist.* 6.41). By his repeated use of the phrase, Jesus clearly implies that God's final decision concerning each person 'is irreversible and entails eternal consequences'.[63] Or to borrow words written a century ago,

> The expressions of . . . 'unquenchable fire,' may mean merely that there is to be no deliverance, – no revival, – no restoration, – of the condemned. 'Death,' simply, does not shut out the hope of being brought to life again: 'eternal death' does. 'Fire' may be quenched before it has entirely consumed what it is burning: 'unquenchable fire' would seem most naturally to mean that which destroys it utterly.[64]

Mark continues with a cryptic saying he alone records:

'Everyone will be salted with fire' (Mk 9:49).

In the next verse Jesus admonishes, 'Have salt in yourselves, and be at peace with each other.' Some traditionalists have presented v. 49 in support of everlasting conscious torment. 'Fire is usually destructive,' says Strong, 'but this unquenchable fire will act like salt, preserving instead of destroying.'[65] A. B. Bruce mentions this interpretation in EGT but sees 'no necessity to regard' it as correct.[66] The interpretation not only lacks scriptural precedent; it aligns v. 49 against v. 48. Given this meaning, the ambiguous salt contradicts the unquenchable fire as that term is defined by numerous other passages which are quite clear.

Conditionalist Edward White suggests another approach. 'The meaning may be,' he surmises, 'that every such sacrifice to the avenging Justice will be, like "Lot's wife," "salted with fire," preserved as a monument in death of the tremendous results of rebellion against the Omnipotent'.[67] While

---

63. Lane, *Mark* p. 347.
64. Richard Whately, *View of the Scripture Revelations concerning a Future State* p. 183.
65. *Theology* 3:1036. A. W. Pink compares this preservation as by salt to God's preserving the burning bush (Exod. 3) and keeping the bodies of the three Hebrews in the fiery furnace (Dan. 3) (*Eternal Punishment* p. 27). We agree that God is able to so preserve the bodies of the wicked to endure eternal conscious torment. We simply see nothing in Scripture to indicate that he will, and much there to indicate that he will not.
66. EGT Vol. 1 p. 407.
67. *Life in Christ* p. 409.

this suggestion at least builds on the biblical precedent of a notable prototype of divine punishment, it is also less than convincing.

Salmond offers still another interpretation. He reminds us that 'salt was the sign of the binding obligation of the covenant, and the covenant-relation had its terrible side to the faithless as well as its gracious side to the faithful'.[68] Wrath and righteousness are both covenant concepts. But having raised this intriguing point, he fails to use his insight to illuminate this mysterious saying.

The interpretation with the best support is probably that given by Lane. Having already shown the close relation between Mark's Gospel and the fires of persecution, he reads this passage in that light.

> The thought of the sacrifice of an offending member of the body (verses 43–47) is here carried a step further: every disciple is to be a sacrifice for God (cf. Rom. 12:1). In the OT the Temple sacrifices had to be accompanied by salt (Lev. 2:13; Ezek. 43:24; cf. Ex. 30:35). The salt-sacrifice metaphor is appropriate to a situation of suffering and trial in which the principle of sacrifice cultivated with respect to the individual members of the body is now severely tested. The disciples must be seasoned with salt, like the sacrifice. This will take place through fiery trials (cf. 1 Pet. 1:7; 4:12).[69]

This explanation enjoys the support of its immediate context, the outlook of the book of Mark as a whole, and the background material regarding salt and sacrifices in the Old Testament. Jesus offers his disciples a choice: the fire of persecution now or the fire of Gehenna later. He speaks straight from the shoulder – on this decision hangs our eternal destiny.

Nestle's Greek text gives two cross-references here: Isa. 66:24 and Judith 16:21. (They are discussed above on pages 62 and 75.) They offer opposing pictures of the end of the wicked, so our options are clearly set forth. We choose to follow Isaiah and ignore Judith.

Matthew 21:33–44

Jesus re-presents Isaiah's Song of the Vineyard (Isa. 5:1–7) to drive home his own warning that God will again reject faithless Israel. The parable comes in a series of parables and confrontations during the final days of the ministry. These intensify the rage of the Pharisees and chief priests until it culminates in Jesus' arrest and their demand for his crucifixion (Matt. 21:45f.).

The parable does not deal directly with the end of the world. Matt. 24, and perhaps 1 Thess. 2:15f suggest that *this* judgment might have been inflicted – along with the destruction of Jewish national hopes – by the hands of the Romans in AD 69–70. Yet temporal judgments often prefigure the great and final one, so even this interpretation leaves room for the passage in our present study. But how does it picture the judgment it threatens? 'What' is the punishment, regardless of its 'when'?

In Matthew's account Jesus' hearers acknowledge that the owner 'will bring those wretches to a wretched end' (v. 41). Jesus then changes from

---

68. *Immortality* p. 377, note 1.
69. Lane, *Mark* p. 349.

parabolic narrative to address his hearers directly. 'Therefore I tell you that the kingdom of God will be taken away from you and given to a people who will produce its fruit' (v. 43). Mark and Luke add that the vineyard-owner will 'kill those tenants' (Mark 12:9; Luke 20:16). Matthew[70] and Luke then add Jesus' statement that 'he who falls on this stone will be broken to pieces, but he on whom it falls will be crushed' (Matt. 21:44; Luke 20:18), language based on Daniel's interpretation of the great image in Nebuchadnezzar's dream (Dan. 2:34f., 44f.). We may incidentally note that Daniel (2:35) compares the ruined and broken image to 'chaff on a threshing floor in the summer' which 'the wind swept ... away without leaving a trace' – the same figure Psalm 1 uses for the wicked's end. Daniel applies the language to human kingdoms; Jesus particularizes it to individual persons.

Whatever its relevance to the individual destiny of the wicked, we may summarize the parable's judgment like this. The offenders lose all privileges of the kingdom; they are brought to death in a wretched end. If we include the data from Daniel, the wind blows them away without leaving a trace. We cannot be sure if the judgment is temporal or eschatological, but these are the terms Jesus used to describe it.

Matthew 22:13

The Parable of the Wedding Banquet also ends on a tragic note. The king discovers a guest unsuitably dressed. The man has no excuse; he is speechless (Matt. 22:12). The climax is reached in verses 13 and 14:

> The king orders the attendants: 'Tie him hand and foot, and throw him outside, into the darkness, where there will be weeping and gnashing of teeth.' For many are invited, but few are chosen.

Found only in Matthew, this parable serves there as a sort of epilogue to the Parable of the Great Banquet, which Luke also reports (Matt. 22:1–14; Luke 14:15–24). Jesus' saying that 'many are invited, but few are chosen' has a close parallel in 4 Ezra. When Ezra laments the small number who are saved and the great crowds of the damned, he is told, 'Many have been created, but few shall be saved' (4 Ezra 8:3).

Jesus may mean only that the generosity of God's invitation dwarfs the meagreness of human response. Those 'chosen' are few compared to the many God 'invites'. In the parable the spotlight finally rests on the improperly dressed guest rather than those who ignored the invitation. Apparently the 'few' are even fewer than the guests who come. The warning is for those who accept God's invitation, not for those who reject it.

There seems to be no historical support for the explanation that the Palestinian host would provide his guests with a wedding garment. Jeremias suggests that this is not a special festive garment at all but a freshly-washed garment still unsoiled. He cites a similar parable from a first-century rabbi which identifies the clean garment as repentance –

---

70. Matt. 21:44 does not appear in some Greek manuscripts and the RSV omits it. It is unquestioned in Luke.

preferably on the day before one dies. 'But here', Jeremias says, 'we must choose between the rabbinic answer and the Gospel's.' He refers to Isa. 61:10 and Rev. 22:14, where the robes are God's forgiveness and imputed righteousness.[71] The contrast between Matthew and rabbi may not be accidental. 'What has not been sufficiently recognized,' writes W. D. Davies, 'is the extent to which . . . the period when Matthew emerged was one of the codification of Law in Judaism and of the reformulation or reformation of worship.'[72]

In respect of final punishment, this parable provides nothing new. The language is familiar – the expulsion into the outside darkness and the weeping and grinding of teeth. It underscores the truth that those who accept Christ's invitation must come only in the robes woven by his perfect obedience to God and made spotless by his cleansing blood (Gal. 3:27; Rev. 7:14; cf. Zech. 3:1–8; Rev. 3:18).[73]

Matthew 24:50f.

Jesus alternates his warnings – first to the self-righteous Pharisees, who presume that they will inherit God's kingdom – then to his own disciples, who are beginning to recognize the Pharisees' error but stand in danger of repeating it themselves. The Lord exhorts us to watchfulness in this illustration of a reckless and profligate servant suddenly surprised when his master returns. The story ends with a warning:

> The master of that servant will come on a day when he does not expect him and at an hour he is not aware of. He will cut him to pieces and assign him a place with the hypocrites, where there will be weeping and gnashing of teeth.

Luke omits 'weeping and gnashing of teeth' and puts 'unbelievers' instead of 'hypocrites.' Both changes are easily explained in terms of intended audiences. Luke writes for Gentiles, and Matthew for Jews. Luke also supplies Jesus' conclusion, providing the parable's only unique contribution to our study. Jesus says:

> That servant who knows his master's will and does not get ready or does not do what his master wants will be beaten with many blows. But the one who does not know and does things deserving punishment will be beaten with few blows. From everyone who has been given much, much will be demanded; and

---

71. *Parables* pp. 65, 188f.

72. *Sermon on the Mount* p. 300. He warns that his remarks concerning a possible relationship between rabbinic Judaism and Matthean Christianity are 'tentative and exploratory'.

73. Rev. 19:8 has the saved dressed in 'fine linen, bright and clean,' which 'stands for the righteous acts of the saints'. This is spoken in a different frame of reference from our passage in the Gospels or even Isaiah 64:6, where 'all our righteous acts are like filthy [lit. 'menstruous'] rags'. On the paradox of grace and works in judgment see C. Leslie Mitton, 'Present Justification and Final Judgment: A Discussion of the Parable of the Sheep and the Goats,' *ET* 68, no. 2 (Nov. 1956) p. 46–50, and especially Ridderbos, *Paul* pp. 178–181. Ridderbos further recommends G. C. Berkouwer (*Faith and Justification* pp. 103–112) and Schrenk (*TDNT* 2:208).

from the one who has been entrusted with much, much more will be asked (Luke 12:47f.).

These words clearly imply degrees of punishment in proportion to light spurned and opportunity neglected. Here traditionalists and conditionalists fully agree, though at times each camp has used the point as an argument against the other.[74] A close reading of the text raises another question, however, which neither side seems to have considered.

The villain in the story is cut in pieces and thrown out to the hypocrites/unbelievers. But of the other two servants, beaten with stripes few and many, the parable says no such thing. Are they of a character entirely different from the villain? If the man cut in pieces and thrown out stands for those God will finally banish to hell, as common opinion holds on both sides of the controversy, whom do the beaten servants represent? Do they return to the master's good graces following their beatings? Do they represent some finally saved though punished first in a degree appropriate to their guilt? Does the free grace of God leave any place for such a scheme, which many very orthodox theologians have entertained in some form? If so, the phrase 'degrees of punishment' assumes even greater significance. Or do we press the text too literally in even raising such a question?

Whatever the answer to these questions, no one in the story is tormented for ever. One man receives a few blows; another many. The worst fellow is cut in pieces and thrown out – a terrible punishment indeed, but still far from eternal conscious torment.

Luke takes us further yet. 'I have come to bring fire on the earth,' Jesus says, 'and how I wish it were already kindled!' (Luke 12:49). This is the first 'fire' in the passage, and it is evidently the same judgment-fire which John had before announced that Jesus would bring (Matt. 3:10ff.). But the fire falls on Jesus first, in the 'baptism' awaiting him on Golgotha (Luke 12:50).

Matthew 25:30

Today the 'one-talent man' is often an object of pity. Jesus' parable is less sympathetic; there he is 'lazy' and 'worthless.' At the end he loses what little capital he had, then is thrown 'outside, into the darkness where there will be weeping and gnashing of teeth'.

Mark summarizes the story as a lesson on vigilance but omits Matthew's ending describing the master's return (Mark 13:32–36). Luke gives the parable in detail, also without Matthew's ending, but he introduces a subplot and some new characters. Early in his story a group of citizens refuse to acknowledge the master's authority (Luke 19:14). At the end the master has them arrested and executed before his eyes (v. 27).

---

74. Traditionalists: Louis Berkhof, *Reformed Dogmatics* 2:345; A. A. Hodge, *Outlines of Theology* pp. 580f; Shedd, *Punishment* p. 131, note 1; E. B. Pusey, *What Is of Faith?* pp. 9f. Pusey here even says that 'we cannot tell how far the exposure of infants may be a sin in China . . . or cannibalism in a nation of cannibals.'
Conditionalists: Constable, *Punishment* pp. 1f; Froom, *Conditionalist Faith* 1:496.

Neither Mark nor Luke adds to our picture of final punishment, though each gives his own special admonition or warning.

Matthew 25:41, 46

The sayings in these two verses, concluding the parable of the Sheep and the Goats, are perhaps the most famous of all Jesus' words concerning final punishment. The parable itself closes a series of crisis parables in which Jesus exhorts the disciples to keep their eyes open and their hands busy in view of his future glorious coming.[75] The three parables are a challenging conclusion to the fifth and last discourse in Matthew's carefully-worked arrangement of material.[76] In each of these Jesus' teaching climaxes with a story or saying concerning the stakes of discipleship, so that (in Matthew at least) we may say Jesus' teaching always brings us to this same point regardless of where it starts.

The parable has been interpreted many ways. Dispensationalists see here a judgment of individual Gentiles who are alive at Christ's second coming, based on their treatment of Jews during the great tribulation just ended.[77] Most exegetes, however, probably agree with Jeremias and Hunter that it speaks of the great judgment at the end of the world,[78] although they disagree on the identity of 'the least of these brothers,' whose treatment becomes the standard of judgment.[79]

J. A. T. Robinson has defended the parable's authenticity; Theo Preiss has beautifully shown its poetic structure.[80] Perhaps 'the most sombre and haunting' of all Christ's parables, this one has as its burden 'doomsday and eternal separation'.[81] The gathering of God's scattered flock is a familiar feature of the Messianic age (Isa. 40:11; Ezek. 34:11–31; John 10:1–16; 11:52). In Ezekiel 34:17 God promises to 'judge ... between rams and goats'. According to Dalman, flocks in Palestine were often mixed. Shepherds separated sheep from goats each night, the goats requiring protection from the cold, the sheep preferring open air.[82] This is the setting of Jesus' story, which is incidental to the contrasting judgments.

---

75. They are The Ten Virgins (Matt. 25:1–13), The Talents (Matt. 25:14–30) and this one. For a lively, practical discussion of their different emphases, see Eller, *Most Revealing* pp. 11–14, esp. p. 18.

76. Besides an introduction (ch. 1–4) and an epilogue (ch. 28), Matthew presents his material in five units, each consisting of a discourse by Jesus followed by a section of narrative. Each discourse is followed by a similar formula. e.g. : 'When Jesus had finished saying these things ... ' (Matt. 7:28; 11:1; 13:53; 19:1; 26:1).

77. *Scofield.*

78. Jeremias, *Parables* pp. 206ff; A.M. Hunter, *The Parables Then and Now* pp. 115ff.

79. Davies, *Sermon on the Mount* pp. 98f argues that they are Christ's disciples among the nations. Hunter and Jeremias see them as simply the needy, whether disciples or not (*op. cit*). The context seems to support Davies, as does the use of 'brothers' throughout Matthew; Hunter's and Jeremias' point is made in the Parable of the Good Samaritan, though without a specific judgment scene.

80. Both cited in A.M. Hunter, *Interpreting the Parables*; Robinson on p. 118, Preiss on pp. 88f.

81. Hunter, *The Parables Then and Now* p. 115.

82. G. Dalman, *Arbeit und Sitte in Palastina* (Gutersloh, 1939) 6:99; reference in Jeremias, *Parables* p. 206.

Those on the right hand are told to 'take your inheritance, the kingdom prepared for you since the creation of the world' (v. 34). Jesus' first discourse in Matthew refers to some who receive the kingdom (Matt. 5:3), and now so does his last. In Matt. 5 they are the 'poor in spirit'; here they are those who have been generous to the needy.

To those on the left hand the Son of Man says: 'Depart from me, you who are cursed, into the eternal fire prepared for the devil and his angels' (v. 41). Again Jesus speaks of banishment and the 'eternal fire.' We have examined both figures already. Here the point lies in the contrast. Sheep and goats alike are sent to an appropriate destiny. In each case it has been 'prepared' (see p. 112f for a discussion of Matt. 18:8,9); in each case it is described as 'eternal'. That the language flows along parallel channels highlights the split into opposite directions looming just ahead.

Cursed

To be 'cursed' by God is a disaster but the word itself says nothing of what this involves. The word used is the common word for human curses, as opposed to blessings, both in its verb form (Ps. 62:4; Matt. 5:44; Rom. 12:14; James 3:9) and as a noun (Judges. 9:57). Sometimes it describes one who has died a horrible death or has been executed: a hanged corpse (Deut. 21:22f.), Jezebel (2 Kings 9:34) or the exterminated Canaanites (Wisd. 12:11; cf. Sir. 41:9).The noun is used a few times in connection with fire. Worthless land is 'cursed' and burned (Heb. 6:8); Jotham's curse is fulfilled when a tower of people are burned to death (Judg. 9:57). When Jesus cursed the fig tree, it withered and died (Mark 11:21).

Throughout the Bible sin carries a curse. There is a curse on the ground after the first sin (Gen. 3:17), and through the law when broken (Gal. 3:10, 13), and always in connection with God's covenant (Deut. 11:26; 30:1; Mal. 2:2). In the case of the covenant it is once said to be death (Deut. 30:19), the fate that befell Jesus when he became a 'curse' for us (Gal. 3:10,13). Seductive amoral teachers will be cursed, according to 2 Peter 2:14; the context describes their fate as destruction and perishing (v. 12) or as 'blackest darkness' (v. 17).

Eternal fire

Here the curse is banishment into the eternal fire. Prepared for the devil and his angels, it is also the fire of the Age to Come. It is difficult to avoid the qualitative force of 'eternal' in this passage – though applied in the starkest contrast imaginable and though its quantitative meaning is not denied.[83] We may fear human wrath or covet human blessing. Compared to the issues of God's great judgment, both become mere specks on the horizon.

Bligh claims the parable's flavour is that of contemporary Judaism, and argues that 'only the original twists – that which jars with the perspective of His contemporary patriots' – are unique to Jesus. He cites other cases where Jesus quotes his opponents' own words against them and uses their

---

83. See previous discussion of this word in chapter 2 on the adjective 'eternal'.

rhetoric to ridicule them. They could have agreed wholeheartedly with every detail of this parable except two – who goes each direction and why. These things alone, according to Bligh, are the points Jesus wishes to make.[84] We can appreciate his reasoning and agree that those are the chief emphases, but are happy to follow Jesus' words.

We have already seen how the New Testament uses the adjective *aiōnios* of the result of processes and acts (Heb. 5:9; 6:2; 9:12). The entire Old Testament and the teaching of Jesus suggest we understand it thus here. Whatever *aiōnios* means, one should have good cause for not translating it the same way when it appears twice in one verse! The KJV translators betrayed theological bias by translating 'everlasting' punishment but 'eternal' life, 'a purely wanton and arbitrary variation'.[85]

Neither the fire nor the punishment is of this age, in origin or in quality. When the wicked have perished, it will be for ever – their destruction and punishment is unending as well as qualitatively different from anything we now know. The fire is also 'eternal' in this sense, just as Sodom was destroyed by 'eternal fire' since its results were to last for ever (Jude 7). The life is also 'eternal' in quality as well as quantity. Because both ideas fit the case so that we cannot choose one to the exclusion of the other, and because both 'eternal' and 'everlasting' tend to do this very thing, we repeat without embarrassment our earlier (unoriginal) invitation for a new English adjective – perhaps a neutral transliteration such as 'aionic' or 'aionian'.[86]

We must be careful in pressing the parallel between 'eternal' life and 'eternal' punishment that we do not fall into any spirit of vindictiveness at the fate of the wicked. Since Augustine, traditionalists have argued that unless 'eternal punishment' means endless torment, we have no assurance that 'eternal life' secures our endless joy. Many have cautioned against taking delight in the fate of the lost, a sure sign that some have done just that.

Regardless of his other weaknesses, F. W. Farrar deserves to be heard every time the parallel is drawn. 'Our sure and certain hope of everlasting happiness rests on no such miserable foundation as the disputed meaning of a Greek adjective which is used over and over again of things transitory', he begins. 'If we need texts on which to rest it we may find plenty' (Isa. 25:6ff; Hos. 13:14; Luke 20:36; 1 Cor. 15; 2 Tim. 1:10; 1 Pet. 1:4; 5:4; Rev. 21:4). Furthermore, he argues, the meaning of this

---

84. P. H. Bligh, 'Eternal Fire, Eternal Punishment, Eternal Life (Mt 25:41, 46),' *ET* 83, no. 1 (Oct. 1971) pp. 9ff. Bligh cites as other examples Matt. 22:41–46; Luke 5:32; 18:11f.; John 10:34f.

85. Farrar, *Eternal Hope* p. 198. The NIV corrects this inconsistency in Matt. 25 but lapses into it in 2 Thess. 1:9. Harmon's argument ('Case' p. 212, n.57) that 'eternal' must refer to the *result* of 'life' and of 'punishment' alike overlooks the difference between an ordinary noun ('life') and a noun formed from a verb involving process ('punishment'). Dixon denies that 'eternal' refers to results in this passage but gives no basis for his denial (*Other Side* p. 91). Blanchard discounts this explanation as well, not because the evidence for it is faulty but because he cannot explain certain other passages if it is correct (*Hell* p. 226).

86. In my article, 'Putting Hell in Its Place,' *CT* 6 Aug. 1976, pp. 14–17. The suggestion has been made for centuries by men whose shoes I am unworthy to untie.

same adjective *aiōnios* may be altered by the word it modifies, even in the same verse, citing as examples Habakkuk 3:6 and Romans 16:25f.

But Farrar was also a great preacher, and his soberest words are directed to any who ask how they can be confident of everlasting happiness unless they know the damned will suffer without end. This question Farrar regarded as wicked and selfish, and his response exploded from the heart:

> I call God to witness that so far from regretting the possible loss of some billions of aeons of bliss by attaching to the word *aiōnios* a sense in which scores of times it is undeniably found, I would here, and now, and kneeling on my knees, ask Him that I might die as the beasts that perish, and for ever cease to be, rather than that my worst enemy should, for one single year, endure the hell described by Tertullian, or Minucius Felix, or Jonathan Edwards, or Dr. Pusey, or Mr. Furniss, or Mr. Moody, or Mr. Spurgeon.[87]

We do not follow Farrar's interpretation of 'eternal', but we acknowledge his unselfish spirit, which rates a place alongside Moses (Exod. 32:32) and Paul (Rom. 9:3) in a charity that can only be described as like that of Jesus Christ, who is God himself (John 3:16; Gal. 2:20).

Punishment

The 'goats' go away into everlasting punishment (*kolasis*). The meaning of the word is disputed.

What is *kolasis* here is *timōria* in Hebrews 10:29. Synonyms by nature are agreeably interchangeable, but they reserve the right at times to stand on their own feet and have their individual say! Moulton-Milligan[88] say that the original sense of the word, seems to have been 'cut short', with 'prune' or 'cutting down' a derived but familiar meaning in the time of Jesus. The only other New Testament occurrence of *kolasis* (1 John 4:18) fits this definition, they say, for fear 'checks development,' and in that sense it has to do with punishment (NIV). Moulton-Milligan here see 'the idea of "deprivation," a kind of *poena damni*'.

The Septuagint puts *kolasis* for *mikshol*, which means a stumbling-block that leads to ruin. The word Jesus uses is applied to the plagues of the Egyptians (Wisd. of Sol. 11:13; 16:2,24) and to their death in the Red Sea (Wisd. 19:4). It refers to punishment by death in 1 Samuel 25:31 and Ezekiel 21:15. 'Punishment' may certainly include conscious pain, as in all the examples above, but it does not have to. The same word is applied to an idol of wood or stone in Wisdom 4:10 : '. . . that which was made [idol] shall be punished together with him that made it'.

It is interesting to compare Jesus' statement of contrasting fates here with the one he gives in John 5:29, and both of those with Daniel's (Dan. 12:2). This is what we find:

Matthew   go away to eternal life   go away to eternal punishment;

John   rise to live   rise to be condemned;

---

87. Farrar, *Eternal Hope* pp. 197–202; quotation on p. 202.
88. *Vocabulary* p. 352.

Daniel awake to everlasting life awake to shame and everlasting contempt.

What is said of the righteous is in each case the same. They rise/go to everlasting (eternal) life. On the basis of the comparison, the 'condemnation' of 'shame and everlasting contempt' is the same as the 'eternal punishment' awaiting the wicked. If we may take Isaiah 66:24 as a further inspired description of the 'contempt' mentioned in Daniel, the picture clearly involves the total destruction by fire and worms of corpses the Lord has slain. It is an 'everlasting' contempt because the state is irreversible. Because it is God's judgment against sin, it is not mere happenstance but an everlasting 'punishment'.[89]

Traditionalists sometimes object that irreversible (therefore endless) extinction is actually no 'punishment' at all. Yet throughout human history people have willingly chosen the severest tortures, life imprisonment, or exile into intolerable circumstances and total isolation rather than lose their expected years of life. A. W. Pink argues for conscious torment, but he makes the conditionalist point when explaining why 'second death' is a symbol of hell. 'To the normal man death is the object he fears above all others,' he writes. 'It is that from which he naturally shrinks. It is that which he most dreads.'[90] Salmond, defending the traditional view, acknowledges this innate dread of non-existence, even among primitive peoples.

> 'The idea of annihilation,' says Plutarch, 'was intolerable to the Greek mind. If they had no choice left them between entire extinction and an eternity of torment in Hades, they would have chosen the latter; almost all, men and women both, would have surrendered themselves to the teeth of Cerberus, or the buckets of the Danaidae, rather than to nonentity.'[91]

T. H. Huxley is reported to have said he would prefer the traditionalist's hell to annihilation, as did Milton's Belial in *Paradise Lost*.[92]

Augustine made the same point in *The City of God*. 'Where a very serious crime is punished by death and the execution of the sentence takes only a minute, no laws consider that minute as the measure of the punishment, but rather the fact that the criminal is for ever removed from the community of the living' (pp. 369–370, *Fathers of the Church*, 1954).

On this basis we regard a 20-year prison sentence to be greater than a 10-year sentence, a 50-year sentence worse than one for 20, and life imprisonment greater than these all. Yet, as Constable pointed out,

> From the earliest records of our race capital punishment has been reckoned as not only the greatest but also the most lasting of all punishments; and it is only reckoned the greatest because it is the most lasting. A flogging, inflicted on a

---

89. The Bible emphasizes in many places that man's final destiny will be pronounced by the sovereign God, whether good or bad. See Ps. 62:12; Prov. 24:12; Rom. 2:6; 2 Cor. 5:10; Eph. 6:8; Col. 3:25; Rev. 2:23; 20:12; 22:11f.
90. *Eternal Punishment* p. 22.
91. *Immortality* pp. 608f. Although Salmond offers the data as evidence against extinction, his argument appears to backfire.
92. According to T. F. Glasson, 'Human Destiny: Has Christian Teaching Changed?' *Modern Churchman* 12, no. 4 (July 1969) p. 294.

petty thief, inflicts more actual pain than decapitation or hanging inflicts upon a murderer. Why then is it greater and more lasting? Because it has deprived the sufferer of every hour of that life which but for it he would have had. *Its duration is supposed co-existent with the period of his natural life.*[93]

Indeed, 'to cease to be is the final tragedy which can befall a living soul who is able to receive the gift of eternal life.'[94]

Some insist that 'annihilation is an extremely abstract idea, too philosophical, in fact, to find a natural place within the limits of the realistic biblical eschatology.'[95] Most conditionalists have steered away from the term for that very reason, preferring such biblical verbs as 'die,' 'destroy' or 'perish'. But if it is objected that laws of thermodynamics do not allow anything to be truly destroyed, we will do well to consider that the same laws say nothing is truly created either. We are in a different realm from the inductive physicists. The God of the Bible is a God who calls into being things which do not exist, who gives life to the dead, and who is 'able to destroy both body and soul in hell'!

Jonathan Edwards, too, concedes this point. In a chapter entitled 'Concerning the Endless Punishment of Those Who Die Impenitent,' Edwards writes approximately 15,000 words opposing various ideas of restoration or universal salvation. Apart from a two-sentence denial of annihilation in his opening paragraph, he mentions it only once. In a lengthy paragraph (#31) Edwards responds to the idea that the wicked will suffer penal pains according to the precise measure of divine justice, then will be exterminated.

'On this,' he writes, 'I would observe that there is nothing got by such a scheme; no relief from the arguments taken from Scripture, for the proper eternity of future punishment.' In other words, sinners can find no comfort in this understanding of hell, for it is as properly eternal and scripturally horrible as the common view of unending conscious torment!'[96] He is arguing *ad hominem* in response to those who insisted on a very lengthy period of pain which would be followed by extinction. He is not agreeing to the view we present. Yet he raises no scriptural objection to eternal extinction – only that 'the supposition of the length of their torments [before death] is brought in without any necessity'.[97]

Froom repeats A. Holmes Forbes's statement (in *The Last Enemy*, p. 69) that C. H. Spurgeon also said in later life: 'I have no quarrel with the Conditional Immortality doctrine.'[98] Froom also relates a personal conversation with W. Graham Scroggie, a well-known devotional speaker and pastor for seven years of Spurgeon's Metropolitan Tabernacle in London, when Scroggie gave him explicit permission to quote him as a believer in conditionalism.[99]

93. Ibid. p. 12.
94. Strawson, *Future Life* p. 155.
95. Geerhardus Vos, *The Pauline Eschatology* p. 294.
96. Jonathan Edwards, *Works* 2:515–525; quotation on p. 524.
97. Ibid. p. 524.
98. *Conditionalist Faith* 2:797.
99. Ibid. pp. 910f. Froom says the meeting took place on Dec. 22, 1957. He reports that Scroggie sat up in his sickbed, grasped Froom's hand and said, 'Brother Froom, I believe that God has raised you up for this great task. I am praying for you every day. You

A contemporary evangelical author says he can 'strike hands in a momentary bargain' with the idea of eternal extinction if it can 'be held in balance with seemingly contrary teachings' such as unquenchable fire, undying worm, and wailing and gnashing of teeth.[100] And John Wenham insists that 'the possibility that the lost will eventually pass out of existence, needs much more serious attention'.[101] He concludes his chapter on hell with a call for just such open-minded study of this alternative, saying, 'We shall consider ourselves under no obligation to defend the notion of unending torment, until the arguments of the conditionalists have been refuted.'[102]

Conclusion

In this parable Jesus teaches an end-time judgment which divides humankind into two categories and sentences them to corresponding but opposite dooms. In this apocalyptic picture the wicked are banished into eschatological fire prepared for the satanic angels. There they will eventually be destroyed for ever, both body and soul, as the divine penalty for sin. The process may well involve a period of conscious pain involving body and soul, but the 'eternal punishment' itself is the capital execution, the everlasting loss of existence, the everlasting loss of the eternal life of joy and blessing in company with God and the redeemed. Jude but repeats the Master's thought here when he gives Sodom and Gomorrah as the prototype of those 'who suffer the punishment of eternal fire' (Jude 7), as does Peter in saying that God 'made them an example of what is going to happen to the ungodly' by 'burning them to ashes' (2 Pet. 2:6).

Matthew 26:24

As Jesus' last evening meal with his disciples draws to a close, he predicts that one of them will betray him. They protest, but Jesus insists:

> The Son of Man will go just as it is written about him. But woe to that man who betrays the Son of Man! It would be better for him if he had not been born.

The saying appears in Matthew 26:24 and Mark 14:21. Instead of scriptural prediction, Luke points to divine foreordination and he stops short of the final sentence (Luke 22:22).

Supporters of conscious unending torment often cite this saying of Jesus as if only such suffering is a condition worse than never having been born. Jesus does not say, however, that this is a fate worse than death, but a fate worse than non-birth. The idea occurs also in a parable in the pseudepigraphical 1 (Ethiopic) Enoch. There it is said of sinners in

---

may quote me whenever and wherever you please as being a believer in Conditionalism.' Froom clearly intends to present Scroggie as holding to the final extinction of the wicked.
  100. Calvin D. Linton, 'The Sorrows of Hell,' *CT* 16 (19 Nov. 1971) p. 13.
  101. *Goodness* p. 34.
  102. Ibid. pp. 40f.

126   *The Fire That Consumes*

judgment, 'It had been good for them if they had not been born' (1 En. 38:2). In the verses following, the sinners are destroyed: 'the kings and the mighty perish . . . and . . . none . . . seek . . . mercy . . . for their life is at an end' (vv. 5, 6). Is it not far worse to lose a cherished possession than never to have known it? Who is happier – the man born with empty eye-sockets who never sees the sun, or the man whose sight is suddenly cut off in the middle of a busy life? Do we not regard the death of the young as specially tragic simply because of the expected years they lost?

Job, too, wishes he had never been born (Job 3). In his case the desire is prompted by severe and painful suffering. The language can therefore fit either view of final punishment, but it demands neither.

Luke 16:19–31

As Jesus taught on stewardship and covetousness, 'the Pharisees . . . were sneering at him'. Jesus' reply culminated with this parable. A close comparison of the parable to its immediate context reveals so many parallels that one marvels at the intricate connection. Yet many advocates of eternal conscious torment write as though the story had no context at all, as if its primary point were to be found elsewhere. Thus Buis says: 'This parable so clearly teaches the orthodox doctrine of eternal punishment that the opponents of the doctrine are hard pressed to know what to do with it.'[103]

The plot of the parable, the reversal of earthly fortunes after death, was familiar in popular Palestinian stories of Jesus' time. Gressmann cites a Greek parallel from a first-century Egyptian papyrus and he says there are at least seven versions of the story in Jewish literature.[104] There are

---

103. *Eternal Punishment* p. 39. However, Geldenhuys concludes that Jesus 'related this parable not in order to satisfy our curiosity about life after death but to emphasize vividly the tremendous seriousness of life on this side of the grave.' The story is therefore 'a parable and not . . . a real occurrence from which various questions in connection with the hereafter may be answered' (*Luke*, NICNT pp. 427; 429, note 10; see also notes 5,6, 7,12).

Dixon devotes over half of his discussion of Jesus' teaching to this parable, stretching hermeneutical limits to find here the post-judgment destiny of the lost (*Other Side* pp. 130–144). Even taken literally (no one really does) and out of context, this story offers no hint of how long the Rich Man's suffering will last, but portrays at most the intermediate state of a pre-Christian Jew. Blanchard summarizes the parable's two primary points more modestly: 'the eternal destinies of the righteous and unrighteous are vastly different, and their destinies are settled while they are here on earth' (*Hell* p. 39). Morey acknowledges that Jesus borrowed this story from a common rabbinical tale of the time and that it should not be pressed into a literal preview of the world to come (*Afterlife* pp. 30f, 84f).

104. See K. Hanhart, *Intermediate State in the New Testament* pp. 192f., who also refers to R. Bultmann, *Geschichte der synoptischen Tradition* [*History of the synoptic tradition*] (1931), pp. 212f, 221f; in Reichenbach, *Phoenix* p. 184. For a summary of the tales, Reichenbach refers also to H. M. Creed, *Luke* pp. 208ff. Some protest the label 'parable,' arguing that since Jesus began, 'There was a certain rich man,' what follows must be history and not parable. This argument falls, however, in the light of other parables in Luke's Gospel which began with similar or identical statements (Luke 12:16; 13:6; 14:16; 15:11; 16:1; 18:1f; 18:9, 10; 19:11f; 20:9). Blanchard acknowledges that this story is a parable (*Hell* pp. 38f.)

differences between these stories and Jesus', of course, and therein lies the Lord's uniqueness. But the basic plot was well-known folklore.

Froom cites a discourse of Josephus concerning Hades which paints almost precisely the same picture found in Luke. He concludes that 'Jesus was clearly using a then-common tradition of the Jews to press home a moral lesson in a related field.'[105] (Although the Whiston edition of Josephus offers a lengthy defence of the treatise's authenticity on internal and external grounds,[106] most scholars today regard it as spurious, as conditionalists Edward White and Henry Constable both note.)[107]

Traditionalists generally begin their interpretation of the parable with the word 'Hades,' which they ordinarily regard as the place of punishment entered by the lost at death, to be changed at the last judgment only in intensity and permanence. This understanding became prominent in the Middle Ages and it was mediated into Protestantism largely through the influence of Calvin (see earlier chapters on immortality and the fathers). It stresses the pagan Greek background of 'Hades' but fails to appreciate sufficiently the biblical usage of the term in either Old or New Testament.

Hades

In Greek mythology Hades was the god of the underworld, then the name of the nether world itself. Charon ferried the souls of the dead across the rivers Styx or Acheron into this abode, where the watchdog Cerberus guarded the gate so none might escape. The pagan myth contained all the elements for medieval eschatology: there was the pleasant Elysium, the gloomy and miserable Tartarus, and even the Plains of Asphodel, where ghosts could wander who were suited for neither of the above. Ruling beside the god was his queen Proserpine (or Persephone), whom he had raped from the world above.[108]

The word *hades* came into biblical usage when the Septuagint translators chose it to represent the Hebrew *sheol*, a vastly different concept. *Sheol* too received all the dead (see pp. 41–46 above), but the Old Testament mentions no specific division there for punishment or reward. Intertestamental Judaism held at least two opinions on Hades. Those who expected a partial resurrection (of the righteous only) saw Hades as everlasting (for the wicked); those who looked for a general resurrection naturally thought of it as temporary.[109] Rabbinic opinion was so varied, and the terminology in such a state of flux, that both *hades* and *gehenna* are sometimes the abode of the dead, sometimes the place of final punishment, sometimes interchangeable, sometimes distinct. Modern scholars also disagree on the terms. Jeremias sees a sharp distinction between the two words in the New Testament,[110] while Hanhart argues

---

105. Froom, *Conditionalist Faith* 1:252–256. The complete text is on pp 637f of Whiston's Josephus.
106. Whiston, Josephus, pp. 708–715.
107. White, *Life in Christ* p. 183; Constable, *Punishment* pp. 46f.
108. Arndt and Gingrich, *Lexicon* p. 16; E. Royston Pike, *Encyclopaedia of Religion and Religions* p. 170.
109. J. Jeremias, 'Hades' *TDNT* 1:147–148.
110. Ibid.

that the New Testament usage of *hades* does not go beyond the Old Testament meaning of *sheol*.[111]

In all the confusion, we can best achieve certainty by looking at specific texts. Jesus' statement that Capernaum will go down to Hades (Matt. 11:23; Luke 10:15) needs no pagan background; it finds ample precedent in both Isaiah (Isa. 14:10–15) and Ezekiel (Ezek. 32:17–32). 'Sheol is the great leveller.'[112] The Lord's confidence that the 'gates of Hades' will not prevail against his church (Matt. 16:18)[113] is illuminated by other Jewish literature using the same expression, usually as a synonym for death itself (Job 38:17; Isa. 38:18; cf. 3 Macc. 5:51; Wisd. of Sol. 16:13).[114]

Sheol's gates are no longer one-way, its fortress no longer is impregnable, for Jesus has come in the power of God's kingdom. He will destroy death's hold if he has to carry off the gates like Samson! In quoting Hosea 13:14, Paul substitutes 'death' for 'Hades/Sheol' (1 Cor. 15:55), indicating the close relationship between the two. Jesus went to 'Hades' like all the dead, but unlike the rest he broke out in victory (Acts 2:27, 31). He now holds the keys to 'death and Hades' (Rev. 1:18), which, when he comes again to judge, will both yield their dead, before being cast into the 'lake of fire' (Rev. 20:13ff). It is in keeping with the historical nature of biblical religion that the New Testament speaks thus of Hades – not theoretically or systematically, but in terms of what has really happened in the case of Jesus Christ. We should not build a whole doctrine, therefore, on a single use of a word, even if it were elsewhere than in a parable on a different subject!

Context

The parable's interpretation must include its context[115] and nothing in the context remotely suggests concern with the final state of the wicked[116]. Jesus clearly intends to teach other lessons. He has been preaching on covetousness and stewardship (Luke 16:1–13); the rich man's only implied sin is his selfish neglect of Lazarus.[117] When the Pharisees[118] sneer at Jesus' teaching, he warns them against self-justification,

---

111. Hanhart, *Intermediate State* pp. 32, 35.

112. Strawson, *Future Life* p. 138.

113. That Jesus is referring to the church (*ekklēsia*) rather than his promise to build it is seen in his use of the feminine pronoun ('will not prevail against her'). The other fact is implied in this one.

114. The possible exception is Pss. Sol. 16:1f, which associates the 'gates of hades' with sinners. Even there, however, the phrase denotes death.

115. Hanhart notes several studies involving the context. Two which link the parable to all sections of the chapter are by J. D. M. Derrett, in *NTS* 7, no. 3, pp. 198ff; 7, no. 4, pp. 364ff (Hanhart, *Intermediate State* pp. 191f.).

116. Hanhart disagrees, claiming that 'most recent commentators' hold the opposite view to that here stated (Hanhart, *Intermediate State* pp. 190f., 198).

117. Hanhart disagrees again. He argues that the rich man's distinction was not his character but his wealth. 'While the sinner must seek this righteousness, the oppressed have it already' (Ibid. pp. 195ff.).

118. For some reason, many modern commentators pass over the context entirely and say the parable was directed to the Sadducees. I cannot set aside the biblical text on the basis of critical methodology.

reminding them that God knows their hearts and that what men highly value God often detests (vv. 14f). The rich man and Lazarus provide perfect illustrations of this truth: the parable twice contrasts them, showing first human estimation and then God's (vv. 19, 25). Perhaps the most important point is that the Pharisees are wasting every opportunity to hear and obey God, though they live in the most critical of times (vv. 16f). This was the rich man's mistake, and his brothers continue to make it after his death.[119] It is also the only conclusion Jesus specifically draws in the 'punch line' that ends the story (v. 31). (The saying about divorce in verse 18 seems totally out of place regardless of the parable's interpretation, but even that may reflect an Old Testament arrangement of material. In Deuteronomy 23:19–24:22 Moses also discusses selfishness, then divorce, then concern for the poor.)

Jeremias classes the parable with three others he calls 'double-edged' (Matt. 22:1–14; 20:1–16; Luke 15:11–32). In each Jesus begins with a story familiar to his hearers. Having thus gained an interested hearing, he adds an 'epilogue' containing his real message. The stress falls on the second point – in this case the plight of the five living brothers who are ignoring the Word of God. The parable should not be called The Rich Man and Lazarus, says Jeremias, but The Six Brothers.[120]

Hunter discerns the same emphasis, and summarizes Jesus' message thus: 'If a man cannot be humane with the Old Testament in his hand and Lazarus on his doorstep, nothing – neither a visitant from the other world nor a revelation of the horrors of Hell – will teach him otherwise.'[121] In the event, the Pharisees prove Jesus right. Having ignored Moses and the prophets, when the apostles confront them with a risen Jesus, they ignore that message as well.

This, then, is Jesus' stated message. These are the points, raised already in his context and illustrated by his parable. Conditions after death are a vehicle for the story, and they involve language familiar to Jesus' hearers – language drawn, not from the divine revelation of the Old Testament, but from intertestamental and first-century folklore. Even if that language were thought to teach something of punishment after death, the story antedates the final judgment since others are still living on the earth, even before the gospel becomes a reality and people turn from Moses and the prophets to hear Jesus. Luke 16 supplies no clear exegetical basis for any conclusions concerning the final end of the wicked.

John 3:16

In this verse 'eternal life' contrasts with 'perish'. God's love in the gift of his Son guarantees true believers the first; the passage says absolutely nothing to illuminate the second. 'Perish' is a common descriptive verb for

---

119. Vv. 27ff. Even if the parable intends to teach about post-mortem concerns (which the context nowhere indicates), this point alone would identify the scene as contemporary with ongoing earth life.
120. Jeremias, p. 186.
121. Hunter, *Interpreting the Parables* p. 84.

the fate of the wicked throughout the Bible. Taken at face value, it agrees with all the biblical material we have seen.

John 3:36

Again 'eternal life' stands as an alternative, this time to 'God's wrath remaining.' The realized aspect of both is emphasized. 'Already' eternal life is here for the believer; 'already' God's wrath rests (and continues to rest) on one who rejects the Son of God, who is Life. The statement recalls Deuteronomy 29:20, where the covenant curses not only come ('fall,' NIV) on the high-handed rebel, but 'rest' (NASB) on him as well. The text literally says the curses 'lie down' on him, evoking an image of a beast of prey. So long as one rejects Jesus, God's wrath 'remains', for nothing else can turn it away.

John 5:28f.

This passage was briefly considered at Matthew 25:46. The words recall Daniel 12:2. Jesus says 'a time is coming when all who are in their graves will hear his voice and come out – those who have done good will rise to live, and those who have done evil will rise to be condemned.'

'Condemnation' is a judicial verdict; it implies nothing about the sentence or its execution. Again the emphasis is on the 'already' – what will happen then is determined by the response to Jesus now (vv. 21–27).

The Sadducees denied any resurrection, but it was the strong hope of the Pharisees and many in Israel.[122] Even so, F. F. Bruce warns against assuming too much uniformity in Jewish belief at the time.[123] Regardless of the popular expectation, we rest here on the word of the Son of God. Since Jesus is speaking, we must hear what he says and stop where he stops.

Summary and conclusion

When considering the subject of final punishment, traditionalists have often ignored the Old Testament, oversimplified the intertestamental material, and read the New Testament in the light of that misunderstanding. They have been strong in defence of biblical authority but weak in using the Bible. Conditionalists have walked through the Old Testament, picking up nuggets, but they have shown little interest in mining deeper. Usually they look long enough to gather evidence favouring their beliefs without going into more detail. A truly 'biblical' view must include both Old and New Testament witnesses, noting the distinctive teaching of each as well as the areas of repetition. Ebeling offers this challenge to biblical theologians in general:

---

122. Acts 23:6; 24:20f; 26:6f; 28:20. Robert J. Kepple, 'The Hope of Israel, the Resurrection of the Dead, and Jesus: A Study of Their Relationship in Acts with particular Regard to the Understanding of Paul's Trial Defense,' *JETS* 20, no. 3 (Sep. 1977) pp. 231–242.
123. *Paul* pp. 300f.

In 'biblical theology' the theologian who devotes himself specially to studying the connexion of the Old and New Testaments must give account of his understanding of the Bible as a whole, that is, above all of the theological problems that arise from the variety of the biblical witness considered in relation to its inner unity .... But, be it noted, this 'biblical theology' would not be an independent substitute for dogmatics and would hardly correspond to the pietist ideal of a simple theology, but would be a task for historical theology of uncommon complexity.[124]

Gerhard Hasel summarizes the relationship between Old Testament and New like this:

The NT completes the OT's incompleteness and yet moves beyond to the final *eschaton*. From the OT to the NT and beyond there is one continuous movement in the direction of the *eschaton*, the coming of the Day of the Lord ... On this pilgrimage there are many stops, many initial fulfillments, but each one of them becomes a point of departure again until all promises will finally be fulfilled at the end of time.[125]

Hasel calls for a 'multiplex approach' which recognizes 'similarity and dissimilarity, old and new, continuity and discontinuity, etc., without in the least distorting the original historical witness and literal sense nor falling short in the larger kerygmatic intention and context to which the OT itself testifies and which the NT assumes.'[126]

In examining Jesus' own teaching on final punishment, we have found it in every point agreeable to the Old Testament witness and limited in its major figures to teaching found there. Rather than absorbing the fanciful details of intertestamental apocalyptic, Jesus borrowed some of its language when this might assist communication, but he expressed ideas found in the prophets and illustrated by Old Testament examples of divine judgment.

Strawson compares Jesus' teaching on hell with that of his contemporaries.[127] There is no suggestion that the righteous will gloat over the wicked. Jesus gives no idea that the delights of heaven are increased by contrast with the torments of hell. There is no levity in Jesus' teaching on this subject. Rather, what he says about Gehenna reinforces his appeal for personal self-discipline and obedience. Jesus never talks about the danger of hell to people other than his listeners – his teaching always warns 'you,' whether disciple, Pharisee or scribe. There is no dwelling on torture, no stirring up nationalist feelings against the Romans, no mention of foreigners being consigned to hell. Contemporary Jewish literature illustrates exceptions at every point.

G. C. Berkouwer, the great contemporary Reformed theologian, is concerned that we take Christ's warnings with the utmost seriousness and always in the light of the gospel.

124. Gerhard Ebeling, 'The Meaning of 'Biblical Theology,'" *JTS*, New Series 6, no. 2 (Oct. 1955) pp. 224f.
125. Gerhard F. Hasel, *New Testament Theology: Basic Issues in the Current Debate* p. 196.
126. Ibid. p. 198.
127. *Future Life* pp. 147–150.

> The proclamation of salvation is a witness of profound seriousness. The New Testament constantly presents an apparent ultimatum that is inextricably connected with this proclamation. . . . The Word speaks of being cast away and rejected, of curse and judgment. The proclamation of the gospel contains a warning against unbelief, and the way of unbelief is portrayed as the way of outermost darkness and lostness and the severance of all relationships. In a variety of images and concepts, the Gospels warn against the possibility of a 'definitive destruction'. Such warnings are not meant to orient us to the *eschaton*, but continually to confront us with an admonition to open our eyes to the light and see the salvation, not to harden our hearts (cf. Heb. 3).[128]

People often fail to appreciate the seriousness of Christ's warnings, he continues, because they do not view them under the light of the salvation Christ offers first.

> It is in the context of that gospel that the subject of the outer darkness arises . . . All such threats are not arranged symmetrically beside the gospel, but proceed from it and can be understood only in its light. The outer darkness is contrasted to the brilliant light; the gospel's saving disturbance penetrates the religious terrain where everyone presumes to be safe and secure . . . On the one side the gospel proclaims the Kingdom, the wedding feast, the light, the opened door; on the opposite side darkness, desertion, the flames of the unquenchable fire (Mark 9:43,48). The relationship of this to the gospel accentuates and illuminates the seriousness of these warnings.[129]

Failure to guard this relationship can result in the complete distortion of the biblical perspective on final punishment. Berkouwer explains how this has often happened.

> In the course of time, the word 'hell,' as translation of the Greek *geénna*, was divorced from the relationships in which it is invariably found in Scripture, and came to be treated by many as a ruthless threat, an expression of extreme harshness, in which all feelings of compassion had perished. When this happened, the critical relationship in the New Testament between 'Gehenna' and the invitation, love, and covenant of God was lost . . . People speak of 'heaven' and 'hell' as if they were objective magnitudes like any other thing, situation, or place. Who knows how much damage is done, for example, in the life of a young child who is subjected to moralistic preaching of 'hell' as the final outcome of 'sin' without the light of the joy of the gospel? 'Hell' can easily assume a magical, terrifying dimension that speaks only of the incalculable, all-consuming wrath of God, and says nothing of His love . . . It is not difficult to understand why the word 'hell' has come to be associated only with cruelty and hatred if it is proclaimed without regard for the preaching of the only way out.[130]

Not only does such preaching miss the mark of the biblical witness; it is finally ineffective in motivating the hearers. Berkouwer describes how that happens:

128. G. C. Berkouwer, *Return of Christ* p. 413.
129. Berkouwer, *Return of Christ* pp. 414f..
130. Ibid. p. 416.

As a result, every treatment of 'hell' as an independent topic lacks genuine seriousness. It may assume the appearance of earnestness, but such seriousness is not of the biblical kind, which talks about the beauty 'of the feet of those who preach good news' (Rom. 10:15). This seriousness is not something that can be analyzed on psychological or anthropological grounds, but only on the basis of the salvation proclaimed (cf. Heb. 2:3). If this is ignored, salvation and judgment become far removed from each other, and the preaching of the judgment becomes an isolated, intimidating prophecy of doom, which ultimately will fall on deaf ears. The call to faith and the warning can only go out in the light of Christ's abandonment and His encounter with the outer darkness. Thus the preaching of judgment does not relativize the depth and universality of the gospel, but confirms it according to the incontrovertible witness of the whole New Testament.[131]

This gospel which Jesus came preaching – and doing in his kingdom miracles – is the unique element he introduces. David knew a thousand years earlier that the wages of sin is death. What he was unable to see then was how God could save the sinner out of death and still be true to his law. Jesus stood in the place of both law and sinner, and resolved the dilemma.

It is impossible to separate Jesus' own person from what he teaches, so we may also say that Jesus is the unique element of the New Testament.[132] However wide the circles of Jesus' teaching, they grow concentrically smaller until finally they rest on him. The Son of Man must be killed and rise again. This means that he himself finally demonstrates both God's wrath and his salvation.

The gospel, Paul would later write, already 'reveals' both sides of God's judgment-verdict – his vindication (righteousness) on the one hand, his wrath on the other (Rom. 1:16ff.). We can learn the same truth in the Gospels as we read Jesus' parables and watch what happens to him. 'This is one of the inevitable conclusions toward which the logic of the love, the wrath, the imperative, and the condition of God's justice has been driving us.'[133] It is not a matter of a few passages here and there. It is 'an essential element of the very nature of God as the tension between his love and wrath results in imperative and condition.'[134]

As John's Gospel says so often, light has invaded the darkness, bringing an inescapable challenge. The crisis is here now – in that sense judgment has already arrived. God is on the throne, and the Son of Man stands in the dock. Prosecutor and defender are at hand. Over Jesus' head hangs the heavy cloud of sin, but he himself is spotless. Ultimate conflict is inescapable. When light and darkness finally come crashing together, the

---

131. Ibid. pp. 421f.
132. See e.g. Forestell, 'Christian Revelation' pp. 180f.; Hanhart, *Intermediate State* p. 33; Pilcher, *Hereafter* p. 100; Max Wilcox, 'On Investigating the Use of the Old Testament in the New Testament,' *Text and Interpretation* pp. 242f. Wilcox concludes that 'early Christian Bible-exegesis is part of the contemporary Jewish Bible-exegesis, distinguished from the latter first and foremost by acceptance of the resurrection and the resultant implied "messianic" role of Jesus' (p. 243).
133. Baird, *Justice* p. 234.
134. Ibid. pp. 234f.

universe will quake with the impact. If we look quickly, we will see for a moment the end of the world. Jesus' greatest revelation comes not in his parables but in his history – at Golgotha and at the Garden Tomb. Nowhere in all the Bible will we find a clearer, more concrete picture of the victory of life – or of the reality and horror of hell.

11

Golgotha and Gehenna:
Jesus' Death and the Punishment of the Lost

The literature concerning final punishment contains a number of surprises, and one of the greatest is the scant attention given to the death of Jesus Christ. For the New Testament is quite clear that Jesus' died because of sin and in the place of sinners. More than that, his death was in some sense the sinner's death – the death required by sin – the death we should have died and must finally have died had Jesus not taken it upon himself. Thus Paul says not only that 'Christ died for the ungodly' (Rom. 5:6, 8) but also that 'Christ redeemed us from the curse of the law by becoming a curse for us' (Gal. 3:13). Jesus, says the writer to the Hebrews, 'suffered death, so that by the grace of God he might taste death for everyone' (Heb. 2:9) and 'He was sacrificed once to take away the sins of many people' (9:28). Peter and John also emphasize that Jesus died instead of sinners (1 Pet. 2:24; 3:18; 1 Jn. 2:2; 3:16).

We grasp this 'secret wisdom' of God's eternal purpose only by the Holy Spirit's revelation through the gospel proclamation (1 Cor. 2:10; Eph. 3:1–5; 1 Pet. 1: 10ff). By that gospel light, however, the central cross on Golgotha becomes a window into God's final judgment-verdicts of acquittal and of condemnation (Rom. 1:17f; 3:23–26).

Eschatology is an aspect of christology

To a remarkable extent, different New Testament scholars today agree that eschatology is essentially christology. Jesus is himself the key to the Last Things. This is in contrast to the view which defines the Last Things as a series of events having no integral relation to the life, death and resurrection of Jesus Christ.[1]

The New Testament pattern of interpretation, by contrast, explains prophecy, not by identifying isolated segments and relating these exclusively to the future, but by reading it all in the light of the past, particularly that chain of events 'when through the cross and resurrection Christ fought and won the decisive battle which makes the eventual victory sure'.[2] The future still holds many unanswered questions, but

---

1. William C Berkemeyer, 'The Eschatological Dilemma,' *Lutheran Quarterly* 7, no. 3 (Aug. 1955) p. 234.
2. Ibid.

whatever those answers may be, they all will 'be controlled by and consistent with this Christ-event of the past'.³

F. F. Bruce suggests that perhaps 'we should say that the New Testament reveals the "last thing" to be really the "Last One," Jesus being himself the *Eschatos* (cf. "The First and the Last" as a title of Jesus in Rev. 1:17, 2:8, 22:13)'.⁴ C. H. Dodd says that 'At the last frontier-post we shall encounter God in Christ.'⁵ The 1955 Evanston Assembly of the World Council of Churches put it this way:

> We do not know what is coming to us. But we know who is coming. It is he who meets us every day and who meets us at the end – Jesus Christ our Lord.⁶

Although New Testament writers interpret the gospel by a wide variety of figures and in many different frameworks, they 'unite in affirming that with Jesus the New Age has dawned, but that the consummation of that Age awaits future realization'.⁷ They also agree that consummation has been anticipated in the inauguration, so that the end will only complete and make evident what is already true in Jesus Christ. With Christ's death and resurrection, eschatology has already begun. On the Day of Pentecost Peter announced the 'beginning of the End'. The details of that day were 'last-times' details, whether we think of the announcement that the resurrection had begun, the outpouring of the Spirit, or the actual remission of sins. But 'inauguration points on to the consummation,' and 'this consummation, this goal, must be as truly bound up with [Jesus'] person as the inauguration was'.⁸

This perspective guided the Reformers past whirlpools of prophetic speculation and held them steady through the rapids of imaginative interpretation. Holwerda regards such a Christ-centred understanding of prophecy as a fundamental part of Calvin's heritage. For Calvin, he says, Christ 'incorporates within Himself both Advent and Return: both the fulfillment already completed and the fulfillment that will one day be fully revealed.'⁹ For Calvin, a given prophecy 'can contain only what as a matter of fact has happened and will happen in Christ. Thus every prophecy announcing final victory receives a twofold fulfillment in the Advent and Return of Christ.'¹⁰ We suggest that the same may be said of every prophecy announcing God's judgment and punishment of sin.

G. R. Beasley-Murray, a specialist in the field of apocalyptic, makes the

---

3. Ibid.
4. 'Eschatology,' *London Quarterly and Holborn Review* Apr. 1958 p. 100.
5. *The Coming of Christ* p. 58, quoted by Bruce, 'Eschatology' p. 100. Dodd's words quoted here are fully biblical, though in his earlier works he stressed the 'already' aspect of eschatology at the expense of the 'not yet.' In later works he corrected this imbalance.
6. *The Evanston Report: The Second Assembly of the World Council of Churches* (New York, 1955) p. 3. We can applaud these words even while lamenting the virtual abandonment of biblical evangelism in recent decades by the World Council of Churches.
7. Howard C. Kee, 'The Development of Eschatology in the New Testament,' *JBR* 20, no. 3 (July 1952) p. 193.
8. Bruce, 'Eschatology' p. 103.
9. David E. Holwerda, 'Eschatology and History: A Look at Calvin's Eschatological Vision,' *Exploring the Heritage of John Calvin* p. 125.
10. Ibid p. 126.

same point. 'Christ is the agent of God in that judgment on history which leads to its goal in the kingdom of God; and alike the judgments and the kingdom are the issue of the judgment and redemption wrought in and through the life, death, and resurrection of the Son of God.'[11] Jesus not only inaugurates the end-time events; he also concludes them. He is the Last as well as the First in eschatology as well as in God's saving purpose in general. This means that

> for Christian faith eschatology is an aspect of christology. Whether we are thinking in terms of the history of mankind, or the destiny of the individual, or the meaning of the universe, we are driven back ultimately to the significance of the incarnation and the redemption wrought by God in Christ.[12]

Pannenberg is even more explicit. For him, the end of history has erupted within history, particularly in the resurrection of Jesus Christ. The gospel not only declares the past; it pronounces the future.[13]

Jesus indeed says that 'a time is coming' when all men will rise to be judged, then part company for ever. But because he is 'the Last,' eschatology is subsumed under christology, and thus he says in the same passage that that time 'has now come' (John 5:24–29).

Calvary reveals God's final judgment

The Old Testament prophets spoke of 'the sufferings of the Messiah' and 'glories that would follow' (1 Pet. 1:11), as Jesus himself said more than once (Matt. 16:21; Luke 18:31ff; 24:25ff, 44–48; John 17:1–5). Yet what is this suffering and glory if not the eschatological judgment of God – seen both as divine vengeance on sin and the vindication and exaltation of righteousness? In his exhaustive study J. A. Baird finds that Jesus personified all he taught on this subject, so that Jesus himself 'was absolutely consumed by his involvement in the crisis of God'.

> His life and message was a prism that brought the rays of God's being and nature to flaming focus in himself. He saw his own mission and person as the symbol, the agent, and the very incarnation of the judgment of God.[14]

A little later Baird suggests the 'very interesting possibility' that 'Jesus went to the cross as the last great acted parable of his life, wherein he portrayed in ways beyond comprehension the justice of God and his own involvement therein.' Thus the cross became 'Jesus' creative extension of Moses' great acted parable of judgment, Ebal and Gerizim'.[15]

Alan Richardson comes from a different direction but reaches the same conclusion. Jesus 'clearly regards himself as related to *orgē* [wrath] and *krisis* [judgment] as he is related to *basileia* [kingdom], *zōē* [life] or *doxa* [glory].' More than that, Richardson says, 'it is Christ himself who is the

---

11. 'New Testament Apocalyptic – A Christological Eschatology,' *Review and Expositor* 72, no. 3 (Summer 1975) p. 330.
12. Ibid.
13. [See] E. Frank Tupper, 'The Revival of Apocalyptic in Biblical and Theological Studies,' *Review and Expositor* 72, no. 3 (Summer 1975) p. 296.
14. *Justice* p. 237.
15. Ibid. p. 251.

actual bearer of the divine *orgē.*' The outcome is that the cross of Christ 'is the visible, historical manifestation of the *orgē tou theou* [wrath of God]: it is the supreme revelation of the wrath of God against all ungodliness and unrighteousness of men (Rom. 1:18; cf. 2 Cor. 5:21; Mark 15:34).'[16]

C. K. Barrett agrees. He believes Romans 1–3 reveals the fundamental pattern of Paul's theology. 'Righteousness' and 'wrath' are both eschatological words – words related to the effects of the last judgment. Yet the gospel proclaims that 'both belong to the present' because of what has happened to Jesus of Nazareth.[17] This means 'the last event has already begun, precipitated by the life, death and resurrection of Jesus, who clearly is the central figure in the whole scheme'.[18] Ridderbos too acknowledges that in Christ's death 'God has sat in judgment, has judged sin, and in this way he has caused his eschatological judgment to be revealed in the present time.'[19] Hans Conzelmann says that divine anger against sin has always been poured out but that the gospel shows us what it was. He continues:

> The new element since Christ is that now, through the proclamation of the gospel, man can recognize what God's judgment on sin always was . . . . Thus, wrath is made visible to me by the preaching of the gospel.[20]

These writers represent a variety of theological perspectives, and they differ on the fine points involved here. Yet they all agree that the Passion of Jesus Christ uniquely revealed God's judgment against sin – in general and at the end of the world. The writer to the Hebrews drew Jesus' experience and man's final judgment along parallel lines. 'As' it is ordained that man must be judged, 'so' it happened to Christ. What is more, Christ stood in the place of the sinner in judgment, since he died for sin (Heb. 9:27f).

Jesus' death was 'for sin'

The cross of Christ was no mere example of divine judgment; it was God's supreme judgment – the judgment withheld already for centuries from many to whom it was due (Rom. 3:25; Heb. 9:15, 26ff; cf. NIV footnote to Isa. 53:8). Here Jesus experiences the anguish of being forsaken by God – and it is the consistent view of the Old Testament that God turns away from the one with whom he is angry. Even if Scripture never expressly states that Jesus stood under the divine wrath, all it says about his death forces us to that conclusion.[21]

---

16. *Introduction* p. 77.
17. C. K. Barrett, 'New Testament Eschatology: Part I,' *SJT* 6, no. 2 (June 1953) p. 147.
18. Ibid. p. 150.
19. *Paul* p. 168.
20. Hans Conzelmann, *Outline of the Theology of the N. T.* p. 241. Conzelmann says very little in the book about God's wrath, judgment or hell. His remark here has obvious validity but should not detract from the uniqueness of the cross as God's great judgment-event.
21. G. Stahlin, '*Orgē*' *TDNT* 5:446.

Jesus himself approached this death with 'prayers and petitions,' with 'loud cries and tears' (Heb. 5:7). Though he moved resolutely toward it, he was 'deeply distressed and troubled,' his soul 'overwhelmed with sorrow to the point of death' (Mark 14:33f).

He prayed 'in anguish,' and his sweat 'was like drops of blood falling to the ground' (Luke 22:44). In the words of John Wenham:

> There was something so solemn about the way that he spoke of his death that the disciples were afraid to ask him what he meant. There was something so frightening about his demeanour as he strode ahead of them that they were 'filled with awe'.[22]

Oscar Cullmann refers to the horror with which Jesus viewed his death, a dread Cullmann attributes to Jesus' understanding of death in general. But more is at stake here than anthropology, as Leon Morris reminds us:

> It was not death as such that He feared. It was the particular death that He was to die, that death which is 'the wages of sin' as Paul puts it (Rom. 6:23), the death in which He was at one with sinners, sharing their lot, bearing their sins, dying their Death.[23]

Not only did Jesus view his own death as 'a ransom' for sinners; New Testament writers likewise make that connection. For Paul in particular, notes Ridderbos, 'Christ's death is determined primarily by its connection with the power and guilt of sin.'[24] For Paul the young rabbi, 'the fact that God allowed Jesus to hang on a tree was the decisive disproof of his Messiahship,' for Jesus 'was plainly cursed by God'.[25] There was no escaping this scandal of a crucified Messiah. For Paul it was 'worse than a contradiction in terms; the very idea was an outrageous blasphemy'.[26]

Yet this death for sin was the reason why Jesus had come into this world. 'What shall I say?' He had agonized on the way to Jerusalem. 'Father, save me from this hour?' His answer was quick and firm. 'No, it was for this very reason I came to this hour. Father, glorify Your name!' (John 12:27f).

At Jesus' baptism, we see the others figuratively washing their sins away in the water, but we may rightly picture the sinless Jesus there taking them all on himself.[27] He is both scapegoat and sacrifice – 'for atonement' and 'for Azazel'. The Greek word for 'forgive' (*aphiēmi*) used most often by the Evangelists in reporting what Jesus said has as its root two words which mean 'to take away'.

But that baptism in water required another in blood, and Jesus had no inner rest until this too was accomplished (Luke 12:50). Only then could

---

22. *Goodness* p. 169.
23. *The Cross in the New Testament* p. 47.
24. *Paul* p. 55.
25. Wenham, *Goodness* p. 168.
26. F. F. Bruce, *Paul* p. 71.
27. G. Stahlin ('*Orgē*' p. 466) speaks of Jesus' baptism in Jordan as 'the figure of wrathful judgment'. Meredith G. Kline discusses this concept of covenantal malediction in the light of Old Testament covenants in *By Oath Consigned* pp. 39–49.

he say, 'It is finished' (John 19:30). At Jordan, Jesus had been 'numbered with the transgressors'; at Golgotha he 'bore the sin of many' (Isa. 53:12). Jesus Christ is he 'who came by water and blood'. This is the testimony God has given about his Son (1 John 5:6, 9).

The gospel story is presented against an Old Testament background, including the important concept of 'covenant'. The word evoked not only Jerusalem and Sinai but also Eden. Jesus was 'born of a woman, born under law' (Gal. 4:4). The first statement speaks of his humanity. He is the Second Adam, the second representative Man. The latter identifies Jesus as a Son of the Torah – but even more. He is True Israel, the true Vine of God's planting (John 15:1). The two figures are concentric circles picturing God's covenant, and Jesus now encompasses them both. Integral to each is the recurring pattern of covenantal stipulations, covenantal blessings and covenantal curses. As Second Adam and True Israel, Jesus does what neither Adam nor Israel had ever been able to do. He keeps the stipulations, earns the blessings, then takes on himself all the curses of the broken covenant.

Brinsmead describes these as:

> ... awful threats which may first appear out of all proportion to the sins committed. But sin, being a breach of the covenant, is an affront to the covenant God and an insult to His infinite majesty .... The curses included hunger and thirst (Deut. 28:48; Isa. 65:13), desolation (Isa. 5:6; Zeph. 1:15), poverty (Deut. 28:31), the scorn of passers-by (Jer. 19:8), darkness (Isa. 13:10; Amos 5:18–20), earthquake (Isa. 13:13; Amos 1:1), being 'cut off' from among the people (Ex. 12:15, 19; 31:14; Lev. 7:25; Jer. 44:7–11), death by hanging on a tree (Deut. 21:23), a brass heaven (Deut. 28:23) and no help when one cries for help (Deut. 28:31; Isa. 10:3).[28]
>
> Christ ... was hungry (Matt. 4:2; 21:18). He was so poor he had nowhere to lay his head (Matt. 8:20). On the cross he cried, 'I am thirsty!' (John 19:28). He was mocked and derided (Mark 15:29ff) and deserted by his friends (Malt. 26:56, 69–75). He was hanged on a tree as a cursed man (Gal. 3:13) and 'cut off' from his people (Isa. 53:8). As he hung on the cross, the heavens were as brass. He was as one who cries for help and receives none (Mark 15:34). He died as the great covenant breaker and endured the unabated fury of all the covenantal curses. The cosmic scope of the curses is portrayed in Matthew. As Christ bore the sins of the broken covenant, darkness descended over the land (Matt. 27:45), the earth shook, and the rocks split (Matt. 27:51). But by dying Jesus carried away the curses of the covenant.[29]

A reader familiar with the Old Testament alone could view the scene of Good Friday and know that Jesus is 'stricken by God, smitten by him, and afflicted' (Isa. 53:4). The Law makes that plain enough. But the Gospel tells us why the Sinless One is so treated. Patristic and medieval theologians tended to devise arguments based on human philosophies of justice to explain and justify everlasting punishment. The New Testament

---

28. Brinsmead, *Covenant* p. 81.
29. Ibid. p. 83.

does nothing of the sort. It begins with God's law, with God's covenants, with the divine wrath which accompanies such covenants. Then it leads the reader to a place outside the Holy City.[30]

There it shows us the ultimate penalty for sin. This time it does not take us to the rocky valley of Hinnom – the worst symbol intertestamental apocalyptists could imagine. Instead, it takes us to a stone hill in the shape of a skull. Here, it says, is the greatest revelation of God's wrath against all the ungodliness and wickedness of men.

This is no impersonal transaction, as if divine wrath were a matter of mere mechanics. Nor does it partake of any sinful vindictiveness as human wrath is so prone to do. We cannot begin to comprehend, far less express, what it meant that 'God the mighty Maker died/For man, the creature's sin.' Righteousness and peace kissed that day (Ps. 85:10). God became both 'just and the justifier' (Rom. 3:26).

Markus Barth captures something of the sense of the cosmic judgment which occurred at Calvary.

> With this the proceedings before God's throne reach their most abysmal point. No wonder Jesus cries out to the Father who sent him, 'My God, my God, why hast thou forsaken me?' No wonder darkness shrouds the whole world. This is the horrible judgment of the living God. The words 'anger,' 'curse', 'sin,' 'cross,' 'crucified with him' cannot be sweetened. They cannot be relativized. They present an offence . . . that cannot be removed by any wisdom . . . . In spite of Jesus' truthfulness and love, all of God's anger reigns here. Here is hellish thirst and torment, the Godforsakenness of God's own child . . . .
>
> In the death of his Son, God does not merely make felt what it means to bear sins and die under the curse; he feels it himself. Sin and death are no longer alien to God. Now everything that has to do with the living, obeying, hoping, achieving, doing, suffering, and dying of men has been incorporated into the relation between Father and Son. As it is manifested, it cries out to heaven . . . .
>
> Here God openly stands against God, the Father against the Son, the benevolent, promising God addressed in prayers, against what God makes and allows in the world of facts and events. No theoretical or doctrinal theodicy is able to break in and save the day. Even the true and loving Son can only ask, 'Why have you . . . ?'
>
> The earth trembles. The sun fades away. This is the horror of the judgment:

---

30. T. G. Dunning writes: 'Hell, like Gehenna of old, is out of bounds to the Holy City. Hell's deepest meaning is the loss of the divine presence, the complete absence of fellowship with God and a condition of final unalterable alienation from Him' (T. G. Dunning, 'Heaven and Hell' p. 357). This is precisely what we see at Calvary. Jesus was cast outside Jerusalem to die. God refused to come to his aid, and Jesus was never again to be known as he once had been known in the flesh (cf 2 Cor. 5:16, 19, 21). Jesus became a reject from the covenant society of Yahweh, a man under God's ban and curse, totally 'cut off' from fellowship (life) with God and God's people.

Yet in the light of Jesus' subsequent resurrection, this exclusion from Jerusalem became a symbol of encouragement for the recipients of Hebrews (Heb. 13:12ff). When a city thrusts God out (as the resurrection showed Jerusalem had done in excluding Jesus) and it is about to crumble, absence from it is no longer so bad!

God is silent. An eclipse of the living God, a victory of death over life, the end of all religion, all law and justice, all morality – it is this that comes in at 3:00 p.m. on Good Friday. A Hell, deeper and hotter than anything one might imagine ... has opened its maw, devoured God's Son, and become all-victorious ....

The judgment is adjourned at this time, to reconvene day after tomorrow at the crack of dawn.[31]

Jesus died the sinner's own death

Jesus not only died 'for sin'; he died in the very place of sinners. He does not remain a third party, even one acting on behalf of another. He becomes man in order to be 'made sin' (2 Cor. 5:21, KJV), to 'become a curse' (Gal. 3:13). It is in his 'physical body' that he reconciled us through death (Col. 1:22). He bore our sins 'in his body' on the cross (1 Pet. 2:24). God gave Jesus a body in which to perform perfect human obedience, to 'do the will of God,' and having done that will, Jesus sacrificed that body once for all (Heb. 10:5–10). He 'took up our infirmities and carried our sorrows' (Isa. 53:4). The following verses emphasize that Jesus bore his people's iniquities and their sin – he took it all on himself, the totality in general and its specific manifestations (Isa. 53:11f).

Orthodox theologians have rightly insisted on this personal identification of Jesus with the actual punishment due the sinner. Calvin wrote:

> This is our acquittal: the guilt that held us liable for punishment has been transferred to the head of the Son of God [Isa. 53:12]. We must, above all, remember this substitution, lest we tremble and remain anxious throughout life – as if God's righteous vengeance, which the Son of God has taken upon himself, still hung over us.[32]

Calvin saw Jesus as the Lamb of God, 'taking upon himself the penalty that we owe' so that 'he has wiped out our guilt before God's judgment'.[33] This is what Peter meant in saying that Jesus 'bare our sins in his own body.' Calvin explained that Jesus 'bore the punishment and vengeance due for our sins' so that we 'see plainly that Christ bore the penalty of sins to deliver his own people from them'.[34]

Calvin goes even further: Jesus endured the pains of hell for his people.

> If Christ had died only a bodily death, it would have been ineffectual. No – it was expedient at the same time for him to undergo the severity of God's vengeance, to appease his wrath and satisfy his just judgment. For this reason, he must also grapple hand to hand with the armies of hell and the dread of everlasting death .... No wonder, then, if he is said to have descended into

---

31. Markus Barth, *Justification: Pauline Texts Interpreted in the Light of the Old and New Testaments* pp. 47f.
32. *Institutes* 2.16.5.
33. Ibid. 3.4.26.
34. Ibid. 3.4.30.

hell,[35] for he suffered the death that God in his wrath had inflicted upon the wicked![36]

Jesus' death involved total destruction

Here is the point to which we must finally come. If Jesus' death 'reveals' God's last judgment, if his death was 'for sin' and 'instead of sinner,' if it entailed the penalty and curse and condemnation of sin pronounced throughout the Bible, what does the cross teach us about final punishment? J. D. G. Dunn, not known as an advocate in particular of either a conditionalist or a traditionalist view, sees total destruction as the essence of the Levitical sacrifices which foreshadowed Christ's offering.

> Paul saw the death of the sacrificial animal as the death of the sinner *qua sinner*, that is, the destruction of his sin. The manner in which the sin offering dealt with sin was by its death. The sacrificial animal, identified with the offerer in his sin, had to be destroyed in order to destroy the sin which it embodied, The sprinkling, smearing and pouring away of the sacrificial blood in the sight of God indicated that the life was wholly destroyed, and with it the sin of the sinner.[37]

This utter destruction, Dunn continues, is the just doom also of sinful humanity:

> Had there been a way for fallen man to overcome his fallenness Christ would

---

35. The Apostles' Creed says of Christ that 'he descended into Hades'. The first appearance of this clause is evidently in the so-called Fourth Formula of Sirmium (A.D. 359). Originally it was intended to mean only that Jesus truly died. Rufinus, presbyter of Aquileia, said the phrase explained an old doctrine rather than adding a new one, and for that reason the Aquileian creed omitted the clause 'was crucified, dead, and buried', replacing it with the new expression. Most medieval and modern forms of the Apostles' Creed include the clause but also retain the original statement that Jesus 'was crucified, dead, and buried'.

In the Latin church of the West a related doctrine evolved of a triumphal procession of Christ through the underworld, redeeming Old Testament saints and taking them with him in his ascension to heaven. This 'harrowing of hell' became a very popular theme in medieval literature and plays. Some later developments have Christ redeeming all human souls from hell at his second coming.

On the *decensus* clause of the creed see Jürgen Moltmann, 'Descent into Hell,' *Duke Divinity School Review* 33, no. 2 (Spring 1968) p. 117; Martin H. Scharlemann, 'He Descended into Hell,' *Concordia Theological Monthly* 27, no. 2 (Feb. 1956) pp. 81ff; Shedd, *Punishment* p. 70. On 'the harrowing of hell' see J. A. MacCulloch, *The Harrowing of Hell*, and – what was probably its original seed – the third-century *Gospel of Nicodemus* (also known as *The Acts of Pontius Pilate*), especially chapters 15–19. The *Gospel of Nicodemus* is contained, among other places, in *Apocryphal Books of the New Testament* ed. M. R. James.

36. *Institutes* 2.16.10.

37. Dunn, *Death of Jesus* p. 136. Dunn is no universalist, as two quotations suffice to illustrate. On p. 137 he writes: 'But only those who, like the offerer of old, identify themselves with the sacrifice, may know the other half of the chiasmus, the life of Christ beyond the death of sin, the righteousness of God in Christ.' On pp. 130ff he writes: 'In his risen life he represents only those who identify themselves with him, with his death (in baptism), only those who acknowledge the Risen One as Lord (2 Cor. 5:15) . . . . In short, as Last Adam Jesus represents only those who experience life-giving Spirit (1 Cor. 15:45).'

not have died.... But Christ, Man, died because there is no other way for man – any man. His death is an acknowledgement that there is no way out for fallen men except through death – no answer to sinful flesh except its destruction in death. Man could not be helped other than through his annihilation.[38]

This is the meaning of Jesus' death, according to Dunn, as touching the consequences of sin. He takes issue with those who say Jesus' death simply 'turns away' God's wrath. Jesus did not turn it away, Dunn argues. Rather, he accepted it fully on himself, draining it until no drop is left for any whom he saves.

The destructive consequences of sin do not suddenly evaporate. On the contrary, they are focused in fuller intensity on the sin – that is, on fallen humanity in Jesus. In Jesus on the cross was focused not only man's sin, but the wrath which follows upon that sin. The destructive consequences of sin are such that if they were allowed to work themselves out fully in man himself they would destroy him as a spiritual being. This process of destruction is speeded up in the case of Jesus, the representative man, the *hilastērion*, and destroys him. The wrath of God destroys the sin by letting the full destructive consequences of sin work themselves out and exhaust themselves in Jesus.... If we have understood Paul's theology of sacrifice aright the primary thought is the *destruction* of the malignant, poisonous organism of sin. Any thought of *punishment* is secondary.[39]

The Bible exhausts the vocabulary of dying in speaking of what happened to Jesus. He 'died for our sins' (1 Cor. 15:3). He laid down his 'life [*psychē*]' (John 10:15). He was destroyed (Matt. 27:20, KJV) or killed (Acts 3:15). Jesus compared his own death to the dissolution of a kernel of wheat in the same passage that mentions losing one's life (*psychē*) rather than loving it in order to find life eternal (John 12:23–26). Jesus 'poured out his life (*psychē*) unto death' and was thus 'numbered with the transgressors' (Isa. 53:12).

In the beginning God gave the man and the woman being instead of nonbeing, and warned them that sin would bring death in the place of life (Gen. 2:17). From the first the wages of sin was death, and Jesus underwent the sentence pronounced in Eden.

We can only bow before such amazing grace, saying with John, 'This is how we know what love is: Jesus Christ laid down his life for us' (1 John 3:16), or with Paul, that 'God demonstrates his own love for us in this: While we were still sinners, Christ died for us' (Rom. 5:8).

Some protest that Christ's death was not a true pattern of the judgment awaiting sinners in hell, since Jesus was an infinite person and could absorb infinite punishment in a single moment. Finite sinners, this argument goes, will require conscious punishment in infinite duration for justice to have its way. This whole logic of 'finite' and 'infinite'

---

38. Ibid. p. 130. Blanchard agrees that 'Jesus suffered everything the Bible means when it describes hell as a pit, a prison, darkness and a lake of fire ...' (*Hell* p. 277). Nevertheless he argues that the lost must live for ever in torment because 'Jesus was not annihilated' (p. 228).

39. Ibid. p. 139.

punishment and victims is totally without biblical basis, springing instead from medieval speculation grounded in feudalistic canons of justice. The entire approach is protested today on philosophical grounds, which is proper since that was also its origin.[40] More than that, this philosophy itself leaves room for the question whether the 'infinite' punishment of hell might not be defined in some terms other than conscious torment for endless time. If death is seen to be destruction without limitation (which the traditional view has not allowed), then is not penal death itself an infinite punishment, especially if it is an eternal death which is for ever irreversible? Karl Barth speaks, for example, of Christ 'suffering the eternal wrath of God,' a phrase Stahlin quotes with apparent approval.[41]

The 'abnormal act' of God saving sinners belongs to the 'mystery of godliness' (1 Tim. 3:16). As such, it is not explained on the basis of anything we can see in nature, find in law, discover by human reason or observe in all creation. We will try in vain to analyze and explain this 'hidden wisdom' in terms of human philosophy or judicial theory – whether medieval or modern! Only the innermost mind of the godhead fathoms these depths. We should leave the matter there.

Strong writes, 'Hell, as well as the Cross, indicates God's estimate of sin.'[42] In the light of the words of Isaiah and John, Peter and Paul, and Jesus himself, the sentence would better read: 'Hell, as *revealed* in the Cross, indicates God's estimate of sin.'

Every scriptural implication is that if Jesus had not been raised, he – like those fallen asleep in him – would simply have perished (1 Cor. 15:18). Scriptures such as 2 Timothy 1:10; Hebrews 2:14; Revelation 20:14 affirm that his resurrection reverses every such estimation of affairs, assuring us instead of the death of Death.

---

40. Marilyn McCord Adams ('Hell and the God of Justice,' *Religious Studies* 11 no. 4 (Dec. 1975) p. 433–47) criticizes it on philosophical grounds. Ms. Adams also does away with infinite bliss on philosophical grounds. Her article therefore reaffirms the necessity of beginning with biblical exegesis and basing all reasoning on an authoritative Word of God, a sword which cuts two directions!
41. '*Orgē*' p. 445.
42. *Theology* 3:1050.

12

The Wages of Sin in the Writings of Paul

It is widely held that Jesus taught much about final punishment but that Paul said relatively little.[1] In fact, compared to the apocalyptic literature of his day and the previous two centuries, Jesus gave very few details on the end of the wicked. And if one examines Paul's language in the light of its Old Testament background – especially as it appears in Septuagint Greek – then the few key terms Paul does use may say far more than was previously suggested. Phrases that first appear bland and colourless begin to darken with the smoke of Sinai and to echo the thunderous tones of the prophets.

We will consider Paul's letters in general groups in the order they are commonly held to have been written, beginning with the Thessalonian correspondence and concluding with the so-called Prison Epistles to the Ephesians, Colossians and Philippians.[2] Words sometimes alter in meaning with the passing of time and events. Paul himself received an abundance of successive revelations (2 Cor. 12:1, 7; Gal. 1:11f.; Eph. 3:3–6, 9; 1 Tim. 4:1). While not wishing to 'homogenize' words that should express a rich variety of meaning, we do desire to be sensitive to any developments of doctrine as Scripture progressively unfolds.[3]

The Thessalonian correspondence

1 Thessalonians 1:9f. Paul reminds the believers at Thessalonica of how they had 'turned to God from idols to serve the living and true God, and to wait for his Son from heaven, whom he raised from the dead – Jesus, who rescues us from the coming wrath'.

In these words, surely among our earliest from Paul's hand, he mentions four themes which characterize his preaching (as reported in Acts) and which reappear whenever he discusses the end of the world.

---

1. Buis refers to only five Pauline passages (Rom. 2:3–9, 12; 1 Cor. 3:17; 2 Cor. 5:10; 1 Thess. 5:3; 2 Thess. 1:6–9). He says that 'much less is stated about punishment in the future state than was revealed by Jesus' but acknowledges that there is even in Paul's writings 'a strong conviction regarding the serious alternatives which are involved' (*Eternal Punishment* p. 43).

2. There is no mention of final punishment in Timothy and Titus, probably Paul's final canonical works.

3. Some prefer Clark Pinnock's phrase 'cumulative revelation,' by which he means 'the teleological direction of revelation with the emphasis on the building up of the total truth picture'. Because revelation came 'gradually in chronological progression,' Pinnock says, Scripture 'needs to be read with regard for the place each passage occupies in the revelation process'. The pinnacle of divine revelation was the appearance of Jesus Christ,

1. The gospel calls hearers (here largely pagan idolaters) to know and serve the one, true, living God. This is none other than the Creator God of Israel, as Paul affirms in both his recorded addresses to pagan audiences (Acts 14:15ff; 17:22–31). Paul speaks in the name of the God of his fathers. He presents the gospel as the continuation and fulfilment of the Old Testament story, not as a competitor to it.

2. God has raised Jesus from the dead, so declaring him to be his Son (Rom. 1:4).

3. Jesus has returned to the Father in heaven, but believers are to eagerly await his promised return (1 Cor. 1:7; Phil. 3:20).

4. Jesus' return will mark the end of the present world order. God will then pour out his wrath on the unrepentant, but Jesus will save believers from that wrath.

Wrath to come was no new theme with Paul. We have already found it integral to the message of John the Baptist as he presented Jesus to Israel (Matt. 3:7; Luke 3:7). This wrath is linked to Jesus so closely that it already impends on whoever rejects him (John 3:36). On Calvary Jesus himself bears this wrath (Gal. 3:13; 2 Cor. 5:21; John 1:29; 1 Pet. 2:24). Already the gospel reveals this wrath of the end-time (Rom. 1:18). Jerusalem's destruction by the Romans is viewed as a partial demonstration of the same wrath against unbelieving Israel, who rejected Jesus (Luke 21:23; cf. 1 Thess. 2:16). We will examine Paul's elaboration on the eschatological wrath as we proceed.

There is a popular notion that the Old Testament reveals a God of wrath, the New Testament a God of mercy and love. Nothing could be further from the truth. In a perceptive discussion, John Wenham shows how the theme of divine wrath runs through the entire Bible. Rather than omitting or softening the Old Testament wrath of God, Wenham concludes, the New Testament complements it, completes it, agrees with it, highlights and quotes it, and sometimes 'outdoes' it.[4] Gustav Stahlin agrees. In his *TDNT* article on 'wrath' he insists that in no sense does the New Testament regard God's wrath as 'an inconsistent bit of Old Testament religion which has been dragged in, as though reference to God's wrath belonged only to the Old Testament and reference to his love were confined to the New'.[5]

Still less does the New Testament picture Jesus as the spineless figure of liberal imagination, indifferent to God's law and honour, the author of a painless atonement who stands ready to bypass repentance, sweep all sin under a cosmic rug, and dispense cheap grace to one and all. Nor does Jesus show us the unsympathetic god of a certain distorted fundamentalism, who stands over people, ready at the slightest slip to thrash them and throw them into hell. Jesus always shows us a God of infinite

---

who also is himself the key to interpreting Scripture both before and after his coming (*Biblical Revelation* p. 214).

The same thought may be expressed by the common phrase 'progressive revelation' so long as the term is kept free of humanistic evolutionary ideas.

4. Wenham, *Goodness* pp. 16–23. Paul speaks of God's eschatological wrath' in Rom. 1:18; 2:8; Eph. 5:6; Col. 3:6; 1 Thess. 1:10; 5:9; He speaks of Jesus saving his people from that wrath in Phil. 1:28; 3:20; 1 Thess. 1:10.

5. Stahlin, '*Orgē*' *TDNT* 5:422.

mercy but of equal holiness. His mercy is totally undeserved and absolutely free, so that those who reject this gracious offer merit greater wrath. Jesus teaches this in his parables and demonstrates it in his own substitutionary death for sinners. Mercy and wrath go together in the Bible; each highlights the other. As Stahlin observes:

> Only he who knows the greatness of wrath will be mastered by the greatness of mercy. The converse is also true: Only he who has experienced the greatness of mercy can measure how great wrath must be. For the wrath of God arises from His love and mercy. Where mercy meets with the ungodly will of man rather than faith and gratitude, with goodwill and the response of love, love becomes wrath .... In Christ mankind is divided into those who are freed from wrath inasmuch as they are ready to be saved by His mercy, and those who remain under wrath because they despise His mercy.[6]

It is significant that even in the Old Testament, nouns for God's wrath are consistently linked with the covenant name Yahweh / Jehovah, an association which occurs more than 50 times. Interestingly, Genesis contains no term for the wrath of God, though numerous words fill that place from the Exodus onward.[7] In Romans and Galatians Paul reasons from the Old Testament, as he relates God's wrath to God's law (Gal. 3:10) or when he insists that God is within the bounds of his own justice in condemning Jew and Gentile alike (Rom. 1–4). We have already seen throughout the Old Testament that God's wrath against sin results in the total destruction of the sinner.

It should not surprise us to read, therefore, that in the Old Testament 'the wrath of Yahweh aims at destruction, at full extirpation'.[8] Whenever God's sovereign anger breaks forth, 'the existence of those concerned is at stake'. And whenever his existence is at stake, 'the man of the old covenant detects the wrath of his God'.[9] This is why the Old Testament's metaphors and figures for judgment convey such 'destructive power and irresistible force,'[10] such 'annihilating might and irresistible power'.[11]

Scholars are still debating whether God's wrath is the personal fury of an offended Being or the impersonal outworking of sin's inbuilt self-destruction.[12] We must agree with the first group that God's wrath is as

---

6. Ibid. p. 425.7.

7. J. Fichtner, 'Orgē' *TDNT* 5:396. Morris, too, observes that judgment for the Israelite was exercised in the context of the covenant under God in community with the people. 'It is no accident,' he says, 'that judgment is often linked with words like *chesed* [kindness] and *tsedeq* [justice, righteousness], which are integral to the whole conception of covenant' (*Judgment* p. 19).

8. Fichtner, 'Orgē' *TDNT* 5:400. An earlier translation by Dorothea M. Barton and P. R. Ackroyd is far more forceful. The same sentence there reads: 'The basic effect of Yahweh's wrath is intended to be annihilation, complete obliteration' (J. Fichtner, 'Orgē' Bible Key Words, 4:33).

9. Fichtner, 'Orgē' *TDNT* 5:399.

10. Ibid.

11. Fichtner, 'Orgē' Bible Key Words p. 29. The full sentence says: 'The annihilating might of God's wrath and his irresistible power are displayed in the metaphors and pictorial phrases used for what that wrath brings about.'

12. Wenham has a bibliography covering this controversy (*Goodness* p. 187). Among those holding the personalized view are G. Stahlin, R. V. G. Tasker and Leon Morris.

fully personal as his mercy, that one who views a wrath apart from the personal God very easily rationalizes an impersonal 'God' without wrath.[13] At the same time, since sin at its root expresses rebellion against God, who alone gives and sustains life, we fully agree with J. D. G. Dunn that 'the outworking of the destructive consequences of sin' is 'destructive for the wholeness of man in his relationships'.[14] God's wrath is not capricious, nor is it vindictive in any way that is unjust. Paul carefully pictures God's final wrath in personal terms (Rom. 2:8f), but he insists with equal vigour that God is both longsuffering (Rom. 9:22; 1 Thess. 2:16) and just (Rom. 3:5f).

When Paul reminds the Thessalonians that the Jesus for whom they wait will deliver them from the coming wrath, he writes as a Jew, reared in the Old Testament Scriptures. When he writes later in more detail, he likewise uses language and symbols already established by the Jewish prophets. The wrath to come was no new revelation. The Saviour Jesus Christ was. The first was known by the Law. The second is the good news of the Gospel.

1 Thessalonians 4:6 Gentile converts faced special temptation to sexual immorality, for they lacked the training the Jews had received from the Law. Paul urges holiness within the church, therefore, in matters of sexual purity. Fornication is forbidden, and 'the Lord will punish men for all such sins'. Literally, he writes that the 'Lord is Avenger'. The same phrase appears in Psalm 94:1 (LXX). Neither that passage nor this context adds to the picture, stating only the fact with its implicit threat of punishment from such a God.

1 Thessalonians 5:2f. God will avenge in wrath on the day he has appointed (cf. Acts 17:30f.), here called 'the day of the Lord'. The later prophets of the Old Testament had used this expression for temporal and local judgments as well as for the final universal judgment. They use identical language to describe the effects of such a day in either case. Paul once contrasts God's day with a 'human day,' the literal term translated 'man's judgment' in 1 Cor.4:3 (KJV). Today man has his say. Tomorrow God will have his. God's present forbearance indicates merciful restraint, not ignorance or unconcern. Those who resist present mercy will discover that God has actually been 'storing up' his wrath for them all the while (Rom. 2:4ff.). Paul describes this day in Old Testament terms as 'the day of the Lord' (1 Cor. 5:5; cf. 2 Pet. 3:10, 12). Throughout Scripture that

---

Those holding the depersonalized view include C. H. Dodd, G. H. C. MacGregor, A. T. Hanson and D. E. H. Whiteley.

13. Wenham writes: 'It is uncomfortable to sinful people to live continually under the all-seeing eye of the all-knowing Judge. Therefore Christians have been tempted to soft-pedal the theme of judgment. The theme of hell has been quietly omitted, and the wrath of God has been de-personalized. The wrath of God is thought of as the outworking of a deistic machine, in which God is not immediately and personally involved. But it is because wrath is personal that mercy is personal' (*Goodness* p. 187).

14. 'Paul's Understanding', p. 139. Dunn refers 'particularly' to S. H. Travis's unpublished doctoral dissertation 'Divine Retribution in the Thought of Paul' (Cambridge University 1970).

day brings both wrath and salvation.[15] Paul speaks therefore of 'the day of God's wrath' (Rom. 2:5) and also 'the day of redemption' (Eph. 4:30), but they are the same day. Both wrath and redemption manifest God's righteousness, so this is also 'the day [Christ] comes to be glorified ... and to be marvelled at' (2 Thess. 1:10). Since Jesus will be God's Saviour and Destroyer, this is also 'the day of Christ' (Phil. 2:16) or 'the day of our Lord Jesus Christ' (1 Cor. 1:8; cf. Rev. 6:17). Peter also mentions 'the day [God] visits us' (1 Pet. 2:12). This will be 'the great day' (Jude 6), 'the last day' (John 6:39), 'the day of judgment' (1 John 4:17).

Whatever we call the day on which it occurs, the event of final judgment is most important, and it encompasses many important truths.

> It stresses man's accountability and the certainty that justice will finally triumph over all the wrongs which are part and parcel of life here and now .... This doctrine gives meaning to life .... The Christian view of judgment means that history moves to a goal .... Judgment protects the idea of the triumph of God and of good. It is unthinkable that the present conflict between good and evil should last throughout eternity. Judgment means that evil will be disposed of authoritatively, decisively, finally. Judgment means that in the end God's will will be perfectly done.[16]

The Bible insists that there will be a resurrection of the wicked as well as the good and that all must stand before God to give account and be judged (Dan. 12:2; John 5:29; Acts 24:15; Rev. 21:8). Scripture holds no brief for those who say the existence of the wicked ends with the first death. Paul here describes God's 'day' as unexpected (1 Thess. 5:2), sudden (v. 3) and inescapable (v. 3). In all three respects it will resemble God's previous judgments on sinners, particularly the Flood (Matt. 24:36–44; Luke 17:26–35). Although men assure each other with words of 'peace and safety,' Paul insists that 'destruction will come on them suddenly ... ' (v. 3).

The 'destruction' (*olethros*) that is here 'sudden' is later said to be 'everlasting' (2 Thess. 1:9). Only Paul uses the word in the New Testament. The sinful man at Corinth is to be delivered over to Satan for the 'destruction' of the flesh (1 Cor. 5:5). The desire for riches may lead to 'destruction' ('ruin,' NIV) even now (1 Tim. 6:9). Paul uses a cognate noun for the destroyer that wiped out a generation of Israelites in the wilderness (1 Cor. 10:10). The author of Hebrews uses a verb form for the destroyer who slaughtered the firstborn throughout Egypt (Heb. 11:28). The last two passages clearly involve execution and extermination, though the meaning of the first is ambiguous and the second is metaphorical. None of them hints at conscious unending torment. The description of God's judgment in this passage brings to mind the Flood's extinction of the wicked – a judgment they were unable to escape then or to reverse for ever.

1 Thessalonians 5:9 Paul's readers need not fear, however. 'For God did not appoint us to suffer wrath but to receive salvation through our

---

15. For an excellent discussion of this point, see Robert D. Brinsmead's monographs, *Covenant* (pp. 41–55) and *The Pattern of Redemptive History* (pp. 135–152).
16. Morris, *Judgment* p. 72.

Lord Jesus Christ.' The Epistle closes as it opened, with the alternate fates of 'wrath' from God and 'salvation' through Jesus. The two stand side by side as opposing destinies. Verse 10 says the righteous will 'live together with him,' an outcome exactly opposite to the kind of 'destruction' we have already suggested.

2 Thessalonians 1:5–10 Present persecution and trials inspire hope and joy when viewed in the perspective of God's coming judgment. The greater the suffering for Jesus now, the greater the anticipation of the day when God will settle accounts! Similarly, rest is most inviting to the person who labours the hardest now. Suffering believers may know that 'God is just' and will finally even the score. Paul spells out what this means.

The Thessalonian Christians now knew 'trouble'; then they will find 'relief' (*anesin*). Those who now oppress will then receive the 'trouble' they have been inflicting. 'Trouble' translates *thlipsis*, which literally means 'pressure'. The word is frequently used by New Testament writers for the kind of pressure which comes to believers caught between the 'pull' of the old age (flesh and sin) and the 'pull' of the new age (Spirit and righteousness). The word clearly requires conscious agony, and there will be plenty of time for that, even if it finally ends in extermination. We recall that Jesus spoke of 'weeping and grinding of teeth'. Paul does not stop with reference to the 'trouble,' however. The KJV says Jesus will 'be revealed from heaven with his mighty angels, in flaming fire taking vengeance' (vv. 7, 8). The NIV and RSV place the 'flaming fire' with the phrase preceding it rather than the one following. Jesus 'is revealed from heaven in blazing fire with his powerful angels' (NIV) or 'is revealed from heaven with his mighty angels in flaming fire' (RSV). Both meanings are possible from the Greek, and commentators are divided. Leon Morris argues for the latter, primarily to preserve the unity of the three prepositional phrases. Jesus will be 'revealed' (*apokalypsis* – apocalypse)

[1] from heaven
[2] in blazing fire
[3] with his powerful angels.[17]

Thus accompanied by his angels, robed in fire, descending from heaven, Jesus will then be seen as he is (see Matt. 25:31; Jude 14; Rev. 1:1, 7, 13–16). In this interpretation the 'blazing fire' has to do with the glory of Jesus' person, not specifically the punishment inflicted on the wicked.

But there is another consideration. The entire passage contains several conceptual points of contact and even verbal parallels with Isaiah 66, an important Old Testament apocalyptic passage already noted, which also contrasts judgment and hope. The Thessalonians are presently excluded by their fellow citizens; so were the faithful Israelites Isaiah comforted (1 Thess. 2:14ff; Isa. 66:5). In each case the faithful hope for a day when

---

17. Leon Morris, *Thessalonians* (NICNT) p. 202. One might question the propriety of the NIV translators in here reversing the order of Paul's last two prepositional phrases in the interest of their favoured interpretation. The same meaning could be signified by merely adding a comma, as in the RSV.

circumstances will be reversed (2 Thess. 1:5ff; Isa. 66:6, 14), a standard characteristic of apocalyptic literature. Both passages speak of 'inflicting' or 'repaying' 'vengeance' (2 Thess. 1:6,8; Isa. 66:7,15).[18] Both passages have the Lord coming 'in fire' (2 Thess. 1:7; Isa. 66:15).[19]

If we may read Paul against this background of Isaiah 66, Morris's suggestion still holds true. Indeed, he cites the verse himself to illustrate his point. But while the fire belongs to Christ's revelation in glory, may it not also be a means of his vengeance? This possibility is clearly supported by Isaiah, is a possible interpretation of what follows in Thessalonians, and is explicitly declared in several other passages.

In Isaiah 66, God not only comes with fire; he also brings down 'his rebuke with flames of fire' (v. 15) and 'with fire' executes judgment (v. 16). The rebuke and judgment of fire result in 'many . . . slain by the Lord' (v. 16). The chapter ends with the 'dead bodies' of the slain being given over to fire and worm so that they become 'loathsome to all mankind.' We have considered this passage both in the chapter on the Old Testament and with reference to the teaching of Jesus. The same picture, with vivid apocalyptic symbols, appears also in Revelation 19:21 and 20:9. There God's foes are destroyed respectively by sword and by fire from heaven. It may also be in view in 2 Peter 3:7, where the present heavens and earth are said to be 'reserved for fire, being kept for the day of judgment and destruction of ungodly men'. It is in keeping with the biblical picture that the fire which symbolizes God's holiness destroys those who do not reverence it. The same fire from heaven which lit the altar also destroyed Aaron's irreverent sons (Lev. 9:24–10:3). The God who is called 'a consuming fire' (Heb. 12:29) is jealous for his glory. Those who reject the sin-offering he has provided are not only left without a sacrifice for sin; they also must anticipate 'fearful . . . judgment' and the 'raging fire that will consume the enemies of God' (Heb. 10:26f.). An acceptable offering or the sinner himself: those are still the only options. We suggest that this 'consuming fire' will be the means of the 'everlasting destruction' of 2 Thessalonians 1:9. Commenting on this passage, Ridderbos says that 'there is in this fire an indication of the inexorableness of punishment and the irretrievableness of those who fall under the judgment of God (2 Thess. 1:8), a punishment and a fate from which Christ will keep and deliver his own' (1 Thess. 1:10; 5:9; Rom. 5:9).[20] We have met this fire of God's holiness, with which no unforgiven sinner can long dwell, in Isaiah 33:10–17. Here we meet it again. It consumes all that is not holy.

The wicked are here 'punished' with everlasting destruction. Such destruction is the just penalty of a righteous God. The word translated

---

18. Both RSV and KJV correctly translate the phrase in v. 8 as 'inflicting' or 'taking vengeance'. There appears to be no textual basis for the NIV, 'He will punish those. . . .' Paul uses the participial phrase *didontos ekdikēsin*, and Isaiah 66:15 (LXX) has the infinitival phrase *apodounai ekdikēsin*. On the other hand, it is unfortunate that the English words 'vengeance' and 'revenge' have popularly taken on a tone of ungodly vindictiveness so that the NIV translators were somewhat limited in final options.

19. Isaiah has *en phlogi pyros* and Paul has *en pyri phlogos*. Several lesser Greek MSS of Thessalonians have words identical to those found in Isaiah.

20. Ridderbos, *Paul* p. 554.

'penalty' emphasizes the idea of a lawful process, 'of a punishment meted out as the result of an even-handed assessment of the rights of the case'.[21] It is from the same root word as 'just' in verse 6 and 'vengeance' ('punish', NIV) in verse 8.

The punishment is *aiōnios* in both senses. It is 'eternal' in quality since it belongs to the Age to Come. It is 'everlasting' in quantity since it will never end. It is not only inescapable; having once occurred, it is also irreversible. Like 'eternal judgment' (Heb. 6:2), 'eternal redemption' (Heb. 9:12) and 'eternal salvation' (Heb. 5:9) – all the everlasting results of actions once completed – we suggest that this 'everlasting destruction' also is the unending result of an action or process of destroying, not the process or action itself. However short or long may be the time of the destroying, a point on which Scripture maintains an awesome and mysterious silence, its result is made clear. The wicked, once destroyed, will never be seen again.

The wicked are so 'punished with everlasting destruction from the presence of the Lord, and from the glory of his power' (2 Thess. 1:9, KJV). This reading accurately reflects the ambiguity of the original, which may be interpreted two ways. Either (a) the everlasting destruction issues from the presence of the Lord, or (b) it consists of exclusion from the presence of the Lord. The KJV allows the first; the RSV, NASB and NIV all translate to mean the second.

Pétavel, an advocate of conditionalism, argues for the first view – that the wicked are 'consumed by the "fire of the face" of the Lord'.[22] So, interestingly, does Strong, an advocate of the traditional understanding of hell.[23] Thayer's lexicon also gives the pronoun this meaning, translating the passage as 'destruction proceeding from the (incensed, wrathful) countenance of the Lord'.[24] Moffatt also favours this interpretation, noting that the 'overwhelming manifestation of the divine glory sweeps from before it ... into endless ruin the disobedient'.[25] The same prepositional phrase is used in Acts 3:19, where it clearly has the idea of source or origin. It also appears in Jeremiah 4:26 (LXX), which speaks of cities burned with fire 'from the face of the Lord' (*apo prosōpou kyriou*), evidently with the same sense of origin or cause.

Arndt and Gingrich, on the other hand, think the pronoun *apo* here means 'away from the presence of',[26] as does Morris, who contrasts this fate with that of the righteous who are for ever 'with the Lord' (1 Thess. 4:17).[27]

But again we ask whether we must choose either to the exclusion of the other? May we not affirm that both interpretations are true? There is Old

---

21. Morris, *Thessalonians* p. 205.
22. *Problem* p. 571.
23. *Theology* 3:1034.
24. Thayer, *Lexicon* p. 59.
25. *Thessalonians* p. 46. Eryl Davies observes that '[t]he verb "punished" here means "to pay a penalty", which is then specified as "everlasting destruction"' but claims that the adjective 'everlasting' calls for unending torment rather than irreversible extinction (*Angry God?* p. 115).
26. *Lexicon*, '*apo*' p. 86.
27. *Thessalonians* p. 206.

Testament support for this suggestion. Paul's phrase, 'from the presence of the Lord and from the glory of his power', appears verbatim three times in the Greek text of Isaiah 2 (vv. 10, 19, 21), a context which also discusses the Lord's exaltation and the wicked's destruction in the last days.[28] The Hebrew text uses an idiom: 'from the face (presence) of the fear of the Lord'. Standard English versions translate it variously as: 'for fear of' (KJV), 'from before the terror of' (RSV), 'from dread of' (NIV). The Septuagint translators, however, transposed the Hebraism word for word into Greek, creating the phrase Paul quotes here (only dropping the word 'fear'). But what does Isaiah describe?

The prophet first warns, then predicts that men will flee to the rocks and caves for fear when God appears to judge. They flee because of dread of the Lord (KJV, NIV) but also away from his approaching terror (RSV).[29] Both meanings are included here, and both seem to fit Paul's similar description in Thessalonians. But God's appearance affects more than the human race alone.

It is important that when God comes to punish sinners, the whole earth suffers in the consequences. God 'rises to shake the earth' (Isa. 2:21). Delitzsch remarks:

> Thus the judgment would fall upon the earth without any limitation, upon men universally . . . and upon the totality of nature . . . . When Jehovah rose up, i.e. stood up from His heavenly throne, to reveal the glory manifested in heaven, and turn its judicial fiery side towards the sinful earth, the earth would receive such a shock as would throw it into a state resembling the chaos of the beginning. We may see very clearly from Rev. vi. 15, where this description is borrowed, that the prophet is here describing the last judgment, although from a national point of view and bounded by a national horizon.[30]

---

28. In each case the Septuagint of Isaiah has *apo prosōpou tou phobou kyriou kai apo tēs doxēs tēs ischyos autou*. Paul has the same words in the same order except he drops the single word *phobou*.

29. The figure probably comes from actual practice, as when Israel fled from enemies to hide in rocks, holes and caves (Judg. 6:2; 1 Sam. 13:6; 14:11). The same picture reappears in Rev. 6:15f.

30. Franz Delitzsch, *Biblical Commentary on the Prophecies of Isaiah* 1:125f. Harmon emphasizes this image of exclusion which he charges that I ignore or overlook ('Case' p. 213). The charge is curious since the present work probably says more about the image of exclusion than any book advocating the traditional notion of everlasting torment. (For example, at pages 99f, 102–104, 109, 112, 117, 118, 153–155, 158, 165). Indeed the image of exclusion is very fruitful with implications that have yet to be explicated in teaching on this subject. The more that occurs, the greater will be the impetus away from the traditional doctrine and toward the view which expects the final extinction of the lost. As mortal creatures, humans did not exist until God made them; their only source of existence is God himself; cut off entirely from God, they cannot expect to exist for even one moment. However it is couched, the traditional view ultimately depends on the unscriptural presupposition that human beings who reject God are necessarily indestructible in body and/or soul, and therefore cannot possibly perish even in hell. For example, Davies acknowledges that those in hell also will be in God's presence and that '[t]o be in the presence of God without a Saviour is to be in hell, for our God is a consuming fire (Heb. 12:29)', explaining later that God will keep those in hell alive as he once kept alive the three Hebrews in the Babylonian furnace (*Angry God?* pp 109, 115).

The same return to primeval chaos figures in the judgment scene of Isaiah 24:1-6, 18ff. and in Jeremiah 4:23-26. In the first the earth finally 'falls – never to rise again' (Isa. 24:20); its inhabitants 'are burned up, and very few are left' (Isa. 24:6). In the second Jeremiah watches as the judgment unfolds. It is a reversal of the creation story. Man disappears from the land and birds from the air, the fruitful ground becomes a barren desert (v. 26), the mountains tremble and shake (v. 24), the lights go out of the heavens (v. 23). The earth is left 'formless and empty' (v. 23), just as it once began. We are also reminded of the time of Noah, when once before the floodgates of heaven opened and the earth's foundations crumbled (Gen. 7:11; Isa. 24:18f); of the judgment at Golgotha, when again the earth trembled under the curse of the broken covenant (Matt. 27:51); and of similar New Testament predictions regarding the end of the world (Heb. 12:26-29; 2 Pet. 3:10-13).

Although it takes on slightly different forms throughout the Bible, this is a recurring pattern. God, who created the earth and gave life to humankind, can also take away that life and destroy the earth. Yet believers in any age may look beyond even that. For when the fire has consumed sinners and the earth has shaken from its place, there will be new heavens and a new earth – the unshakable kingdom of God in which righteousness will dwell for ever (Rom. 8:21; Heb. 12:28f; 2 Pet. 3:13).

Here we have come full circle. Paul tells the Thessalonians that the wicked will be punished with everlasting destruction. It will proceed from God's glorious, fiery presence. It will also remove the wicked away from his presence for ever (2 Thess. 1:9).[31] The faithful will then be counted worthy of the kingdom of God for which they had once suffered (v. 5). Perfect justice will balance the books against every ungodly persecutor (vv. 6ff). The last word is that Jesus Christ will be glorified and marvelled at among the believers (v. 10). This, too, was part of Isaiah's vision of God's great day:

> They raise their voices, they shout for joy; from the west they acclaim the Lord's majesty.

---

31. The ultimate state of perfection which Paul describes in 1 Cor. 15:27f will then have arrived, the time when 'God himself again fills all things with his glorious presence' (Ridderbos, *Paul* p. 561). Yet (Ridderbos does not make this connection) Jesus and Paul both tell us that the wicked will be expelled from God's presence (Matt. 25:41, 46; 2 Thess. 1:9). Conditionalists have reasoned like this: (1) God's presence will fill all that is, in every place; (2) the wicked will not be in his presence; (3) therefore the wicked will no longer exist.

Donald G. Bloesch, on the other hand, believes that while God's 'grace and love will finally encompass all ... this does not mean that his grace and love will be manifest in the same way for every person.' Hell, as well as heaven, he sees as a product of divine love. 'Man is in hell,' Bloesch writes, 'not because God is absent but because he is present, and therefore man is constantly reminded of his guilt and infamy. Hell is exclusion from communion with God, but not exclusion from the presence of God. Even redemptive love is present in hell, but not in the sense that the rejected are brought to redemption; nonetheless, they are ineluctably exposed to redemption' (Donald G. Bloesch, *Essentials* 2:225). Such reasoning is indeed provocative – perhaps even inviting – certainly representative of a keen and dramatic literary mind (Bloesch acknowledges certain credit to C. S. Lewis, *The Great Divorce*). Still the question remains: Where is its exegetical basis in Scripture?

> Therefore in the east give glory to the Lord; exalt the name of the Lord, the God of Israel, in the islands of the sea.
> From the ends of the earth we hear singing: 'Glory to the Righteous One.' (Isa. 24:14ff).

This is one of Paul's most detailed descriptions of the end of the wicked, yet Morris quotes Neil's remark that its

> most notable feature is the reticence of the description. What in normal apocalyptic literature would have included a lurid picture of the tortures of the damned and the bliss of the righteous, in Paul's hands becomes a restrained background of Judgment with the light focussed on the Person of Christ as Judge.[32]

If it does not share the 'lurid details' of much apocalyptic literature, it nevertheless is saturated in the prophetic symbolism of the Old Testament. Certain intertestamental writers took the Old Testament language and added everlasting conscious torment. Paul takes the Old Testament language and adds Jesus Christ.

Nothing in the language here requires conscious unending torment. Repeatedly, however, Paul's words, inspired by the Holy Spirit, send us to the former Scriptures, where the doom of sinners is made clear. They will perish, be destroyed, be burned up, be gone for ever. When God rises to judge the earth, creation itself returns to chaos! How much more vulnerable is man, Isaiah (2:22) asks us, 'who has but a breath in his nostrils. Of what account is he?'

The Major Epistles

The Epistles to the Corinthians, the Galatians and the Romans are described as 'major' because of their extensive development of important themes and in view of their influence on the later Christian church. In them all, Paul touches on the final destiny of the wicked, and they exemplify his most detailed teaching during the prime of his ministry.

Galatians 1:8f. Paul insists that the gospel he preaches is the only message worthy of that name. He offers a double warning to those who are perverting the gospel:

> But even if we or an angel from heaven should preach a gospel other than the one we preached to you, let him be eternally condemned! As we have already said, so now I say again: If anybody is preaching to you a gospel other than what you accepted, let him be eternally condemned!

The NIV's 'eternally condemned' is interpretive though probably correct. The RSV and KJV translate more precisely, 'accursed', though none of the three consistently translates the same word everywhere it appears. Paul actually wrote *anathema* (see 1 Cor. 16:22, KJV). The word literally meant something set up or laid by to be kept, as a votive offering might be hung on a temple wall after being devoted to a god. Because offerings devoted to the true God were commonly burnt in their entirety or

---

32. Morris, *Thessalonians* p. 202.

otherwise destroyed, the word in biblical usage signifies something 'accursed' or doomed to destruction.

Paul uses it thus in two other letters. He tells the Romans that he would sacrifice himself as one marked for destruction (*anathema*) if this would save his Israelite brethren (Rom. 9:3). Moses had made a similar offer to God (Exod. 32:32). Neither Moses nor Paul could fill such a function since both were themselves sinners, also in need of a substitute. The Lord Jesus did bear the full penalty given one accursed by God, though Paul warns that it is blasphemy to say Jesus himself deserved what he received (1 Cor. 12:3). What happened to Jesus on Golgotha was the proper fate of one made *anathema*, however, though the innocent Jesus there stood in the place of us sinners.

Death by execution was the sentence this word called for, as seen in the case of Jesus and in the Old Testament background. A verb form of the word appears four times in the New Testament, in each case meaning to swear an oath calling down God's anathema curse if one is not telling the truth (Mark 14:71; Acts 23:12, 14, 21). The Septuagint had ordinarily used *anathema* as the Greek translation of the Hebrew *herem*, the usual term for something 'devoted' to God and therefore, under normal circumstances, to be totally destroyed. It is used of the Canaanites whom God tells Israel to 'totally destroy' and whom they do 'completely destroy' (Num. 21:2f; words in quotation marks represent *herem*, Heb.; or *anathema*, Gk). A NIV footnote to this passage says the Hebrew word 'refers to the irrevocable giving over of things or persons to the Lord, often by totally destroying them'. The site of this destruction is called Hormah (from *herem*), which the Greek text gives as *Anathema*. The same name is given the town of Zephath during the time of the Judges for the very same reason (Judg. 1:17).[33] When Zechariah promises that glorified Jerusalem will always be inhabited, he uses the same word, saying that it will never be anathema ('destroyed', Zech. 14:11, NIV).[34]

When the Canaanite spoils are 'set apart for destruction', the Septuagint uses *anathema* (Deut. 7:26). The most famous incident involved Achan and Jericho. The city and all its spoils were *anathema* or 'devoted to destruction', as would be any Israelite who took from its spoils for himself (Josh. 6:17f; 7:12). Achan did so and paid the precise penalty the word demanded. He was utterly destroyed – in this case stoned to death, burned with fire and covered with rocks (Josh. 7:25f). No Israelite would have doubted that Achan was destroyed because there were physical remains. None would argue that Achan was not chemically 'annihilated'! Nor did they think that 'destruction' meant he should be fastened in a cage and tortured endlessly. They knew what it meant to be *herem/anathema*, and they carried out that sentence.

This is the word's meaning throughout the Scriptures, including the present passage. Because Paul refers to a punishment of the Age to

---

33. The word is *anathema* in Codex Vaticanus. Codex Alexandrinus has *exolethreusis*, formed from the verb Peter uses in Acts 3:23. This apparent interchangeability is especially interesting since NT writers use both words in connection with the fate of the wicked.

34. Zechariah's words seem to be in view in Revelation 22:3, where John uses *katathema* ('curse'), a slightly different form of the same noun.

Come, we need not automatically assign *anathema* a meaning it has never had before. The method of God's punishment will surely be different, but the meaning will be the same. If even an angel from heaven preaches a different gospel, Paul says he comes under this sentence. He is *anathema / herem* – devoted to utter destruction.

Galatians 5:21 Believers are not tied down by Law, but neither are they free to live out their sinful desires. The same Spirit who liberates from legalism also legislates against fleshly license (Gal. 5:16ff). Believers must not give in to their sinful nature, and Paul regards it as obvious what kind of life that forbids (vv. 19ff). Those who 'live like this will not inherit the kingdom of God' (v. 21). Paul makes a similar statement to the Ephesians (Eph. 5:5) and to the Corinthians (1 Cor. 6:9f).

His words speak of exclusion rather than infliction; they describe what sinners will lose, not what they will find. Paul may well be echoing the Master in these pronouncements, for Jesus, too, spoke often of being thrown out of God's kingdom and excluded from eternal bliss. (See comments earlier on Matt. 5:20; 7:23; 8:11f; 13:40–43; 22:13; 25:31–46.) Paul here adds nothing to what Jesus had said already.

Galatians 6:8 The epistle ends on a similar note. 'The one who sows to please his sinful nature, from that nature will reap destruction; the one who sows to please the Spirit, from the Spirit will reap eternal life.'

The NIV expands Paul's 'flesh' (*sarx* – not *sōma*, 'body') to 'sinful nature', but we are more concerned here with the consequences than with the crime. One wonders however why the NIV translators chose 'destruction' instead of 'corruption' to represent *phthora*, especially since the latter was already familiar through the KJV, RSV and NASB, and preferred by the NIV at least once elsewhere (2 Pet. 1:4).

In ordinary Greek this word spoke of 'ruin, destruction, dissolution, deterioration, corruption'.[35] Paul uses it of perishable food (Col. 2:22) and of the world which is decaying (Rom. 8:21). Peter applies it to animals destined to be killed (2 Peter 2:12, NIV 'destroyed'). Arndt and Gingrich cite nonbiblical sources where the word refers to an abortion or a miscarriage; it had the same meaning in Christian literature of the second century. 'You shall not murder a child by abortion' is the injunction of both Barnabas (19:5) and the Didache (2:2). 'Abortion' is *phthora*, which Paul uses here. Metaphorically, the word could be used in a moral sense as in the 'depravity' of wicked men (2 Pet. 2:12). The verb (*phtheirō*) meant to 'corrupt' or to ruin and can be used of destroying a house (1 Cor. 3:17), seducing a virgin (2 Cor. 11:3), ruining a man financially (2 Cor. 7:2), or corrupting someone's morals (1 Cor. 15:33; Eph. 4:22; Rev. 19:2). We merely observe that the maiden's virginity is for ever gone though she continues to live, the man's financial security is annihilated though he personally survives, the building as a building is destroyed even if its blocks remain, and the good character which once existed is no longer to be found.

Annihilation, in the scientific sense of modern physics, is not under

---

35. Arndt & Gingrich, *Lexicon* p. 865.

consideration, but that in no way lessens the true ruin, corruption or destruction of what once was but is no more. This would hardly be worth mentioning except for its relevance to an argument frequently used. According to many traditionalists, when these words are applied to final punishment they cannot have their normal meaning, since even such biblical figures as ashes under foot or smoke rising in the air do not signify literal annihilation. Having ruled out this supposed 'literal' sense of 'destroy', 'ruin' and 'perish', this argument goes on to point out that only figurative or metaphorical meanings are left. The conclusion is then drawn that 'destroy', 'ruin' and 'perish' must mean eternal conscious torment, not extinction. Words which on their face would seem to suggest 'loss of life' are said to signify a 'life of loss' instead. Buis, for example, writes:

> The annihilationist places a great emphasis on the fact that the figure of 'fire' is used in the Bible to describe future punishment; and fire, they point out, always destroys .... But the fact is that when you burn something it is not annihilated, it simply changes form.[36]

Salmond insists that if terms such as death, destruction and perdition 'are used of objects whose nature it is to cease to be, they will have the literal sense. But if they are employed of objects whose nature is the opposite, they will have a larger meaning.'[37] He really means that 'they will have an opposite meaning', and that immortal souls cannot die, perish or be destroyed.

It is strange to object that because biblical figures of eschatological destruction do not fit our scientific view of physical annihilation, they must be emptied of their ordinary meaning altogether. Scripture uses them to say something; surely that 'something' is not the precise opposite of their usual sense. The greatest orthodox theologians have always insisted that God, who created, can also destroy. In this they have merely echoed the words of the Son of God himself (Mt 10:28). Even if the wicked should be assumed immortal, God is able to destroy them. But it is always to the glorified bodies of the righteous that Scripture attributes incorruptibility and immortality in the Age to Come, never to 'souls' apart from bodies, of the righteous now, or of the wicked at any time.

There is no good reason not to take Paul's primary words in their most normal sense. He says the wicked will 'perish', 'die', be 'corrupted' or be 'destroyed'. Those terms have very definite connotations to the most simple person. We need not all become advanced physicists discussing material 'annihilation'. When we speak of final punishment, we are speaking of a realm which transcends the present space-time world with all its laws of energy, matter and thermodynamics.

We recognize that these key terms are used at times in a figurative or metaphorical sense. Yet the very fact that a word can have such an extended sense presupposes an ordinary and literal sense in the first place. Furthermore, the ordinary sense gives meaning to the figurative or extended usage, not the other way around. It is highly questionable,

---

36. *Eternal Punishment* pp. 125ff.
37. *Immortality* p. 615.

therefore, whether one should so casually dismiss Paul's word 'corruption' or its verb form 'to corrupt' when used of the sinner's doom (1 Cor. 3:17; Gal. 6:8; cf. Jude 10), especially when the only reason given is a dogmatic argument concerning the nature of hell — itself the subject under consideration.

The adjective member of this family is *phthartos*, and all agree that it means subject to corruption or decay. It occurs six times in the New Testament, four times in Paul's writings, and twice in Peter's. In every case it is used in a specific contrast between something that passes away (perishes or decays) and something that endures.

Paul contrasts 'mortal' creatures with the immortal God (Rom. 1:23), the crown that 'will not last' with one that lasts for ever (1 Cor. 9:25). He contrasts our present body, which is 'perishable,' with the glorified resurrection body, which will not be (1 Cor. 15:53f). Peter contrasts 'perishable' silver and gold with the eternal redemptive blood of Jesus Christ (1 Pet. 1:18), or 'perishable' seed with the imperishable word of God (1 Pet. 1:23).

What comfort is there in the thought of an 'imperishable' God, crown or resurrection body if the 'perishable' thing really also lasts for ever? Why is it so clear that the adjective signifies things which come to an end, but the noun and the verb, used in the same eschatological connection, suddenly take on figurative and metaphorical meanings? Is this sober exegesis, or is it dodging a dogmatic weakness?

In Galatians 6:8 Paul explicitly contrasts the issue of the flesh ('sinful nature', *sarx*) on the one hand and the harvest of the Spirit on the other. The first brings forth corruption (possibly we should think of a miscarriage). The second brings eternal life.

The most natural way to understand the opposite of life is as death or non-life — not life in misery. The fact that 'eternal life' involves so much more than mere existence only heightens Paul's contrast involving 'corruption'. If ordinary life stands over against death, can the opposite of 'eternal' life be any less drastic? By what means can 'loss of life' be converted to a 'life of loss'? If the 'life' is of a more precious and enduring quality than any we now fully experience, that makes the loss of it all the more tragic, but it is more terrible precisely because it is loss.

1 Corinthians 3:17 'If anyone destroys God's temple,' Paul warns, 'God will destroy him.' Paul is concerned about divisions in the church and adds a word of explanation: 'You [plural] are that temple.' Such factions are among the obvious acts of the sinful nature which, as Paul told the Galatians, result in 'destruction or corruption' (Gal. 5:20; 6:8). Now he warns the Corinthians similarly. The verb he uses here (*phtheirō*, 'destroy') is cognate with the noun 'corruption' or 'destruction' used in Galatians.

The unity of God's temple must be kept intact if there is truly to be a temple. A heap of broken blocks is no building. Such physical remains only increase the sense of loss felt by those who observe them. Even if the Old Testament pictures of corpses eaten by worms and fire or of rising smoke were intended to be literal, physical descriptions of the end of sinners (which we need not suppose), such material remains as ashes or smoke would not cancel the threat of this passage that 'God will destroy' the one who destroys his temple. Yet again we recall Matthew 10:28.

1 Corinthians 6:9 Again Paul says that the immoral will not inherit the kingdom of God. (See on Galatians 5:21 above.)

1 Corinthians 16:22 'If anyone does not love the Lord – a curse be on him.' The KJV says 'let him be anathema'; the RSV, 'let him be accursed'. The word is the same one Paul used in Galatians 1:8, 9 (see above).

Romans 1:18 'The wrath of God is being revealed from heaven against all the godlessness and wickedness of men who suppress the truth by their wickedness.' 'Revealed' has eschatological overtones here and in the verse preceding. There Paul had said that 'in the gospel a righteousness from God is revealed'. Both times he uses the verb *apokalyptō* – to 'uncover' or 'reveal'.

The last day will be a time for uncovering all that is now hidden. We have already noted Paul's statement that Jesus himself will then be revealed as he is (2 Thess. 1:7; cf. 1 Cor. 4:3ff; 1 John 3:2). The last day has not yet come, but already the gospel story of Jesus Christ's death and resurrection 'reveals' its most important features. Those features are the divine righteousness (or verdict of acquittal) and divine wrath. God's judgment means either vindication or condemnation.

As representative Man, Jesus has already been vindicated before God's tribunal. Those who believe the gospel will enter the judgment empty-handed, pointing in that day only to the work Jesus has accomplished apart from them and on their behalf. Since they already know the standard of God's judgment (perfection), the plea they will present before the divine tribunal (Jesus Christ alone, by faith), and the estimate God places on that appeal (justification, righteousness, vindication or acquittal), the last day will not take them by surprise, and they can anticipate it now without doubt or fear.

In a similar way the gospel already uncovers God's negative verdict of judgment. But divine wrath against sin is uncovered in the very same preview that reveals divine righteousness – that is, the death and resurrection of Jesus Christ. This very 'revealing' character of the gospel makes the period of time it is preached the 'last days', for it declares that the act of resurrection and judgment has already begun with the Man, Jesus of Nazareth. The consummation remains, but it will be just that – the completion and fulfilment of what is already known in principle through the gospel.

The death of Jesus Christ 'reveals' the divine wrath in a way no apocalyptic literature ever could, however powerful its imagination or picturesque its terms, as we have seen in Chapter 11 above.

Romans 1:32 It is 'God's righteous decree' that those who give themselves over to the depravity described in Romans 1:21–31 'deserve death'. Twice more in Romans Paul says that sin leads to 'death' (Rom. 6:21, 23). That was God's sentence pronounced in Eden (Gen. 2:17). Plato taught that death was a friend which separated the immortal soul from the imprisoning body. But no Hebrew prophet ever spoke in such terms, nor does any word of Scripture. Death is God's punishment for sin, and in Romans 6:23 it stands in stark contrast to eternal 'life'. (See above on Galatians 6:8.)

Romans 2:6–11 Along with 2 Thessalonians 1:6–10, these verses contain Paul's most detailed teaching concerning the fate of the lost. In both places the context concerns the justice of God's judgment – as it involves suffering Christians and their persecutors (Thessalonians), and as it concerns the impenitent and the faithful (Romans). In Thessalonians God's justice gives comfort and inspires hope; in Romans it warns against carelessness and rebukes indifference. These are the pertinent phrases:

> God 'will give to each person according to what he has done.' To those who by persistence in doing good seek glory, honour and immortality, he will give eternal life. But for those who are self-seeking and who reject the truth and follow evil, there will be wrath and anger. There will be trouble and distress for every human being who does evil: first for the Jew, then for the Gentile; but glory, honour and peace for everyone who does good: first for the Jew, then for the Gentile. For God does not show favouritism.

Paul first states the principle that God will recompense individually and fairly. He echoes Psalm 62:12 (LXX, v. 13) where the same words are used of God's strength and love. Proverbs 24:12 has the words in a warning against cowardice and moral neutrality. Both settings figure also in Paul's discussion that follows.

Some individuals persistently do the good, by this demonstrating their search for glory, honour and immortality. God will give these eternal life (v. 7), a kind of summary term which also includes 'glory, honour and immortality' (vv. 7, 10). For Paul, immortality is always God's gift to the faithful, to be awarded in the resurrection. He never views it as an inherent characteristic nor does he ever attribute it to the wicked. This fact bears repeating since it is so often overlooked. 'Eternal life' is not mere existence – it is the deathless life of God's glorified people, who share in Christ's own honour in the Age to Come.

Over against these (Paul uses the contrasting *men / de* construction in vv. 7f) are others who prefer evil to truth, pleasing themselves to pleasing God. God will award them 'wrath and anger, trouble and distress'. The first pair (wrath and anger) describe the retribution from the standpoint of God's displeasure and contrast with the eternal life promised the righteous a verse earlier. The second pair (trouble and distress) describe the same punishment from the standpoint of its recipients in contrast to the bliss promised the righteous a verse later.[38]

'Wrath' is *orgē* (see above on 1 Thess. 1:10). When the synonym 'anger' (*thymos*) accompanies it, it is usually to strengthen or intensify the meaning. The pair occur together of human anger (Eph. 4:31; Col. 3:8) and of God's (Rev. 14:10; 16:19; 19:15). Righteous judgment does not exclude God's personal fury against wilful and unrepentant sinners. Justice, in fact, demands it!

The pair 'trouble' (*thlipsis*) and 'distress' (*stenochōria*) also appear in

---

38. So also Murray, *Romans* (NICNT), p. 66. The NIV brings out Paul's contrast.

combination elsewhere in Paul. God's people encounter these opponents in the present world, he says, but they cannot separate the believer from God's love (Rom. 8:35). Such 'trouble and hardship' actually mark the faithful as God's true servants (2 Cor. 6:4). Paul is one of those who are 'hard pressed . . . but not crushed', and he uses these same two words in participle form to say so (2 Cor. 4:8). This last translation is suggestive for our present verse. Judgment day will find the wicked 'hard pressed' – to the point of being 'crushed'.

Paul's readers who knew the Septuagint would likely remember Zephaniah 1:14–18 as they read these words. Time and again Paul repeats in this gospel setting the words and phrases Zephaniah had used in his classic description of the great day of the Lord. Zephaniah spoke of 'the day of the Lord's wrath' (v. 18), and so did Paul (v. 5).[39] Zephaniah pictured 'wrath' (*orgē*, v. 15) and 'distress' (*thlipsis*, vv. 15, 17; Paul's 'trouble') as well as 'trouble' (v. 15, not Paul's Greek word).

If we read the prophet as a background to the apostle, Paul's description pales by comparison. Romans emphasizes God's justice (vv. 5, 6, 11) and includes the wicked's punishment under that. Zephaniah's portrayal of the day of wrath is unmixed terror. He mixes metaphors freely: the blood of sinners 'will be poured out like dust and their entrails like filth' (v. 17) and God will 'consume' the whole world in 'the fire of his jealousy' (v. 18). Literalists could probably arrange a scenario, but Zephaniah does not. He is painting a picture. Both scenes have a single meaning: God 'will make a sudden end of all who live in the earth' (v. 18).

Is not Paul making the same point? He says nothing about everlasting torment. For him, immortality (like incorruption, glory, honour and eternal life) is always God's gift to the saved. Paul, like Jesus, freely borrows from the Old Testament's prophetic vocabulary. Also like Jesus, he adds to the Old Testament picture – not details of unending tortures, as did some of his contemporaries and many of his successors, but the shining, single beam of the gospel and in particular the figure of Jesus. What the New Testament adds to the content of previous apocalyptic literature is not lurid details of conscious torment, but Jesus.

The cross has replaced the Valley of Hinnom as the best picture of God's wrath. In advance of the cross, Jesus spoke of his death in guarded terms and used the intertestamental term 'Gehenna' of the fate of the wicked. After the cross and Pentecost, however, no New Testament writer ever again uses that phrase of final punishment.[40] Paul, who says more on the subject than any of the others, points continually to Jesus' death as its clearest revelation. With the death and resurrection of Jesus, judgment day has already begun. The gospel 'reveals' it to men and women everywhere. It is God's last call to repent!

Romans 2:12 God gave the Jews greater privileges than the Gentiles, and with them greater responsibilities. But God will judge both righteously.

---

39. Zephaniah refers to the 'Day of the Lord' (LXX – *kyriou*). Paul omits *kyriou* in his expression 'the day of wrath'. For Paul the title of 'Lord' now belongs to the exalted and glorified Jesus.

40. The Gospels were written after the fact, of course, but they represent the teaching they contain to be that given by Jesus while on earth.

'All who sin apart from the law will also perish apart from the law.' John Murray comments:

> The perishing ... can be none other than that defined in the preceding verses as consisting in the infliction of God's wrath and indignation and the endurance of tribulation and anguish in contrast with the glory, honour, incorruption, and peace bestowed upon the heirs of eternal life.[41]

Murray rightly perceives that Paul contrasts those who 'perish' with those who receive 'immortality'. Perishing therefore comes down on the side of mortality. That Paul always attributes immortality exclusively to the saved, while associating corruption, death, destruction and perishing with the wicked, strongly suggests that the wicked will be revived[42] in a mortal and corruptible body, suffer according to God's exact justice, then pass away for ever in the penal extinction John calls the 'second death'.

Traditionalist writers often urge that 'perish' (*apollymi*) is used of ruined wineskins (Matt. 9:17) and spoiled food (John 6:12); consequently casual readers may assume that the word's primary meaning must be very mild indeed. Here are the facts. *Apollymi* appears 92 times in the New Testament, 13 times in Paul's letters. Most often it refers to actual death.[43] Sometimes it is contrasted with enduring, eternal life.[44] It is the regular term for the 'lost' or for those who are 'perishing.'[45] Several times it describes the final state of the wicked in the Age to Come.[46]

To those who are 'perishing' (*appollymenois*) the gospel has a 'stench of death' – a fact in keeping with our earlier suggestion that they will be raised mortal, then return to corruption and final extinction (2 Cor. 2:16). Peter uses this word of the fate which befell the world before the Flood (2 Pet. 3:6). Paul (1 Cor. 10:9, 10) and Jude (Jude 5) use it to describe Israel's destruction in the wilderness.

Jesus once drew a specific picture in which this word stands for one possibility and the resurrection to life represents the other (John 6:39). Similarly, Paul says that if Christ has not been raised, then 'those who have fallen asleep in Christ are lost' (1 Cor. 15:18; the same word). What would be the state of dead believers without Christ's resurrection? This picture, alongside the great Flood, Israelite corpses scattered across the desert, the 'stench of death', and the common use of this term to describe ordinary death, all make it plain that we should think of something more than burst wineskins or wasted food when it is used of the doom of the ungodly. Taken literally, these various pictures contradict each other. Taken seriously, they paint a single picture of utter, shameful extinction.

Romans 6:21, 23 Twice Paul says that sin leads to 'death', which he places in opposition to 'eternal life'. In our present experience, life and

---

41. Murray, *Romans* p. 70.
42. See the discussion on Matt. 10:28 in the previous chapter.
43. Matt. 2:13; 8:25; 12:14; 16:25; 21:41; 22:7; 26:52; 27:20; John 10:10; 11:50; 18:14; Acts 5:37; 1 Cor. 10:9f.; Jude 5, 11.
44. John 6:27; 10:28; 12:25; Heb. 1:11; 1 Pet. 1:7.
45. Matt. 10:6; 15:24; 18:11; 1 Cor. 1:18f.; 2 Cor. 2:15; 4:3; 2 Thess. 2:10; etc.
46. Matt. 5:29, 30; 10:28; John 3:16; 17:12; 2 Pet. 3:9.

death are opposites, and the dead are no longer among the living. Eternal life is the opposite of eternal death. Paul never gives us reason to suppose that eternal death is anything other than what it sounds like. Rather, he strengthens these connotations by such words as 'perish', 'destruction' and 'corruption'.

Ephesians 5:5f Paul warns against immorality and the deceitfulness of sin: 'No immoral, impure or greedy person – such a man is an idolater – has any inheritance in the kingdom of Christ and of God. Let no one deceive you with empty words, for because of such things God's wrath comes on those who are disobedient.'

We have met both of Paul's expressions already. On exclusion from the kingdom, see above on 1 Corinthians 6:9f. On the wrath of God, see on Romans 2:8 and 1 Thessalonians 1:10.

Philippians 1:28 Like their fellow Greeks at Thessalonica, the Philippian disciples met opposition from their neighbours. Paul encourages them with the prospect that their very persecution is a present sign of God's impending judgment – and their full salvation! Do not be 'frightened in any way by those who oppose you', he says. 'This is a sign to them that they will be destroyed, but that you will be saved – and that by God.'

'Destruction' here is *apōleias*, from *apollymi*. See the discussion on Romans 2:12. Paul contrasts this fate of the wicked with the reward of the righteous, who will be saved (*sōtēria*). Cf 1 Thessalonians 1:10. Jesus also pointed believers to God, who is able to 'save' and to 'destroy' (Matt.10:28; cf. James 4:12).

Philippians 3:19 Paul has just noted (v. 18) that some 'live as enemies of the cross of Christ'. 'Their destiny', he now says, 'is destruction, their god is their stomach, and their glory is in their shame. Their mind is on earthly things.'

The end ('destiny', *telos*) of such sinners is 'destruction'. The word is *apōleia*, the same used in Philippians 1:28, from *apollymi*, which Paul uses in Romans 2:12, discussed above. Here the apostle contrasts 'destruction' with being immortalized in glory. Though they suffer now, he says, believers look forward to the coming of a Saviour, the Lord Jesus (v. 20). He will then 'transform our lowly bodies so that they will be like his glorious body' (v. 21). Paul discusses this change in the bodies of the saved in his great resurrection chapter (1 Cor. 15:42–54). Again we observe that, for Paul, immortality is God's resurrection boon to the righteous. The wicked will also rise to face judgment, but their 'destiny is destruction'. They have served their stomach (carnal appetites) as their god; it cannot give immortality but will perish itself (1 Cor. 6:13; note contrast in v. 14).

Colossians 3:6 Sins of the earthly nature may give pleasure now, but because of them 'the wrath of God is coming'. On the expression see previous comments (Rom. 2:8; 1 Thess. 1:10).

Paul's language in its philosophical context

In his classic conditionalist work, Henry Constable developed an argument about the meaning of Paul's major words for the end of the wicked, based on their usage in the philosophical discussion both before and during the time of Paul. Edward White, Constable's contemporary and himself a noted advocate of conditional immortality, adopted a similar approach. Like many other conditionalist arguments, this one has been completely ignored by traditionalist writers. If there is no satisfactory answer, perhaps this should be acknowledged. If there is a good answer, someone ought to bring it forward and refute Constable's argument.

Constable began by pointing out that the subject of immortality was a topic of lively discussion in Paul's day both by philosophers and also among the common people. Paul's terms for the fate of the wicked — 'corrupt', 'die', 'destroy' — were all stock words in this discussion. According to Constable,

> In every school the question before us was discussed in the phrases and language of the New Testament. In Jerusalem and Rome, at Athens and Corinth, in Ephesus and Antioch — wherever a Christian preacher opened his mouth to speak to man of his future destiny — were Platonists, or Epicureans, or Stoics, or Alexandrians, to whom the question of immortality was a question of solemn thought, with whom the phrases in which the preacher addressed them as to their solemn future were familiar household words.[47]

Particularly well known was Plato's work entitled the *Phaedo*, a dialogue written to advance the philosopher's concept of the immortality of every soul. It told the story of the martyrdom of Socrates, who, on the day he was to die, discoursed with his friends about death and his hope beyond it. Socrates' hope was the immortality of the soul. He believed that any philosopher should not only meet death courageously but actually welcome it, since death restored the immortal soul from imprisonment in the mortal body to its former, natural state.

White says the *Phaedo* 'was as well known among the reading population of the Macedonian and Roman empires as any tragedy of Shakespeare is known among English readers'[48] and both well known and widely studied in Paul's day, 400 years after it was written. The words Plato used to express his leading ideas, according to White, 'formed a fixed element of thought and speech over the wide area where his works were studied in the numerous academies and schools around the Mediterranean shores'.[49]

At one point in the conversation, Socrates' friend Cebes disagrees with the philosopher. Socrates held that the soul continued after death in a state preferable to the one it occupied before. Cebes, however, was inclined to think that the soul, 'when it has departed from the body, *nowhere any longer exists*, but on whatever day a man dies, on that day it is destroyed (*diaphtheiretai*) and perishes (*apollyetai*); the moment it departs and goes forth from the body it is dispersed like breath or smoke,

---

47. *Punishment* pp. 42f.
48. *Life in Christ* p. 260.
49. Ibid.

and flies abroad, and is gone, and *no longer exists anywhere.*'⁵⁰ Whether Cebes was right or wrong matters less for our study than the terminology he used to express his view. For the two words which he uses to describe the utter annihilation of the soul, are two of the primary words Paul employs to describe the end of the wicked.

Plato argues that every soul is immortal by nature. He therefore denies that any soul can ever become extinct or pass out of existence. In what terms does Plato express this denial? Constable answers with conviction:

> *In the very terms in which the punishment of the wicked is asserted in the New Testament!* When the latter says the soul shall die, Plato says it shall not die; when the latter says it shall be destroyed, Plato says it shall not be destroyed; when the latter says it shall perish and suffer corruption, Plato says it shall not perish and is incorruptible. The phrases are the very same, only that what Plato denies of all souls alike the New Testament asserts of some of the souls of men.⁵¹

White makes the same observation. Both Plato and Paul use the terms 'death' (*thanatos*), 'destruction' (*apōleia*), 'corruption' (*phthora*), 'perish' (*olethros*) and 'die' *(apothnēsko)* – but with this difference: Plato says none of these things will ever befall the soul, for it possesses immortality; Paul says these words define the destiny of those who resist God and refuse to believe in Jesus. Furthermore, White continues,

> In Plato's dialogue these words stand for extinction of life, for that idea only, and in the strongest possible contrast to the idea of perpetuation of being. Our argument is that in the New Testament they signify precisely the same doom, – the final and absolute extinction of life in the case of the wicked.⁵²

Interestingly, Plato believed that some would be punished for ever (or at least for a very long time after death). Such reprobate souls can continue in misery, he said, because they possess 'immortality', are 'indestructible' and 'immortal'. Yet 'not one of these terms is ever used in the New Testament to describe the future condition of the lost.'⁵³ Others in Paul's day taught universal annihilation, believing that when people died they perished completely and for ever, both body and soul, and there was no future life of any kind for any person. The Epicureans represented such a view among the Greeks, and the Sadducees did among the Jews. 'Now,' asks Constable, 'in what terms and by what language did such men set forth their views? Simply and entirely by their application to all men alike of the very terms which the New Testament applies to the future punishment of the wicked.'⁵⁴

50. R. F. Weymouth, from a letter to E. Pétavel. Quoted in Pétavel. *Immortality* pp. 493f. Italics original.
51. *Future Punishment* p. 42. Italics original.
52. *Life in Christ* p. 361. White discusses the Greek words and their familiar usage in the philosophical dialogue concerning immortality on pages 362ff. Constable gives quotations from the same discourses in both Greek and English in *Future Punishment* pp. 42–45.
53. *Future Punishment* p. 48.
54. Ibid. pp. 48f.

Such a mass of evidence calls for careful consideration. R. F. Weymouth, a Greek scholar and translator of the New Testament, wrote:

> My mind fails to conceive a grosser misinterpretation of language than when the five or six strongest words which the Greek tongue possesses, signifying 'destroy', or 'destruction', are explained to mean maintaining an everlasting but wretched existence. To translate black as white is nothing to this.[55]

Weymouth's challenge is daring and unequivocal. Constable and White also press their point with vigour. Is there a traditionalist answer which can meet this evidence fairly and squarely? The literature of the past does not reveal it. Are these conditionalist challengers enemy Goliaths wrongfully provoking God's people? Or are they modern Gideons sent to tear down a hollow Baal which is powerless to make a response?

---

55. Quoted by White in *Life in Christ* p. 365, from a letter. Modern examples of the practice Weymouth denounced include Stahlin's statement that 'eschatological *apōleia* in its most terrible form is not, of course, annihilation or extinction of being; it is eternal *basanismos* [torment]' Stahlin, 'Orgē,' *TDNT* 5:444). Another is O. Oepke's remark concerning *apōleia* ('destruction') that 'What is meant here is not a simple extinction of existence, but an everlasting state of torment and death' (O. Oepke, *'Apōleia' TDNT* 1:397). These are conclusions to be proved, not presuppositions from which to begin reading the Bible.

13

Final Punishment in the Rest of the New Testament

We have briefly examined final punishment in the teaching of Jesus, as revealed in the great judgment on Calvary, and as presented in the writings of Paul. In this chapter we summarize the evidence to be found in the rest of the New Testament.

James, Hebrews and the sermons found in Acts all speak from a 'Jewish' standpoint and may present such teaching as was commonly given or received within a Palestinian messianic community. Hebrews may be written by someone outside Palestine, and Luke of course was a Gentile, but the generalization still has merit. Peter, Jude and John also are Hebrews of Palestinian origin, but they evidently address their works to churches composed of either Gentiles or Diaspora Jews. 2 Peter and Jude are very much alike, and both use apocalyptic language as a vehicle for expression. Revelation gives its Greek name ('Apocalypse') to other literature which shares its characteristic style. Formerly many scholars looked largely to Gentile literature for help in deciphering its symbols. Today they are increasingly recognizing the book's dependence on the Old Testament. itself.[1] 2 Peter, Jude or possibly the book of Revelation were in all likelihood the last New Testament books to be written.

Hebrews

The authorship, audience, time and place of origin of Hebrews are all still in question.[2] Internal evidence suggests that this sermonic exhortation was written for Hebrew-Christian believers who at some time beyond their initial conversion and experience of the new life had second thoughts about the commitment they had made and what they had left behind. The author constantly explains the new covenant in terms of the old one it has superseded. He uses Old Testament Scripture frequently, and points

---

1. Numerous illustrative quotations could be supplied and some will be offered later. Here we merely note that not only Revelation but the entire N.T. from Jesus onward builds on the foundation of O.T. teaching and eschatology. This is taken for granted in most areas by biblical theologians, but has been overlooked in most traditionalist literature when it comes to interpreting N.T. symbols and terms describing final punishment. Evangelicals who hold a high view of Scripture should surely lead the way in making this relationship clear in theory and useful in practice. Instead, they have often talked as if the O.T. had little or nothing to offer, then have turned to the uninspired intertestamental literature to give content to N.T. language. Without doubt, that literature must be considered, but it ought never to take precedence over the O.T. Word of God.

2. I have attempted a popular summary of these matters in *Our Man in Heaven: An Exposition of the Epistle to the Hebrews* pp. 11–14.

always to Jesus Christ. In the matter of final punishment the book of Hebrews also speaks with Jesus Christ in view, using familiar Old Testament terms and pictures.

Hebrews 2:2 Because Jesus is so much greater than the angels in his person and in his position, his hearers are under special responsibility. Moses' law was mediated by angels (Acts 7:38; Gal. 3:19), and its violators were punished severely. 'How shall we escape if we ignore such a great salvation . . . announced by the Lord?' the writer asks. The answer is obvious — there will be no escape. This passage gives no details of that terrible and certain punishment, but it does make those two points plain.

Some have argued that this punishment 'worse than death' must be everlasting conscious torment. That is a possibility, so far as the silence of this passage goes, but it is not the only possibility. Jesus warned that God can 'destroy body and soul in hell.' Even the Mosaic executioners could not do that. The death penalty now will be as nothing compared to the horror of rising in the 'resurrection unto condemnation' only to perish eternally in the second and final death. Yet even that is not all the punishment involved, as Hebrews itself later will make clear.

Hebrews 6:1 The resurrection of the dead (*anastaseōs nekrōn*, not *ek tōn nekrōn*) is a foundational teaching of Christianity, as is the doctrine of eternal judgment. Both resurrection and judgment are eschatological events, part of the end-time agenda. Yet both have already started in the case of Jesus of Nazareth (Heb. 9:27f.).[3] A day of reckoning is coming when all who have lived will rise to hear God's final word of judgment. This is so integral to true Christianity that our author here calls it 'elementary'.

Regardless of the precise nature of hell, there is absolutely no argument between conditionalists and traditionalists on this point.[4] Biblical ortho-

---

3. This is one key to understanding the gospel principle of justification by faith and certainly a key to Heb.9:27f. in its larger context.

4. Thus Guillebaud, a traditionalist who embraced conditionalism: 'We are living in days when the awful possibilities of human wickedness are being revealed as they have not been for centuries, and faith would have a hard task indeed, if it could not be sure that God will demand a full account for all the abominable cruelties and wrongs that are done on earth. And this would be impossible, if the only alternative to eternal life were a painless end to existence at the time of bodily death. The resurrection to judgment, and the infliction of penal suffering, are absolutely essential to the justice of God' (Guillebaud, *Righteous Judge* p. 65).

Henry Constable, making the same point, sharply distinguishes his position from that which denies that the wicked will rise to face judgment : 'We have no sympathy with those who deny the resurrection of the wicked. We know that there are writers who hold our view of the destruction of the ungodly, who also . . . hold that they will never rise to judgment . . . But now, once for all, we disavow any connection or sympathy with them on this point. We think their view false, and mischievous in the extreme . . . For ourselves, we have no doubt that the resurrection of the wicked is taught as plainly as that of the just, and that if we give up the one we may quite as well give up the other' (*Judgment* pp. 78f.).

In spite of such statements, traditionalist authors often lump together all who question the received understanding of final punishment. According to Frank S. Mead's *Handbook of Denominations in the United States*, the Advent Christian Church, the Church of God

doxy requires a final, universal resurrection and judgment before God which issues in opposing verdicts of everlasting consequence. Such 'catholic' creeds as the Apostles' and the Nicene go no further.

Judgment is 'eternal' in quality since it belongs to the Age to Come. It is 'eternal' in quantity since its results (though not its action) endure for ever. On this point see the discussion regarding *aiōnios* and words of action in chapter 3.

Hebrews 6:8 Those who have tasted the new life in Christ are urged to go on to maturity. The author warns that apostasy is nothing short of recrucifying the Son of God (Heb. 6:4ff). If Jesus is not all he claimed to be – and therefore worthy of worship and allegiance even to death – he is neither a good man nor a person about whom one might choose to be indifferent, but rather a blasphemer to be denounced and himself condemned. Apostasy reaffirms the judgment the Jewish scribes demanded and Pilate made official. God, who blesses farm land when it is fruitful (v. 7), will surely do no less for his people (vv. 9f). But unproductive land also serves to warn professing believers. For 'land that produces thorns and thistles is worthless and is in danger of being cursed. In the end it will be burned'.

Thorns and thistles are directly related to sin, as is the 'curse' (Gen. 3:17f). Can the land here be anything other than a figure of 'worthless' disciples who claim to know Christ but bear no fruit? God had used the figure before to warn his people; why not here (Isa. 5:1ff; Matt. 21:33ff)? The reason for burning a field of briars is not to cause pain but to destroy what is useless; and though the burnt-off land remains, those thorns and thistles are for ever gone. Is this figure intended to illustrate something directly opposite to what it pictures?

Hebrews 10:27–31 Christ's atonement sacrifice was offered once for all time. Those who come to God on this basis may therefore come boldly,

---

(General Conference) and the Primitive Advent Christian Church all hold to the view, expressed by Constable and Guillebaud, that the wicked will rise to face God in judgment and finally be exterminated in the lake of fire. The Seventh-day Adventists hold the same view, which, because of their numbers, is generally associated with their name (pp. 20ff.). 'Jehovah's Witnesses', by contrast, hold that the incorrigibly wicked will never be resurrected at all; their only 'hell' is the grave (p. 156; see *Let God Be True* pp, 283–291). Bloesch overlooks this important distinction, making SDAs of the JWs; Jon Braun errs the other direction and implies that all but traditionalists hold the JW position (Bloesch, *Essentials* 2:219; Braun, *Whatever?* p. 49).

Buis repeats the common view that 'Jehovah's Witness' founder, Charles T. Russell, borrowed his doctrine of annihilation from the Seventh-day Adventists (*Eternal Punishment* p. 145). Seventh-day Adventist author, LeRoy Edwin Froom, vehemently denies the association and disavows any connection with the 'un-Christian positions' of Russell and his followers. He says Russell was indebted instead to the mainstream evangelical Advent Christian Church for his original thought, which he then perverted into its present form (Froom, *Conditionalist Faith* 2:667). So long as the confusion of positions remains, however, Froom's historical technicality will do little to alleviate the common guilt by association. Prospects for this are not too bright since, according to Norman T. Burns, such confusion of resurrectionists and anti-resurrectionists has characterized much of the literature concerning mortalism for several centuries (*Christian Mortalism* pp. 13f).

confidently and continually (Heb. 10:12ff., 19–25). But this very truth also carries a dire warning. For if someone rejects this offering, nowhere in the universe or in all human history is there another one God will approve and accept. Any who 'deliberately keep on sinning' therefore thrust away their only hope (Heb.10:26; cf. Num.15:30f.) For such people there remains 'only a fearful expectation of judgment and of raging fire that will consume the enemies of God' (v. 27).

Now the author makes explicit what he hinted at earlier. Those who to the end reject God's offers of mercy will then find only judgment – and a raging, consuming fire. A. W. Pink, a Calvinist commentator, says this term denotes 'the resistless, tormenting, destroying efficacy of God's terrible wrath, and emphasizes its dreadful fierceness'.[5] We note that this fire consumes or devours God's enemies, an allusion to the fate of Nadab and Abihu, who were similarly devoured by fire from God (Lev. 10:2).[6] We meet such a fire frequently in the Old Testament as well as in the teaching of John the Baptist, Jesus and the apostle Paul. Even before the fire there is the torture of awaiting sentence, already knowing the outcome; of being pursued with no hope of escape; of beholding the righteous Judge face to face with the full knowledge of wilful rebellion and crimes. Fiction offers earthly illustrations of such horror. We remember the burdened criminal of *Crime and Punishment*, the runaway slave of *Uncle Tom's Cabin* or *Roots*, who desperately flees from bloodthirsty hounds. We think of the fugitive of Hugo's *Les Misérables*, with never a moment of rest without fear.

Who can imagine the dread the condemned murderer feels on the morning of his execution as he first wakes, then lies in anticipation like a man sunk in a silent pond, crushed beneath its stagnant weight?

Who can say that is not worse than the act of dying itself? Yet how much worse – infinitely worse indeed – to face the God whose love one has knowingly spurned time and time again, to hear his judgment sentence echo across the vast silence of eternity, and to see the consuming flames just ahead? We should understand this imagery symbolically and not literally, but God's symbols accurately portray the truth they express.[7]

Rebels who rejected the law of Moses 'died without mercy' (v. 28). Again the author implies that a greater salvation carries greater responsibility, so those who reject it will be punished even 'more severely' (v. 29). 'It is a dreadful thing to fall into the hands of the living God' (v. 31).

Hebrews 10:39 Though the author warns his readers repeatedly against apostasy or unbelief, he also reassures them time and again with expressions of confidence that they will do what is right. They are to

---

5. *Hebrews* p. 613.
6. Pink says the term 'consuming fire' probably alludes to the case of Nadab and Abihu, but he then quotes John Owen: '. . . this fire shall ever prey upon them, and never utterly consume them'. The result is an allusion which pictures the exact opposite of what it is used to illustrate!
7. Traditionalists who say such a view is an 'easy way out' not only pass over Scripture passages such as this; they also fail to consider seriously the very real torment involved in the case the passage describes.

persevere, remembering the warning of Habakkuk 2:3f. (Heb. 10:38). 'But we are not of those who shrink back and are destroyed,' our author writes, 'but of those who believe and are saved.' As we have seen other places already, 'destruction' here also is opposed to being 'saved'. This is the same word (*apōleian*) Paul so often used.

Hebrews 12:25, 29 Again the contrast is made between old and new covenants, again in terms of accountability and ultimate punishment. 'If they did not escape,' the author asks, 'how much less will we, if we turn away from him who warns us from heaven?' The epistle opened almost with such a question (Heb. 2:3), which it repeated (Heb. 10:29) and repeats again. The plain answer is that there is no escape.[8]

Verse 29 picks up a thought expressed in Hebrews 10:27. There the author had spoken of 'raging fire that will consume the enemies of God'. Here he says that 'our God is a consuming fire'. We have seen already the thought that God's very holiness is a fire which consumes all that is not pure (Isa. 33:14; 2 Thess. 1:7). 'As a fire consumes combustible matter cast into it, so God will destroy sinners.'[9]

The expression 'consuming fire' (*pyr katanaliskon*) occurs twice in Deuteronomy (4:24; 9:3, LXX). Both verses have 'your' God;[10] Hebrews has 'our' God. The author himself takes this warning seriously. Dare we regard it less lightly than he?

James

James 1:15 Throughout this letter, James admonishes some who are long on words but short on work. If people today blame the devil for their sins, some known to James wanted to blame God. He corrects this error by fingering evil desire as the culprit. Desire, James says, conceives; then

---

8. Conditionalists and traditionalists generally agree that there is no escape after this life, although such a respected Reformed author as Donald G. Bloesch says: 'We do not wish to build fences around God's grace, however, and we do not preclude the possibility that some in hell might finally be translated into heaven' (Bloesch, *Essentials* 2:226). We will develop the thought further in a later chapter, but it seems the traditionalist view will always tempt to belief in such 'restoration' or Apocatastasis, if only on the maxim that 'where there's life there's hope.' If hell's fire is truly irresistible ('unquenchable') and its results irreversible ('eternal') so that it is indeed a 'consuming fire,' there is no universalist or restorationist possibility. Then it becomes evident that 'today is the day of salvation' and the gospel's offer of pardon is seen in all its urgency.

9. Pink, *Hebrews* pp. 1102f. Pink elsewhere denies what he here states, so that in the end dogmatic theology triumphs over biblical exegesis. Davies (*Angry God?* p. 115) likewise affirms: 'Both in the realm of the body and the soul unbelievers will suffer the fire of God's wrath without being themselves consumed, just as in a very different situation the three Hebrews in Babylon stood inside the burning furnace without being burnt in any way (Dan. 3). In their respective books advocating the traditionalist interpretation, Buis and Braun both completely ignore Hebrews 12:29 as well as the same picture every place it appears in Scripture.

10. Both passages in Deuteronomy refer to the Canaanites. Deuteronomy 9:3 says also that God will *exolethreuō* the Canaanites and the Israelites will *apollymi* them. Both verbs are applied to final punishment in the N.T. The Canaanites were to be totally exterminated.

'it gives birth to sin; and sin when it is full-grown, gives birth to death.' Evil Desire may be enticing, and its offspring, Sin, may appear charming indeed; but when Sin matures and bears its own natural child, that child will surely be Death.

The figure is akin to Paul's when he says that whoever sows to please the sinful nature will from it reap 'corruption' (Gal. 6:8), a word used among other things for a miscarriage or abortion. The contrast in James is with verse 18 – God gave us birth through the word of truth so we might be a firstfruit of his new creation. The new creation stands over against death; they are the two alternatives when the Present Age has passed away.

James 4:12 Our responsibility toward God's law ought to be obedience, not sitting in judgment. James both cautions and informs us:

> There is only one Lawgiver and Judge, the One who is able to save and destroy. But you – who are you to judge your neighbour?

Since God gave the law, only he has the right to call men into account regarding it. Besides, only God can bring to pass any judgment sentence, for good or for ill. The contrast here is between 'save' and 'destroy'. Surely James is remembering the words of Jesus in Matthew 10:28. [11]

James 5:1-6 'Misery' awaits the wicked rich. Corroded gold and silver will 'eat your flesh like fire,' James warns. Like the rich man of Luke 16:19-31, those James rebukes 'have lived on earth in luxury and self-indulgence'. Little did they know they were 'fattening' themselves 'in the day of slaughter'. The well-spread banquet table appears in a different light to the man who knows he will be executed tomorrow! On the figure see Isaiah 3:11-26; Amos 4:1-3; especially Jude 10.

James 5:19 Christians have a mutual responsibility to watch for the welfare of one another. 'Whoever turns a sinner away from his error will save him from death and cover a multitude of sins.' The NIV has 'him' for *psychē*, a common biblical usage, correcting KJV 'soul', which has been so long read in alien terms of Grecian dualism. 'Salvation' is from 'death'. James nowhere hints that he really means anything else. Four times James refers to the final outcome of sin. Twice it is 'death', once misery followed by 'slaughter', and once 'destruction'.

Acts of the Apostles

For all its accounts of evangelism and summaries of apostolic proclamation, Acts says little about final punishment. Peter's warning here seems to be the only statement in the book. The stress in the earliest preaching seems to have been on the blessings of salvation offered in the name of Jesus.

Acts 3:23 Here Peter paraphrases Deuteronomy 18:15,19. Jesus is the Prophet of all prophets, and Moses had warned that if anyone does not listen to

---

11. It is instructive to compare James's teaching throughout the Epistle with the words of Jesus, particularly in the Sermon on the Mount.

God's prophet, God himself 'will call him to account' ('will require it of him,' KJV, RSV, NASB). Peter changes the statement to the third person and uses a different, passive verb: such a one 'will be completely cut off from among his people.' This word (*exolothreuō*) means 'to destroy utterly, to root out' according to Arndt and Gingrich.[12] A cognate word is translated as 'the destroyer' in two other places (1 Cor. 10:10; Heb. 11:28).

Peter's word is the ordinary translation in the Septuagint for the Hebrew *karath*, the usual Old Testament verb for capital punishment or total extermination. It is the fate prescribed for the man who refuses circumcision (Gen. 17:14), for those who eat leaven during the Passover period (Exod. 12:15, 19), and for whoever fails to bring his offering to the Tent of Meeting in the wilderness (Lev. 17:4, 9). It is also used of God's destruction in the Flood (Gen. 9:11). The same word describes the fate of evildoers in general in the Old Testament,[13] and it is applied specifically to the Messiah, who would later suffer the fate due to sinners (Dan. 9:26).[14]

The verb appears only here in the New Testament, where it 'signifies the utterness of the destruction from the people,' though not necessarily more than capital punishment. 'If the word has any eschatological bearing,' observes EGT, 'it would support the theory of annihilation more easily.'[15]

1 Peter

Peter's first Epistle can be described as a combined handbook and travel guide for Christian pilgrims who are passing through this world en route to their heavenly home. Several passages suggest a connection with the Christian initiation of water baptism. Peter is especially concerned that the new believers live holy and fruitful lives before their pagan neighbours and that they be ready to endure suffering if God calls them to that. Over and over the book mentions 'suffering' and 'glory,' and always in that order. The emphasis is on Christian faith and life; little is said about the end of the wicked. One passage touches on this.

1 Peter 4:17 If you suffer for Christ's sake, Peter urges, do not be ashamed but praise God for the privilege (cf. Matt. 5:11f.; Phil. 1:29). 'For it is time for judgment to begin with the family of God; and if it begins with us, what will the outcome be for those who do not obey the gospel of God?'

> 'If it is hard for the righteous to be saved, what will become of the ungodly and the sinner?'

Again we meet the principle that great privilege brings great responsi-

---

12. *Lexicon* p. 276.
13. In Ps. 37:9, 22, 28, 34, 38 and Prov.2:22 among others.
14. The English text also says the Suffering Servant will be 'cut off' (Isa. 53:8), but that is a different Hebrew verb (*gazar*) from this.
15. *Acts*, EGT vol. 2 p. 118.

bility. In saying that judgment is about to begin with the house of God, Peter evokes an Old Testament incident. In the days of Judah's captivity Ezekiel saw a vision explaining why the tragedy had occurred. He observed idolatry in the very precincts of the sanctuary (Ezek. 8). God's glory rose from above the cherubim and prepared to desert the temple (Ezek. 9:3). All who grieved for the abominations received a mark on their foreheads for protection; all others were to be slaughtered without compassion or pity (Ezek. 9:4ff.). Then came the order: 'Begin at my sanctuary' (Ezek. 9:6).

The time has come again, Peter says, for judgment. Again it goes out from God's house.[16] Persecution proves the faith of some, the essential unbelief of others. In either case it manifests the quality of the profession. It also serves as a warning to the persecutors, as another Old Testament prophet of the Exile had also made clear.

Jeremiah also explains the captivity to Israel and reveals that it will be for 70 years (Jer. 25:1-11). At the end of that time God will utterly destroy Babylon for ever, then punish all the nations of the earth (Jer. 25:12-16). If pagan kingdoms hesitate to receive this word of judgment, God points them to Israel's own fate as proof that he is in earnest. 'See, I am beginning to bring disaster on the city that bears my Name, and will you indeed go unpunished?' (Jer. 25:29). If God judges his own people, he will certainly judge their enemies!

Peter now makes the same point. If judgment 'begins with us,' he asks, viewing the tribulations through which believers must here pass, 'what will the outcome be for those who do not obey the gospel of God?' In context, God judges his family by present afflictions, though that judgment relates to the final judgment as we have already seen. Present judgments also come at times on the wicked (throughout the Old Testament there are temporal judgments; we note the destruction of Jerusalem and Rome in the New), but these are also related to the issues of the last day.

Peter's next statement shows that he views present troubles, though it may also suggest a final reckoning. He quotes a proverb: 'If it is hard for the righteous to be saved, what will become of the ungodly and the sinner?' This is the Septuagint translation of Proverbs 11:31. Even the godly must pass along a rough and thorny trail on their way to final salvation, and they have the gift of faith to sustain them. How will those who do not know God ever make it through life? Even in this world, the implication is, God's people are blessed in their suffering.

The Hebrew proverb was slightly different. The NIV translates: 'If the righteous receive their due on earth, how much more the ungodly and the sinner?' In light of the teaching of both Psalms and Proverbs concerning the end of the wicked, this statement may well point to future punishment. Surely the time is coming that the wicked will be recompensed and in such a manifest way that faith in God's justice will be thoroughly vindicated.

---

16. The Greek has *oikos*, by which Peter evidently refers to God's family, the church. The NIV obscures the Old Testament background, however, by interpreting the word as 'family' rather than translating it ('house' = 'temple' in Ezekiel).

2 Peter

The traditional date and authorship of this Epistle are disputed, but conservative scholars point to the lack of conclusive proof otherwise as well as to the care taken by the early councils to exclude unauthentic works from the canon. We accept it as from the apostle whose name it bears and as a sequel to 1 Peter.

Peter responds to sceptics who scoff at Christ's delayed return. He reassures believers of the reliability of the apostles' eyewitness testimony and of the divine origin of Scripture. He assures them that licentious and spurious (false) teachers will certainly come to a terrible but appropriate end. There is an obvious correspondence between 2 Peter 2 and the Epistle of Jude in wording as well as in thought.

2 Peter 2:1–21 Pseudo-teachers bringing seductive heresies will finally meet condemnation (v. 3) and swift destruction (vv. 1, 3). Both 'condemnation' (*krima*) and 'destruction' (*apōleia*) are familiar New Testament words for the end of the lost. Each expresses an aspect of God's sovereignty, who alone can recall even the dead to give account and who alone can totally and eternally destroy. Neither word carries any inherent meaning of everlasting conscious torment, although that meaning has been read into 'destruction' since Tertullian and Augustine.

Peter gives three examples to illustrate the certainty of his warning. Two have already been examined at length – namely, the Flood, which destroyed the old world (v. 5), and the destruction of Sodom and Gomorrah by fire from heaven (v. 6). Throughout the Bible we have found these two events mentioned as prototypes of God's judgment against sin. Each involved a total destruction with sinners exterminated and their sinful way of life annihilated for ever. When evildoers obstinately refused to quit their wickedness, even with God's judgment beating at the door, God had no other choice: sin and sinners perished together. (This is a thought worth pondering when someone suggests that sinners in hell will continue to sin for ever, so that both sin and sinners are eternal, only out of sight.)

Peter particularly displays Sodom and Gomorrah as an example of final condemnation and the end of the wicked. God condemned the twin cities, he says, 'by burning them to ashes, and made them an example of what is going to happen to the ungodly' (v. 6). Other translations do not change the sense. The RSV says that 'by turning to ashes he condemned them to extinction'; the KJV has 'turning into ashes, condemned with an overthrow'. Peter's verb (*tephrō*) is a rare word found only here in the New Testament. Moulton-Milligan cite non-biblical sources where the word describes an eruption of the volcano, Vesuvius, and they say the verb means either 'cover with ashes' or 'reduce to ashes.'[17] Thayer's lexicon has 'reduce to ashes,' and Arndt-Gingrich suggest 'cover with or reduce to ashes.' EGT prefers 'cover up with' over 'reduce to'.[18] This is the same picture we met in Isaiah 66:24, Malachi 4:1ff., Matthew 3:10, 12 and other places in both Testaments. It portrays total destruction by fire from God, a scene strengthened by the adjectives 'unquenchable' (it cannot be

---

17. *Vocabulary* p. 632.
18. *Lexicon* p. 621; *Lexicon* p. 821; R. H. Strachan, *2 Peter* EGT, vol. 5, p. 135.

stopped in its destruction) and 'eternal' (its effects will never be reversed). Peter's language here is so clear and forceful that traditionalist authors are simply at a loss to comment on it at all.[19]

As a third illustration of God's ability to hold the ungodly for judgment, Peter cites the fallen angels. God sent even them to 'hell,' where they are held in 'gloomy dungeons' for judgment. These fallen angels held special fascination for certain apocalyptic writers between the Testaments; we observed several references to them in the books attributed to Enoch. Peter appears to reflect this literature more than once, and Jude quotes from Enoch by name (Jude 14f.). Peter probably has the fallen angels in mind when he writes of the 'spirits in prison' (1 Pet. 3:19f., 22).[20]

Here he says that they are kept 'in Tartarus', which most English versions strangely render as 'hell.' The word appears only once in Scripture, here borrowed from the literature of classical Greek. In Homer's *Odyssey* (11. 575) Tartarus is the place where the Titans were enchained for endless punishment. Both Homer and Plato also call the place Hades, which is the Septuagint's usual choice in translating the Hebrew *sheol*.[21] Whatever one might make of this passage and the angels in Tartarus, it adds nothing to our understanding of the final doom of human sinners, since (1) it concerns angels, not men, and (2) it speaks of detention before the judgment rather than punishment following.[22]

After describing the pseudo-teachers' crimes, Peter returns to their punishment. Like brute beasts 'born only to be caught and destroyed,' they too 'will perish' (v. 12). Both 'destroy' and 'perish' translate the same word (*phthora*, see Gal. 6:8). Peter pictures brute beasts and wicked men coming to the same final end, though the men must first face God's judgment, sentence and consuming fire.

'Blackest darkness is reserved for them' (v. 17). Jude completes the simile, comparing the spurious teachers to 'wandering stars, for whom blackest darkness has been reserved for ever' (Jude 13). Like the comparison with Sodom and the death of brute beasts, this figure also suggests and harmonizes with the idea of final, total extinction.

The apostate's fate is worse than that of one who never knew the way of righteousness (2 Pet. 2:20ff.). We are reminded of similar comparative

---

19. Neither Buis *(Eternal Punishment)* nor Braun *(Whatever ?)* explains this passage. Nor does Donald G. Bloesch in his chapter, 'Heaven and Hell' *(Essentials* vol. 2). Even R. C. H. Lenski, whose exposition is frequently marked by concern with minute detail, is oddly silent here *(The Interpretation of the Epistles of St. Peter, St. John and St. Jude).*

20. This is R. T. France's conclusion, following a thorough and critical examination of the passage, in 'Exegesis in Practice: Two Samples,' *New Testament Interpretation* pp. 264–281.

21. A. R. Fausset, *Englishman's Critical and Expository Bible Cyclopaedia* p. 281; Shedd, *Punishment* p. 42.

22. Buis *(Eternal Punishment* p. 45) describes the language of this chapter as 'very forceful' but makes almost no comment on it. Braun *(Whatever?* pp. 151ff.) ignores everything in the chapter except the word 'Tartarus,' which he calls 'extremely illuminating on the subject of the judgment of God and ensuing punishment,' and on which he writes more than a page.

The NIV and RSV ('continuing their punishment') represent the Greek better than KJV ('to be punished') in v.9. This idea, also found in Enoch, has to do with angels, and it can be extended to men only on the basis of more evidence than this passage gives.

statements in Hebrews (Heb. 2:2f.; 10:27–31; 12:25). Traditionalists and conditionalists affirm together that there will be degrees of conscious punishment: by varying external circumstances or internal sensitivity to them, and, say some conditionalists, by length of time in hell prior to the second death. Another interpretation of the passage sees an entirely different point: the difficulty or impossibility of reclaiming one who has rejected known truth (cf. Heb. 6:4ff.; 12:16f.). This text certainly does not require or even support eternal conscious torment.

2 Peter 3:6–9 Scoffers conclude that 'everything goes on as it has' and mock at Christ's promised coming (v. 4). Peter points out that the same opinion was expressed by the generation which perished in the Flood and that God's judgment again will crash into man's comfortable routine. Once before, the world 'was deluged and destroyed' by water at God's command. By the same word 'the present heavens and earth are reserved for fire, being kept for the day of judgment and destruction of ungodly men'.

The implication here is that the fire which will melt the elements will also accomplish the destruction of ungodly men. 'The 'tares' are to be 'burned' on the field where they grew'.[23] Whether Peter speaks of the old world being 'destroyed' or the future end of ungodly men ('destruction,' v. 7; 'perish,' v. 9), he uses the same verb (*apollymi*) or noun (*apōleia*). Both words were among Paul's most familiar terms for the end of the wicked. Peter's alternatives of repentance or perishing (v. 9) echo a similar warning of Jesus himself (Luke 13:3). The disciple remembers the Master's words, and the Spirit leads him into further truth than Jesus had clearly spoken on earth (John 14:26; 16:12ff.).

Jude

Jude 4–7 We have noted already the similarity between 2 Peter 2 and Jude. The infiltration of some 'godless men, who change the grace of our God into a license for immorality and deny Jesus Christ our only Sovereign and Lord,' prompts Jude to urge his readers everywhere to 'contend for the faith that [God has] once for all entrusted to the saints' (vv. 3f.). God will surely punish such men, and is well able to guard all who abide in his love. The first fact takes away frustration; the second removes anxiety.

Like Peter, Jude points to past examples of God's righteous judgment. Unbelieving Israel was 'destroyed' (*apollymi*) in the wilderness (cf. 1 Cor. 10:5–11; Heb. 3:16–19). Angels who sinned have been kept in 'everlasting chains' in darkness, awaiting judgment. Sodom and Gomorrah in particular 'serve as an example of those who suffer the punishment of eternal fire'.

There is some question as to the nature of Sodom's 'example'. Lenski says these cities are an 'indication or sign (not "example," – our versions), that points like a finger to "eternal fire" '.[24] The NIV could be read this

---

23. White, *Life in Christ* p. 352.
24. *Interpretation* p. 625.

way, as it inserts 'of those who' between Peter's 'serve as an example' and 'suffer . . . punishment of eternal fire.' Bietenhard calls attention to a contemporary Jewish idea that the people of Sodom and Gomorrah were even then suffering fiery punishment.[25] One might read this into the RSV: 'serve as an example by undergoing a punishment of eternal fire'.

Neither view seems best to fit the evidence. Jude's word translated 'example' (*deigma*) simply does not mean 'indication or sign,' as Lenski suggests, but rather (as English versions agree) 'example'. Moulton-Milligan find numerous references in non-biblical Greek where the word is used of 'samples of corn and produce'.[26] Though the precise word appears only here in the New Testament, several other forms of it are used elsewhere. Yet *deigmatizō* (Col. 2:15), *paradeigmatizō* (Matt. 1:19; Heb. 9:9) and *hypodeigma* (John 13:15; Heb. 4:11; 8:5; 9:23; James 5:10; 2 Pet. 2:6) all speak of 'examples,' whether of good or bad. Nor does Jude say that Sodomites are a vague and general example of those who actually will suffer the punishment of eternal fire, but that they themselves exemplify that very punishment.

There is no biblical hint that Sodom and Gomorrah's inhabitants presently endure conscious torment; several passages, in fact, make a point of their abiding extinction.[27] One of the Jewish texts cited for the view actually teaches the opposite, and another reflects a source well outside mainstream Judaism.[28]

In the end, Jude says just what he seems to say, and the KJV may translate it most faithfully after all. The sinners of Sodom are 'set forth for an example, suffering the vengeance of eternal fire'. The passage defines 'eternal fire.' It is a fire from God which destroys sinners totally and for ever. Sodom illustrates it, and the ungodly should heed the warning. Peter makes the same point unequivocally: God condemned these cities 'by burning them to ashes, and made them an example of what is going to happen to the ungodly' (2 Pet. 2:6). Jude will also bring our thoughts back to Sodom's fire.

Jude 13. These wicked teachers are 'wandering stars, for whom blackest darkness has been reserved for ever'. (See the remarks on 2 Pet. 2:17.)

Jude 23. God is able to keep his own people from falling; Jude urges his readers to build themselves up, pray in the Spirit, and keep themselves in God's love (vv. 20f., 24). They are also to care for one another: be tender with some; 'snatch others from the fire and save them; to others show

---

25. H. Bietenhard, 'Fire' *NIDNTT* 1:657.
26. *Vocabulary* p. 137.
27. OT allusions to Sodom's destruction include Deut. 29:23; Isa. 13:19–22; 34:10; Jer. 49:18; 50:40; Lam. 4:6; Zeph. 2:9.
28. J. B. Mayor *EGT* p. 261 cites Wisdom 10:7 and a passage from Philo. Wisdom says that of Sodom's wickedness '. . . a smoking waste still witnesseth, and plants bearing fair fruit that cometh not to ripeness . . .'. This pictures Sodom as a desolate ruin (as Abraham saw it after its judgment), not the Sodomites in fiery torment as Mayor suggests. Philo's opinion is better documented, but he does not represent a majority opinion within Judaism either in Palestine or among the Diaspora. The legend of fruit growing at Sodom's site

mercy, mixed with fear – hating even the clothing stained by corrupted flesh.'

The figure of being snatched from the fire comes from Amos 4:11. The prophet reminds a remnant: 'You were like a burning stick snatched from the fire' when God overthrew some as he once had Sodom and Gomorrah. When total destruction and extinction came on some, Amos says to the survivors, you were snatched from the fire in the bare nick of time – like a stick already beginning to burn!

The same language reappears in Zechariah 3:2. God there says to Satan: 'The Lord rebuke you! . . . Is not this man [Joshua the high priest] a burning stick snatched from the fire?' Here the 'fire' was the Babylonian Exile, from which many never returned. Joshua had been spared, and Satan now seeks his destruction. Jude's 'clothing stained by corrupted flesh' may well reflect this same passage in Zechariah. The next verses tell how Joshua stood in filthy clothes before the angel. These are removed and replaced by rich garments and a clean turban. The angel tells Joshua: 'See, I have taken away your sin, and I will put rich garments on you' (Zech. 3:3ff.). There is an obvious connection between this symbolic incident and New Testament teaching about being 'clothed' with Christ and dressed in perfect righteousness to stand before God (Gal. 3:27; Eph. 4:22ff.; Phil. 3:9; Rev. 3:18).

For Jude, those 'snatched from the fire' are given 'eternal life' (v. 21). To be sure, 'life' means far more than mere existence, but it includes that as well; why should not its denial exclude everything 'life' encompasses, existence included? Jude's picture of contrasting fates allows no survival whatsoever for those thrown into the fire. He has said earlier that 'eternal fire' (the opposite of 'eternal life') is the punishment which befell Sodom and Gomorrah. It is everlasting destruction, blackest darkness for ever. In this he agrees with Peter, Hebrews, James, Acts, Paul, Jesus and the entire Old Testament.

1 John

John says relatively little about final punishment in his Gospel, as we noted earlier, and the same is true of the Epistles. Of the three letters, only the first touches on the subject, and that once only.

1 John 5:16 'There is a sin that leads to death and there is sin that does not lead to death' (v. 17). Whatever the distinction, the outcomes are made clear. They are 'death' and 'not death'. One is either dead or not dead. Over against death stands life. In our present experience there is no sharper contrast than life and death. God could not possibly use a clearer, more expressive word than 'death,' or one grasped any easier by common people of all times and places. Paul spoke of 'death' as the end of sin, and he coloured that word with terms like 'corruption' and 'destruction'.

Even figurative usages depend on an actual, literal sense of words. When 'death' is used as a figure, it is in order to convey the feelings

---

which crumbled at a touch was still current in the fifth century, since Augustine refers to it in Book 21 of *The City of God.*

conjured by our literal understanding of the term. Nowhere does Scripture indicate that it uses these words in a figurative sense when it applies them to the end of the wicked. Few things are stated more often throughout the whole Bible than that the wicked will 'die,' 'perish,' 'be destroyed,' pass away, be no more, and be forgotten for ever. The fact that we deal with the language of divine law and justice only strengthens the case for giving the words their most essential and ordinary meanings. Constable stresses this point at some length.

> The accepted principle of interpretation among mankind is this: 'that all language relative to law and jurisprudence, all language descriptive of the sanctions of government, all language setting forth the penalties of crime and disobedience, is to be accepted in its primary sense and in no other ... Thus when death is announced as a penalty for crime, no controversy would for an instant be admitted as to its meaning. No lawyer, for or against the criminal, would search for dramatic or poetic secondary senses ... A secondary sense may be more usual and more proper elsewhere, but not here. Poetry and the drama, the literature of passion, imagination, and feeling, may use these terms differently; but their use is not to affect in the smallest degree the interpretation of a law. Here we take our stand. Here we are on sure and steady ground. The terms we have been discussing are the terms of the Divine Law: the jurisprudence we have been discussing is God's jurisprudence. The Great Governor is laying before His subjects the penalties which attach to sin. He speaks to them in the only language they can understand – their own language. He puts no new rules of interpretation upon it when He addresses them. He accepts, adopts, and uses the language of those to whom He speaks. We can then only interpret the divine penalty for sin in the sense which man has put upon all such penalties, viz. in the primary sense.'[29]

Revelation

In the very nature of things, talk about final punishment involves realities which our present knowledge based on experience cannot reach. The end of the world, the visible appearance of Jesus Christ, judgment before Almighty God, the new heavens and earth on one hand and the lake of fire on the other – these all transcend any categories our finite minds have yet learned to comprehend. How can we even imagine what it means that this created order of space and time will actually come to an end? Little wonder that when Scripture speaks of Last Things, it speaks in symbols, directing its message to our emotions as much and perhaps even more than to our mind. Jeremias bluntly states, 'When Jesus speaks of the consummation he always uses symbols.'[30] Ridderbos says the same about Paul's teaching on the final events:

> Paul's pronouncements here bear the character of flashing, prophetic warnings, which illuminate for an instant the awful seriousness of the great future, not of a doctrine that in fixed order and piece by piece indicates the component parts of the picture of the future and combines them with each

---

29. Constable, *Future Punishment* p. 54.
30. Jeremias, *The Parables of Jesus* p. 221.

other into an integral unity. This applies in particular to the punitive judgment on unbelievers and the ungodly. Paul declares the certainty of this judgment in an unmistakable way, in many respects with words that have been derived from the Old Testament preaching of judgment. He speaks of it as ruin, death, payment with an eternal destruction ...; wrath, indignation, tribulation, anguish ... But nowhere is the how, the where or the how long 'treated' as a separate 'subject' of Christian doctrine in the epistles of Paul that have been preserved to us.[31]

What is true of Jesus and Paul is even more obvious in the last book of the Bible. Robert H. Mounce insists that 'the essential question' in approaching a study of Revelation is the kind of literature we are dealing with, so that an 'informed sensitivity to the thought forms and vocabulary of apocalyptic is the *sine qua non* of satisfactory exegesis.' Many contemporary writers have lacked that insight, Mounce charges, and as a result have fallen into 'either an indefensible literalism or a highly imaginative subjectivism.'[32]

To say that Revelation uses sign language does not detract from the seriousness of what it says. Liberals and literalists alike have misunderstood the evangelical's approach at this point according to Buis: 'The liberal must recognize that he fails to understand our position when he thinks we take these symbols literally ...' On the other hand, 'the ultra conservative literalist must be made to understand that we have in no way abandoned the belief in eternal punishment when we advocate such a symbolical interpretation.'[33]

But shunning literalism does not give us license to invent our own meanings for John's graphic visions. Even John did not invent his symbols, nor were they original with this book. They belonged to what was almost a language of its own, drawn from an ancient tradition which had thrived already for 200 years, with biblical origins even more ancient. Beasley-Murray compares this apocalyptic imagery to the stereotypes of the modern political cartoon. Long usage has made certain figures familiar around the world, he says, pointing to Uncle Sam and John Bull, to the Russian Bear, the British Lion, the American Eagle and the Chinese Dragon. In a similar way, he explains, 'Jewish apocalyptists had a veritable art gallery of well-known images from which to draw in their portrayals of the future.'[34]

A century ago most critical scholars tried to decode Revelation on the basis of pagan mythologies, seeking parallels in the literature of Rome and

31. *Paul* p. 554. C. F. D. Moule mentions Paul's discussion of 'the unimaginable dimensions of the Christian verities' in connection with last things (C. F. D. Moule, *JTS*, New Series 15, no.1, p. 4, quoted by C. Leslie Mitton, 'Life after Death: The After-Life in the New Testament,' *ET*, Aug. 1965, p. 334).
32. *Revelation* NICNT p. 12. Wenham (*Goodness* pp. 27f.) reminds us: 'Twentieth-century man does not and cannot come to the Bible with an empty mind. The very word "hell" comes to us laden with literary and artistic associations of many centuries. Platonic philosophy clearly had a great influence on Christian thought and Greek mythology on Christian art.'
33. *Eternal Punishment* p. 131.
34. 'The Contribution of the Book of Revelation to the Christian Belief in Immortality,' *SJT* 27, no. 1 (Feb. 1974) p. 78.

Greece, of Persia and Babylon and Egypt. Seventy-five years ago they were beginning to unravel the mysteries of the Jewish literature between the Testaments, literature so like that of the Apocalypse that to describe it they coined the adjective 'apocalyptic'. Now that the initial excitement of discovery has somewhat passed, they are taking a closer look at that literature and noting the differences as well as the similarities between it and the Revelation given to John.

Mounce lists some of the differences. The author of Revelation gives his own name – 'John'; he speaks as one who is himself a prophet; he sees history as having both purpose and a centre, with God firmly in charge of it all. Apocalyptic literature did not carry the true author's name, was often pseudonymous, being written in the name of an individual regarded as having authority, and perceived no redemptive meaning in history.[35]

For evangelical Christians, however, the greatest difference between Revelation and intertestamental apocalyptic literature is more than format, style or even world-view. It is a matter of origin. For John's Apocalypse came from the Spirit of the living Lord, the same Spirit who inspired the Old Testament prophets. And those Old Testament writings are still our best guide to understanding this final book of Scripture.

Beasley-Murray notes that John's portrayals of divine judgment 'employ traditional images, above all those connected with the typology of the second exodus – hence his elaboration of the plagues of Egypt which fall on the kingdom of the new Pharaoh'. Sodom's fate is also reflected here. Sometimes the figures are literally inconsistent, Beasley-Murray observes, but even then 'their use of the Scripture precedents for judgment is comprehensible'.[36] This is only true, however, in the light of the Old Testament.

'Revelation is rooted in the Old Testament. This is where we find the clues to the meaning of the various symbols – comparing scripture with scripture.'[37] Hendriksen stresses the same point. 'Revelation is rooted in and is in full harmony with the rest of the sacred scriptures and must be explained on the basis of the clear teaching of the Bible everywhere.'[38]

The symbols of Revelation are not given to satisfy our curiosity or to write history in advance. Their function is to challenge, warn and inspire us. We must remember also that while many of the same symbols also appeared in the uninspired apocalyptic literature of the previous two centuries, their primary meaning will be learned from the prophetic literature of the Old Testament. There is a unity to divine revelation which transcends the fantasies of imaginative fiction writers, however pious and well-intentioned.

We must also keep in mind the universally-accepted rule of interpretation that obscure passages must be interpreted in the light of passages that are clear and not the other way around. The survey that follows will not supply all the answers. It may appear unsensational. But in such a course we can surely have strong confidence that we are never far off the trail. If one cannot find understanding by searching the Scriptures,

35. *Revelation* pp. 23f.
36. 'Contribution of Revelation,' p. 92.
37. Lion/Eerdmans *Handbook to the Bible* pp. 645f.
38. *More Than Conquerors* p. 63.

praying for wisdom and keeping one's eyes on Jesus, surely understanding is not to be had.

Revelation 2:16, 22 Some at Pergamum followed the errors of Balaam, and others held the teaching of the 'Nicolaitans'. Unless these repent, Jesus warns, he will 'come . . . and will fight against them with the sword of my mouth.' At Thyatira, too, the false prophetess 'Jezebel' led some into idolatry and sexual immorality. Seeing no repentance, Christ warns that he is about to 'cast her on a bed of suffering,' make those who commit adultery with her 'suffer intensely,' and 'strike her children dead'.

All this may refer to temporal judgments, perhaps of lingering or even terminal disease. Insofar as they describe final punishment, they picture a suffering that ends in death.[39]

Revelation 11:18 When the seventh trumpet sounds, John hears loud voices in heaven. They announce good news: God has triumphed over his enemies! The kingdom is the Lord's! In response the twenty-four heavenly elders say:

> 'The time has come for judging the dead . . . and for destroying those who destroy the earth.'

Here 'destroy[ing]' is an intensive Greek verb (*diaphtheirō*) which John uses but once more. There (Rev. 8:8, 9) a burning mountain is thrown into the sea, turning waters into blood, killing living creatures, and 'destroying' a third of the ships in passage . Luke uses the word once of moths devouring clothes (Luke 12:33). Paul has the same verb when he says that 'outwardly we are wasting away' (2 Cor. 4:16) and as he describes the 'corrupt' mind of certain men (1 Tim. 6:5). On the special justice involved in God's 'destroying those who destroy the earth,' compare comments on 1 Corinthians 3:17, where Paul uses a cognate verb (*phtheirō*) in a similar framework.

Certainly destruction involves torment, but the stress here is on the destruction and not the accompanying torture. The New Testament probably describes the pain of final punishment in greatest detail in Romans 2:8f., followed closely by 2 Thessalonians 1:7–10. Both these passages also end with destruction, as does the 'painful' passage, Hebrews 10:26–31. God is just and he is severe, but he does not delight in the death even of the wicked; certainly he is no sadistic torturer. This is a major difference between the Bible's picture of final punishment and that found nearly everywhere else – whether from venerated churchmen or bloodthirsty pagans.

Revelation 14:9ff. Following the appearance of the beast from the sea and the beast from the earth, John sees Mount Zion. There stands the Lamb, accompanied by 144,000 of his people, the earth's redeemed

---

39. Mounce gives this explanation (pp. 99,105), noting that the expression 'to "kill with death" is a Hebraism that means "to slay utterly" . . . or (preferably) "to kill by pestilence."' At the same time, he believes that such a judgment would have been viewed by those visited as also the second or final coming of Jesus.

firstfruits in God's spiritual harvest (Rev. 14:1–5). Three angels announce God's judgment in language progressively stronger. The third angel cries:

> 'If anyone worships the beast and his image and receives his mark on the forehead or on the hand, he, too, will drink of the wine of God's fury, which has been poured full strength into the cup of his wrath. He will be tormented with burning sulphur in the presence of the holy angels and of the Lamb. And the smoke of their torment rises for ever and ever. There is no rest day or night.'

The announcement includes four penal elements involving punishment. They are: (1) drinking the wine of God's fury poured out full strength into the cup of his wrath; (2) being tormented with burning sulphur in the sight of the angels and of the Lamb; (3) the smoke of their torment rising for ever and ever; and (4) having no rest day or night. Let us turn to the former scriptures as we ask what these pictures mean.

Wine of God's Fury

The cup of God's wrath is a well-established Old Testament symbol of divine judgment in the books of poetry (Job 21:20; Ps. 60:3; 75:8) as well as prophecy (Isa. 51:17, 22: Jer. 25:15–38; Obad. 16). The figure points to God, who mixes the drink (Ps. 75:8; Jer. 25:15–38), and also to the staggering effect the potion has on those drinking it (Ps. 60:3; Isa. 51:17, 22). Since God concocts this cup, he can adjust its potency according to his own purpose, diluting it (as with water) or strengthening it (as with spices or perhaps even poison). To be handed the cup means being singled out for divine punishment and so entails agony, terror and fear.

Since the cup's strength reflects the degree of God's wrath, the intensity of the punishment may also vary. For God's own people it may be a stroke which sends them reeling but from which they recover (Ps. 60:3; Isa. 51:22). For his enemies it often ends in total and irreversible extinction. 'They will drink and drink and be as if they had never been' (Obad. 16). They 'drink, get drunk and vomit, and fall to rise no more' (Jer. 25:27). In the end their corpses are everywhere. 'They will not be mourned or gathered up or buried, but will be like refuse lying on the ground' (v. 33). They become 'a ruin and an object of horror and scorn and cursing' (v. 18).

Such was the cup Jesus accepted from God's hand in Gethsemane, and to drink it unmixed he refused even the numbing wine offered by his murderers (Matt. 26:39, 42, 44; 27:34). He suffered torment of body and soul. More than that, he drained the cup of God's wrath, passively enduring the simultaneous extinction of his own life into total death. Because his death was neither partial nor pretence, his resurrection was God's ultimate triumph over Satan and signalled the coming annihilation of death itself. That could not be so had Jesus not experienced to the full everything that death involves. Because he accepted that cup, his people will not have to. The cup he leaves for us is a constant reminder that he has taken our place (Matt. 26:27ff.).

John sees the same figure of God's cup of wrath in Revelation (Rev. 16:19; 18:6; 19:15). Here it also includes 'torture and grief,' but it ends in 'death, mourning and famine' and in consumption by fire (Rev. 18:7ff.).

While Jesus 'treads the winepress of the fury of the wrath of God Almighty,' an angel is already calling the birds of prey to gather for a grisly feast (Rev. 19:15–18). The fact that divine punishment ends in total destruction and death does not minimize the terror or pain. Two of the other three figures found in Revelation 14:9ff. suggest that same end for those who drink God's unmixed cup there, and the third figure possibly does as well.

Burning Sulphur

In the NIV, 'burning sulphur' replaces the 'fire and brimstone' of older English translations. The new phrase seems easier to understand, though it probably does not 'preach' as well. In the Bible the symbol derives its meaning from the annihilation of Sodom and Gomorrah, and the Old Testament uses it often to signify complete and total desolation.

At Sodom (see discussion of Genesis 19) God 'rained down burning sulphur ... out of the heavens,' and the overthrow was so total that nothing remained next morning but 'dense smoke rising from the land' (Gen. 19:23, 28). One of the curses of God's covenant with Israel was that the land would become 'a burning waste of salt and sulphur – nothing planted, nothing sprouting, no vegetation growing on it' – so that it would 'be like the destruction of Sodom and Gomorrah' (Deut. 29:23). In this passage the people are removed from the land and not actually exterminated, but the point of the figure remains. From the standpoint of the land they become as Sodom; where there is burning sulphur there are no people!

Bildad pictures the same fate for the wicked man. Fire and burning sulphur mark the place he once resided; his roots dry and his branches wither; his memory perishes from the earth (Job 18:15ff.; cf. Ps. 11:6). For the king of Assyria, Isaiah says, God has prepared the fires of Topheth. 'The breath of the Lord, like a stream of burning sulphur, sets it ablaze' (Isa. 30:33). This 'burning anger' is a 'consuming fire' as God 'shakes the nations in the sieve of destruction' (Isa. 30:27–30). Although this picture ends in consumption by fire, it includes strokes from God's punishing rod which first strikes down and shatters (vv. 31f.).

Edom's dust and land will also become 'burning sulphur' and 'blazing pitch' (Isa. 34:9) when God stretches out 'the measuring line of chaos and the plumb line of desolation' (v. 11). The same picture seen in Sodom's destruction is predicted for Gog and his hordes by Ezekiel (Ezek. 38:22). This is literally inconsistent with the picture that follows, where carrion birds eat the corpses and Israel salvages the spoils, but both pictures are in perfect harmony as they proclaim a message of utter extinction. Revelation 19:20f. has both figures and distinguishes between them, but it gives no indication of changing this basic meaning of either. (The figure also appears in Revelation 20:10 and 21:8, which we will discuss later.)

Outside the book of Revelation there can be little question that burning sulphur signifies extinction, destruction, eradication, extermination and annihilation. Sometimes this is explicit; sometimes it is implied. But it is always there.

The victims in Revelation 14:9ff suffer in the presence of the angels and the Lamb. Mounce refers to some intertestamental passages in which the righteous watch the wicked's torment with some delight, but he notes that in Revelation 'there is no suggestion that the suffering of the damned takes place in the presence of martyred believers who now rejoice to see their oppressors burning in hell.'[40] The Old Testament often speaks of the righteous beholding the evidence of the wicked's destruction, but it does not have them gloating over their actual pain either. (See comments on Isa. 66:24.) God sees the whole process, however, and here the angels do as well. Actual torment is meted out according to the mixture of God's cup. Then, as the next image points out, it is for ever memorialized in the smoke which remains.

Rising Smoke

It is clear that these figures often overlap and that a number of Old Testament passages which mention one also mention others. Sodom, which presents the figure of burning sulphur, also contributes the imagery of rising smoke. When Abraham went out the next morning, all he saw was 'dense smoke rising from the land, like smoke from a furnace' (Gen. 19:28). Nothing else remained. The blanket of smoke spoke eloquently of an annihilated city and an ungodly population who would never be seen on earth again.

Isaiah uses the same picture to describe Edom's destruction (Isa. 34:10). We have already looked at v. 9, which says that Edom's dust will become 'burning sulphur' and her land 'blazing pitch.' Verse 10 adds that the fire 'will not be quenched night and day' and that 'its smoke will rise for ever.' The fire here is unquenchable precisely because it is not put out until it has completely destroyed (v. 11). It consumes by night and by day. There is no relief from its burning, until it has finished its work. Then the actual burning ceases, but the smoke remains. In saying the smoke 'will rise for ever,' the prophet evidently means what he describes in vv. 11–15 – so long as time goes on, nothing but devastation will remain at the site which once was Edom. Again the picture of destruction by fire overlaps that of slaughter by sword (vv. 1–7). The wicked die a tormented death; the smoke reminds all onlookers that the Sovereign God has the last word. That the smoke lingers for ever in the air means that the judgment's effect will last for ever.

Conditionalist writers can point out that the same word translated 'torment' here is applied elsewhere (in verb form) to the tossing of an inanimate boat. Traditionalists can respond that it also describes the rich man's conscious suffering in fire in Jesus' story of the Six Brothers (Luke 16:23, 28) or the excruciating pain of a scorpion sting (Rev. 9:5). We agree fully with Mounce that what the angel 'has proclaimed so vividly must not be undermined by euphemistic redefinition'.[41] One refrains from doing that by letting the Scripture interpret itself, which is all we are asking here.

John's later vision of the fall of Babylon clearly focuses on the point at

---

40. *Revelation* p. 276.
41. Ibid., p. 277. Mounce does not mention the O.T. background for the smoke which goes up for ever.

issue (Rev. 18). A voice from heaven calls on God to balance the wicked city's glory and luxury with equal measure of 'torture' and grief (v. 7). Here is the same word, and it clearly calls for conscious suffering. But after answering this prayer with plagues of death, mourning and famine, God destroys the city with a consuming fire (v. 8). Merchants and kings bewail the 'torment' they see, but all they behold is the rising smoke of a destruction now completed (vv. 10,18). The scene evokes Abraham looking out over the site of what had been Sodom, seeing nothing now but rising smoke. The conscious torment is past; the reality of its destruction continues; the smoke is its silent but powerful witness (cf. Rev.19:3).[42]

No rest day or night

We may describe an action or event several ways with reference to time. We might talk of a kind of time. Paul worked and prayed 'night and day' (1 Thess. 2:9; 3:10), but he did neither non-stop. Sometimes he prayed at night, sometimes by day; the same may be said for his working. Greek expresses this kind-of-time by the genitive case form.[43] Or we might speak of a point of time. Peter would deny Jesus in a particular night (Mark 14:30). Greek expresses point-of-time by the locative case.[44] Or one might speak of a duration of time. Jesus spoke of the seed which sprouts and grows 'night and day' (Mark 4:27). All day the seed is growing; all night it is growing too. Greek expresses such duration-of-time by the accusative case.[45]

The use here of the genitive shows that 'day and night' refers to the kind of time. The wicked are not guaranteed rest during the day; there is no certain hope that relief will come at night. This does not necessarily imply that the suffering lasts all day and all night (although that may be true), but that in neither case are they immune to it. John uses the same genitival 'day and night' to describe the living creatures praising (Rev. 4:8), the martyrs serving (Rev. 7:15), Satan accusing (Rev. 12:10), and the unholy trinity being tormented (Rev. 20:10). In each case the thought is the same: the action described is not by nature a daytime action, nor is it a nighttime action. It happens either and both. Guillebaud is therefore correct when he concludes that these words suggest there will be 'no

---

42. Because they do not permit Scripture to interpret its own metaphors, traditionalists such as Dixon (*Other Side* p. 80) and Blanchard (*Hell* p. 229) are at a loss to explain the figure of ascending smoke in this passage and in Rev. 19:3.

43. H. E. Dana and Julius R. Mantey, *A Manual Grammar of the Greek New Testament* p. 77.
The expression 'day and night' (or 'night and day') appears with this genitival construction outside Revelation in Mark 5:5; Luke 18:7; Acts 9:24; 1 Thess. 2:9; 3:10; 2 Thess. 3:8; 1 Tim. 5:5; 2 Tim. 1:3; in the Septuagint in Ps. 2:1; 32:4 (31:4, LXX); 42:3 (41:3); 55:10 (54:11); Isa. 34:10; 60:11; Jer. 9:1 (8:23); 14:17; Lam. 2:18. There appears to be no significance in the word order since John has 'day and night' while Isaiah 34:10, which he seems to build on, has 'night and day.'

44. Ibid. p. 87. I could not find 'day and night' in this dative case form. Evidently the locative point-of-time does not consistently call for such a usage.

45. Ibid. p. 93. The 'day and night' expression appears with the accusative sense of duration-of-time in Mark 4:27; Luke 2:37; Acts 20:31; 26:7; Isa. 62:6 (LXX). The first and last passage seem literal; the rest appear to be hyperbole based on the literal meaning.

break or intermission in the suffering of the followers of the Beast, while it continues; but in themselves they do not say that it will continue for ever'.[46]

The first three figures in the passage all either indicate or are agreeable to the idea that the suffering finally ends in total extinction and desolation.

The same form of 'night and day' is used in Isaiah 34:10, a context noted already for its association of burning sulphur and rising smoke. There Edom's fire is not quenched 'night and day,' with the same sentence concluding, 'its smoke will rise for ever.' Edom's fire would not be limited to a day shift or a night shift; it burned in the daytime and in the night-time. But when it had consumed all that was there, it went out; and then its smoke ascended as a memorial to God's thorough destruction.

We have examined the four figures used in Rev. 14:9ff. The wine of God's fury signifies a penal judgment from the Almighty; that it is poured full strength strongly suggests a judgment culminating in absolute extinction. This extinction is apparently preceded by some degree of conscious torment pictured as a storm of burning sulphur. That figure, too, takes us back to Sodom. There and elsewhere it results in a silent wasteland devoid of inhabitant. Scripture uses the third figure of rising smoke to indicate a continuing reminder of God's just judgment. Those so destroyed have no guarantee of relief, whether by day or night, so long as their suffering lasts.[47]

Not all commentators understand this passage as even referring to the final end of the wicked.[48] If it does, its figures must still be interpreted in the light of the Old Testament. To be sure, the New Testament may add its own new light or meaning, but such redefinition ought to be clearly justified by the text itself. There is no justification for lifting the figures out of their biblical context and explaining them in the light of later dogmatic developments.

Revelation 18. Here, as in the Old Testament, 'Babylon' is a symbol of opposition to God's kingdom. John's readers would take the name as a

---

46. *Righteous Judge* p. 24.

47. Harmon ('Case' p. 210) charges that this work is 'exegetically flawed' because it 'often introduces a chronological lapse of time in New Testament passages which is not there in the texts themselves.' He thus charges me with importing into the biblical texts a chronology consisting of banishment – conscious punishment – extinction which he does not believe the texts naturally contain (pp. 210ff). However, Harmon himself concludes that the Bible leaves us with three overpowering themes regarding final punishment: exclusion, conscious punishment and destruction (pp. 212f.) Unless one wishes to say it is wrong to attempt to think in chronological terms at all on this subject, how can one who takes language seriously possibly conceive of any sequence other than the one I have proposed? Is not 'exclusion' the first step in any scenario? If 'destruction' really means what it sounds like, how can anything else follow after it? The truth is that the traditional position is forced to define 'death,' 'destruction' and 'corruption' alike as 'eternal existence under painful circumstances.' It is that definition, not some exegetical error on my part, which requires anyone to reject the simple order I suggest.

48. Hailey says the picture is 'in harmony with Jesus' teaching' concerning final punishment, but he does not believe Revelation describes the End until later. Hailey

cipher for Rome. This chapter describes the fall of Rome – of 'Babylon' – of ungodly world power which vaunts itself in any age under any name. The description is borrowed almost wholly from Old Testament pictures of divine judgment against ungodly cities, whether Babylon (Isa. 21:1–10), Nineveh (Nahum) or especially Tyre (Ezek. 27).

One should not look to this chapter for a description of final punishment, therefore; but because some of the language occurs in passages which do seem to speak of that, a brief survey may be in order. This judgment against Babylon includes plagues (v. 4), torture and grief (v. 7), death, mourning and famine, and finally ends in consumption by fire (v. 8). Having been so brought to ruin (vv. 17, 19), a ruin including torment (vv. 10, 15), the smoke of the city goes up for all to see (vv. 9, 18). That the smoke goes up for ever (Rev. 19:3; cf. 14:9ff.) speaks of an eternal destruction but not everlasting conscious torment. It is a perpetual reminder of God's devastating judgment.[49]

Revelation 19:20; 20:10, 15; 21:8 The *lake of fire* is the last description in the Bible of final punishment. This fiery lake of burning sulphur does not appear anywhere else in the Bible. Even so, conditionalists and traditionalists agree that it stands for the same ultimate destiny which in the Gospels (but nowhere else in Scripture) is pictured under the name 'Gehenna'. The pseudepigraphical book of 1 (Ethiopic) Enoch paints a similar picture of the place where fallen angels are punished (1 En. 18:11–16; 21:7–10) as well as wicked shepherds and apostates (1 En. 90:24–27). One passage has them imprisoned forever (1 En. 21:10); another implies that they are totally burned up (1 En. 90:27).

It has been customary to say that the intertestamental literature clearly and generally taught eternal conscious torment and that Jesus and New Testament writers borrowed the language, thereby endorsing and continuing the same understanding.[50] Strack and Billerbeck, however, raise the question whether all the intertestamental material might really intend to describe total annihilation.[51] We have already seen (Chapter 9).

---

regards this as a judgment against imperial Rome with its emperor cult (Hailey, *Revelation* p. 310).

The dispensational interpretation in *Scofield* sees this as a picture of suffering encountered by the wicked during the great tribulation.

49. Although the chapter does not describe final punishment, its picture of destruction by fire is commonly used in Scripture for that fate. Hailey sees the significance of the picture in Revelation 18:8 thus: 'The end comes to the great city, followed by mourning over the death and famine from the economic collapse, for "she shall be utterly burned with fire" – totally destroyed (Rev. 17:16)' (Hailey, *Revelation* p. 363).

50. Buis writes: 'It is an inescapable fact that Jesus ... places the stamp of his approval upon the general Gehenna concept which had developed during the Inter-Testamental period ... Jesus' teaching further proves that the Inter-Testamental development of the doctrine was in reality a sound extension of the beginnings of that doctrine which are found in the Old Testament' (*Eternal Punishment* p. 42).

51. 'The punishment of the godless, regardless if they were judged in the catastrophic judgment or the regular judgment, lasts for ever. But the Pseudepigrapha also speaks about the destruction or the annihilation of the godless, so that one may be in doubt if to them the everlasting condemnation of the (judged) guilty simply had become synonymous

that the Old Testament picture of utter extinction clearly continues alongside those passages which appear to teach everlasting conscious torment, well into the first century after Christ. We reiterate that the New Testament must be allowed to speak for itself and that the Old Testament Scriptures rather than the uninspired apocalyptic literature must be its primary interpreter.

Daniel's dream of four beasts provides the nearest Old Testament parallel (Dan. 7:9–12). There the Ancient of Days takes his seat on a throne that flames with fire (v. 9). A river of fire flows from before him (v. 10). The terrible fourth beast is 'slain and its body destroyed and thrown into the blazing fire'. This is in specific contrast to the other beasts, who are stripped of authority but allowed to live for a period of time (vv. 11f.). Unless this vision of world powers under the imagery of beasts sheds light on the lake of fire in Revelation, no light is to be had from the Old Testament. If the passage in Daniel is its background, that light reveals a fiery destruction which is expressly not a mere stripping of authority with a survival of life. It is more helpful to compare the four occurrences of the lake of fire in the Apocalypse itself.

The beast and the false prophet are the first beings thrown into the lake (Rev. 19:20). They symbolize persecuting civil government and corrupting false religion. Neither institution will be perpetuated for ever, nor could either suffer conscious, sensible pain. In their case the lake of fire cannot indicate that kind of everlasting punishment. Hailey does not regard the passage as a description of Christ's second coming at all but of 'the victorious war against the forces that have been under discussion'.[52] Thus the whole passage means the 'Roman Empire and emperor worship backed by the imperial power were now being brought to a final and complete end, never to rise again.'[53]

Hanns Lilje, who finished his commentary while imprisoned under Hitler's Gestapo, marvels that John gives no description here of any battle. 'The very moment when this purpose of God is fulfilled,' he writes, 'the mighty power of the beast shrivels up like a collapsed balloon, as if it had never been. It has been unmasked, and its true character revealed: it was empty, futile presumption.' So far as the meaning of the lake of fire is

---

with everlasting annihilation' (Strack & Billerbeck 2:1096). For the German text see ch. 7, note 18, p. 82.

52. *Revelation* p. 381. Yet he understands the figures here to signify 'defeat and destruction' (p. 382). The armies, sword and rod he sees 'destroying by divine judgment, reducing to chaff, burning, and carrying away' (p. 385). In the end the birds pick the corpses so that 'not a vestige of the anti-Christian forces was left; the destruction was complete' (p. 388). If the figures here signify such annihilation and extinction of anti-Christian forces, why would they not have the same meaning when applied elsewhere to the end of the ungodly?

53. Ibid. p. 388. Scofield makes this the fourth item on an agenda of 10 final events. Here it sees the destruction of earth's 'last and most awful tyrant,' whom Satan gives power to rule during the world's final days. Mounce takes a middle course between Scofield's dispensationalism and Hailey's 'historical background' approach. He speaks of 'the eschatological defeat of Antichrist (an event which takes place in time and brings to a close this age as we know it) but does not require that we accept in a literal fashion the specific imagery with which the event is described' (*Revelation* p. 349).

concerned. Lilje is content to use the word 'annihilated'.[54] In the case of the beast and false prophet, therefore, the lake of fire stands for utter, absolute, irreversible annihilation.

Satan also is judged. In Revelation 20:7–10 John views Evil's last great assault against Good, issuing in Evil's final downfall and everlasting destruction. The picture is built on the imagery of Ezekiel 38 and 39, down to the code names 'Gog' and 'Magog.' Satan's hordes surround the camp of God's people, but as in the days of Elijah (2 Ki.1), fire from heaven devours them. Satan is reserved for more singular punishment. He is 'thrown into the lake of burning sulphur, where the beast and the false prophet had been thrown.' Together, the vision has these three – beast, false prophet and the devil – 'tormented day and night for ever and ever'.

The language is symbolic, and a literal interpretation is impossible. Political power and apostate religious beguilement are not persons who can be tortured in fire. Even the vision would be impossible if these forces were not personified as creatures. We can imagine Satan being kept in deathless torment, but how does one even picture that situation in the case of impersonal abstractions? On the other hand, if the lake of fire means here what it did in Revelation 19:20, it is simply a symbol for annihilation.[55] But if that is its meaning, how does John see the devil 'tormented day and night for ever and ever'? There is no easy solution. Yet to this point no human beings are involved in the lake of fire, nor does this passage say that any of Adam's race are tormented for ever and ever.

Death and Hade share Satan's fate. Earth and sky flee away as the dead assemble to be judged before the great white throne (Rev. 20:11ff.). 'Then death and Hades were thrown into the lake of fire' (v. 14). Isaiah foretold a time when God would 'destroy the shroud that enfolds all peoples, the sheet that covers all nations,' when 'he will swallow up death for ever' (Isa. 25:7f.). Paul had written, 'The last enemy to be destroyed is death' (1 Cor. 15:26), and he had pictured the resurrection unto life when death would be 'swallowed up' in victory (v. 54). This is the consummation of God's victory. Lilje notes:

> Annihilation is itself annihilated. All that remains is the majesty of life, which is God himself. He will be all in all (1 Cor. 15:23, 28).[56]

As in the case of the beast and false prophet, so with death and Hades

---

54. Lilje, *The Last Book of the Bible* (TFTC 256).

55. Lilje writes: 'Fire from heaven falls upon these hosts, and annihilates Satan and his armies. God's will has triumphed gloriously; the "lake of fire" means no more than this' (ibid. p. 254).

Seventh-day Adventists (and others) believe that Ezek. 28:11–19 describes the devil under the figure of the 'King of Tyre', with vv. 18–19 prophesying Satan's final annihilation. See Ellen G. White, *The Great Controversy between Christ and Satan* pp. 672f.

Scofield also extends Ezekiel's lament beyond the earthly king of Tyre to Satan himself, but then explicitly denies that these verses teach Satan's cessation of being.

C. F. Keil, among others, explains the text in detail, with recourse only to the human king of Tyre, in his *Biblical Commentary on the Prophecies of Ezekiel* 1:409–425.

56. Lilje, *Last Book* p. 256.

(abstractions and not persons) the lake of fire here means annihilation. In this case it can mean nothing else. Death will be no more – for ever. Now John makes the identification clear. 'The lake of fire is the second death.'

In other such expressions throughout Revelation, the second term used inteprets the first. The bowls of incense in 5:8 'are' prayers of the saints. The fine linen of 19:8 'is' the righteous acts of the saints. The thousand year reign with Christ in 20:5 'is' the first resurrection. So what is the lake of fire? It is the second death (Rev. 20:14). On this pattern 'lake of fire' is the expression to be defined; 'second death' is its clearer meaning. Such a formal observation is not conclusive, but it deserves serious consideration, and it is in keeping with all that we can understand throughout the rest of Scripture.[57] Death itself will die. What sense does it make to say 'separation will be separated'? But what a powerful thought it is that 'annihilation will be annihilated'! Then it will be true that death itself has passed away (Rev. 21:4).

Sinners are only now included in this dreadful fate. 'If anyone's name was not found written in the book of life, he was thrown into the lake of fire' (Rev. 20:15). The next chapter repeats the fact with elaboration. Overcomers will inherit the new heavens and new earth, but all classes of sinners 'will be in the fiery lake of burning sulphur'. Again John says: 'This is the second death' (Rev. 21:8). Twice John tells us the wicked end in the lake of fire. Both times he identifies the lake of fire as 'the second death'.

Traditionalist authors always read the equation the other direction, as if it said 'the second death' (which is indefinite) is 'the lake of fire' (which is clear). In fact, however, John says that 'the lake of fire' (his symbol) is 'the second death' (a clearer reality). Because John's statement is so clear, writers who hold to everlasting conscious torment are very careful to contradict what it seems to say.

Thus Roger Nicole explains that the second death 'does not mean that the soul or personality lapses into non-being, but rather that it is ultimately and finally deprived of that presence of God, and fellowship with Him which is the chief end of man and the essential condition of worthwhile existence.'[58] Salmond says 'the second death' means 'existence without the resurrection of life and the crown of life, the existence that is eternal loss and dying,' and he quotes Philo, who speaks of a 'kind of death remaining deathless and dying'.[59] This kind of language is everywhere in patristic literature from about the fourth century onward,

---

57. Guillebaud notes this structure in *Righteous Judge* p. 14.
Blanchard (*Hell* pp 40, 139) believes that the Lake of Fire in Revelation shows that Hades cannot be eternal, and Dixon (*Other Side* p. 119) says that it clearly signifies the end of Death. Neither allows it to mean the end of lost humans, although the Bible twice calls it the 'second death' (Rev. 20:15; 21:8). Instead, Blanchard (*Hell* p. 154) quotes Chrysostom of Constantinople who said, in pure Alice-in-Wonderland style: 'The damned shall suffer an end without end, a death without death, a decay without decay.'
58. 'The Punishment of the Wicked,' *ChrT*, 9 (Sept. 1958) p. 13.
59. *Immortality* pp. 428f.

but it is nowhere found in Scripture. Rather than the wicked experiencing a 'deathless death,' John tells us that death itself will die and be no more.

Even George Beasley-Murray says the lake of fire does not signify annihilation but 'torturous existence in the society of evil in opposition to life in the society of God'.[60] Mounce is more in line with the text when he writes: 'It is the second death, that is, the destiny of those whose temporary resurrection results only in a return to death and its punishment.' Both Mounce and Hailey quote Alford, who explained:

> 'As there is a second and higher life, so there is also a second and deeper death. And as after that life there is no more death (ch. xxi. 4), so after that death there is no more life' (pp. 735f).[61]

As we have seen, for the beast and false prophet as for death and Hades, the lake of fire clearly means annihilation and cessation of existence. In the case of impenitent sinners, nothing in the text prevents this meaning. The context twice suggests it by explaining the lake of fire as the 'second death'. Everything we have seen in the rest of the Bible is in keeping with this meaning.

So far as the devil is concerned, the expression itself would seem to have the same meaning, but it becomes ambiguous and disputable in light of the specific statement that he will be tormented for ever and ever. Other prophetic passages might reverse that understanding, however, if they intend to picture Satan's destiny. Furthermore, in Revelation itself John writes 'torment' when describing lifeless desolation. Whatever the case with Satan, the final punishment of the wicked is a different subject.[62]

---

60. Quoted in Mounce, *Revelation* p. 367.

61. Ibid. p. 367; Hailey, *Revelation* p. 403. Mounce comments: 'The grim simplicity of the narrative stands in contrast with the lurid descriptions found in Jewish apocalypticism.'

This is no mere slipping into oblivion, as Bernard emphasizes: 'Things do not melt quietly into the peace of the kingdom of God. There is a crash of ruin, and a winepress of the wrath of Almighty God, and a lake that burns with fire and brimstone. And this judgment falls, not only on principles and powers of evil, but on nations of men; and not only on nations, but on separate persons, even on "every one who is not found written in the book of life"' (*Progress of Doctrine in the New Testament* p. 205).

62. Hailey notes Jesus' parallel of 'eternal punishment' and 'eternal life' (Matt. 25:46), and John's parallel between service 'day and night' (Rev. 7:15) and no rest 'day and night' (Rev. 14:11). He then reasons: 'Since the day is in heaven and the night in hell, and since the one group serves Him day and night while the other group is tormented night and day, it follows that the night endures as long as the day. But since God is the light of the eternal day, the day (and, consequently, the night) will never end. The period of this torment, "for ever and ever," is the same in duration as God, for He lives "for ever and ever" (Rev. 4:9). If there shall be total annihilation of the devil and the wicked it is not revealed' (*Revelation* pp. 398f).

By way of dialogue with my respected teacher, I quickly acknowledge the parallel statements of both Jesus and John, and fully agree that the 'night' lasts as long as the 'day.' This is a telling argument against every form of universal restorationism. But if 'day' equals 'heaven,' and 'night' equals 'hell,' how can there be either service or torment 'day and night' unless the righteous serve in heaven and hell, and the wicked suffer in hell and heaven? Does not the genitival 'day and night' simply stress the quality of both blessing

The element of mystery

We close this investigation of New Testament teaching on final punishment with a word of caution. God has spoken on this subject in symbolic language.[63] He has not given a physical, let alone a scientific description of the end of the wicked. 'We need to recognize anew the element of mystery in revelation', exhorts Donald G. Bloesch.[64] If that is true in general, it is especially true concerning the Last Things. Even the much-used word 'eschatology' can itself 'become a substitute for careful thought' so that it leads 'only to ambiguities and confusions', warns I. Howard Marshall.[65] When we study the subject of this book, we are peering at 'the dark side of the far hereafter'[66] and 'vagrant speculation' needs to give way to a 'reverent agnosticism'.[67]

Alan Richardson writes of the atonement, but his words are equally applicable to our subject:

> One can construct theories and offer them as solutions of problems, but one cannot theorize about the deep mystery . . . The NT does not do so; it offers to us not theories but vivid metaphors, which can, if we will let them operate in our imagination, make real to us the . . . truth . . . The desire to rationalize these metaphors into theories . . . has created much division and rigidity amongst Christian bodies; the curious combination of Renaissance rationalism and evangelical zeal, which has characterized much Reformed and sect-type Christianity in recent centuries, has resulted in an unfortunate kind of sophistication which believes that the only thing to do with metaphors is to turn them into theories.[68]

James Orr makes the same point.

> The conclusion I arrive at is that we have not the elements of a complete solution, and we ought not to attempt it. What visions beyond there may be, what larger hopes, what ultimate harmonies, if such there are in store, will come in God's good time; it is not for us to anticipate them, or lift the veil where God has left it down.[69]

---

and suffering, that neither is limited to the day or the night (as we think of it)? Does not the above reasoning expect too much of John's figures of speech?

There is no question in the present book that the wicked are destroyed for ever – as everlastingly as the redeemed enjoy life in immortality. But the 'quantitative' meaning of 'eternal' does not answer the question of the nature of final punishment. As to the purported silence of Scripture on the extinction of the wicked, this study leads us to conclude that the Bible reveals a great deal more than has commonly been affirmed. Traditionalists have simply failed in many cases (as Hailey often put it) to 'grapple with the text.'

63. Strong, *Theology* 3:1035.
64. 'Crisis in Biblical Authority,' *Theology Today* 35, no. 4 (Jan. 1979) p. 462.
65. 'Slippery Words: Eschatology,' *ET*, June 1978 p. 268.
66. The title Gerald C. Studer uses for his chapter on hell in *After Death, What?* pp. 108–130.
67. David W. Lotz, 'Heaven and Hell in the Christian Tradition,' *Religion in Life* 48 (Spring 1979) p. 90.
68. *Introduction* pp. 222f.
69. *Christian View of God and the World* (1893), p. 397, quoted in *Encyc. Brit.*8:704. Harmon faults the present work because it 'fails to understand that the apocalyptic images used for the doom of the ungodly have a single referent, and instead claims that different

In another place he warns against dogmatism:

It is . . . necessary to guard against dogmatisms . . . as if eternity must not, in the nature of the case, have its undisclosed mysteries of which we here in time can frame no conception . . . Scripture . . . with its uniformly practical aim . . . does not seek to satisfy an idle curiosity. Its language is bold, popular, figurative, intense; the essential idea is to be held fast, but what is said cannot be taken as a directory to all that is to transpire in the ages upon ages of an unending duration. God's methods of dealing with sin in the eternities may prove to be as much above our present thoughts as His dealings now are with men in grace. In His hands we must be content to leave it, only using such light as His immediate revelation yields.[70]

Many have failed to heed such warnings, regardless of the point they wished to establish. The literature abounds in half-truths, historical inaccuracies, assertions without proof, dogmatic assumptions, presuppositional argument, circular reasoning, and examples of 'eisegesis' instead of exegesis. More literalistic authors on both sides of this question have drawn their calendars with such precision that the Lord will need a stopwatch to meet their programme. This applies to many traditionalists (whether fundamentalist dispensationalists or Calvinistic scholastics), but also to certain doctrinaire conditionalists who leave no room for the mysteries of the Age to Come and an order that transcends our experience in the present space-time creation.[71]

---

images refer to differing aspects of the wicked's final fate' ('Case' p. 213). He argues rather that biblical images of personal exclusion, conscious suffering and destruction 'need to be understood as giving us hints at the same eschatological reality' (ibid). Why should we suppose these images are all exactly parallel? If they are parallel, why does Scripture utilizes several images instead of one? Does not each biblical image impact us in its own unique manner? Can we not distinguish at all between the primary meaning of each image? Must we assume that they all overlay each other precisely with no differentiation?

70. 'Everlasting Punishment' (IV, 1), *ISBE* (1915, 1929), 2:2503. When Orr's admonition is forgotten, 'conditionalism looks like an attempt to evade difficulties in the apostolic witness by wrapping up these problems in a neater package than that in which they came' (Harmon, 'Case' p. 215). The intent of the present book is not to tie up doctrinal packages at all, but rather to open up relevant biblical passages and to display their contents in plain view for all to see.

71. At times Froom seems to leave nothing to the realm of mystery and transcendence in his *Conditionalist Faith*. Edward White, one of Froom's conditionalist predecessors, was more cautious, as illustrated by the following warning: 'The doctrine of the Second Death . . . is represented in the Divine Revelation amidst "blackness, and darkness, and tempest," like that which covered Mount Sinai at the giving of the law; and, therefore, none can break through to gaze into the abyss whence bursts the fire that "burns into the midst of heaven." To venture into those scenes with a design of exploring the shadows, on which even the flashes of Divine vengeance throw no light but rather render darkness visible, be far from us. A certain part of the moral effect of the prospect of judgment to come depends on its mystery' (*Life in Christ* p. 345).

To insist that we leave room for an element of mystery concerning God's final disposition of evil is another matter than the question of how Scripture – so far as it does – reveals that end to us. On that question we must answer with those who hope for a perfect universe where God is 'all in all' and evil will exist no more. Scripture does not allow us, however, to anticipate a precise timetable of events, nor does it speak to us other than in language understandable to our present experience.

We simply cannot pinpoint the events of the last day. All that the Bible says, with the possible exception of one or two highly figurative passages in Revelation, indicates that the wicked will perish in the consuming fire of the holiness of the coming God. At the same time, we are unable to visualize exactly what will happen, or to speak with the authority of one who has been there. We know only what we are told, and on this subject God has spoken with his hand over his mouth.

Most of all, God points us to the cross of Jesus. Under the shadow of Golgotha we remember who and what we are. Rather than speculate, we need to pray. Rather than letting our imaginations run wild, we need to repent. And when the last day does come in all its glory and all its terror, we will realize that even our repentance needs to be repented of and even our prayers need praying for. We will fall on our faces before the risen Lord, who was dead and is alive, dissolved in prayer and praise until he touches us to rise and calls us to follow him home.

We will do well to remember that while all God's prophecies are true, so that what they say really comes to pass, their fulfilment is often a matter of correspondence rather than mechanical literalism. E. F. Kevan reminds us that the 'fulfilment of the acorn is the oak, and the fulfilment of the apple blossom is the apple.'[72] Yet who possibly could have looked at the acorn or the blossom and known that in advance? We would do well also to remember how the Jews, who had so many prophecies of the promised Messiah, failed in such large part to recognize him when he finally came and fulfilled those prophecies perfectly.[73] God's fulfilments, like his thoughts, are higher than ours.

---

72. 'The Principles of Interpretation,' *Revelation and the Bible*, ed. Carl F. H. Henry, p. 298. T. G. Dunning ('Heaven and Hell' *Bapt Qtrly*. 20. no. 8 [Oct. 1964] p. 356) critiques traditionalism, conditionalism and restorationism, and suggests that each view may have 'a partial truth which will find its place in a synthesis beyond human comprehension'.

73. Vernard Eller makes the point. 'There is, of course,' he writes, 'the fact that some Bible prophecies have been fulfilled ... the nature of those prophecies was such that, when the event itself took place, they could be cited as confirmation that it had been prophesied ahead of time. However, there is no evidence ... that the prophecies ever made it possible for anyone to make an accurate prediction as to just when, where, and how the event would occur, The accomplished fulfillment of some Bible prophecies provides no excuse or justification for contemporary calendarizing' (*Most Revealing* pp. 13f.).

Although Daniel knew from Jeremiah's prophecy when the Babylonian Exile would end, and Herod's scribes knew from prophecy where Jesus would be born, Eller's point is still valid. Peter stresses the unknown element from the standpoint of the prophets themselves (1 Pet. 1:10ff.), and Paul makes the same point from the standpoint of the fulfilment (1 Cor. 2:8f.).

14

Universalism's New Face

We have not so far mentioned the belief that all will be saved. Yet universalism has formed part of the creed of a significant minority. During the last few centuries the doctrine has been most generally associated with 'liberal' theology and Shedd was responding to the universalism of classical liberalism when he criticized it thus:

> Universalism has a slender exegetical basis. The Biblical data are found to be unmanageable, and resort is had to human feeling and sympathy. Its advocates quote sparingly from scripture. In particular, the words of Christ relating to eschatology are left with little citation or interpretation.[1]

Yet today this doctrine seems to hold a growing fascination for a number of scholars whose roots are evangelical or Reformed. They begin with the traditional view of conscious everlasting torment but allow it to lead them in unexpected directions. Thus they perceive hell not so much as demonstrating divine wrath and punishment, but as manifesting divine mercy and love. While traditional orthodoxy saw hell's 'apartness' as penal exile, these writers turn it into a refuge where sinners can escape the unbearable presence of the all-holy God.

Some of them go further. If hell is the product of divine love, may not that love eventually reclaim at least some who initially go there? Might hell not have an exit or perhaps a back door? At the very least, might not its front door be locked only on the inside? Thus hell ceases to be 'the ultimate horror,' and becomes at best a refining purgatory and at worst a 'painful refuge'.[2]

---

1. *Punishment* p. 9.
2. Dante offered this explanation as a kind of theodicy in his *Divine Comedy*; L. A. King repeated Dante's concept in modern form in 'Hell, the Painful Refuge,' *Eternity*, Jan. 1979, pp. 27ff, with no suggestion that hell might have an exit. C. S. Lewis seems to have popularized the notion in *The Great Divorce* (New York: Macmillan & Co., 1946) although in the introduction he said the work was intended as a fantasy with a moral and was not intended to provide either a guess or speculation about the actual facts. Lewis went a step further in his 'fantasy,' suggesting that if hell's inhabitants actually chose to be there rather than in the presence of God, they might some day have a change of heart and go to heaven instead. Bloesch begins at the same point and argues theologically for a possible restoration from hell in *Essentials*, 2:224–230. Eller reasons for the same possibility on exegetical grounds (*Most Revealing*, pp. 200–205). It would be most unfair to suggest that these men all say the same thing or that any of them is a 'universalist' as the word is commonly used. Both Bloesch and Eller appeal to the statement of Rev. 21:25 that the gates of the New Jerusalem are always open. Could this not simply mean there are no enemies that threaten and that it is always day? One might describe his crimeless village by saying, 'We never lock our doors.' He would not mean that he was expecting company but

This presentation has obvious apologetic advantages, but if the picture which has emerged in our study of final punishment is at all valid, then such restoration is totally out of the question. If the wicked are to be consumed, they can never be reformed. If God kills and destroys the unrepentant in the lake of fire so that they die, corrupt and perish, we must dismiss any thought that heaven might be their eventual destination. If the fire of hell is truly 'unquenchable' so that it cannot be resisted, and if its punishment of destruction is 'eternal' so that it will never be reversed, it is inconceivable that anyone sentenced to its fate could ever be found alive again once the fire had accomplished its work.

If, by contrast, the wicked are made immortal, if hell is also a form of God's mercy, and if God for ever loves even those he finally banishes from his presence, restorationism will always be a persuasive option. In fact, the traditionalist answer, which has so long charged conditionalism with being an 'easy way out', has itself become the basis for restorationist speculations which conditionalism precluded from the beginning. What once presented itself as the only explanation *severe* enough to serve justice is now seen marching under a banner proclaiming the *mercy* of God.

This is clearly a different sort of universalism than nineteenth century liberal theologians proposed. Because it has sprung from reformed and evangelical soil this restorationism is immune to the arguments of an earlier time. Shedd's criticisms are no longer valid. As a notable reformed theologian points out, the modern face of universalism

> does not wish to deny the guilt or sin or weaken the wrath of God. But it sees sin and wrath as *temporary*, on the ground that God's wrath and punishment are aimed at the salvation of all men. In any case there is no intention of making human feelings the basis of this doctrine.[3]

Wenham points out that 'universalism is usually argued [today] in terms of man as a free being living for ever within the influence of God's infinitely patient love. In his selfishness and pride man may long resist God's gentle attraction, but in the end Love will win his free and full response.'[4]

The older universalism sprang from an obviously deficient view of Christ and his atonement. The newer universalism, however, 'continues to be advocated in strongly Christological and doxological terms,' Berkouwer notes, and for this very reason 'it cannot be summarily dismissed'. The philosophical arguments for the traditionalist's hell are also perceived as broken reeds:

> It would be inadequate, for example, to challenge universalism on the ground

---

that he was certainly *not*. Eller also calls attention to the 'kings of the earth' who bring their glory and honour into the city (Rev. 21:24ff). Since nothing impure enters (v. 27), he asks whether these kings might have been purified outside the city and then found entry. He is very careful to distinguish between his suggestion and 'univeralism' as it is usually conceived. With his qualifications the issue becomes an exegetical one regarding passages on final punishment, not a matter to be dismissed on dogmatic grounds involving sin, the atonement, divine wrath or human responsibility.

3. G. C. Berkouwer, *Return* p. 390.
4. *Goodness* p. 33.

that eternal punishment is a self-evident consequence of the idea of retribution. This is the notion behind the argument that there is such an appalling breadth of evil in the world that it is impossible for all of it to be absorbed in the final divine remission that would cover all guilt . . . . Such a duality breaks down because God's justice is revealed precisely in the cross. Because of this, any argument against apocatastasis [restoration] that requires the justice of God to be satisfied in an eternal punishment is invalid and unbiblical.[5]

Rather than decrying appeals to Scripture, many modern universalists appear to make it a basis for their case. As the wise woman of Tekoa described a wise king as one who 'devises ways so that a banished person may not remain estranged from him' (2 Sam. 14:14), so modern advocates of restorationism picture the all-powerful and all-merciful God. Any successful confrontation must take this fundamental approach and stance into account.

The present chapter makes no attempt or claim to be exhaustive. Here we simply note the phenomenon of modern universalism, observe the essential weakness of its major 'proof-texts,' and summarize the critique and response of one theologian who is thoroughly in touch with the modern discussion.

Some 'Proof-Texts' of Universalism

The universalism of old liberalism made less appeal to Scripture than the restorationism of today, no doubt in part because of its lower view of revelation. Historically, however, there were four 'important considerations' which 'helped to bring a measure of amelioration' from the majority view of everlasting torment. Accordng to T. F. Glasson,[6] those considerations were

1. the 'every man' statement in the prologue to John's Gospel (John 1:9),
2. Peter's statement concerning spirits in prison (1 Peter 3:18ff),
3. the rise of the doctrine of purgatory,
4. the idea that any man can prepare himself for saving faith on the basis of natural reason and so be saved by God's grace.

A careful reading of the text, however, refutes these appeals. John's prologue states clearly that while the Word became publicly incarnate in Jesus, many refused to accept him when he came. The same context also makes clear that spiritual rebirth is the work of God, not of any human agency, and that only God, and not natural reason, can illuminate the heart to acknowledge and receive Jesus as God's Son. The idea of purgatory lacks solid exegetical support, and Peter's statement about 'spirits in prison' probably refers to just what it says – 'spirits', not people. Even if it does refer to human beings, it says nothing about the situation beyond the judgment, nor does it mention a second chance or offer of salvation beyond the present life.

5. *Return*, pp. 392f.
6. T. F. Glasson, 'Human Destiny: Has Christian Teaching Changed?' *Modern Churchman* 12, no. 4 (July 1969) pp. 284–298.

It is true that Scripture in several places speaks of purification or testing by fire in both the Old (Mal. 3:2) and New (1 Cor: 3:13ff; 1 Pet. 1:7) Testaments. Even so, the context sometimes concerns present afflictions; when final judgment is in view, only those are under consideration who have served God in this life.

One might also recall Paul's universalistic statements: God's purpose is to reconcile 'all things' in Christ (Col. 1:19f), who will at the last be 'all in all' (1 Cor. 15:26ff). Or one may recall John's vision of the time when God makes 'everything new,' when there will be neither pain nor mourning, crying nor curse (Rev. 21:4f.; 22:3). These statements, however, often appear as one side of a study in contrasts; at other times they involve the vital word 'if'.

Guillebaud raises another interesting question. Philippians 2:9f speaks of every tongue confessing Jesus' sovereignty, whether in heaven, in earth or *under the earth*. But, Guillebaud points out, when Paul says God will 'sum up all things' in Christ, he includes things in heaven and earth but makes no mention of subterranean beings (Eph. 1:9f). Does this mean, Guillebaud asks, that the infernal creatures will *confess* Christ but not be included in his *saving consummation*?[7]

Universalists have appealed also to certain texts in the Gospels. But after making a detailed study, J. Arthur Baird concludes that those texts teach no such thing. 'It is necessary therefore to reaffirm what many who hold this position admit: there is no valid evidence in the Synoptics for the doctrine of universal salvation. 'Such a view', he says, 'must find its support in more philosophic argument and in certain debated portions of Paul and John.'[8]

We have spoken of John already in passing, but note another Johannine proof-text. Revelation 5:13 describes a beautiful scene in which all creatures everywhere praise God together. But this vision is followed by the central drama of evil's temporary triumph, preceding its ultimate downfall.

Paul's bold claim that one day every knee will bow before Jesus (Phil. 2:9ff.) is based on Isaiah 45:23 (quoted also in Rom. 14:11). Yet Isaiah's next verse says some will be incensed and ashamed; these, according to Isaiah 41:11, will finally perish and become as nothing.

But does not Rom. 11 hold out a hope that all will finally come to a saving knowledge of Christ? Kümmel notes that Paul's preaching of salvation ends with a 'worshipful note of praise and not a rationally sensible answer'. He concludes that we are 'unable to assert that Paul could not venture to cherish such a hope in God's all-encompassing grace', yet he points out that the total context of Romans 9–11 includes statements in Romans 9:32 and 11:22 which contradict this view. 'Paul', he says, 'reckons with the fact that there are men who are condemned by God and lost, and he warns even the Christians not to take God's wrath and condemnation lightly (Rom. 2:5; 11:22).'[9]

When one views the lost as immortalized in everlasting consciousness,

---

7. *Righteous Judge* pp. 5f.
8. *Justice* pp. 230ff.
9. W. G. Kümmel, *The Theology of the NT According to its Major Witnesses*: pp. 243f.

the picture will occasionally blur and fade, momentarily overpowered by the other biblical picture of universal harmony and praise. The most compelling answer to the challenge of universalism is actually the scriptural teaching of the fire that *consumes*. Only when we take the second *death* with absolute seriousness are we totally free of lingering thoughts that the damned eventually will come to know second *life*.

A Twofold Criticism

In his book on the last things, G. C. Berkouwer devotes one chapter to the question of *apocatastasis* or restorationism.[10] Berkouwer does not spend much time on universalism's alleged scriptural support, nor does he attempt to answer it by the 'proof-text' method. Instead, he stands backs from the subject, in order to examine it critically in the light of the gospel as a whole.

Berkouwer argues that the crucial mistake of advocates of universal restoration is to begin with a single doctrine or tenet rather than (as the Scripture does) with the biblical gospel in the framework of history. Universalism starts with the unconquerable love of God and reasons from there. It thus rests on a weak foundation, because what it says about hell and salvation is divorced from the gospel itself. Christian theologians may include verses of Scripture in their thinking but unless they stand under the shadow of the cross when they consider final punishment, says Berkouwer, they have little advantage over the Greek philosophers on Mars Hill.

Berkouwer contrasts the universalist approach to salvation with that of the New Testament. Essentially universalism looks at salvation as *eschaton* – something beyond space-time and outside the realm of gospel proclamation. The point of departure for this reasoning is the love of God in isolation; it has lost connection with the proclamation of salvation and the warning of eternal judgment.

Since this doctrine of *apocatastasis* is static and timeless, unconnected with gospel proclamation, it becomes a form of abstract belief standing over against God and his active love.

> In contrast, the biblical witness to the love of God always treats it in a kerygmatic [proclamation] context and never announces it as a static eschatological 'fact' that goes over the heads of those to whom it is addressed . . . . Outside of this correlative application of the seriousness of the gospel, nothing can be said about the future that would make one any the wiser. If one tries to concern himself with it objectively [in terms of a theological system], he finds himself ending up in a certain coldness, able to draw conclusions, but conclusions that have lost their comforting and admonishing character.[11]

However, Berkouwer charges that modern universalists are reacting in part to two errors made by the rest of the church. If he is correct, some of those who oppose restoration most vehemently have actually helped to bring it about.

10. *Return* pp. 387–423.
11. Ibid., pp. 412f.

One possible reason for the development of universalism is 'intemperate and unbiblical' preaching on hell which equally separates it from the gospel. This happens whenever final punishment is preached as a topic of curiosity or of mere intellectual interest and whenever hell is used merely to intimidate or threaten.[12] Such preaching actually detracts from the seriousness of the gospel. For the true seriousness of the gospel is that it tells all indiscriminately (not only the elect) what God has done in Christ for sinners, calls for repentance and faith, and warns of the dreadful fate of those who reject such a great salvation. Whenever hell is preached outside of this setting, or ignoring the fact that 'judgment begins with the house of God', the doctrine loses its biblical character. In the end, Berkouwer notes, such preaching generally leads to extremes, abuses and, finally, indifference.

Berkouwer also sees universalism as a reaction against a scholastic understanding of election which weakens the genuine offer of the gospel. The New Testament declares repeatedly that God is rich in grace and mercy in a measure that we cannot now fully understand or appreciate. 'When the Bible talks about salvation, it does so in a way that calls up the idea of a truly overflowing abundance .... Time and again this abundance leads ... to exclamations of praise.'[13] Thus election as well as hell have both been expounded apart from the gospel – and with similar harmful results.

Berkouwer acknowledges that the church throughout history has often

---

12. Harry Buis chides Origen for teaching eternal damnation to the masses as a deterrent to sin while privately believing in universalism. Buis calls this 'an admission of the fact that the denial of eternal punishment undermines morals' (*Eternal Punishment*, p. 57). We agree with this assessment. Origen, however, has not been alone in using hell as a means of intimidation. Pusey speaks of one of Tertullian's hellish descriptions 'which he probably uttered to scare the heathen' (*What is of Faith?* p. 11). Pusey himself said that 'neither the Church nor any portion of it has so laid down any doctrine in regard to [corporeal sufferings] as to make the acceptance of them an integral part of the doctrine itself' (p. 18), yet he comments without hesitation that 'dread of hell peoples heaven; perhaps millions have been scared back from sin by the dread of it' (p. 19). Later he remarks concerning terrifying literalistic sermons on hell: 'In the early part of this century such sermons were favourite sermons with the poor, because they were stirred up by them to reverent and awe-stricken thoughts' (p. 263). Is Pusey more righteous than Origen if he preaches literal suffering to scare the poor while admitting to his sophisticated readers that corporeal suffering is not essential to the doctrine? Berkouwer believes that when hell is spoken of 'more for its psychological effect than out of truly evangelical concern,' the preaching lacks the gospel's sound and is ineffectual in the end (*Return* p. 420).

13. *Return*, pp. 395f. In *Unconditional Good News* (Eerdmans 1980) Neal Punt begins with passages of Scripture which speak of salvation or the atonement in terms of 'all', 'the world' or 'every man', and argues from a Calvinistic basis that all are elect in Christ except those the Bible says explicitly will be lost. If Calvinists can allow the Scripture has no divine decree of reprobation (so God has no part in peoples' being lost), and if Arminians can allow that Christ's atonement accomplished salvation for the elect rather than merely making it a possibility (so God has all the glory in our being saved), Punt's 'biblical universalism' might provide a profitable meeting place at least for further discussion. More important to our thesis, Punt recognizes the scriptural teaching that at least *some* will be finally lost.

Clark H. Pinnock similarly challenges his fellow non-Calvinists to re-examine God's love for all the world (*A Wideness in God's Mercy*, Zondervan 1992).

failed to take the 'universal' passages of Scripture seriously and the doctrine of *apocatastasis* has flourished in consequence. Sometimes the depreciation of these passages has been associated in Reformed circles with 'a particular doctrine of election that leaves no room for the universal invitation to salvation, on the ground that salvation could honestly and truly be offered only to the elect . . . . Obviously this extreme does as much violence to the seriousness of the proclamation as *apocatastasis* does.'[14] For the Bible demands that we preach the gospel to all without discrimination. The proclamation of salvation is not some kind of game, some cruel charade which has God saying one thing and meaning something altogether different. Berkouwer stresses the need to be faithful in preaching the gospel, leaving the unanswerable questions of election in the hands of the sovereign God.

Those who believe that God intends the gospel call for the elect only often appeal to the Synod of Dort which in 1618–19 affirmed that Christ's death was for the elect only. In response Berkouwer quotes another eminent Calvinist theologian, Herman Bavinck, who, after 'profound analysis,' concluded that 'the authors of the Canons of Dort did not proceed in response to an "all or not at all" dilemma'.

The issue involved at Dort, says Bavinck, was not whether God loves all men or only a few, or whether the gospel call to salvation is seriously intended for all. It was rather whether Christ's atoning work only made salvation *possible* or whether it made it *accomplished fact*. The Arminian party held the first view; the party of Dort contended for the second. Berkouwer summarizes Bavinck in these words:

> The objection [at Dort] to the Arminian Remonstrants was directed against their idea that the sense of 'Christ's sacrifice for all' was that the *possibility* of salvation was obtained for all through him. The objection . . . was to the doctrine of *potential reconciliation*, according to which human decision must lead to the realization of this possibility.[15]

Berkouwer quotes Bavinck concerning the gospel call to salvation, which keeps its meaning even for those who reject it, because it is 'the proof of God's unending love for all sinners without distinction and seals the word that he has no pleasure in the death of a sinner'.[16] Berkouwer would urge those who treasure the doctrines expressed by the Canons of Dort not to minimize the seriousness of the gospel's proclamation or to abbreviate God's genuine offer in the name of a 'logical' but unscriptural doctrine.

Regardless of where one begins, Berkouwer warns, problems will always arise whenever one tries to deduce answers to questions on the

---

14. Ibid., p. 408.
15. Ibid., pp. 410f.
16. Ibid., p. 411. Both Berkouwer and Bloesch discuss Karl Barth's view on hell. They concur that Barth's concern grows out of the desire to overcome the tension between the 'universal' and 'particular' aspects of the gospel. Bloesch says: 'The logic of [Barth's] theology drives him toward an ultimate universalism, though his intention is to transcend the polarity between universalism and particularism' (*Essentials*, 2:224). Berkouwer however denies that Barth was a universalist, noting that he emphatically rejected the doctrine numerous times (*Return*, p. 399).

divine mercy or the divine wrath apart from the cross and the proclamation of the gospel. Jesus did not come to satisfy our curiosity or to make us wise as God. He came to reveal *God* – and to call men to faith and obedience. Berkouwer ends on this note:

> Over and over again the question addressed to Jesus arises in the history of the church: 'Lord, will those who are saved be few?' Jesus' answer seems so noncommital, so evasive: 'Strive to enter by the narrow door' (Luke 13:23f.). But this evasiveness is only apparent. This *is* the answer to *this* question. As long as we see only in a mirror, in riddles, many questions will remain unanswered. But *this* question has been answered, once and for all time.[17]

---

17. *Return* p. 423.

15

Doubts: and How to Resolve Them

The object of this study has been to examine the biblical teaching on the destiny of the wicked. The conclusion has been that the the ultimate punishment of hell is total everlasting extinction. Some readers, however, may be left with lingering doubts. Most of these will be best dealt with by taking another look at the relevant Scriptures as set out above. But others are of a different nature and what follows is a response to some of the most common.

Not Forever

It is sometimes argued that everlasting extinction implies something less than an 'eternal' punishment. The question is discussed above (pp. 11–20) but it may be worth while re-emphasizing that the *duration* of final punishment is clear; the question concerns its *nature*. We measure capital punishment, for example, by its permanency, not by the time required for its execution.

In the same way, the permanence of the second death is not minimized by the duration of the conscious suffering which precedes it. Somebody facing capital punishment will derive little comfort from the thought that their actual pain will be brief. The sentence is not measured in terms of pain. This same reality, recognized by courts and criminals throughout the earth, also answers the objection that eternal extinction is really no *punishment*. For all agree that instant death before a firing squad is rightly regarded as a far greater penalty than even a lifetime in prison. Whatever conscious suffering hell may involve, such torment will correspond precisely to the sentence of divine justice in every case. God is severe but he is not a sadist.

Not Possible

Some have objected that 'annihilation' is physically impossible. But surely no martyr approaching the stake ever took comfort from the thought that their smoke and ashes would remain. In any case, Scripture does not address us in terms of Newtonian physics but of life and death; we have intentionally spoken of 'extinction' rather than 'annihilation' most of the time to avoid this cavil. The events of the Age to Come are not subject to physicists' inductive generalizations drawn from experience now. In addition, the same law of thermodynamics which says that nothing is destroyed also says nothing is created. God is greater than either part of the statement, and he is fully able to destroy both body and soul in hell.

A Dangerous View

Quite often the fear is expressed (sometimes with extreme stridency) that this view of final punishment endangers the faith. Constable responded very well to this objection. Precisely *what*, he asked, is at risk?

> Does it imperil our faith in God? What attribute of his is attacked? His love! Is it the part of love to inflict eternal pain if it can be helped? His mercy! Is it part of mercy never to be satisfied with the misery of others? His holiness! Can justice only be satisfied with everlasting agonies? No; we do not endanger faith. We strengthen it, by allying it once more with the divine principles of mercy, equity and justice. It is the Augustinian theory which endangers faith, and has made shipwreck of faith in the case of multitudes, by representing God as a Being of boundless injustice, caprice and cruelty.

This is not, course, the basis on which we rest our case. We merely urge that this particular criticism is not valid.

Not Noble

It is said that extinction contradicts the 'great value' of each individual. Is that value better secured by preserving a person alive for ever in unspeakable torment? This argument is essentially humanistic and most at home in a nineteenth-century case for universalism. The Bible nowhere presents human worth as something inherent (in truth, we are creatures of clay) but in terms of our relationship with God. Traditionalists, on the other hand, also feel free to speak of man's sense of 'total worthlessness' in hell, so this argument cuts both ways.

Not Moral

What about the danger that eternal extinction removes the fear of hell and thus encourages sin? Conditionalists point to the remarkable results of the traditionalist view. Augustine responded to the traditional doctrine by inventing purgatory, Origen by formulating restorationism. Sceptics turn the idea into a joke or use it as an excuse to charge God with injustice. Even those who say they believe the doctrine usually think eternal torment is for someone else and thus contrive to protect themselves from the shock value the belief supposedly has.

Most certainly our age desperately needs to learn the fear of the Almighty, and that is one reason for the proper preaching of hell. We have attempted to stress this biblical emphasis throughout the present study. We all have violated God's voice in nature and conscience. Those who reject his final word of mercy in Jesus Christ are warned in the most awesome terms. Nothing remains for such a one, Scripture say, but fearful anticipation of judgment – and fiery indignation which will devour every adversary! One of the greatest benefits to come by recovering the scriptural teaching on hell will be to loose preachers' tongues to make very clear this alternative to salvation in the power of the Holy Spirit and in the wholesome and truthful language of the Word of God.

This 'argument by (supposed) results' can settle the issue neither way since it begins with the human response rather than with God's revelation. The only question that should concern us is to ask what the Bible teaches. If it teaches eternal torment, peoples' reactions will not lessen that one whit. If it teaches eternal extinction, no supposedly 'practical' objection can make it less true. Such objections are unworthy of Christians who profess to repose final authority in the Word of God.

Not Reasonable

Others object that it seems an uncalled-for act of severity to raise the wicked for judgment, only to destroy them eternally. Conditionalists, however, are amazed that advocates of eternal torment should raise the question of severity. It is clear from Scripture that God will indeed raise the wicked from death and that he will do this in order to deal with them according to their actions performed when in the body. Even human feelings of moral necessity agree to this (though these by themselves prove nothing), for many evils evidently go unpunished in the present life.

But in the last resort the final answer to this objection must be the one given by traditionalists to those questioning the *justice* of their own view. God, not man, is the judge of the world, and he will do what is right. Once more, the question reverts to one of exegesis. What does Scripture say God will do? When we look there, we find it stated in dozens of ways that the wages of sin is *death*.

Not Vindictive

A quite different objection is that final extinction has more to with grace than justice, being rooted in a false conception that sees hell as a form or manifestation of benevolence rather than righteousness and wrath. Yet no conditionalist discovered in this study ever argued along these lines although more than one traditionalist has! It is the advocate of eternal torment, not of final extinction, who reasons that divine grace reaches to hell as well as to heaven, and that hell's very existence is a sign of God's mercy to those who cannot stand to be in his immediate presence. This is an interesting question, but it is the traditionalist's problem, not the conditionalist's.

Life is more than Existence

Advocates of eternal torment frequently make a great deal of the fact that eternal *life* means far more than 'mere existence'. The implication is that 'mere existence' is included in the second *death*. Surely the *non sequitur* is obvious. God has promised abundant life to all who believe in Jesus and death to those who will not do so. 'Abundant' life certainly means more than 'mere existence' in this case, but death is simply *death*. It would be foolish indeed for somebody who has rejected the gospel to demand that their life should be spared on the basis of such an argument as this.

The simple truth is that none of these objections is valid. They are all irrelevant to the main question. Equally, the issue between eternal extinction and eternal conscious torment is not be settled by disputing whether the pains of hell are spiritual or physical or a combination of both. The answer does not even depend on a 'right' view of human personality. Christians who hold to a separate and conscious 'soul' which survives bodily death freely acknowledge that God is well able to destroy both soul and body in hell – if he so desires. On the other hand, those who hold that human beings are unitary, so that the body / soul distinction is functional rather than substantial, do not doubt that God could grant immortality to the wicked as easily as to the righteous – if he so desired. Some 'conditionalists' have even believed in a conscious 'soul' which survives physical death; others have held that it dies with the body; others that it sleeps.

Even less is the issue one of cowardice, 'liberalism' or wishful thinking. Such charges add pepper to a sermon, but they are unbecoming, uninformed and unfair to most conditionalists. Traditionalist writers frequently equate their own position with respect for the Bible. Considering some of their critics over the last four centuries, one can understand why. To traditionalists who share my commitment to the authority of Scripture, I can only reiterate what was said at the beginning of this book. It was as a result of careful study that my beliefs were changed. Mere assertion and denunciation will not refute the evidence presented in this book, nor will a reaffirmation of ecclesiastical tradition. The case finally rests on Scripture. Only Scripture can disprove it.

Selective Bibliography

Where a short title is used in the notes, this is shown in bold type after the entry.

1. Primary Texts

Ante-Nicene Christian Library (Edinburgh: T. & T. Clark, 1867–, Grand Rapids: Eerdmans 1950 rp)
Bettenson, H. ed. *Documents of the Christian Church* (London & New York: OUP 1943)
Bihlmeyer, Karl ed. *Die Apostolischen Vater* (Tubingen: J. C. B. Mohr 1956²)
Charles, R. H. ed. *Apocrypha and Pseudepigrapha of the OT* (Oxford: Clarendon 1913)
Dupont-Sommer, A. ed. *The Essene Writings from Qumran* (Cleveland & New York: World 1962)
Goodspeed, E. J. *The Apostolic Fathers* (New York: Harper 1950)
Nestle, E. ed. *Novum Testamentum Graece* (New York: American Bible Society 24th edn)
New Scofield Reference Bible (New York: Oxford 1967) **Scofield**
Nicodemus, Gospel of, in *Apocryphal Books of the NT* (Philadelphia: David McKay 1901)
Pritchard, J. B. ed. *Ancient Near Eastern Texts Relating to the OT* (Princeton, N.J.: Princeton UP, 1969³) **ANET**
Rahlfs, A. ed. *Septuaginta* (Stuttgart: Wurttembergische Bibelanstalt 1966⁷)
Whiston, W, trans. *Josephus* (Grand Rapids: Kregel 1969 rp)

2. Dictionaries and Reference works

Alexander, D. & P. eds. *Lion/Eerdman's Handbook to the Bible.* (Tring/Grand Rapids: Lion/Eerdmans 1973)
Arndt, W. F. & Gingrich, F. W. trs. *Greek-English Lexicon of the NT* (Chicago: Univ. of Chicago, 1957) **Lexicon**
Baker's Dictionary of Theology Harrison E. F. ed. (Grand Rapids: Baker 1960)
Bible Key Words, vol. 4 'Law,' 'Wrath.' Barton D. M. & Ackroyd P. R. trans (New York: Harper & Row 1962)
Catholic Dictionary Attwater D. ed (New York: Macmillan 1957²)
Dana, H. E. & Mantey, J. R. *Manual, Grammar of the Greek NT* (New York: Macmillan 1960 rp)
Dictionary of Christian Bibliography Smith W. & Wace H. eds. (London: Murray 1880)
Dictionary of Religion and Ethics Mathews S. & Smith G. B. eds (London: Waverley 1921)
Dictionary of the Bible Hastings J. ed, Grant F. C. & Rowley H. H. revd (Edinburgh: T.& T. Clark 1963²) **HDB**

Dictionary of Christ and the Gospels Hastings J. ed. (Edinburgh/New York: T & T Clark/Scribner 1906)
Dowley, T. *Lion/Eerdmans' Handbook to the History of Christianity* Grand Rapids/Tring: Lion/Eerdmans 1977)
Encyclopaedia of Religion and Religions Pike E. Royston ed. (London: Allen & Unwin 1951)
Encylopaedia of Religion Ferm V. ed. (New York: Philosophical Library 1945)
Encyclopaedia Biblica Cheyne T. K. & Black J. S. eds. (London: Black 1901)
Encyclopaedia of Religion and Ethics Hastings J. ed. (New York: Scribner 1912)
Englishman's Critical and Expository Bible Cyclopaedia Fausset A. R. (London: Hodder 1878)
International Standard Bible Encyclopaedia Bromiley G. W. ed (Grand Rapids: Eerdmans 1979–88³)
International Standard Bible Encyclopaedia Kyle M. ed (Chicago: Howard-Severance 1929²)
Interpreter's Dictionary of the Bible (New York & Nashville: Abingdon 1962) **IDB**
Jewish Encyclopaedia Singer I. ed. (New York: Funk & Wagnalls 1925) **JW**
Mead, F. S. *Handbook of Denominations in the United States* (Nashville: Abingdon 1975⁶)
Moulton, J. H. & Milligan, G. *Vocabulary of the Greek Testament* (London: Hodder 1963)
New Schaff-Herzog Encyclopedia of Religious Knowledge Jackson S. M. ed. (New York & London: Funk & Wagnalls 1911) **Vocabulary**
New Catholic Encyclopaedia (Washington D.C.: Catholic Univ. of America 1967) **NCE**
New Bible Dictionary Douglas J. D. ed. Grand Rapids: IVP/Eerdmans 1974)
New International Dictionary of NT Theology Brown C. ed. (Exeter/Grand Rapids: Paternoster/Zondervan 1975)
Protestant Dictionary Carter C. S & Weeks G. E. A. eds. (London: Harrison Trust 1933)
Religious Encyclopaedia Schaff P. ed. (New York: Funk & Wagnalls 1891³)
Thayer, J. H. *Greek-English Lexicon of the NT* (Grand Rapids: Zondervan 1963) **Lexicon**
Theological Dictionary of the NT Kittel G. & Friedrich G. eds, G.W. Bromiley trans. (Grand Rapids: Eerdmans 1964–)
Zondervan Pictorial Bible Dictionary Tenney M. C. ed. (Grand Rapids: Zondervan 1963)

3. Journals and Periodicals

Adams, M. 'Hell and the God of Justice' *Religious Studies* 2, no.4 (Dec. 1975) 433–447

Badham, P. 'Recent Thinking on Christian Beliefs: The Future Life' *ET* (Apr. 1977) 197–202

Barbour, R. S. 'Gethsemane in the Tradition of the Passion' *NTS* 16, no. 3 (Apr. 1970) 231–251

Barrett, C. K. 'NT Eschatology: Pt I,' *SJT* 6, no. 2 (June 1953) 136–155

Barrett, C. K. 'NT Eschatology: Pt II – The Gospels' *SJT* 6, no. 3 (Sep. 1953) 225–243

Beardslee, W. E. 'NT Apocalyptic in Recent Interpretation' *Interpretation* 25, no. 4 (Oct. 1971) 419–435

Beasley-Murray, G. R. A 'New Testament Apocalyptic – A Christological Eschatology' *Review & Expositor* 72, no. 3 (Summer 1975) 317–330

Beasley–Murray, G.R. 'The Contribution of the Book of Revelation to the Christian Belief in Immortality' *SJT* 27, no. 1 (Feb. 1974) 76–93

Berkemeyer, W. C. 'The Eschatological Dilemma' *Lutheran Quarterly* 7, no. 3 (Aug. 1955) 233–239
Bligh, P. H. 'Eternal Fire, Eternal Punishment, Eternal Life (Mt. 25:41, 46,)' *ET* 83, no. 1 (Oct. 1971) 9–11
Bloesch, D. G. 'Crisis in Biblical Authority,' *Theology Today* 35, no. 4 (Jan. 1979) 455–462
Brandon, S. G. F. 'Life after Death: The After-Life in Ancient Egyptian Faith and Practice' *ET* (Apr. 1965) 217–220
Brinsmead, R. D. 'Man' parts 1–3. *Verdict*, Aug., Sep., Dec. 1978
Bruce, F. F. 'A Reappraisal of Jewish Apocalyptic Literature' *Review & Expositor* 72, no. 3 (Summer 1975) 305–315
Bruce, F. F. 'Paul on Immortality' *SJT* 24, no. 4 (Nov. 1971) 457–472
Bruce, F. F. 'Eschatology.' *London Quarterly and Holborn Review* (Apr. 1958) 99–103
Bultmann, R. 'History and Eschatology in the NT' *NTS* 1, no.1 (Sep. 1954) 5–16
Burns, J. B. 'Mythology of Death in the OT' *SJT* no. 3 (Aug. 1973) 327–340
Cupitt, D. 'The Language of Eschatology: F. D. Maurice's Treatment of Heaven and Hell' *Anglican Theological Review* 54 no. 4 (Oct. 1972) 305–317
Davies, J. G. 'Factors Leading to the Emergence of Belief in the Resurrection of the Flesh' *JTS* 23 (1972) 448–455
Dockx, S. 'Man's Eschatological Condition' *SJT* 27, no. 1 (Feb. 1974) 20–34
Dunning, T.G. 'What has Become of Heaven and Hell?' *Baptist Quarterly* 20, no. 8 (Oct. 1964) 352–361 **Heaven and Hell**
Ebeling, G. 'The Meaning of "Biblical Theology" ' *JTS*, NS 6, no. 2 (Oct. 1955) 210–255
Fairhurst, A. M. 'The Problem Posed by the Severe Sayings Attributed to Jesus in the Synoptic Gospels' *SJT* 23 (1970) 77–91
Forestell, J. T. 'Christian Revelation and the Resurrection of the Wicked' *CBQ* 19, no. 2 (Apr. 1957) 165–189 **Christian Revelation**
Fudge, E. 'The Eschatology of Ignatius of Antioch: Christocentric and Historical' *JETS* 15, no. 4 (Fall 1972) 231–237
Fudge, E. 'Putting Hell in its Place' *ChrT*, 6 Aug. 1976, 14–17
Glasson, T. F. 'Human Destiny: Has Christian Teaching Changed?' *Modern Churchman* 12 no. 4 (July 1969) 284–298
Goen, C. C. 'The Modern Discussion of Eschatology' *Review & Expositor* 57, no. 2 (Apr. 1960) 107–125
Gundry, D. W. 'The Ghost in the Machine and the Body of the Resurrection' *SJT* 18, no. 2 (June 1965) 164–169
Hamilton, N. Q. 'The Last Things in the Last Decade: The Significance of Recent Study in the Field of Eschatology' *Interpretation* 14, no. 2 (Apr. 1960) 131–142
Harris, Murray 'Resurrection and Immortality: Eight Theses' *Themelios* 1, no. 2 (Spring 1976) 50–55
Heinitz, K. 'Eschatology in the Teaching of Jesus' *Concordia Theological Monthly* 41, no. 8 (Sep. 1970) 451–461
Heller, J. J. 'The Resurrection of Man' *Theology Today* 15, no. 2 (July 1958) 217–229
Herhold, R. M. 'Kubler-Ross and Life after Death.' *Christian Century*, 14 Apr. 1976, 363–364
Hodgson, L. 'Life after Death: the Philosophers Plato and Kant' *ET* (Jan. 1965) 107–109
Hofmann, H. 'Immortality or Life' *Theology Today* 15, no. 2 (July 1958) 230–245
Hooke, S. H. 'Life after Death: Israel and the After-Life' *ET* (May 1965) 236–239

Hooke, S. H. 'Life after Death: the Extra-Canonical Literature' *ET* (June 1965) 273–276
Howard C. 'The Development of Eschatology in the NT' *JBR* 20, no. 3 (July 1952) 187–193
Hoyles, J. A. 'The Punishment of the Wicked after Death' *London Quarterly and Holborn Review* (Apr. 1957) 118–123
Inbody, T. 'Process Theology and Personal Survival' *Iliff Review* 31, no. 2 (Spring 1974) 31–42
Jeremias, J. ' "Flesh and Blood Cannot Inherit the Kingdom of God" (1 Cor. xv.50)' *NTS* 2, no. 3 (Feb. 1956) 151–159
Kepple, R. J. 'The Hope of Israel, the Resurrection of the Dead, and Jesus' *JETS* 20, no. 3 (Sep. 1977) 231–242
King, L. A. 'Hell, the Painful Refuge' *Eternity* (Jan. 1979) 27, 29, 39
Knight, G. A. F. 'Eschatology in the OT' *SJT*, no. 4 (Dec. 1951) 355–362
Linton, C. D. 'The Sorrows of Hell' *ChrT* (19 Nov. 1971) 12–14
Logan, N.A. 'The OT and a Future Life' *SJT* 6, no. 2 (June 1953) 165–172
Lotz, D. W. 'Heaven and Hell in the Christian Tradition' *Religion in Life* 48 (Spring 1979)
Macquarrie, J. 'Death and Eternal Life' *ET* 89 (Nov. 1977) 46–48
Marshall, I. H. 'Slippery Words: Eschatology' *ET* (June 1978) 264–269
Martin, W. B. J. 'Life after Death: The Poets-Victorian and Modern.' *ET* (Feb. 1965) 140–143
Mattill, A. J. Jr. 'The Way of Tribulation' *JBL* 98, no. 4 (Dec. 1979) 531–546
Mitton, C. Leslie 'Present Justification and Final Judgment: A Discussion of the Parable of the Sheep and the Goats.' *ET* 68, no. 2 (Nov. 1956) 46–50
Mitton, C. Leslie 'Life after Death: The After-Life in the NT' *ET* (Aug. 1965) 332–337
Moltmann, J. 'Descent into Hell' *Duke Divinity School Review* 33, no. 2 (Spring 1968) 115–119
Motyer, J. A. 'The Final State' *ChrT*, (28 Sep. 1962) 30–31
Nicole, R. 'The Punishment of the Wicked' *ChrT* (9 June 1958) 13–15
Müller, G. 'Ungeheuerliche Ontologie: Erwagungen zur christlichen Lehre uber Holle und Allversohnung' *Evangelische Theologie*, no. 3 (1974) 256–275
Noll, M. 'Who Sets the Stage for Understanding Scripture?' *ChrT* (23 May 1980) 14–18
O'Laughlin, M. 'Scripture and Tradition' *Again* 2, no. 3 (July–Sep. 1979) 14–15
Peel, M. L. 'Gnostic Eschatology and the NT '*Novum Testamentum* 12, no. 2 (Apr. 1970) 141–165
Rex, H. H. 'Immortality of the Soul, or Resurrection of the Dead, or What?' *Reformed Theological Review* 17, no. 3 (Oct. 1958) 73–82
Ridenhour, T. E. 'Immortality and Resurrection in the OT' *Dialog* 15 (Spring 1976) 104–109
Roberts, J. W. 'Some Observations on the Meaning of 'Eternal Life' in the Gospel of John' *Restoration Quarterly* 7, no. 4 (4th Qter, 1963) 186–193 Immortality
Scharlemann, R. P. 'Afterlife and the Eternal as a Question' *Dialog* 15, no. 2 (Spring 1976) 118–122
Scharlemann, M. H. 'He Descended into Hell' *Concordia Theological Monthly* 27, no. 2 (Feb. 1956) 81–94
Scott, J. J. 'Some Problems in Hermeneutics for Contemporary Evangelicals' *JETS* 22, no. 1 (Mar. 1979) 67–78
Selwyn, E. G. 'Image, Fact and Faith' *NTS* 1, no. 4 (May 1955) 235–247
Shutt, R. J. H. 'The NT Doctrine of the Hereafter: Universalism or Conditional Immortality' *ET* 67, no. 5 (Feb. 1956) 131–135

Smith, G. V. 'Structure and Purpose in Genesis 1–11' *JETS* 20, no. 4 (Dec. 1977) 307–320
Snaith, N. 'Justice and Immortality,' *SJT* no. 3 (Sep. 1964) 309–324
Strawson, W. 'Life after Death: The Future Life in Contemporary Theology' *ET* (Oct. 1965) 9–13
Suchocki, M. 'The Question of Immortality' *Journal of Religion* 57, No. 3 (July 1977) 288–306
Sutherland, S. R. 'What Happens after Death?' *SJT* 22, no. 4 (Dec. 1969) 404–418
Taylor, Vincent 'Life after Death: the Modern Situation' *ET* 76, no. 3 (Dec. 1964) 76–78
Thomson, J. G. S. 'Death and Immortality' *ChrT* (3 Aug. 1962) 18–19
Tupper, E. F. 'The Revival of Apocalyptic in Biblical and Theological Studies' *Review & Expositor* 72, no. 3 (Summer 1975) 279–304
Vawter, B. 'Intimations of Immortality and the OT' *JBL* 91, no. 2 (June 1972) 158–171
Wahle, Hedwig. 'Die Lehren des rabbinischen Judentums uber das Leben dem Tod.' *Kairos: Zeitschrift fur Religionswissenschaft und Theologie* 14, no. 4 (Jahrgang 1972) 291–309
Whiteley, D. E. H. 'Liberal Christianity in the NT' *Modern Churchman* 13, no. 1 (Oct. 1969)
Widengren, G. 'Life after Death: Eschatological Ideas in Indian and Iranian Religion' *ET* (Sep. 1965) 364–367
Wilken, R. L. 'The Immortality of the Soul and Christian Hope' *Dialog* 15, no. 2 (Spring 1976) 110–117
Wolfson, H. A. 'Notes on Patristic Philosophy' *Harvard Theological Review* 57, no. 2 (Apr. 1964) 119–132
Zens, J. 'Do the Flames Ever Stop in Hell?' *Free Grace Broadcaster* (Mar.–Apr. 1978) 1–8

4. Commentaries and other books

Abbot, E. 'The Literature of the Doctrine of a Future Life' in *Destiny of the Soul* Alger, W. R. (Boston: Roberts 1880[10]. rp. N.Y.: Greenwood 1968)
Abbot, L. ed. *That Unknown Country* (Springfield, Mass.: C. A. Nichols 1891)
Alger, W. R. *Destiny of the Soul* (2 vols. Boston: Roberts 1880[10] rp N. Y.: Greenwood 1968)
Ankerberg, J. *The Facts on Life after Death* (Harvest House 1992)
Atkinson, B. F. C. *Life and Immortality* (Taunton, England: Phoenix/Goodman n.d.) **Life and Immortality**
Badham, P. *Christian Beliefs about Life after Death* (London: Macmillan 1976)
Baird, J. A. *Justice of God in the Teaching of Jesus* (London: SCM 1963) **Justice**
Baker, C. F. *Dispensational Theology* (Grand Rapids: Grace Bible College 1971)
Bardy, Abbe *Christian Latin Literature of the First Six Centuries* (St Louis: Herder 1930)
Barth, M. *Justification* (Grand Rapids: Eerdmans 1971)
Barth, K. *Romans* (London: Oxford UP 1933)
Beasley-Murray, G. R. *Christ is Alive!* (London: Lutterworth 1947)
Beecher, E. *History of Opinions on the Scriptural Doctrine of Retribution* (N.Y.: Appleton 1878) **Opinions**
Belcastro, J. 'The Permanent Validity of the Idea of Hell' (S.T.M. thesis, Oberlin [Ohio] College 1937)
Berkhof, L. *Principles of Biblical Interpretation* (Grand Rapids: Baker 1950)
Berkhof, L. *Reformed Dogmatics*, vol. 2. (Grand Rapids: Eerdmans 1932) **Berkhof**
Berkhof, L. *Vicarious Atonement through Christ* (Grand Rapids: Eerdmans 1936)

Berkouwer, G. C. *Return of Christ* (Grand Rapids: Eerdmans 1972) **Return**
Bernard, T. D. *Progress of Doctrine in the NT* (N.Y.: American Tract Soc. 1907)
Blenkinsopp, J. 'Theological Synthesis and Hermeneutical Conclusions' in *Immortality and Resurrection,* Benoit, P. & Murphy, R. eds. (London: Herder 1970)
Blanchard, J. *Whatever Happened to Hell?* (Durham: Evangelical Press 1993) **Hell**
Bloesch, D. G. *Essentials of Evangelical Theology*, vol. 2. (San Francisco: Harper 1979) **Essentials**
Boatman, R. E. *Beyond Death* (Author [245 N. Elizabeth, Florissant, Mo. 63033] 1980)
Boettner, L. *Person of Christ* (Grand Rapids: Eerdmans 1943)
Boliek, L. *Resurrection of the Flesh* (Grand Rapids: Eerdmans 1962)
Braun, J. E. *Whatever Happened to Hell?* (Nashville: Nelson 1979) **Whatever?**
Brinsmead, R. D. *Pattern of Redemptive History* (Fallbrook, Calif.: Verdict 1979) **Pattern**
Brinsmead, R. D. *Covenant.* (Fallbrook, Calif.: Verdict 1979)
Bruce, F. F. *Paul . . .* (Exeter/Grand Rapids: Paternoster/Eerdmans 1977) **Paul**
Bruce, F. F. *Answers to Questions* (Exeter/Grand Rapids: Paternoster/Zondervan 1973)
Buis, H. *Doctrine of Eternal Punishment* (Philadelphia: Presbyterian and Reformed 1957) **Eternal Punishment**
Burns, N. T. *Christian Mortalism from Tyndale to Milton* (Cambridge, Mass.: Harvard U.P. 1972) **Christian Mortalism**
Buswell, J. O. Jr. *Systematic Theology* (1-vol. ed., 3rd rp. Grand Rapids: Zondervan 1969)
Calvin, J. *Isaiah* (Grand Rapids: Eerdmans 1948 rp)
Calvin, J. *Harmony of the Evangelists* (Grand Rapids: Eerdmans 1957 rp)
Calvin, J. *Institutes* trans. Ford Lewis Battles (Philadelphia: Westminster 1960)
Cameron, N. M. de S. ed. *Universalism and the Doctrine of Hell* (GrandRapids/Carlisle: Baker/Paternoster 1993)
Carnell, Edward John *Introduction to Christian Apologetics* (Grand Rapids: Eerdmans 1948)
Charles, R. H. *A Critical History of the Doctrine of a Future Life* (London: Black, 1913^2)
Charlesworth, J. H. *Pseudepigrapha and Modern Research* Septuagint and Cognate Studies, no. 7 (Missoula, Mont.: Scholars 1976) **Pseudepigrapha**
Constable, H. *Duration and Nature of Future Punishment* (London: Hobbs 1886^6) **Punishment**
Conzelmann, H. *Outline of the Theology of the NT* (New York: Harper 1969)
Cross, F. L. *Early Christian Fathers* (London: Duckworth 1960)
Cullman, O. *Immortality of the Soul or Resurrection of the Dead?* (London: Epworth 1958) **Immortality or Resurrection?**
Davies, E. *An Angry God?* (Bryntirion: Evl. Press of Wales 1991) **Angry?**
Davies, W. D. *Setting of the Sermon on the Mount* (London: Cambridge UP 1963)
Davis, A. P. *Isaac Watts* (London: Independent 1943)
Delitzsch, F. *Hebrews* (Grand Rapids: Eerdmans 1952 rp)
Delitzsch, F. *Isaiah* (Grand Rapids: Eerdmans 1965 rp)
Dixon, L. *Other Side of the Good News* (BridgePoint, 1992) **Other Side**
Dubarle, A-M. 'Belief in Immortality in the Old Testament and Judaism' in *Immortality and Resurrection* Benoit P. & Murphy, R. eds. (London: Herder 1970)
Dunn, J. D. G. 'Paul's Understanding of the Death of Jesus' in *Reconciliation and Hope* ed Banks R. (Grand Rapids/Exeter Eerdmans/Paternoster 1974) **Paul's Understanding**
Dupont-Sommer, A. *Dead Sea Scrolls* (Oxford: Blackwell 1952)

Edwards, Jonathan *Works* Revd. by Hickman E. (2 vols. Carlisle, Penn.: Banner of Truth)
Eller, V. *The Most Revealing Book of the Bible* (Grand Rapids: Eerdmans 1974) **Most Revealing**
Farrar, F. W. *Eternal Hope* (London/New York: Macmillan 1879)
Farrar, F. W. *Mercy and Judgment* (London: Macmillan 1881)
Ferguson, E. *Early Christians Speak* (Austin, Texas: Sweet 1971)
France R. T. 'Exegesis in Practice: Two Samples' in *New Testament Interpretation* I. H. Marshall, ed. (Exeter/Grand Rapids: Paternoster/Eerdmans 1978)
Froom, L. E. *Conditionalist Faith of Our Fathers* (2 vols. Washington D.C.: Review and Herald 1965) **Conditionalist Faith**
Fudge, E. *One Life, Death and Judgment* (Athens, Ala.: Edward Fudge 1978)
Fudge, E. *Our Man in Heaven: An Exposition of the Epistle to the Hebrews* (Grand Rapids: Baker 1974)
Gatch, M. McC. *Death: Meaning and Mortality in Christian Thought and Contemporary Culture* (NewYork.: Seabury 1969) **Death**
Geisler, N. L. *Philosophy of Religion* (Grand Rapids: Zondervan 1974)
Geldenhuys, N. *Luke* (Grand Rapids: Eerdmans 1951)
Guillebaud, H. E. *Righteous Judge* (Taunton England: Phoenix n.d.)
Hailey, H. *Revelation* (Grand Rapids: Baker 1979)
Hailey, H. *Commentary on the Minor Prophets* (Grand Rapids: Baker 1972)
Hanhart, K. *Intermediate State in the N.T.* (Doctoral dissertation at the Univ. of Amsterdam. Franeker: T. Wever Sept. 1966)
Harmon, K. 'The Case against Conditionalism' in *Universalism and the Doctrine of Hell* ed. Cameron, N. M. de S. (GrandRapids/Carlisle: Baker/Paternoster 1993)
Harris, M. J. 'Paul's View of Death' in *New Dimensions in N.T. Study*, Longenecker, R. N. & Tenney, M. C. eds. (Grand Rapids: Zondervan 1974)
Hasel, G. F. *NT Theology: Basic Issues* (Grand Rapids: Eerdmans 1978)
Hendriksen, W. *More Than Conquerors* (Grand Rapids: Baker 1960)
Hendriksen, W. *Gospel According to John* (Grand Rapids: Baker 1967)
Henry, C. F. H., ed. *Revelation and the Bible* (Grand Rapids: Baker 1958)
Hick, J. *Death and Eternal Life* (London: Collins 1976)
Hodge, A. A. *Outlines of Theology* (Grand Rapids: Eerdmans 1957 rp)
Hodge, C. *Systematic Theology* (New York: Scribner 1884)
Hoekema, A. A. *The Bible and the Future* (Grand Rapids/Exeter: Eerdmans/Paternoster 1979)
Holwerda, D. E. 'Eschatology and History: A Look at Calvin's Eschatological Vision' in *Exploring the Heritage of John Calvin* Holwerda, D. E. ed. (Grand Rapids: Baker 1976)
Hunter, A. M. *The Parables Then and Now* (Philadelphia: Westminster 1971)
Hunter, A. M. *Interpreting the Parables* (London: SCM 1960)
Hunter, A. M. *Gospel According to St. Paul* (Philadelphia: Westminster 1966)
Jenkins, F. *Old Testament in the Book of Revelation* (Marion, Ind.: Cogdill – Grand Rapids; Baker pbk 1972) **OT Revelation**
Jeremias, J. *The Parables of Jesus* (London: SCM 1963) **Parables**
Keil C. F. & Delitzsch, F. *Biblical Commentary on the OT* (Grand Rapids: Eerdmans n.d.)
Keil, C. F. *Ezekiel* (Grand Rapids: Eerdmans n.d.)
Kelly, J. N. D. *Early Christian Doctrines* (London: Black 1977[5])
Kennedy, H. A. A. *St. Paul's Conceptions of the Last Things* (London: Hodder and Stoughton 1904[2])
Kevan, E. F. 'The Principles of Interpretation' in *Revelation and the Bible* C. F. Henry ed. (Grand Rapids: Baker 1958)
Kline, M. G. *By Oath Consigned* (Grand Rapids: Eerdmans 1968)

Kummel, W. G. *Theology of the NT* (Nashville: Abingdon 1973)
Ladd, G. E. *Pattern of NT Truth* (Grand Rapids: Eerdmans 1968)
Lane, W. *Mark* (Grand Rapids: Eerdmans 1974)
Lenski, R. C. H. *The Interpretation of the Epistles of St. Peter, St. John and St. Jude* (Columbus, Ohio: Wartburg 1945) **Interpretation**
Let God Be True Anon. (Brooklyn, N.Y.: Watchtower 1946)
Lilje, H. *The Last Book of the Bible* (Philadelphia: Muhlenberg 1957)
Luther, M. *Works* vol. 17, *Lectures on Isaiah 40–66* (St Louis: Concordia 1972)
Luther, Martin *Works* Pelikan, J. (vols. 1–30) and Lehmann H. T. (vols. 31–55) eds. (St. Louis/Philadelphia: Concordia/Muhlenberg 1955–1975)
MacCulloch, J. A. *Harrowing of Hell* (Edinburgh: T. & T. Clark 1930)
Martin, J. P. *Last Judgment in Protestant Theology from Orthodoxy to Ritschl* (Grand Rapids: Eerdmans 1963)
Martin-Achard, R. *From Death to Life* (Edinburgh & London: Oliver & Boyd 1960)
Morey, R. *Death and the Afterlife* (Minneapolis: Bethany 1984) **Afterlife**
Morris, L. *Biblical Doctrine of Judgment* (London: Tyndale Press 1960) **Judgment**
Morris, L. *1 & 2 Thessalonians* (Grand Rapids: Eerdmans 1959)
Morris, L. *Cross in the N.T.* (Grand Rapids/Exeter: Eerdmans/Paternoster 1965)
Mounce, R. *Revelation* (Grand Rapids: Eerdmans 1977)
Murray, J. *Romans* (Grand Rapids: Eerdmans 1959)
Nickelsburg, G. W. E., Jr. *Resurrection, Immortality, and Eternal Life in Intertestamental Judaism* (Harvard Theol. Studs, no. 26. Cambridge, Mass.: Harvard U. P. 1963) **Intertestamental**
Nicoll, W. Robertson, ed. *Expositor's Greek Testament* (Grand Rapids: Eerdmans 1961 rp)
Norris, R. A., Jr. *Manhood and Christ* (London: Oxford U P 1963)
Orr, J. *Resurrection of Jesus* (Grand Rapids: Zondervan 1965)
Packer, J.I. *'Fundamentalism' and the Word of God* (London/Grand Rapids: IVF/Eerdmans 1958)
Pedersen, J. *Israel: Its Life and Culture.* 2 vols. (London: Oxford UP 1926)
Pelikan, J. *Shape of Death* (N.Y: Abingdon 1961)
Petavel, E. *Problem of Immortality* (London: Elliot Stock 1892) **Problem**
Pilcher, C. V. *Hereafter in Jewish and Christian Thought, with Special Reference to the Doctrine of the Resurrection* (London: SPCK, 1940) **Hereafter**
Pink, A. *Hebrews* (Grand Rapids: Baker 1954)
Pink, A. W. *Eternal Punishment* (Swengel, Pa.: Reiner n.d.)
Pinnock, C. H. *Biblical Revelation* (Chicago: Moody 1971)
Pinnock, C. H. 'Prospects for Systematic Theology' in *Toward a Theology for the Future* Wells D. F. & Pinnock C. H. eds. (Carol Stream, Ill.: Creation Hse 1971)
Plass, E. M., comp. *What Luther Says: An Anthology* (St. Louis: Concordia 1959)
Pusey, E. B. *What is of Faith as to Everlasting Punishment?* (Oxford: James Parker 1880)
Quistorp, H. *Calvin's Doctrine of the Last Things* (London: Lutterworth 1955) **Last Things**
Reichenbach, B. R. *Is Man the Phoenix?* (Christian University [subsidiary of Christian College Consortium and Eerdmans], 1978) **Phoenix**
Richardson, A. *Introduction to the Theology of the NT* (London/New York: SCM/Harper 1958) **Introduction**
Ridderbos, H. N. *Paul* (Grand Rapids: Eerdmans 1975)
Ridderbos, H. *Galatians* (Grand Rapids: Eerdmans 1953)
Robinson, H. Wheeler *Christian Doctrine of Man* (Edinburgh: T. & T. Clark 1911)
Rowell, G. *Hell and the Victorians* (Oxford: Clarendon 1974)

Salmond S. D. F. *Christian Doctrine of Immortality* (Edinburgh: T. & T. Clark 1895) **Immortality**
Schwartz, H. 'Luther's Understanding of Heaven and Hell' in *Interpreting Luther's Legacy*. Meuser F. W. & Schneider S. D. eds (Minneapolis: Augsburg 1969)
Scobie, C. H. H. *John the Baptist* (Philadelphia/London: Fortress/SCM) 1964
Sewell, A. *Study in Milton's Christian Doctrine* (London: Oxford U. P 1939)
Shedd, W. G. T. *Doctrine of Endless Punishment* (New York: Scribner 1886) **Punishment**
Strack, H. L. & Billerbeck, P. *Kommentar zum Neuen Testament aus Talmud und Midrasch* (Munich: Beck 1928) **Strack and Billerbeck**
Strauss, L. *Life after Death* (Westchester, Ill.: Good News 1979 – abridged from *We Live for Ever* 1947)
Strawson, W. *Jesus and the Future Life* (Philadelphia/London: Westminster/Epworth 1959) **Future Life**
Strong, A. H. *Dogmatic Theology* (New York: Scribner 1894)
Strong, A. H. *Systematic Theology* vol. 3. (Philadelphia: Judson 1909) **Theology**
Studer, G. C. *After Death, What?* (Scottdale, Pa.: Herald 1976)
Swete, H. B. *Life of the World to Come* N.Y./London: Macmillan/SPCK 1917)
Thielicke, H. *Death and Life* (Philadelphia: Fortress 1970)
Torrance, T. F. *Calvin's Doctrine of Man* (London: Lutterworth 1949)
Torrance, T. F. *Space, Time and Resurrection* (Grand Rapids: Eerdmans 1976)
Travis, S. *Jesus and the Justice of God* (Basingstoke: Marshall 1986)
Truth about Hell Anon. (E. Rutherford, N.J.: Dawn Bible Students Assn., n.d.)
Vos, G. *Pauline Eschatology* (Grand Rapids: Eerdmans, 1961 rp).
Walker, D. P. *Decline of Hell* (Chicago: Univ. of Chicago 1964)
Watts, I. *Ruine and Recovery of Mankind* (London: James Brackstone 1742)
Watts, I. *The World to Come* (Leeds: Davies & Booth 1918 rp)
Webber, R. E. *Common Roots* (Grand Rapids: Zondervan 1978)
Wenham, J. W. *Goodness of God* (London/Downer's Grove, Ill.: Inter-Varsity/IVP 1974)
Westcott, B. F. *Gospel of the Resurrection* (London: Macmillan 1879[4])
Whateley, R. *View of the Scripture Revelations concerning a Future State* (Philadelphia: Smith, English 1873[4])
White, E. *Life in Christ* (London: Elliot Stock 1878[3])
White, E. G. *Great Controversy between Christ and Satan* (Mountain View, Calif.: Pacific 1950 rp)
Wilcox, M. 'On Investigating the Use of the OT in the NT' in *Text and Interpretation* Best, E. & Wilson, R. M. (Cambridge: Cambridge UP 1979)
Wolff, H. W. *Anthropology of the Old Testament* (Philadelphia: Fortress 1974)
Wolfson, H. A. 'Immortality and Resurrection in the Philosophy of the Church Fathers' in *Immortality and Resurrection* Krister Stendahl ed. (New York: Macmillan 1965) Reprint from Wolfson's *Religious Philosophy: A Group of Essays*(1961), first in *Harvard Divinity School Bulletin* 22 (1956–57): 5–40.
Woodson, L. H. *Hell and Salvation* (Old Tappan, N.J.: Revell 1973)
Yarnold, E. J. & Chadwick, H. *Truth and Authority* (London: SPCK & CTS 1977)
Zerwick, M. *Biblical Greek* (Rome: Scripta Pont. Inst. Bib. 1963)

Index of Authors

(Footnote references are, generally, not included.)

Alford, H., 195
Ankerberg, J., 3
Atkinson, B.F.C., 9

Baird., J.A., 101, 106, 137, 202
Barrett, C.K., 138
Barth, Markus, 141
Barth, K., 145
Bavinck, H., 205
Beecher, E., 13
Beasley-Murray, G., 24, 136, 184
Berkhof, L., 6
Berkouwer, G.C., 23, 131f., 203–206
Bernard, T.D., 195
Bietenhard, H., 180
Billerbecke, P., 72, 191
Blanchard, J., 3, 48f., 54, 56, 64, 66, 95, 120f., 126, 144, 189
Bligh, P.H., 120f.
Bloesch, D.G., 30, 155, 196
Braun, J.E., 11, 15, 43, 64f.
Brinsmead, R., 3, 140
Bruce, A.B., 114
Bruce, F.F., 30, 107, 130, 136
Buis, H. 22, 37, 41, 44, 63, 65, 71, 126, 159, 183
Burns, N.T., 37

Carnell, E.J., 31
Charles, R.H. 69, 84, 88
Charlesworth, J. 69
Constable, H., 56, 106, 123, 166f., 182
Conzelmann, H., 138
Cullmann, O., 105, 139

Dalman, G., 119
Darby, J.N., 23
Davies, Eryl, 153, 168, 173
Davies, W.D., 117

Delitzsch, F., 154
Dixon, L., 48, 54, 66, 95, 104, 106, 121, 126, 189, 194
Dodd, C.H., 136
Dunn, J.D.G., 143f., 149

Ebeling, G., 130
Edersheim, A., 71
Eller, V., 58

Farrar, F.W., 5, 12, 15, 71, 111, 121
Forsyth, P.T., 23
Froom, L.E. 14, 24f., 34, 47, 124, 127

Gatch, M., 37
Glasson, T.F., 201
Green, M., 10
Gressmann, H., 126
Guillebaud, H.E., 9f., 15, 19, 99f., 108, 189, 202
Gundry, D.W., 24

Hanhart, K., 127
Harmon, K., 71, 121, 154, 190, 196
Harris, Murray, 31, 107
Hendriksen, W., 184
Hodge, A. A., 7, 21
Hoekema, A., 30
Holwerda, D.E., 37, 136
Hughes, P.E., 10
Hunter, A. M., 119
Huxley T. H., 123

Jeremias, J., 116, 119, 127, 129, 182

Kennedy, H.A.A., 15
Kevan, E.F., 198
Kümmel, W.G., 202

Lane, W.L., 96, 115
LaSor, W., 81
Lenski, R.C., 179
Lilje, H., 192f.

Marshall, I. H., 196
Martin, J.P., 37
Mattill, A.J., 101
Maurice, F.D., 11, 15
Morey, R., 71, 126
Morris, L., 139, 150
Mounce, R.H., 108, 183f., 188, 195
Murray, J., 164

Nickelsburg, G.W.E., 77
Nicole, R., 12, 194
Nikolainen, A., 29

Oehler, G., 44
Orr, J., 23, 196f.

Pannenberg, W., 137
Pétavel, E., 12, 65, 153
Pink, A.W., 114, 123, 172
Pinnock, Clark, 146
Preiss, Theo, 119
Pusey, E.B., 4ff, 21, 34, 71, 111

Quistorp, H., 37

Reichenbach, B.R., 30
Richardson, Alan, 137, 196
Ridderbos, H., 138f., 152, 182
Robinson, H. Wheeler, 27
Robinson, J.A.T., 119

Salmond, S.D.F., 13, 23, 64, 72, 99, 111, 115, 123, 159, 194
Shedd, W.G.T., 11, 15, 21, 43f., 71, 107, 199
Stahlin, G. 138, 147

Stott, J., 10
Strack, H.L., 72, 191
Strauss, Lehman, 1
Strong, A.H., 6, 114, 145, 153

Taylor, V., 40
Thielicke, H., 30, 42

Wenham, J., 9, 10, 24, 93, 125, 139, 147, 200

Westcott, B.F., 23
Whately, Richard, 114
White, E., 114, 166
Wilken, R.L., 34
Wolff, H.W., 29

General Index

American Standard Version, 44
Anabaptists, 36f.
anathema, 156–158, 161
annihilation, 72, 88, 108ff., 123ff., 158ff., 193, 207
anti-supernaturalist, 22, 39
Antiochus IV, 68
apocalyptic, 41, 69, 131
Apocrypha, 69, 73–77
Apostles' Creed, 143
ark, 66f.
Arnobius, 34
Augustine, 33, 64, 121
authority, 2

Babylon, 67, 74, 190
Bible, 10, 92, 209
brimstone, 55
British evangelicals, 8
Bullinger, H., 37

Calvin, J., 36–38, 64, 106, 113, 127, 136, 142
chaos, 154ff.
Christ,
– as the eschaton, 135ff., 170
– baptized in fire, 94, 118
– bearing punishment of sinners, 133f., 144f.
– death of, 135
– descent into hell, 143
– punished as covenant breaker, 140
Conditionalism, -ist, 3, 19, 41, 47, 64, 118, 124, 130, 179, 188, 197
conscience, 64
consume, 61–64, 66
corruption, 158, 160
covenant, 132, 140f.
creation, 42
curse, 56f., 120, 130, 187

darkness, 58f., 103, 117

Day of the Lord, 59, 103, 149f.
'day and night', 189f.
Dead Sea Scrolls, 69, 80
death, 29, 42f., 161f.
– second, 194f.
desolation, 57
destroy, God's power to, 105, 108f.
destruction, 47, 60, 62f., 143, 150, 152, 155, 157f., 165, 185
disagreement, 5
dispensationalists, 119, 191
divine government, 60
dogmatism, 197
Dort, Synod of, 205
Drag-net, Parable of the, 112
dualistic, 39

Edom, 67
Edwards, Jonathan, 124
Epicureans, 167
eschatology, -ical, 2, 61
– and the death of Christ, 135
– judgment, 59
Essenes, 80
eternal, 11–20, 55, 65, 111, 120
– death, 165, 207
– destruction, 16, 18, 90
– fire, 113, 120f., 178, 180
– judgment, 16
– life, 125, 129f., 162
– punishment, 16, 18, 122–125, 153, 156, 207
– redemption, 16f.
– salvation, 16f.
– sin, 17, 110
– torment, 85, 87, 88, 90ff., 99, 118, 191, 193, 195
eternality, 39
etymology, 44
evangelicals, 10
everlasting, 11
– pain, 77
– destruction, 153

exclusion, 95, 112, 158
extinction, 4, 10, 92, 207–209

fear, 172
final judgment, 49
final resurrection, 65
fire and brimstone (see sulphur)
fire, 5f., 55, 57, 63, 66–68, 74f., 113, 118, 151f., 172
– baptism of, 94
– of judgment, 95
– lake of, 191–195
– unquenchable, 63, 97, 114
flesh, 29
Flood, 53, 150
fundamentalism, -ists, 4, 7f.

Gehenna, 70, 84, 89, 96–101, 113, 127, 132, 191
Gilgamesh, 45
Golgotha, 118, 134, 157
gospel, 133, 149, 203–206
government, 48f., 53
grave, 44
Greek philosophy, 6, 26

hades, 127f., (see also *sheol*)
heart, 29
hell, 1f., 5, 43f., 72, 131, 133f., 199–206
Heraclitus, 98
hermeneutics, 3f.
holiness of God, 61
human nature, 41
humanism, 208
Husbandmen, Parable of the Wicked, 115

Ignatius, 34
image of God, 27
image, 42
immortality, -ists 6, 7, 10, 21, 40, 77, 105, 159, 162–166

General Index

– of soul, 21–40
intertestamental period, 68–72, 92
Irenaeus, 34

Jehovah's Witnesses, 26
John the Baptist, 94
Josephus, 27, 71, 80
Judah, 67
judging, 16
judgment (s), 16, 48, 49, 53, 115, 150, 161, 162
– and the death of Christ, 138
– eschatological, 86
Judith, 75, 77
Justin, 34

King James Version, 44, 109, 121, 151
knowledge, theory of, 32

language, 131, 159, 163
– figurative and literal, 182f., 193, 196, 198
– mythological, 45
– symbolic (see under "symbolism")
– used by Paul, 166–168
liberal (s) 7f.
life, 42, 109f.
literalistic, 3
Luther, M., 30, 35, 64, 106

Maccabeans, 68
Messiah, 60f.
modernism, 7f.
mortalism, -ists, 26, 39, 40
mortality, 43
mystery, 196f.
mythological language, 45

Neo-Platonism, 34, 39
Nineveh, 67
New International Version, 18, 41, 44, 151

Old Testament, 31, 41, 169
Origen, 33
orthodoxy, 4ff., 8

pain, 6
Paul,
– characteristic themes, 146
– language used by, 166–168
– wrath of God, 147
penal, 18
perish, 164
Phaedo, 166
Pharisees, 27, 71
Philo, 33, 71
pit, 44
Plato, Platonism, 23, 32ff., 39, 166f.
Protestantism, 8
Pseudepigrapha, 69, 72, 78–91
Psychopannychia, 37
punishment, 6
– proportional, 118
purgatory, 99, 208

Qumran, 80, 82

Reformed, 22
Reformers, 35
restorationism, 99, 200–206, 208
resurrection, 23f., 75–77, 88, 106, 108
– general, 171
– of both good and evil, 65
– of sinners, 49, 150
Revised Standard Version, 151
Rich man and Lazarus, Parable of the, 126

Sadducees, 167
salt, 114f.
Satan, 195
– punishment of, 193
Scripture(s), 2–4, 9f., 210
Scroggie, W. Graham, 124
Septuagint, 146
Seventh Day Adventists, 26
Sheep and Goats, Parable of, 119
silence, 57
smoke, 56, 188f.
Socrates, 43

Sodom, destruction of, 54–57, 177, 179–81, 210
soul, 6, 32–41, 77, 105f., 109, 166f.
soul-sleep, 26, 36f.
spirit, 29
Spurgeon, C.H., 6, 124
Stoics, 98
sulphur, 187
Summary, 19, 38, 46, 52, 66, 77, 91, 130
supernaturalist, 22
symbolic, symbolism, 53, 58f., 62, 66, 156, 172, 182–185, 196f.

Talents, Parable of, 118
Tartarus, 127f.
Tatian, 34
teeth, grinding of, 104, 117
Tertullian, 34
torment, 75
traditionalism, -ists, 3f., 6, 19, 24, 39, 41f., 47, 61, 63, 71f., 78, 106, 118, 121, 127, 130, 179, 188, 197, 208–210
trouble, 151
Tyndale, W., 36

unceasing, 189f.
unending, 75
universalism, 199–206

Verdict Publications, 3

Watts, I., 1
Wedding Banquet, Parable of the, 116
Weeds, Parable of the, 111
weeping, 103f., 117
wine of God's fury, 186
worm(s), 5, 62ff., 67, 75, 77, 113f.
wrath, 146–150, 161
– cup of God's, 186f.

Zoroastrianism, 97

Index of Foreign Words

HEBREW
asham, 99
karath, 175
mikshol, 122
nephesh, 28, 41
neshamah, 28
olam, 12
rephaim, 45
sheol, 41–46, 127f.

GREEK
aiōn, -ios, 11, 121f.
apocatastasis, 203–206
apollymi, 164
exolothreuō, 175
kolasis, 122
psychē, 28, 109, 174
olethros, 150

orgē, 162
pantote, 14
phthartos, 160
phtheirō, 160
phthora, 158
psychē, 28, 109, 174
thlipsis, 151
timōria, 122

Biblical and Extra-Canonical Literature

OLD TESTAMENT		Zechariah		5:28f.	130
		3:2	181	5:29	122
Genesis		Zephaniah		Acts	
1–2	41	1:14–18	59, 163		174
19:24–29	54			3:23	174
6–9	53	Malachi			
		4:1–6	65	Romans	
Deuteronomy				1:18	161
29:18–29	56			1:32	161
		NEW TESTAMENT		2:12	163
Job				2:6–11	162
49	52	Matthew	93	6:21, 23	164
Psalms		3:10, 12	94	1 Corinthians	
1:3–6	59	5:20	95	3:17	160
11:1–7	50	5:22	95	6:9f.	161
2:9–12	60	5:25f.	99	16:22	161
34:8–22	50	5:29f.	100		
37:1–40	50	7:13f.	100	Galatians	
50	51	7:19	101	1:8f.	156
58	51	7:23	102	5:21	158
69:22–28	52, 60	7:27	102	6:8	158
49	52	8:11f.	103	Ephesians	
		10:28	105	5:5f.	165
Proverbs		10:39	109		
49	52	11:22ff	110	Philippians	
		12:31f.	110	1:28	165
Isaiah		13:30	40–43, 111	2:9	202
1:27–31	57	13:48ff.	112	3:19	165
11:4	60	18:8f.	112		
33:10–24	60	22:13	116	Colossians	
5:24f	58	21:33–44	115	3:6	165
51:3–11	61	24:50f.	117	1 Thessalonians	
66	96, 108, 151f.	25:30	118	1:9f.	146
66:24	62, 123	25:41	46, 119	4:6	149
		25:41	122	5:2f.	149
Jeremiah		25:46	18	5:9	150
25	176	26:24	125	2 Thessalonians	
Ezekiel		Mark		1:9	18
8–9	176	3:29	17	1:5–10	151
Daniel		Luke		Timothy and Titus	146
12:2	122	16:19–31	126		
2:34f.	116	John		Hebrews	
7:9–12	192		94		169
12:2f.	30, 60, 130	1:9	201	2:2f.	170
Nahum		3:16	129	5:9	17
1:2–15	58	3:36	130	6:1f.	170

6:2	16	Jude		Jubilees	85–88
6:8	171		179	Judith	75
9:12	17	4–7	179	Life of Adam and Eve	85
10:27–31	171	13	180	1 Maccabees	75
10:39	172	23	180	2 Maccabees	75f.
12:25	29, 173	Revelation		4 Maccabees	91
1 Peter		2:16, 22f.	185	Psalms of Solomon	82f
	175	14:9ff.	185	Sibylline Oracles	79
3:18ff.	201	18	190f.	Sirach, (Ecclesiasticus)	73, 77
4:17f.	175	19:20; 20:10, 15;		Testaments of the Twelve	
2 Peter		21:8	191–195	Patriarchs	84
	177			Tobit	73
2:1–21	177			Wisdom of Solomon	76f.
3:6–9	179	APOCRYPHA,			
1 John		PSEUDEPIGRAPHA ETC		QUMRAN LITERATURE	
	181				
5:16f.	181	Assumption of Moses	84	Damascus Document(CDC)	
James		Baruch	74		81
		2 (Syriac) Baruch	90	Hymn Scroll (1QH)	82
	173	1 (Ethiopic) Enoch	88ff.	Manual of Discipline	
1:15	173	2 (Slavonic) Enoch	91	(1QS)	81
4:12	174	Apocalypse of Ezra		Psalms pesher (1QpPs)	81f
5:1–6	174	(4 Esdras)	83	War Scroll (1QM)	81
5:19f	174	Josephus	80f.	Zadokite Work	79

PATERNOSTER DIGITAL LIBRARY
Titles in this series

George R. Beasley-Murray
Baptism in the New Testament

F. F. Bruce
(Revised by David F. Payne)
Israel and the Nations
The History of Israel from the Exodus to the Fall of the Second Temple

F. F. Bruce
Paul
Apostle of the Free Spirit

F. F. Bruce
The Spreading Flame
The Rise and Progress of Christianity from its First Beginnings to the Conversion of the English

Edward William Fudge
The Fire that Consumes
The Biblical Case for Conditional Immortality

C. E. Gunton
Christ and Creation
A Summary Dogmatic Christology

I. Howard Marshall
Biblical Inspiration

I. Howard Marshall
(Editor)
New Testament Interpretation
Essays on Principles and Methods

I. Howard Marshall
Last Supper and Lord's Supper
A Comprehensive Study of Recent Work on the Lord's Supper in the New Testament

I. Howard Marshall
Kept by the Power of God
A Study of Perseverance and Falling Away

Leon Morris
The Cross in the New Testament
A Book-by-Book Study of the Central Fact of Christianity

David W. Smith
Transforming the World?
The Social Impact of British Evangelicalism

Anthony C. Thiselton
The Two Horizons
New Testament Hermeneutics and Philosophical Description With Special Reference to Heidegger, Bultmann, Gadamer and Wittgenstein

John Wenham
Easter Enigma
Are the Resurrection Accounts in Conflict?

Printed in the United States
43992LVS00004B/112